DOCUMENTS IN WORLD HISTORY

VOLUME 1

DOCUMENTS IN WORLD HISTORY

VOLUME 1

The Great Traditions: From Ancient Times to 1500

FOURTH EDITION

Peter N. Stearns
George Mason University

Stephen S. Gosch
University of Wisconsin, Eau Claire

Erwin P. Grieshaber
Mankato State University

PEARSON
Longman

New York   San Fransisco   Boston
London   Toronto   Sydney   Tokyo   Singapore   Madrid
Mexico City   Munich   Paris   Capetown   Hong Kong   Montreal

Senior Acquisitions Editor: Janet Lanphier
Executive Marketing Manager: Sue Westmoreland
Production Manager: Denise Phillip
Project Coordination, Text Design, and Electronic Page Makeup: WestWords, Inc.
Cover Design Manager: Wendy Ann Fredericks
Cover Designer: Kay Petronio
Cover Art: T'ang Dynasty scroll showing the Emperor Ming Huang and his famous concubine,
     Yang Kuei-fei, on horseback. © The Granger Collection, New York
Photo Researcher: Vivette Porges
Senior Manufacturing Buyer: Alfred C. Dorsey
Printer and Binder: Hamilton Printing
Cover Printer: Coral Graphics Services

Library of Congress Cataloging-in-Publication Data

Documents in world history / [selected by] Peter N. Stearns, Stephen
S. Gosch, Erwin P. Grieshaber.—4th ed.
     v.   cm.
   Contents: v. 1. The great traditions, from ancient times to 1500
   –
   v. 2. The modern centuries, from 1500 to present.
   ISBN 0-321-33054-4 (pbk. : v. 1) – ISBN 0-321-33258-X (pbk. : v. 2)
   1. World history—Sources. I. Stearns, Peter N. II. Gosch,
Stephen S. (Stephen Spencer). III. Grieshaber, Erwin P. (Erwin Peter)

D5.D623 2006
909—dc22

                                   2005003149

Please visit our website at http://www.ablongman.com

ISBN 0-321-33054-4

2345678910—HT—08 07 06 05

CONTENTS

GEOGRAPHICAL CONTENTS: MAJOR SOCIETIES

East Asia and Central Asia

Eastern Europe

Western Europe

TOPICAL CONTENTS

Trade and Cities

Social and Gender Structure

Women and the Family

PREFACE

When many people think of world history, they think of a textbook. World history does have a survey element that textbooks serve very well. But world history also stems from the lives of many people in a variety of environments. The flavor of the human aspect of world history can in no way be captured solely by a progression of names, dates, and main developments. These subtleties come through in a sampling of the expressions people have produced in different societies at various periods. Learning to interpret a document from a distant place or time is a vital part of world history study, yielding skills of interpretation that go well beyond an introductory history course.

This book offers a range of documents to illustrate characteristic features of key civilizations during major stages of world history since the beginnings of written records to the start of the modern age around 1500 C.E. The book has been substantially revised since the previous edition, to offer a wider range of materials at various points in time. But the basic commitment remains: to provide documents that offer insights into the ways people experienced and shaped major passages in world history and that enhance abilities to interpret and analyze.

The documents were not written for posterity; some were not even intended for a wide audience when written. They are collected here to get beneath the survey level and raise issues of understanding and interpretation that can enliven and enrich the world history course.

The book covers several key facets of the human experience, again at various times and in a variety of places. It deals with the organization and functions of the state. It treats philosophy and religion and at points literature and science. It explores contacts among civilizations, such as the diverse impacts of Islam or early contacts between Europe and Asia, plus a number of relationships through trade. It also deals with families and women and with issues of social structure.

The contents of this new edition have a number of features. They add to the range of historical experiences open to discussion, whether the subject is classical China or the merchant guilds of Western Europe. New materials on Africa and Latin America enhance attention to these important regions. Additional contacts between major societies are documented, for example the Christian-Muslim interactions during the crusades. Another important feature involves the presentation of visual evidence, or **Visual Sources** as they are called in the reader, with context and interpretive exercises attached. In volume II, new documents allow exploration of the often changing, sometimes deeply troubling, events of a more global age, including international terrorism and United States involvement in Iraq.

The book's organization facilitates relating it to a core textbook. Major civilizations are represented with several readings—East Asia, the West, India, the Middle East, Eastern Europe, Africa, and Latin America. Thus a course can trace elements of change and continuity within each civilization. A section in each period also focuses explicitly on contacts across civilizations. The readings are also divided by basic time periods: early civilization, the classical era to about 500 C.E., and the spread of civilization and major religions, to roughly 1500 C.E. This chronological coverage focuses on the establishment of the major civilization traditions and contact patterns still present in the world today. The third principle of selection involves topics that can be coherently traced and compared both across different civilizations and across different time periods. A topic table of contents facilitates the ability to identify themes like gender, or religion, or trade, and build readings and analysis accordingly.

Dealing with documents in the world history context in fact involves several related exercises, and the study questions involve these exercises. First, of course, is what the document means—and meanings often have to be teased out of the literal words, as when a set of laws is "asked" about the nature of a social structure, which was not the explicit purpose of the document's author. Second is what relationship the document has to other features of the society or period in question—how representative it is, and what quirks it has. Third—and the **Study questions** in the revised edition pay increased attention to this point—what is the document's relationship to larger world history themes, whether they be comparative or focus on change and continuity over time. Study questions in this revised edition have been reworked to provide a clearer basis for all the desirable levels of document analysis.

Although the book is comprehensive, *particularly in this expanded new edition,* the goal is not maximum coverage. All sorts of attractive and significant documents are left out, of necessity. This book is deliberately intended to be usefully brief and accessible (and at least comparatively affordable). We chose readings that illustrate key facets of an area or period, that raise challenging problems of interpretation, or that—at least in many cases—express some charm and human drama. The readings also invite comparisons across cultures and over time. **Chapter introductory notes** not only identify the readings but also raise some issues that can be explored in class discussion or otherwise. Study questions at the end of each chapter further enrich discussion of issues.

This book was prepared by three world history teachers at work in several kinds of institutions. It is meant, correspondingly, to serve the needs of different kinds of students. It is motivated by two common purposes: first, a strong belief that some perspective on the world is both desirable and possible as a key element in contemporary American education; and second, that understanding world history can be greatly enhanced not just by exposure to an overall factual and interpretive framework, but also by the kinds of challenges and insights raised by primary materials, not written by scholars but by people actually living out the diverse and changing patterns we are grappling to understand.

Dealing with primary sources is not an easy task. Precisely because the materials are not written with American college students in mind, they require some thought. They must be related to other elements we know about the particular society; they must be given meaning; and they must be evaluated more carefully than a secondary account or textbook designed deliberately to pinpoint what should be learned. By the same token, however, gaining some ease with the meaning of primary sources is a skill that carries well beyond a survey history course into all sorts of research endeavors. Gaining this skill in the context of the diverse civilizations that compose the world goes some distance toward understanding how our world has become what it is—which is, in essence, the central purpose of history. The study of primary sources also offers students something of a relief from the demands imposed by a standard world history textbook. This book is composed of a diverse mixture of writings, many of which can be fun to savor and ponder.

Thanks go to the reviewers of this edition. They are Bud Burkhard, University of Maryland; Mark W. Chavalas, University of Wisconsin–LaCrosse; J. Michael Farmer, Brigham Young University; Kerri A. Inglis, Brigham Young University–Hawaii; Lu Liu, University of Tennessee; Aran S. MacKinnon, University of West Georgia; Brendan J. McManus, Bemidji State University; and David Simonelli, Youngstown State University.

Peter N. Stearns
Stephen S. Gosch
Erwin P. Grieshaber

INTRODUCTION

The selections in this volume are designed to provide insight into major developments in the history of leading civilizations and the formation of global connections. They also convey some of the major changes and processes in the field of world history. The selections are source materials that were written during significant periods in the past, but not as formal histories or studies. As documents rather than research pieces, they convey a direct sense of other times and places. They also demand explicit analysis and interpretation to relate them to more general themes and issues.

The need to study world history becomes increasingly apparent. Although the 20th century was hailed as the "American century," it is obvious that even given the United States' claim to some world leadership, it must interact with various other societies and, in part, on their terms. As a power with worldwide military responsibilities or aspirations, the United States maintains increasingly close diplomatic contacts with all the inhabited continents. Economically, American reliance on exports and imports—once a minor footnote to this nation's industrial vigor—grows greater every year. Cultural influences from abroad are significant. Even though the United States remains a leading exporter of consumer fads and styles, we can see among the American people cultural standards imported from Europe, interest in various schools of Buddhism, or a fascination with Japan's gifts at social coordination. Even the composition of the U.S. population reflects growing worldwide contacts. The United States is now experiencing its highest rates of immigration ever, with new arrivals from Latin America and various parts of Asia joining earlier immigrant groups from Europe and Africa.

Enmeshed in this world, shaping it but also shaped by it, U.S. citizens need to know something of how that world has been formed and what major historical forces created its diversities and contacts. We need to know, in sum, something about world history. Study of our own past—that is, U.S. history—or even the larger history of Western civilization from which many American institutions and values spring, risks now being unduly narrow. This explains why the study of world history is receiving renewed attention.

A danger exists, however, in stressing the need to study world history too piously. True, growing global interdependence and communication make knowledge of past world patterns increasingly essential as the basis for interpreting policy options open to American government or business—or simply for grasping the daily headlines in more than a superficial manner. The mission, however, of a world history course does not rest entirely on the desire to create a more informed and mature citizenry. It also rests directly on the intrinsic interest and the analytical challenge world history offers.

World history presents the opportunity to evaluate a fascinating range of human experience. For example, it delves into interactions between humanity and nature through study of disease patterns and the human use of animals. Human interaction with nature went beyond the objective natural environment, of course. Some major cultures venerated particular aspects of nature, removing these from daily use. Thus India held the cow in respect, and Westerners and Middle Easterners—unlike East Asians—refused to eat dog meat. Even human emotions varied by culture and over time. India, though formally a highly patriarchal society, modified the impact of male control in daily family life by strong emphasis on affection and sexual passion. West Europeans, long schooled to view husband-wife relations as an economic arrangement to which emotional attachments were secondary, came to see positive virtues in romance, with suggestions of a new esteem for love some 600 years ago.

Variety and change at the more visible levels of high culture and government are equally familiar themes in world history. Indian society, although successful in commerce and technology, developed an otherworldly emphasis—a concern for spiritual explanations and goals—normally foreign to the higher reaches of Chinese society. Japan built an intricate set of feudal relationships among warriors into a durable tradition of group loyalty, whereas a similar set of warrior relations in Western Europe led less to group cohesion than to institutions—parliaments—that would try to regulate the doings of kings. Culture contact led sub-Saharan Africa to borrow significantly from Islam but not to merge with the Islamic world.

World history is challenging as well as varied. Putting the case mildly, much has happened in the history of the world; and although some developments, particularly in early societies, remain unknown for want of records, the amount we do know is astounding—and steadily expanding. No person can master the whole, and in presenting a manageable course in world history, selectivity is essential. Fortunately, there is considerable agreement on certain developments that are significant to a study of world history. The student must gain, for example, some sense of the special political characteristics of Chinese civilization; or of the nature of Islam; or of the new global trading patterns that Western Europe organized, to its benefit, after about 1500. This list of history basics, of course, is not uniform, and it can change with new interests and new data. The condition of women, for example, as it varied from one civilization to the next and changed over time, has become a staple of up-to-date world history teaching in ways that were unimaginable 20 years ago. Despite changes in the list, though, the idea of approaching world history in terms of basics—key civilizations, key points of change, key factors such as technology or family—begins the process of making the vast menu of information digestible.

In practice, however, the teaching of world history has sometimes obscured the focus on basics with a stream-of-narrative textbook approach. An abundance of important and interesting facts can produce a way of teaching world history so bent on leaving nothing out (though in fact, much must be omitted in even the most ponderous tome) that little besides frenzied memorization takes place. Yet world history, although it must convey knowledge, must also stimulate thought—about why different patterns developed in various key civilizations, about what impact new contacts between civilizations had, about how our present world relates to worlds past.

One way to stimulate thought—and to give a dash of the spice that particular episodes in world history offer—is to provide access to original sources. The purpose of this volume is to facilitate world history teaching by supplementing a purely textbook-survey approach with the immediacy of contact that original source documents offer.

The readings are designed to illustrate several features of various civilizations during key periods in world history through direct evidence. Thus the readings convey some sense of what Buddhism is all about through writings by Buddha's early disciples, or of how Confucianism helped shape China's political institutions and underlying stability, again through direct statements. They require, however, some effort of interpretation. Because the writers were not necessarily trying to persuade others of their beliefs or even reporting what they saw at the time, they did not focus on distilling the essence of a religion, a political movement, or a list of government functions for early-21st-century students of world history. The reader must decide on meaning, aided by the brief contexts provided in the chapter introductions, and the questions provided at the end of each chapter. Analytical thinking is also encouraged and challenged by recurrent comparisons across space and time. Thus documents dealing with social or family structure in China can be compared with documents on the same subject for the Mediterranean world, and a picture of China's bureaucracy 2000 years ago begs for juxtaposition with descriptions of later Chinese politics to see what changes and what persists. Chapter 48 explicitly organizes comparison around the theme of merchants and trade in documents that originate in the post-classical period.

The documents presented are not randomly chosen. The selections follow certain general principles around which one can organize an approach to world history. Quite simply, these principles involve place, time, and topic.

First is the focus on major societies in organizing choice of place. The readings deal with seven parts of the world that have produced durable civilizations that still exist, at least in part. East Asia embraces China and a surrounding zone—most notably Japan—that came under partial Chinese influence. Indian civilization, which constitutes the second case, had considerable influence in other parts of southern Asia. The Middle East and North Africa, where civilization was born, form a third society to be addressed at various points in time, both before and after the advent of its major religion, Islam. Europe, although sharing some common values through Christianity, developed two partially distinct civilizations in the east (centered ultimately on Russia) and west. Both East and West European civilizations innovated as new religion, trade, and political organizations spread northward. Values and institutions from Western Europe would also help shape new settler societies in North America and in Australia and New Zealand. Sub-Saharan Africa, a vast region with great diversity, forms a sixth civilization area. Finally, civilization developed independently in the Americas. Here, though a bit later than in Africa, signs of civilizations showed early. The seven civilizations represented in the readings are not sacrosanct: They do not embrace all the world's cultures, past or present. They overlap at points, and they contain some marked internal divisions, such as the division between China and Japan in East Asia. These civilizations, however, do provide some geographic coherence for the study of world history, and they are all represented repeatedly in the selections that follow.

The second basis of place selection involves contact among different societies as a result of migrations, invasions, trade, deliberate borrowing, or missionary intrusions. Here is a key, recurrent source of change, friction, and creativity. Documents on the nature and results of significant contacts complement those focused on the characteristics of major civilizations. For each period after the earliest, one or more sections on global contacts highlight key interchanges among societies in different parts of the world.

Time is a vital organizing principle. Obviously, some of the civilizations currently important in the world did not exist 1,500 years ago, so chronology is vital just to order the list of civilizations. Further, even ancient civilizations changed over time, and we need a sense of major periods to capture this evolution.

This volume deals with three time periods: First, early civilizations when written records first emerged. Second, the classical period, 1000 B.C.E. to 500 C.E., where larger civilizations took hold in China, India, and the Mediterranean. And third, after the fall of the great classical empires, a post-classical period, 500–1450 C.E.

Although the emphasis of this volume lies in the formation of basic traditions and traditional contacts, the theme of change must be traced as well. New religions and the rise and fall of political systems brought important shifts. Contacts among most of the world's civilizations increased, particularly rapidly after about 800 C.E. Tradition evolved further as it fed into more modern world history.

The third organizing principle in the sources that follow is the topic. In dealing with major periods and civilizations, the readings convey four features inherent in human society. First, every civilization must develop some government structure and political values. Second, it must generate a culture, that is, a system of beliefs and artistic expressions that help explain how the world works. Among these, religion is often a linchpin of a society's culture, but science and art play crucial roles as well. Economic relationships—the nature of agriculture, the level of technology and openness to technological change, the position of merchants—form a third feature of a civilization. And fourth, social groupings, hierarchies, and family institutions—including gender relations—organize human relationships and provide for the training of children. Until recently, world history focused primarily on the political and cultural side of the major societies, with some bows to technology and trade. More recently, the explosion of social history—with its inquiry into popular as well as elite culture, families, and social structure—has broadened world history concerns. Readings in this book provide a sense of all four aspects of the leading civilizations—political, cultural, economic, and social—and a feeling for how they changed under the impact of new religions, the rise and fall of empires, or new contacts among civilizations themselves.

This book aims at providing the flavor of such topics, a sense of how people at the time lived and perceived them, and an understanding of the issues involved in interpreting and comparing diverse documents from the past. The collection is meant to help readers themselves breathe life into world history and grasp some of the ways that both great and ordinary people have lived, suffered, and created in various parts of the world at various points in our rich human past.

One final point takes us back to the art of dealing with documents. The selection of the documents and their topics, and the kinds of questions asked at the end of each chapter, encourage important exercises in analyzing change and continuity and major contrasts and comparisons. But the kinds of documents featured in this collection require analysis in their own right: what do they mean? What do they reveal about societies that the authors did not explicitly intend but nevertheless convey? Who, in fact, are the authors, and what are their points of view? When are accounts by travelers helpful, and when do they mislead? When are participants in a major event useful reporters, and when do they become part of the interpretive problem? How can modern readers best judge bias, or representativeness, in using documents to build arguments about significant aspects of the world's past? Learning to build these interpretive skills helps in handling vital features of world history, and they can also be applied to documents that emerge from the world in the present day.

SECTION ONE

EARLY CIVILIZATIONS

River-valley civilizations developed in several places between 3500 and 500 B.C.E. They set up more formal governments than had existed before and developed important religious and cultural principles. Both areas of achievement depended on the creation of writing, which in turn left more diverse and explicit records than was possible for preliterate societies. Persia, featured in the final document, was part of the sequence of societies that dominated Mesopotamia. But, it also set up institutions and values that still affect Iran and surrounding regions, a more direct legacy than some of the earlier civilizations had achieved.

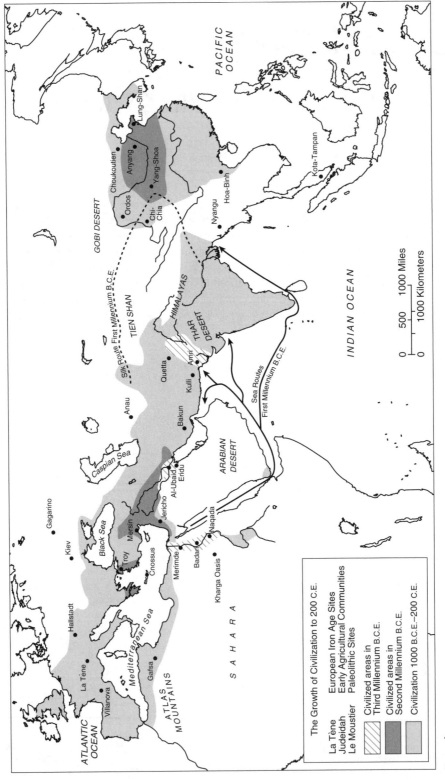

The Growth of Civilization to 200 C.E.

La Tène   European Iron Age Sites
Judeidah   Early Agricultural Communities
Le Moustier   Paleolithic Sites

▨ Civilized areas in
  Third Millennium B.C.E.

▓ Civilized areas in
  Second Millennium B.C.E.

▒ Civilization 1000 B.C.E.–200 C.E.

Eurasia

1 MESOPOTAMIAN VALUES: IDEAS ABOUT THE NATURE OF LIFE AND DEATH

Unlike the waters of the beneficent Nile, whose annual floods were predictable and controllable, those of the Tigris and Euphrates rivers proved erratic and often devastating. This factor, combined with the harshness of the physical terrain, the absence of protective natural barriers, and the steady intrusion of invaders who used the element of surprise, superb leadership, and technological advantage to gain temporary hegemony over the region, prompted a complex outlook that found expression in the eclectic civilization that evolved in ancient Mesopotamia. The Sumerians, whose creative genius provided the cultural foundations of the region, perceived humans as lowly mortal servants to a pantheon of immortal gods and goddesses, and they viewed the state of humanity as a consequence of human failure to obey divine commands. These views, frequently reiterated in the literature of the region, are best expressed in the great Babylonian heroic tale, *The Gilgamesh Epic*. This poem was preserved in 12 tablets that were recovered during 19th-century excavations of Ashurbanipal's (668–627 B.C.E.) palace library in Nineveh. It is the first known piece of written literature in the world.

Heavily indebted to a variety of older oral stories, the epic describes the vain quest of its hero, Gilgamesh (ca. 2800 B.C.E.), fifth ruler of the first dynasty of Uruk, to secure immortality. By recounting the perilous ventures and hardships of Gilgamesh, the poem reaffirms that valiant personal efforts cannot prevent one's inevitable death and suggests that energy should instead be directed toward enjoying and making the most of life. During his quest, Gilgamesh sought and found Per-napishtim, the Babylonian Noah, who had secured immortality because of his piety. Tablet XI focuses on their meeting and provides Per-napishtim's account of the great deluge. A genetic relationship between his account and that of the Hebrews in Genesis is obvious, but the historical relationship between them is uncertain.

Some historians have found *The Gilgamesh Epic* pessimistic, but these views have been disputed. How do you interpret this example of Mesopotamian values?

Epic literature developed in many early civilizations—not only that of Mesopotamia, but also in Hebrew, Greek, and Indian cultures. How would tales like *Gilgamesh* help shape and express a civilization's values? What purpose did these stories serve?

From *Assyrian and Babylonian Literature*, edited by Rossiter Johnson (New York: D. Appleton and Company, 1901), pp. 351–357.

THE GILGAMESH EPIC

Gilgamesh

[From the shore Utnapishtim, the favorite of the gods, now relates the story of the deluge to the hero, who, sitting in his ship, is listening to him.]

Utnapishtim then said unto Gilgamesh:
"I will reveal unto thee, O Gilgamesh, the mysterious story,
and the mystery of the gods I will tell thee.
The city of Shurippak, a city which, as thou knowest,
is situated on the bank of the river Euphrates.
That city was corrupt, so that the gods within it
decided to bring about a deluge, even the great gods,
as many as there were: their father, Anu;
their counsellor, the warrior Bel;
their leader, Ninurta;
their champion, the god Enlil.
But Ea, the lord of unfathomable wisdom, argued with them.
Their plan he told to a reed-hut, (saying):
'Reed-hut, reed-hut, clay-structure, clay-structure!
Reed-hut, hear; clay-structure, pay attention!
Thou man of Shurippak, son of Ubara-Tutu,
Build a house, construct a ship;
Forsake thy possessions, take heed for thy life!
Abandon thy goods, save (thy) life,
and bring living seed of every kind into the ship.
As for the ship, which thou shalt build,
let its proportions be well measured:
Its breadth and its length shall bear proportion each to each,
and into the sea then launch it.'
I took heed, and said to Ea, my lord:
'I will do, my lord, as thou hast commanded;
I will observe and will fulfil the command.
But what shall I answer to (the inquiries of) the city, the
people, and the elders?'
Ea opened his mouth and spoke,
and he said unto me, his servant:
'Man, as an answer say thus unto them:
"I know that Bel hates me.
No longer can I live in your city;
Nor on Bel's territory can I live securely any longer;
I will go down to the 'deep,' I will live with Ea, my lord.
Upon you he will (for a time?) pour down rich blessing.
He will grant you fowl [in plenty] and fish in abundance,
Herds of cattle and an abundant harvest.
Shamash has appointed a time when the rulers of darkness
at eventide will pour down upon you a destructive rain.'"

All that was necessary I collected together.
On the fifth day I drew its design;
In its middle part its sides were ten gar high;
Ten gar also was the extent of its deck;
I added a front-roof to it and closed it in.
I built it in six stories,
thus making seven floors in all;
The interior of each I divided again into nine partitions.
Beaks for water within I cut out.
I selected a pole and added all that was necessary.
Three (variant, five) shar of pitch I smeared on its outside;
three shar of asphalt I used for the inside (so as to make it water-tight).
Three shar of oil the men carried, carrying it in vessels.
One shar of oil I kept out and used it for sacrifices,
while the other two shar the boatman stowed away.
For the temple of the gods (?) I slaughtered oxen;
I killed lambs (?) day by day.
Jugs of cider (?), of oil, and of sweet wine,
Large bowls (filled therewith?), like river water (i.e., freely) I poured out
   as libations.
I made a feast (to the gods) like that of the New-Year's Day.
To god Shamash my hands brought oil.
[* * *] the ship was completed.
[* * *] heavy was the work, and
I added tackling above and below, [and after all was finished,]

The ship sank into water two thirds of its height.
With all that I possessed I filled it;
with all the silver I had I filled it;
with all the gold I had I filled it;
with living creatures of every kind I filled it.
Then I embarked also all my family and my relatives,
cattle of the field, beasts of the field, and the uprighteous people—all them
   I embarked.
A time had Shamash appointed, (namely):
'When the rulers of darkness send at eventide a destructive rain,
then enter into the ship and shut its door.'
This very sign came to pass, and
The rulers of darkness sent a destructive rain at eventide.
I saw the approach of the storm,
and I was afraid to witness the storm;
I entered the ship and shut the door.
I intrusted the guidance of the ship to Purur-bel, the boatman,
the great house, and the contents thereof.
As soon as early dawn appeared,
there rose up from the horizon a black cloud,
within which the weather god (Adad) thundered,

and Nabu and the king of the gods (Marduk) went before.
The destroyers passed across mountain and dale (literally, country).
Dibbara, the great, tore loose the anchor-cable (?).
There went Ninib and he caused the banks to overflow;
the Anunnaki lifted on high (their) torches,
and with the brightness thereof they illuminated the universe.
The storm brought on by Adad swept even up to the heavens,
and all light was turned into darkness.
[* * *] overflooded the land like [* * *]
It blew with violence and in one day (?) it rose above the mountains (?).
Like an onslaught in battle it rushed in on the people.
Not could brother look after brother.
Not were recognised the people from heaven.
The gods even were afraid of the storm;
they retreated and took refuge in the heaven of Anu.
There the gods crouched down like dogs, on the inclosure of heaven they
    sat cowering.
Then Ishtar cried out like a woman in travail,
and the lady of the gods lamented with a loud voice, (saying):
'The world of old has been turned back into clay,
because I assented to this evil in the assembly of the gods.
Alas! that when I assented to this evil in the council of the gods,
I was for the destruction of my own people.
What I have created, where is it?
Like the spawn of fish it fills the sea.'
The gods wailed with her over the Anunnaki.
The gods were bowed down, and sat there weeping.
Their lips were pressed together (in fear and in terror).
Six days and nights
The wind blew, and storm and tempest overwhelmed the country.
When the seventh day drew nigh the tempest, the storm, the battle
which they had waged like a great host began to moderate.

The sea quieted down; hurricane and storm ceased.
I looked out upon the sea and raised loud my voice,
But all mankind had turned back into clay.
Like the surrounding field had become the bed of the rivers.
I opened the air-hole and light fell upon my cheek.
Dumbfounded I sank backward, and sat weeping,
while over my cheek flowed the tears.
I looked in every direction, and behold, all was sea.
Now, after twelve (days?) there rose (out of the water) a strip of land.
To Mount Nisir the ship drifted.
On Mount Nisir the boat stuck fast and it did not slip away.
The first day, the second day, Mount Nisir held the ship fast, and did not let
    it slip away.

The third day, the fourth day, Mount Nisir held the ship fast, and did not
let it slip away.

The fifth day, the sixth day, Mount Nisir held the ship fast, and did not let
it slip away.

When the seventh day drew nigh

I sent out a dove, and let her go.

The dove flew hither and thither,

but as there was no resting-place for her, she returned.

Then I sent out a swallow, and let her go.

The swallow flew hither and thither,

but as there was no resting-place for her she also returned.

Then I sent out a raven, and let her go.

The raven flew away and saw the abatement of the waters.

She settled down to feed, went away, and returned no more.

Then I let everything go out unto the four winds, and I offered a sacrifice.

I poured out a libation upon the peak of the mountain.

I placed the censers seven and seven,

and poured into them calamus, cedar-wood, and sweet-incense.

The gods smelt the savour;

yea, the gods smelt the sweet savour;

the gods gathered like flies around the sacrificer.

STUDY QUESTIONS

1. What are the main features of the flood story?
2. What does the story mean? What values was it meant to impress on the audience?
3. What religious beliefs does *The Gilgamesh Epic* express? What is the nature of divinity? Of evil? What is the relationship of humans to the gods?
4. Is this a pessimistic account? How does it compare to later religions that began in the Middle East—to Judaism, to Christianity, or to Islam?

2 Babylonian Law: How an Early State Regulated Its Subjects

Once he successfully reunited Mesopotamia by victories over Assyria and the neighboring Sumerian city-states, the Babylonian king Hammurabi (ca. 1850–1750 B.C.E.) played a dominant role in the Near East. In his 43-year reign, he earned a reputation for just and efficient administration, secured prosperity within his domain by strict control of western trade routes and judicious regulation of trade, and encouraged the production of extensive literature. Although his ephemeral empire gave way to Kassite tribes after his death, Hammurabi left for posterity the famous Code of Hammurabi, the earliest major collection of laws in history currently extant. Consisting of 282 case laws inscribed in the Akkadian (Semitic) language and presented in a series of horizontal bands on a massive diorite slab (discovered in 1901 at Susa, Iran, and now in the Louvre), the code represented no attempt by Hammurabi to produce a codification of existing statutes and/or common laws into a formal legal system. Rather, it was a formal collection of select decisions rendered by Hammurabi, the "just" judge, on a variety of isolated cases intended for public dissemination that represented recommended rules of justice. As amendments to the Babylonian common law, the code omitted many important areas in the law and virtually ignored procedural law and the judiciary. Extant legal documents and reports indicate that neither judges nor litigants viewed laws in the code as binding or enforceable in Babylonian courts.

Despite the fact that Hammurabi's compilation represents only a minor contribution to the advancement of law and jurisprudence, his laws offer historians important insights into Babylonian social structure, real and personal property, land tenure, trade and commerce, marriage and family, agriculture, wages and prices, slaves, and professions.

Writing down and maintaining formal law are among the chief functions of any organized government, but although certain acts are almost always defined as crimes, other definitions—and related punishments—have varied greatly from one culture to the next. Judging by the following passages, what kind of social and family relations was the Babylonian state trying to uphold? How did it define crime and punishment?

From J. M. Powis Smith, *The Origin and History of Hebrew Law* (Chicago: University of Chicago Press, 1931), pp. 181–183, 186, 190–193, 195, 199–200, 209–213.

THE CODE

When the lofty Anu, king of the Anunnaki, and Enlil, lord of heaven and earth, who determines the destinies of the land, committed the rule of all mankind to Marduk . . . when they pronounced the lofty name of Babylon, made it great among the quarters of the world and in its midst established for him an everlasting kingdom whose foundations were firm as heaven and earth—at that time Anu and Enlil named me, Hammurabi, the exalted prince, the worshiper of the gods, to cause righteousness to prevail in the land, to destroy the wicked and the evil, to prevent the strong from plundering the weak.

· · ·

1

If a man accuse a man, and charge him with murder, but cannot convict him, the accuser shall be put to death.

2

If a man charge a man with sorcery, but cannot convict him, he who is charged with sorcery shall go to the sacred river, and he shall throw himself into the river; if the river overcome him, his prosecutor shall take to himself his house. If the river show that man to be innocent and he come forth unharmed, he that charged him with sorcery shall be put to death. He who threw himself into the river shall take to himself the house of his ancestor.

3

If a man, in a case (before the court), offer testimony concerning deeds of violence, and do not establish the testimony that he has given—if that case be a case involving life, that man shall be put to death.

4

If he offer testimony concerning grain or money, he shall himself bear the penalty imposed in that case.

5

If a judge pronounce a judgment, render a decision, deliver a sealed verdict, and afterward reverse his judgment, they shall convict that judge of varying his judgment and he shall pay twelve-fold the claim in that suit; then they shall remove him from his place on the bench of judges in the assembly, and he shall not (again) sit in judgment with the judges.

22

If a man practice robbery and be captured, that man shall be put to death.

23

If the brigand be not captured, the man who has been robbed shall establish the amount of his loss before the god, and the city and the governor, in whose land or border the robbery was committed, shall compensate him for whatsoever was lost.

24

If there were loss of life, the city and governor shall pay one mana of silver to his heirs.

48

If a man owe a debt and Adad [a god] inundate the field or the flood carry the produce away, or, through lack of water, grain have not grown in the field, in that year he shall not make any return of grain to the creditor, he shall alter his contract-tablet and he need not pay the interest for that year.

49

If a man obtain money from a merchant and give (as security) to the merchant a field prepared for grain or sesame, and say to him, "Cultivate the field, and harvest and take to thyself the grain and sesame which is produced"; and the cultivator raise grain or sesame in the field, at the time of harvest the owner of the field shall receive the grain or sesame which is in the field and he shall give to the merchant grain for the loan which he had obtained from him and for the interest and for the expenses of the cultivation.

55

If a man open his canal for irrigation and neglect it and he let the water carry away an adjacent field, he shall measure out grain on the basis of the adjacent fields.

66

If a man borrow money from a merchant, and his merchant foreclose(?) on him, if he have no money for repayment, but give his orchard, after (it has been) pollinated, to the merchant, and say to him, "The dates, as many as there (are produced) in the orchard, take for your money," that merchant shall not agree. The dates, as many as there are in the orchard, the owner shall take (gather) and shall pay the merchant the money and its interest according to the wording of his tablet; and the remaining dates which are in the orchard the owner shall take (for himself).

87

If he put out money at interest, for one shekel of silver he shall receive one-fifth of a shekel (*lit.,* one-sixth of a shekel plus six SHE) as interest.

105

If the agent be careless and do not take a receipt for the money which he has given to the merchant, the money not receipted for shall not be placed to his account.

127

If a man point the finger at a nun or the wife of a man and cannot justify it, they shall drag that man before the judges and they shall cut the hair of his forehead.

128

If a man take a wife and do not draw up a contract with her, that woman is not a wife.

129

If the wife of a man be taken in lying with another man, they shall bind them and throw them into the water. If the husband of the woman spare the life of his wife, the king shall spare the life of his servant (i.e., subject).

130

If a man force the (betrothed) wife of a man, who has not known a male and is living in her father's house, and lie in her bosom, and they take him, that man shall be put to death and that woman shall go free.

131

If a man accuse his wife and she have not been taken in lying with another man, she shall take an oath in the name of God and she shall return to her house.

132

If the finger have been pointed at the wife of a man because of another man, and she have not been taken in lying with another man, for her husband('s sake) she shall throw herself into the sacred river (i.e., she shall submit to the ordeal).

133 (Partly Restored)

If a man be taken captive and there be something to eat in his house and his wife go out of her house and she do not protect her body and she enter into another house, because that woman did not protect her body and entered into another house they shall convict that woman and they shall throw her into the water.

134

If a man be taken captive and there be nothing to eat in his house and his wife enter into another house, that woman has no blame.

135

If a man be taken captive and there be nothing to eat in his house, and his wife enter into another house and bear children; if later her husband return and reach his city, that woman shall return to her husband; the children shall go to their father.

194

If a man give his son to a nurse and that son die in the hands of the nurse, and without (the knowledge of) his father and mother the nurse come to an agreement (with some other family to substitute) another son, they shall convict her, and because she has made an agreement (to substitute) another son without the consent of the father and mother, they shall cut off her breast.

195

If a man strike his father, they shall cut off his hand.

196

If a man destroy the eye of another man, they shall destroy his eye.

197

If he break a man's bone, they shall break his bone.

198

If he destroy the eye of a common man or break a bone of a common man, he shall pay one mana of silver.

199

If he destroy the eye of a man's slave or break a bone of a man's slave, he shall pay one-half his price.

200

If a man knock out a tooth of a man of his own rank, they shall knock out his tooth.

201

If he knock out a tooth of a common man, he shall pay one-third mana of silver.

202

If a man smite on the cheek a man who is his superior, he shall receive sixty strokes with an oxtail whip in public.

203

If the son of a gentleman smite the son of a gentleman of his own rank on the cheek, he shall pay one mana of silver.

204

If a common man smite a common man on the cheek, he shall pay ten shekels of silver.

205

If a man's slave smite the son of a gentleman on the cheek, they shall cut off his ear.

206

If a man strike (another) man in a quarrel and wound him, that man shall swear, "I did not strike him intentionally," and he shall be responsible for the physician.

207

If he die as the result of the blow, he shall swear (as above), and if it were the son of a gentleman, he shall pay one-half mana of silver.

208

If it were a common man, he shall pay one-third mana of silver.

209

If a man strike the daughter of a man and bring about a miscarriage, he shall pay ten shekels of silver for her miscarriage.

210

If that woman die, they shall put his daughter to death.

211

If through a blow he bring about a miscarriage to the daughter of a common man, he shall pay five shekels of silver.

212

If that woman die, he shall pay one-half mana of silver.

213

If he strike the maidservant of a man and bring about a miscarriage, he shall pay two shekels of silver.

214

If that maidservant die, he shall pay one-third mana of silver.

215

If a physician make a deep incision upon a man (i.e., perform a major operation) with his bronze lancet and save the man's life; or if he operate on the eye socket of a man with his bronze lancet and save that man's eye, he shall receive ten shekels of silver.

216

If it were a common man, he shall receive five shekels.

217

If it were a man's slave, the owner of the slave shall give two shekels of silver to the physician.

218

If a physician make a deep incision upon a man with his bronze lancet and cause the man's death, or operate on the eye socket of a man with his bronze lancet and destroy the man's eye, they shall cut off his hand.

219

If a physician make a deep incision upon a slave of a common man with his bronze lancet and cause his death, he shall substitute a slave of equal value.

226

If a barber without (the consent of) the owner of the slave cut the hair of the forehead of a slave (making him) unrecognizable, they shall cut off the hand of that barber.

235

If a shipbuilder construct a boat for a man and he do not make its construction trustworthy, and that boat develop structural weakness the same year (and) have an accident, the shipbuilder shall dismantle that boat and he shall strengthen it at his own expense and he shall give the strengthened boat to the owner of the boat.

STUDY QUESTIONS

1. Is it apparent that the Hammurabic Code is clearly the product of a civilization, rather than some other kind of early society? Does the code illustrate key elements of what a civilization is?
2. How many social classes did Babylonia have? Does the code suggest wide gaps among them?
3. What protections did women have in Babylonian law? Why is it clear that this was a patriarchal society?
4. Did Babylonia have a powerful state with a large bureaucracy? What state services, now taken for granted in dealing with crimes, were absent in this society? Why was so much attention given to issues of false accusation?
5. What religious beliefs did the code reflect? Are these the same beliefs as those suggested in *The Gilgamesh Epic*?
6. What kind of economy did Babylonia have? What were some common problems relating to economic activity that the code addressed? What principles were used to deal with such problems? How do they compare with principles used in more modern societies?

3   EGYPT: RELIGIOUS CULTURE AND THE AFTERLIFE

Egyptian civilization was the second great river-valley center in the ancient Mediterranean, but this one was in Africa rather than in the Middle East. Egyptian kingdoms, developing from about 3000 B.C.E. onward, had frequent contact with Mesopotamia, particularly in trade but periodically in wars of defense and conquest. Although there was also some cultural interaction, Egyptian religion and art emerged along very distinctive lines. Strong emphasis was placed on the power of the gods, starting with the god of the sun, Re. A host of other gods served other specific purposes and warranted careful propitiation by humans; Osiris, particularly, had power over the passage after death. The strong Egyptian state was headed by a king, or pharaoh, who himself claimed divine status, while working in tandem with powerful priests. Egypt enjoyed political stability over long stretches of time, and this, plus the reliability of irrigation from the river Nile, may have given Egyptians an optimistic sense of control.

Concern about the afterlife was a hallmark of Egyptian civilization, motivating elaborate art for shrines and an active trade in mummification to preserve the body from decay. The following selection deals with Egyptian religious beliefs and their relationship to ethics and to preparations for the afterlife. These preparations not only included awareness of an awesome judgment day in which one's deeds would be tallied but also protection by evocation of magical powers through spells that could help ensure benign treatment in the Netherworld after death. Concern for protection, in other words, did not end with death.

The material is taken from what is now called the *Book of the Dead,* which is a sheet of papyrus (Egyptian writing material made of dried papyrus leaves) covered with magical texts and illustrations that Egyptians placed with their dead to help them pass through the dangers of the Underworld and attain a blissful afterlife in the Field of Reeds, the Egyptian heaven. Even ordinary people frequently ordered texts of this sort, and the rich commissioned elaborate statements. The material dates up to the mid-15th century B.C.E.

From *The Ancient Egyptian Book of the Dead,* edited by Carol Andrews and translated by Raymond O. Faulkner, published for the Trustees of the British Museum (London: British Museum Publications, 1985), pp. 27–29, 31, 36, 153–154. © the British Museum, British Museum Press.

BOOK OF THE DEAD

I. INTRODUCTORY HYMN TO THE SUN-GOD RE

Worship of Re When He Rises in the Eastern Horizon of the Sky by N

He says: Hail to you, you having come as Khepri, even Khepri who is the creator of the gods. You rise and shine on the back of your mother (the sky), having appeared in glory as King of the gods. Your mother Nut shall use her arms on your behalf in making greeting. The Manu-mountain receives you in peace, Maat embraces you at all seasons. May you give power and might in vindication—and a coming forth as a living soul to see Horakhty—to the ka of N.

He says: O all you gods of the Soul-mansion who judge sky and earth in the balance, who give food and provisions; O Tatenen, Unique One, creator of mankind; O Southern, Northern, Western and Eastern Enneads, give praise to Re, Lord of the Sky, the Sovereign who made the gods. Worship him in his goodly shape when he appears in the Day-bark. May those who are above worship you, may those who are below worship you, may Thoth and Maat write to you daily; your serpent-foe has been given over to the fire and the rebel-serpent is fallen, his arms are bound, Re has taken away his movements, and the Children of Impotence are non-existent. The Mansion of the Prince is in festival, the noise of shouting is in the Great Place, the gods are in joy, when they see Re in his appearing, his rays flooding the lands. The Majesty of this noble god proceeds, he has entered the land of Manu, the land is bright at his daily birth, and he has attained his state of yesterday. May you be gracious to me when I see your beauty, having departed from upon earth. May I smite the Ass, may I drive off the rebel-serpent, may I destroy Apep when he acts, for I have seen the abdju-fish in its moment of being and the bulti-fish piloting the canoe on its waterway. I have seen Horus as helmsman, with Thoth and Maat beside him, I have taken hold of the bow-warp of the Night-bark and the stern-warp of the Day-bark. May he grant that I see the sun-disc and behold the moon unceasingly every day; may my soul go forth to travel to every place which it desires; may my name be called out, may it be found at the board of offerings; may there be given to me loaves in the Presence like the Followers of Horus, may a place be made for me in the solar bark on the day when the god ferries across, and may I be received into the presence of Osiris in the Land of Vindication.

For the ka of N.

II. INTRODUCTORY HYMN TO OSIRIS

Worship of Osiris Wennefer, the Great God who dwells in the Thinite nome, King of Eternity, Lord of Everlasting, who passes millions of years in his lifetime, first-born son of Nut, begotten of Geb, Heir, Lord of the Wereret-crown, whose White Crown is tall, Sovereign of gods and men. He has taken the crook and the flail and the office of his forefathers. May your heart which is in the desert land be glad, for your son Horus is firm on your throne, while you have appeared as Lord of Busiris, as the Ruler who is in Abydos. The Two Lands flourish in vindication because of you in the presence of the Lord of All. All that exists is ushered in to him in his name of 'Face to whom men are ushered'; the Two Lands are marshalled for him as leader in this his name of Sokar; his might is far-reaching, one greatly feared in this his name of Osiris; he passes over the length of eternity in his name of Wennefer.

Hail to you, King of Kings, Lord of Lords, Ruler of Rulers, who took possession of the Two Lands even in the womb of Nut; he rules the plains of the Silent Land, even he the golden of body, blue of head, on whose arms is turquoise. O Pillar of Myriads, broad of breast, kindly of countenance, who is in the Sacred Land: May you grant power in the sky, might on earth and vindication in the realm of the dead, a journeying downstream to Busiris as a living soul and a journeying upstream to Abydos as a heron; to go in and out without hindrance at all the gates of the Netherworld. May there be given to me bread from the House of Cool Water and a table of offerings from Heliopolis, my toes being firm-planted in the Field of Rushes. May the barley and emmer which are in it belong to the ka of the Osiris N.

III. THE JUDGMENT OF THE DEAD

The Heart of the Dead Man Is Weighed in the Scales of the Balance against the Feather of Righteousness

Spell 2

Spell for going out into the day and living after death

O you Sole One who shine in the moon, O you Sole One who glow in the sun, may N go forth from among those multitudes of yours who are outside, may those who are in the sunshine release him, may the Netherworld be opened to him when N goes out into the day in order to do what he wishes on earth among the living. . . .

Spell 6

Spell for causing a shabti to do work for a man in the realm of the dead

O shabti, allotted to me, if I be summoned or if I be detailed to do any work which has to be done in the realm of the dead; if indeed obstacles are implanted for you therewith as a man at his duties, you shall detail yourself for me on every occasion of making arable the fields, of flooding the banks or of conveying sand from east to west; 'Here am I,' you shall say.

Spell 30b

O my heart which I had from my mother! O my heart which I had from my mother! O my heart of my different ages! Do not stand up as a witness against me, do not be opposed to me in the tribunal, do not be hostile to me in the presence of the Keeper of the Balance, for you are my ka which was in my body, the protector who made my members hale. Go forth to the happy place whereto we speed; do not make my name stink to the Entourage who make men. Do not tell lies about me in the presence of the god; it is indeed well that you should hear!

Thus says Thoth, judge of truth, to the Great Ennead which is in the presence of Osiris; Hear this word of very truth. I have judged the heart of the deceased, and his soul stands as a witness for him. His deeds are righteous in the great balance, and no sin has been found in him. He did not diminish the offerings in the temples, he did not destroy what had been made, he did not go about with deceitful speech while he was on earth.

Thus says the Great Ennead to Thoth who is in Hermopolis: This utterance of yours is true. The vindicated Osiris N is straightforward, he has no sin, there is no accusation against him before us, Ammit shall not be permitted to have power over him. Let there be given to him the offerings which are issued in the presence of Osiris, and may a grant of land be established in the Field of Offerings as for the Followers of Horus.

Thus says Horus son of Isis: I have come to you, O Wennefer, and I bring N to you. His heart is true, having gone forth from the balance, and he has not sinned against any god or any goddess. Thoth has judged him in writing which has been told to the Ennead, and Maat the great has witnessed. Let there be given to him bread and beer which have been issued in the presence of Osiris, and he will be for ever like the Followers of Horus.

Thus says N: Here I am in your presence, O Lord of the West. There is no wrong-doing in my body, I have not wittingly told lies, there has been no second fault. Grant that I may be like the favoured ones who are in your suite, O Osiris, one greatly favoured by the good god, one loved of the Lord of the Two Lands, N, vindicated before Osiris.

. . . Hail to you, great god, Lord of Justice! I have come to you, my lord, that you may bring me so that I may see your beauty, for I know you and I know your name, and I know the names of the forty-two gods of those who are with you in this Hall of Justice, who live on those who cherish evil and who gulp down their blood on that day of the reckoning of characters in the presence of Wennefer. Behold the double son of the Songstresses; Lord of Truth is your name. Behold, I have come to you, I have brought you truth, I have repelled falsehood for you. I have not done falsehood against men, I have not impoverished my associates, I have done no wrong in the Place of Truth, I have not learnt that which is not, I have done no evil, I have not daily made labour in excess of what was due to be done for me, my name has not reached the offices of those who control slaves, I have not deprived the orphan of his property, I have not done what the gods detest, I have not calumniated a servant to his master, I have not caused pain, I have not made hungry, I have not made to weep, I have not killed, I have not commanded to kill, I have not made suffering for anyone, I have not lessened the food-offerings in the temples, I have not destroyed the loaves of the gods, I have not taken away the food of the spirits, I have not copulated, I have not misbehaved, I have not lessened food-supplies, . . . I have not diminished the aroura, I have not encroached upon fields, I have not laid anything upon the weights of the hand-balance, I have not taken anything from the plummet of the standing scales, I have not taken the milk from the mouths of children, I have not deprived the herds of their pastures, I have not trapped the birds from the preserves of the gods, I have not caught the fish of their marshlands, I have not diverted water at its season, I have not built a dam on flowing water, I have not quenched the fire when it is burning, I have not neglected the dates for offering choice meats, I have not withheld cattle from the god's-offerings, I have not opposed a god in his procession.

I am pure, pure, pure, pure! My purity is the purity of that great phoenix which is in Heracleopolis, because I am indeed the nose of the Lord of Wind who made all men live on that day of completing the Sacred Eye in Heliopolis in the 2nd month of winter last day, in the presence of the lord of this land. I am he who saw the completion of the Sacred Eye in Heliopolis, and nothing evil shall come into being against me in this land in this Hall of Justice, because I know the names of these gods who are in it. . . .

Spell 154

Spell for not letting the corpse perish

Hail to you, my father Osiris! I have come to you to the intent that you may heal my flesh; I am complete like my father Khepri, who is the like of one who does not perish. Come, that my breath may be stronger than yours, O Lord of Breath; where are the likes of him? May I endure longer than you, for I am fashioned as the possessor of a burial; may you permit me to go down into the earth for ever like that one who serves you and your father Atum, and his corpse will not perish; such is he who will not be destroyed. I have not done what you dislike; may your ka love me and not thrust me aside; take me after you. May I not become corrupt, being like that one who served you better than any god or any goddess, than any herds or any snakes who shall perish. May my soul ascend aloft after death; may it descend only after it has perished. Such is he who is decayed; all his bones are corrupt, his flesh is slain, his bones are softened, his flesh is made into foul water, his corruption stinks and he turns into many worms . . .

Now every mortal is thus, one who will die whether (men), herds, fowl, fish, snakes or worms; those who live will die. May no worm at all pass by; may they not come against me in their various shapes; you shall not give me over to that slayer who is in his . . . , who kills the body, who rots the hidden one, who destroys a multitude of corpses, who lives by killing the living, who carries out his business and who does what has been commanded to him. You shall not give me over to his fingers, he shall not have power over me, for I am at your command, O Lord of the Gods.

Hail to you, my father Osiris! You shall possess your body; you shall not become corrupt, you shall not have worms, you shall not be distended, you shall not stink, you shall not become putrid, you shall not become worms. I am Khepri; I will possess my body for ever, for I will not become corrupt, I will not decay, I will not be putrid, I will not become worms . . .

STUDY QUESTIONS

1. What were some of the main features of the Egyptian religion? What kinds of gods did the Egyptians believe in? What was the relationship between people and gods?
2. What did Egyptians expect concerning judgment after death? How might these expectations affect behavior?
3. What was the Egyptian concept of the afterlife? How did it compare with views of heaven in other religions later on? What powers might people have in the afterlife? What was the purpose of special spells and incantations?
4. How did Egyptian views of religion and relationships of humans with the gods compare with those in Mesopotamia, as suggested in *The Gilgamesh Epic*?

EGYPTIAN ARTIFACTS FOR THE DEAD

Themes of travel from Earth to the afterlife were commonplace in Egyptian art, suggesting the tremendous importance of this religious goal. Later pyramids sometimes contained full-sized ships to help transport the pharaoh (king) to the afterlife. Animal-headed gods were another common theme, relating to ideas about how different gods would play different roles in judging people and arranging the transition from this life to the next.

Egyptian art, though largely religious in nature, reveals much about Egyptian life more generally, including, for example, the relatively important position of women.

This sculpture is an early example of Egyptian art, from the twelfth dynasty, about 3000 B.C.E. It is housed in the Museum of Antiquities in Turin, Italy.
(Alinari/Art Resource, NY)

STUDY QUESTIONS

1. How did artistic representations of the transition to the afterlife relate to other aspects of Egyptian society? What ideas are suggested by the image of the boat from this life to the afterlife?
2. What kind of transition to death does this sculpture suggest?

3. What attitudes toward the gods are suggested in the sculpture? How did Egyptian attitudes to the gods compare with those of the Sumerians, as in *The Gilgamesh Epic* featured in Chapter 1?
4. Does the sculpture suggest any particular features of Egyptian society?
5. Does this representation of the passage to death correspond to the ideas about death in the *Book of the Dead* text? Beginning simply with the similar subject matter and the importance given to it, can you trace connections?

4

THE HEBREW BIBLE

The Jewish people settled near the eastern Mediterranean around 1200 B.C.E.—the first fully reliable record of their existence comes from the 1100s, although the Jewish religion urged an earlier history including enslavement in Egypt. Hebrews formed a regional state in the period when the larger river-valley empires in Egypt and Mesopotamia were weakening. Jewish political independence did not last long (the prime period of the Israelite state was 1000 to 922 B.C.E.), but the religion the Jewish leaders had formulated was another story.

The principal gift of the ancient Hebrews to the world's cultural bank was their monotheistic religion, which today thrives as a major religion and in the past served as an essential ingredient for the successor religions of Christianity and Islam. Stressing complete submission to the laws and commands of their omnipotent and omnipresent God, a deity whom Hebrews perceived as outside of nature and comprehensible in intellectual and abstract terms, the religion focused on God's covenant with the Hebrews and the history of their special relationship. As lawgiver and universal upholder of moral order, God is depicted in the Holy Writ of Israel as beneficent and loving but also as a stern and vengeful overseer who unhesitatingly punishes those who refuse to comply. Both the evolution of their unique covenant theology and their laws receive prominent treatment in this canonical text, which offers a history of the ancient Hebrews and serves as a remarkable literary masterpiece as well.

Priests and prophets began spelling out the tenets of the Hebrew religion in oral form, emphasizing not only God's power but a series of laws and ethical obligations that also endowed the religion with distinctive qualities. Elements of the Hebrew Bible began to be written down from the 8th century B.C.E. onward, and were gradually collected into a coherent larger holy text.

The first selection emphasizes two aspects of the religion: first, the definition of a single God and then God's relationship to the Hebrew people. The second selection deals more with laws and ethical codes; here, Hebrew writings emphasized that God gave a series of laws to Moses after the flight from enslavement in Egypt. These laws included the Ten Commandments but also a subsequent series of rules and ethical prescriptions.

From *The Oxford Study Bible: Revised English Bible with the Aprocrypha,* edited by M. Jack Suggs, Katharine Dobb Skenfeld, and James R. Mueller (New York: Oxford University Press, 1992). *Revised English Bible* © Oxford University Press and Cambridge University Press, 1989. Selection 1, Isaiah: pp. 747–748, 40:1–31; 41:1–24. Selection 1, Psalms: p. 615, 93:1–5; 94:1–20. Selection 2, Exodus: pp. 81–86, 19:1–6; 20:1–17; 21:1–7, 33–36; 22:1–5, 16, 21–27; 23:1–8, 13–32.

FROM THE HEBREW BIBLE

I. THE NATURE OF GOD: ISAIAH AND PSALMS

Isaiah

Comfort my people; bring comfort to them,
says your God;
speak kindly to Jerusalem
and proclaim to her
that her term of bondage is served,
her penalty is paid;
for she has received at the LORD's hand
double measure for all her sins.
A voice cries:
'Clear a road through the wilderness for the LORD,
prepare a highway across the desert for our God.
Let every valley be raised,
every mountain and hill be brought low,
uneven ground be made smooth,
and steep places become level.
Then will the glory of the LORD be revealed
and all mankind together will see it.
The LORD himself has spoken.'

A voice says, 'Proclaim!'
and I asked, 'What shall I proclaim?'
'All mortals are grass,
they last no longer than a wild flower of the field.
The grass withers, the flower fades,
when the blast of the LORD blows on them.
Surely the people are grass!
The grass may wither, the flower fade,
but the word of our God will endure for ever.'

Climb to a mountaintop,
you that bring good news to Zion;
raise your voice and shout aloud,
you that carry good news to Jerusalem,
raise it fearlessly;
say to the cities of Judah, 'Your God is here!'
Here is the LORD GOD; he is coming in might,
coming to rule with powerful arm.
His reward is with him,
like recompense before him.
Like a shepherd he will tend his flock
and with his arm keep them together;
he will carry the lambs in his bosom
and lead the ewes to water.

WHO has measured the waters of the sea in the hollow of his hand,
or with its span gauged the heavens?
Who has held all the soil of the earth in a bushel,
or weighed the mountains on a balance,
the hills on a pair of scales?
Who has directed the spirit of the LORD?

What counsellor stood at his side to instruct him?
With whom did he confer to gain discernment?
Who taught him this path of justice,
or taught him knowledge,
or showed him the way of wisdom?

To him nations are but drops from a bucket,
no more than moisture on the scales;
to him coasts and islands weigh as light as specks of dust!
Lebanon does not yield wood enough for fuel,
beasts enough for a whole-offering.
All the nations are as naught in his sight;
he reckons them as less than nothing.

What likeness, then, will you find for GOD
or what form to resemble his?
An image which a craftsman makes,
and a goldsmith overlays with gold
and fits with studs of silver?
Or should someone choose mulberry-wood,
a wood that does not rot,
and seek out a skilful craftsman for the task
of setting up an image and making it secure? . . .
Do you not know, have you not heard,
were you not told long ago,
have you not perceived ever since the world was founded,
that God sits enthroned on the vaulted roof of the world,
and its inhabitants appear as grasshoppers?

He stretches out the skies like a curtain,
spreads them out like a tent to live in;
he reduces the great to naught
and makes earthly rulers as nothing.
Scarcely are they planted, scarcely sown,
scarcely have they taken root in the ground,
before he blows on them and they wither,
and a whirlwind carries them off like chaff.
To whom, then, will you liken me,
whom set up as my equal?
asks the HOLY ONE.
Lift up your eyes to the heavens;
consider who created these,

led out their host one by one,
and summoned each by name.
Through his great might, his strength and power,
not one is missing.

Jacob, why do you complain,
and you, Israel, why do you say,
'My lot is hidden from the LORD,
my cause goes unheeded by my God'?
Do you not know, have you not heard?
The LORD, the eternal God,
creator of earth's farthest bounds,
does not weary or grow faint;
his understanding cannot be fathomed.
He gives vigour to the weary,
new strength to the exhausted.
Young men may grow weary and faint,
even the fittest may stumble and fall;
but those who look to the LORD will win new strength,
they will soar as on eagles' wings;
they will run and not feel faint,
march on and not grow weary.

Listen in silence to me, all you coasts and islands;
let the peoples come to meet me.
Let them draw near, then let them speak up;
together we shall go to the place of judgment.

Who has raised up from the east
one greeted by victory wherever he goes,
making nations his subjects
and overthrowing their kings?
He scatters them with his sword like dust
and with his bow like chaff driven before the wind;
he puts them to flight and passes on unscathed,
swifter than any traveller on foot.
Whose work is this, who has brought it to pass?
Who has summoned the generations from the beginning?
I, the LORD, was with the first of them,
and I am with those who come after . . .

But you, Israel my servant,
Jacob whom I have chosen,
descendants of my friend Abraham,
I have taken you from the ends of the earth,
and summoned you from its farthest corners;
I have called you my servant,
have chosen you and not rejected you:
have no fear, for I am with you;

be not afraid, for I am your God.
I shall strengthen you and give you help
and uphold you with my victorious right hand.

Now all who defy you
will be confounded and put to shame;
all who set themselves against you
will be as nothing and will vanish.
You will look for your assailants
but you will not find them;
those who take up arms against you
will be reduced to nothing.
For I, the LORD your God,
take you by the right hand
and say to you, Have no fear;
it is I who help you.

Have no fear, Jacob you worm and Israel you maggot.
It is I who help you, declares the LORD;
your redeemer is the Holy One of Israel.
See, I shall make of you a sharp threshing-sledge,
new and studded with teeth;
you will thresh mountains and crush them to dust
and reduce the hills to chaff;
you will winnow them; the wind will carry them away
and a gale will scatter them.
Then you will rejoice in the LORD
and glory in the Holy One of Israel.

The poor and the needy look for water and find none;
their tongues are parched with thirst.
But I the LORD shall provide for their wants;
I, the God of Israel, shall not forsake them.
I shall open rivers on the arid heights,
and wells in the valleys;
I shall turn the desert into pools
and dry land into springs of water;
I shall plant cedars in the wilderness,
acacias, myrtles, and wild olives;
I shall grow pines on the barren heath
side by side with fir and box tree,
that everyone may see and know,
may once and for all observe and understand
that the LORD himself has done this:
it is the creation of the Holy One of Israel.

Come, open your plea, says the LORD,
present your case, says Jacob's King;
let these idols come forward

and foretell the future for us.
Let them declare the meaning of these past events
that we may reflect on it;
let them predict the future to us
that we may know what it holds.

Declare what is yet to happen;
then we shall know you are gods.
Do something, whether good or bad,
anything that will strike us with dismay and fear.
You cannot! You are sprung from nothing,
your works are non-existent.
To choose you is outrageous! . . .

Psalms

The LORD has become King, clothed with majesty;
the LORD is robed, girded with might.

The earth is established immovably;
your throne is established from of old;
from all eternity you are God.
LORD, the great deep lifts up,
the deep lifts up its voice;
the deep lifts up its crashing waves.
Mightier than the sound of great waters,
mightier than the breakers of the sea,
mighty on high is the LORD.

Your decrees stand firm,
and holiness befits your house,
LORD, throughout the ages.

GOD of vengeance, LORD,
GOD of vengeance, show yourself!
Rise, judge of the earth;
repay the arrogant as they deserve.
LORD, how long will the wicked,
how long will the wicked exult?
Evildoers are all full of bluster,
boasting and bragging.

They crush your people, LORD,
and oppress your chosen nation;
they murder the widow and the stranger
and put the fatherless to death.
They say, 'The LORD does not see,
the God of Jacob pays no heed.'

Take heed yourselves, most stupid of people;
you fools, when will you be wise?

Can he who implanted the ear not hear,
he who fashioned the eye not see?
Will he who instructs the nations not correct them?
The teacher of mankind, has he no knowledge?
The LORD knows that the thoughts of everyone
are but a puff of wind.

Happy the one whom you, LORD, instruct
and teach from your law,
giving him respite from misfortune
until a pit is dug for the wicked.
The LORD will not abandon his people
or forsake his chosen nation;
for justice will again be joined to right,
and all who are upright in heart will follow it.

Who is on my side against the wicked?
Who will stand up for me against the evildoers?
Had the LORD not been my helper,
I should soon have dwelt in the silent grave
If I said that my foot was slipping,
your love, LORD, continued to hold me up.
When anxious thoughts filled my heart,
your comfort brought me joy.
Will corrupt justice win you as an ally,
contriving mischief under cover of law? . . .

II. HEBREW LAW

Exodus

In the third month after Israel had left Egypt, they came to the wilderness of Sinai. They set out from Rephidim and, entering the wilderness of Sinai, they encamped there, pitching their tents in front of the mountain. Moses went up to God, and the LORD called to him from the mountain and said, 'This is what you are to say to the house of Jacob and tell the sons of Israel:

You yourselves have seen what I did to Egypt, and how I have carried you on eagles' wings and brought you here to me. If only you will now listen to me and keep my covenant, then out of all peoples you will become my special possession; for the whole earth is mine. You will be to me a kingdom of priests, my holy nation. Those are the words you are to speak to the Israelites.' . . .

God spoke all these words:
I am the LORD your God who brought you out of Egypt, out of the land of slavery.

You must have no other god besides me.

You must not make a carved image for yourself, nor the likeness of anything in the heavens above, or on the earth below, or in the waters under the earth.

You must not bow down to them in worship; for I, the LORD your God, am a jealous God, punishing the children for the sins of the parents to the third and fourth generation of those who reject me. But I keep faith with thousands, those who love me and keep my commandments.

You must not make wrong use of the name of the LORD your God; the LORD will not leave unpunished anyone who misuses his name.

Remember to keep the sabbath day holy. You have six days to labour and do all your work; but the seventh day is a sabbath of the LORD your God; that day you must not do any work, neither you, nor your son or your daughter, your slave or your slave-girl, your cattle, or the alien residing among you; for in six days the LORD made the heavens and the earth, the sea, and all that is in them, and on the seventh day he rested. Therefore the LORD blessed the sabbath day and declared it holy.

Honour your father and your mother, so that you may enjoy long life in the land which the LORD your God is giving you.

Do not commit murder.

Do not commit adultery.

Do not steal.

Do not give false evidence against your neighbour.

Do not covet your neighbour's household: you must not covet your neighbour's wife, his slave, his slave-girl, his ox, his donkey, or anything that belongs to him. . . .

These are the laws you are to set before them:

When you purchase a Hebrew as a slave, he will be your slave for six years; in the seventh year he is to go free without paying anything.

If he comes to you alone, he is to go away alone; but if he is already a married man, his wife is to go away with him.

If his master gives him a wife, and she bears him sons or daughters, the woman with her children belongs to her master, and the man must go away alone. But if the slave should say, 'I am devoted to my master and my wife and children; I do not wish to go free,' then his master must bring him to God: he is to be brought to the door or the doorpost, and his master will pierce his ear with an awl; the man will then be his slave for life.

When a man sells his daughter into slavery, she is not to go free as male slaves may.

If she proves unpleasing to her master who had designed her for himself, he must let her be redeemed; he has treated her unfairly, and therefore he has no right to sell her to foreigners. If he assigns her to his son, he must allow her the rights of a daughter. If he takes another woman, he must not deprive the first of meat, clothes, and conjugal rights; if he does not provide her with these three things, she is to go free without payment. . . .

When a man removes the cover of a cistern or digs a cistern and leaves it uncovered, then if an ox or a donkey falls into it, the owner of the cistern must make good the loss; he must pay the owner the price of the animal, and the dead beast will be his.

When one man's ox butts another's and kills it, they must sell the live ox, share the price, and also share the dead beast. But if it is known that the ox has for some time past been vicious and the owner has not kept it under control, he must make good the loss, ox for ox, but the dead beast is his.

When a man steals an ox or a sheep and slaughters or sells it, he must repay five beasts for the ox and four sheep for the sheep. He must pay in full; if he has no means, he is to be sold to pay for the theft. But if the animal is found alive in his possession, be it ox, donkey, or sheep, he must repay two for each one stolen.

If a burglar is caught in the act and receives a fatal injury, it is not murder; but if he breaks in after sunrise and receives a fatal injury, then it is murder.

When a man burns off a field or a vineyard and lets the fire spread so that it burns another man's field, he must make restitution from his own field according to the yield expected; and if the whole field is laid waste, he must make restitution from the best part of his own field or vineyard. . . .

When a man seduces a virgin who is not yet betrothed, he must pay the bride-price for her to be his wife. If her father refuses to give her to him, the seducer must pay in silver a sum equal to the bride-price for virgins. . . .

You must not wrong or oppress an alien; you were yourselves aliens in Egypt.

You must not wrong a widow or a fatherless child. If you do, and they appeal to me, be sure that I shall listen; my anger will be roused and I shall kill you with the sword; your own wives will become widows and your children fatherless.

If you advance money to any poor man amongst my people, you are not to act like a moneylender; you must not exact interest from him.

If you take your neighbour's cloak in pawn, return it to him by sunset, because it is his only covering. It is the cloak in which he wraps his body; in what else can he sleep? If he appeals to me, I shall listen, for I am full of compassion. . . .

You must not be led into wrongdoing by the majority, nor, when you give evidence in a lawsuit, should you side with the majority to pervert justice; nor should you show favouritism to a poor person in his lawsuit.

Should you come upon your enemy's ox or donkey straying, you must take it back to him. Should you see the donkey of someone who hates you lying helpless under its load, however unwilling you may be to help, you must lend a hand with it.

You must not deprive the poor man of justice in his lawsuit. Avoid all lies, and do not cause the death of the innocent and guiltless; for I the LORD will never acquit the guilty. Do not accept a bribe, for bribery makes the discerning person blind and the just person give a crooked answer. . . .

Be attentive to every word of mine. You must not invoke other gods: their names are not to cross your lips.

Three times a year you are to keep a pilgrim-feast to me. You are to celebrate the pilgrim-feast of Unleavened Bread: for seven days, as I have commanded you, you are to eat unleavened bread at the appointed time in the month of Abib, for in that month you came out of Egypt; and no one is to come into my presence without an offering. You are to celebrate the pilgrim-feast of Harvest, with the firstfruits of your work in sowing the land, and the pilgrim-feast of Ingathering at the end of the year, when you gather the fruits of your work in from the land. Those three times a year all your males are to come into the presence of the LORD GOD.

Do not offer the blood of my sacrifice at the same time as anything leavened.

The fat of my festal offering is not to remain overnight till morning.

You must bring the choicest firstfruits of your soil to the house of the LORD your God.

Do not boil a kid in its mother's milk.

And now I am sending an angel before you to guard you on your way and to bring you to the place I have prepared. Heed him and listen to his voice. Do not defy him; he will not pardon your rebelliousness, for my authority rests in him. If you will only listen to his voice and do all I tell you, then I shall be an enemy to your enemies, and I shall harass those who harass you. My angel will go before you and bring you to the Amorites, the Hittites, the Perizzites, the Canaanites, the Hivites, and the Jebusites, and I will make an end of them. You are not to bow down to their gods; you are not to worship them or observe their rites. Rather, you must tear down all their images and smash their sacred pillars. You are to worship the LORD your God, and he will bless your bread and your water. I shall take away all sickness out of your midst. No woman will miscarry or be barren in your land. I shall grant you a full span of life.

I shall send terror of me ahead of you and throw into panic every people you find in your path. I shall make all your enemies turn their backs towards you. I shall spread panic before you to drive out the Hivites, the Canaanites, and the Hittites in front of you.

I shall not drive them out all in one year, or the land would become waste and the wild beasts too many for you, but I shall drive them out little by little until you have grown numerous enough to take possession of the country. I shall establish your frontiers from the Red Sea to the sea of the Philistines, and from the wilderness to the river Ephrates. I shall give the inhabitants of the land into your power, and you will drive them out before you. You are not to make any alliance with them and their gods. They must not stay in your land, for fear they make you sin against me by ensnaring you into the worship of their gods. . . .

STUDY QUESTIONS

1. What were the qualities of the Hebrew God? What were the obligations to God?
2. Why were Hebrews called the chosen people? Does their relationship with God help explain why Judaism did not become an active missionary religion? Does it help explain the durability of Jewish religion in adverse circumstances?
3. Why is the Hebrew insistence on monotheism an important turning point in the history of Mediterranean religions?
4. How did Hebrew law compare with the Hammurabic Code? Did it reflect the same social and gender structure and prescriptions, or were there subtle differences in the treatment of lower social groups and of women?
5. The Hammurabic Code was a royal compilation, though sanctioned by a god; Hebrew law was held to emanate from God. How does this difference emerge in the laws offered—what behaviors they cover, how they are sanctioned? Is a clearer set of ethical obligations involved in Hebrew law?
6. How did the Hebrew approach to God and to divine sanctions for good behavior compare with Egyptian religion? What were the main similarities and differences?
7. What were some of the reasons why, beginning with Judaism, monotheistic religions began to replace polytheistic religions in the Middle East? (See also later chapters on Zoroastrianism, Christianity, and Islam.)

5 HERODOTUS AND THE PERSIAN EMPIRE

Herodotus of Halicarnassus was a Greek historian—Greece's first known historian—who wrote between 450 and 420 B.C.E. He traveled widely in the Eastern Mediterranean world, and based his history on what he was told and observed.

One of his obvious topics was the Persian Empire, which had formed after defeating a previous Empire, that of the Medes, in the area now known as Iran. In 553 B.C.E. Cyrus the Great led a revolt against the Medean king, Astyges, presumably with the help of some dissidents led by Harpagus—Astyges had arranged for his son to marry a Persian and Cyrus was the result of that marriage, hence was the grandson of Astyges. Cyrus quickly expanded the Persian Empire to cover most of the Middle East, in the process attacking the many Greek cities in the region. Much later, a Persian effort to invade Greece, early in the 5th century, resulted in defeat, and later still Persia was conquered by Alexander the Great. Persian culture, however, took deep root in the region, and Persia in many ways constituted a fourth great classical civilization in Eurasia.

In the passage that follows, Herodotus offers his own version of Cyrus's rise (earlier, he repeats a Moses-like story of Cyrus being hidden from the king and brought up in a humble family despite his high birth; the story may have circulated widely but it was not true). He also discusses a variety of Persian characteristics. His account raises two main kinds of questions: first, what aspects of Persian society were unusual, compared to other early civilizations, and what were fairly standard. The second set of questions involves Herodotus's accuracy: he was a sympathetic observer in many ways, despite Greek-Persian hostility before his lifetime. But he almost certainly did not speak Persian and so depended on stories, some of which may not have been true.

THE HISTORIES

When Cyrus grew up to be the bravest and most popular young man in Persia, Harpagus, who was burning for revenge upon Astyges, began to pay him court and send him presents. His own position, he thought, was inadequate to justify hopes of punishing the king without assistance; so when he saw Cyrus coming to maturity, he exerted himself to win his support, saying he had suffered injuries not unlike his own. He had already paved the way to his design by severally persuading the great

Median nobles that it would be to their advantage, in view of the harshness of Astyges' rule, to dethrone him in favour of Cyrus. This done by way of preparation, Harpagus wished to inform Cyrus of his purpose; but, as Cyrus lived in Persia and the roads were guarded, there was only one way he could think of to get a message through to him: this was by slitting open a hare, without pulling the fur off, and inserting into its belly a slip of paper on which he had written what he wanted to say. He then sewed up the hare, gave it to a trusted servant, together with a net to make him look like a huntsman, and sent him off to Persia with orders to present the hare to Cyrus, and tell him by word of mouth to cut it open with his own hands, and to let no one be present while he did so. The orders were obeyed. Cyrus received the hare, cut it open, found the letter inside and read it. 'Son of Cambyses,' it ran, 'since the gods watch over you—for without them you would never have been so fortunate—pay back Astyges, your would-be murderer. Had he achieved his purpose, you would have died; to the gods, and to me, you owe your deliverance. Doubtless you have long known what was done to you, and how Astyges punished me for giving you to the cowherd instead of killing you. Do now as I advise, and you will become master of the whole realm of Astyges. Persuade the Persians to revolt, and march against the Medes. It makes no odds whether I or any other Mede of distinction is appointed by the king to take command against you: you will succeed in either case, for the Median nobility will be the first to desert him and join you in the attempt to pull him down. All our preparations are made. Do what I advise, and do it quickly.'

The letter set Cyrus thinking of the means by which he could most effectively persuade the Persians to revolt, and his deliberations led him to adopt the following plan, which he found best suited to his purpose. He wrote on a roll of paper that Astyges had appointed him to command the Persian army; then he summoned an assembly of the Persians, opened the roll in their presence and read out what he had written. 'And now,' he added, 'I have an order for you: every man is to appear on parade with a sickle.' The Persian nation contains a number of tribes, and the ones which Cyrus assembled and persuaded to revolt were the Pasargadae, Maraphii, and Maspii, upon which all the other tribes are dependent. . . . Other tribes are the Panthialaei, Derusiaei, Germanii, all of which are attached to the soil, the remainder—the Dai, Mardi, Dropici, Sagartii—being nomadic.

The order was obeyed. All the men assembled with their sickles, and Cyrus' next command was that before the day was out they should clear a certain piece of rough land full of thorn bushes, about eighteen or twenty furlongs square. This too was done, whereupon Cyrus issued the further order that they should present themselves again on the following day, after having taken a bath. Meanwhile Cyrus collected and slaughtered all his father's goats, sheep, and oxen in preparation for entertaining the whole Persian army at a banquet, together with the best wine and bread he could procure. The next day the guests assembled, and were told to sit down on the grass and enjoy themselves. After the meal Cyrus asked them which they preferred—yesterday's work or today's amusement; and they replied that it was indeed a far cry from the previous day's misery to their present pleasures. This was the answer which Cyrus wanted; he seized upon it at once and proceeded to lay bare what he had in mind. 'Men of Persia,' he said, 'listen to me: obey my orders, and you will be able to enjoy a thousand pleasures as good as this without ever turning your hands to servile labour; but, if you disobey, yesterday's task will be the pattern of innumerable others you will be forced to perform. Take my advice and win your freedom. I am the man destined to undertake your liberation, and it is my belief that you are a match for the Medes in war as in everything else. It is the truth I tell you. Do not delay, but fling off the yoke of Astyges at once.'

The Persians had long resented their subjection to the Medes. At last they had found a leader, and welcomed with enthusiasm the prospect of liberty.

When news of these events reached Astyges, he summoned Cyrus to appear before him; but Cyrus' answer was to send the messenger back with the threat that he would be there a good deal sooner than Astyges liked. Astyges thereupon armed the Medes to a man, and so far lost his wits as to appoint Harpagus to command them—having apparently forgotten how he had treated him. The result was that when they took the field and engaged the Persian army, a few who were not in the plot did their duty, but of the remainder some deserted to the Persians and the greater number deliberately fought badly and took to their heels. When Astyges learnt of the disgraceful collapse of the Median army, he swore that even so Cyrus should not get away with it so easily; then, having first impaled the Magi who had advised him to let Cyrus go, he armed all Medes, both under and over military age, who had been left in the city, led them out to battle and was defeated. His men were killed and he himself was taken alive.

After the capture of Astyges, Harpagus came and jeered at him, the most bitter of his insults being a reference to the supper at which the king had regaled him with his son's flesh, followed by the question of what it felt like to be a slave instead of a king. Astyges looked at him and countered the question by another: did Harpagus, he asked, claim responsibility for what Cyrus had done? Harpagus replied that he most certainly did, for it was he who wrote the letter urging Cyrus to revolt.

'Then,' said Astyges, 'you are not only the wickedest but the most stupid of men: you are stupid, because when you might have been king yourself (if you really were responsible for what has happened) you gave another man the power; and you are wicked, because merely on account of that supper you have brought the Medes into slavery. If you had to hand the throne over to somebody else rather than keep it to yourself, it would have been more proper to give so fine a prize to a Mede than to a Persian; but as things are, the innocent Medes have become slaves instead of masters, and the Persians masters of the Medes though they were once their slaves.' . . .

On the present occasion the Persians under Cyrus rose against the Medes and from then onwards were masters of Asia. . . .

The following are certain Persian customs which I can describe from personal knowledge. The erection of statues, temples, and altars is not an accepted practice amongst them, and anyone who does such a thing is considered a fool, because, presumably, the Persian religion is not anthropomorphic like the Greek. Zeus, in their system, is the whole circle of the heavens, and they sacrifice to him from the tops of mountains. They also worship the sun, moon, and earth, fire, water, and winds, which are their only original deities . . . it was later that they learned from the Assyrians and Arabians the cult of Uranian Aphrodite. . . . The actual worshipper is not permitted to pray for any personal or private blessing, but only for the king and for the general good of the community, of which he is himself a part. . . .

Of all days in the year a Persian most distinguishes his birthday, and celebrates it with a dinner of special magnificence. A rich Persian on his birthday will have an ox or a horse or a camel or a donkey baked whole in the oven and served up at table, and the poor some smaller beast. The main dishes at their meals are few, but they have many sorts of dessert, the various courses being served separately. It is this custom that has made them say that the Greeks leave the table hungry, because they never have anything worth mentioning after the first course: they think that if the Greeks did, they should go on eating. They are very fond of wine, and no one is allowed to vomit or urinate in the presence of another person.

If an important decision is to be made, they discuss the question when they are drunk, and the following day the master of the house where the discussion was held submits their decision for reconsideration when they are sober. If they still approve it, it is adopted; if not, it is abandoned. Conversely, any decision they make when they are sober, is reconsidered afterwards when they are drunk. . . .

No race is so ready to adopt foreign ways as the Persian; for instance, they wear the Median costume because they think it handsomer than their own, and their soldiers wear the Egyptian corslet. Pleasures, too, of all sorts they are quick to indulge in when they get to know about them—a notable instance is pederasty, which they learned from the Greeks. Every man has a number of wives, and a much greater number of concubines. After prowess in fighting, the chief proof of manliness is to be the father of a large family of boys. Those who have most sons receive an annual present from the king—on the principle that there is strength in numbers.

The period of a boy's education is between the ages of five and twenty, and they are taught three things only: to ride, to use the bow, and to speak the truth. Before the age of five a boy lives with the women and never sees his father, the object being to spare the father distress if the child should die in the early stages of its upbringing. In my view this is a sound practice. I admire also the custom which forbids even the king himself to put a man to death for a single offence, and any Persian under similar circumstances to punish a servant by an irreparable injury. Their way is to balance faults against services, and then, if the faults are greater and more numerous, anger may take its course. . . . They consider telling lies more disgraceful than anything else, and, next to that, owing money. There are many reasons for their horror of debt, but the chief is their conviction that a man who owes money is bound also to tell lies. Sufferers from the scab or from leprosy are isolated and forbidden the city. They say these diseases are punishments for offending the sun, and they expel any stranger who catches them: many Persians drive away even white doves, as if they, too, were guilty of the same offence. They have a profound reverence for rivers: they will never pollute a river with urine or spittle, or even wash their hands in one, or allow anyone else to do so. . . .

All this I am able to state definitely from personal knowledge. There is another practice, however, concerning the burial of the dead, which is not spoken of openly and is something of a mystery: it is that a male Persian is never buried until the body has been torn by a bird or a dog. I know for certain that the Magi have this custom, for they are quite open about it.

STUDY QUESTIONS

1. How does Herodotus explain the rise of Cyrus and the Persian Empire? What kinds of arguments roused the Persians against the Medes? What kind of Empire do these motivations imply? In terms of social classes, how widespread was the Persian revolt?
2. What did Herodotus find most unusual about the Persians? Do you find any of his characterizations improbable, and if so, why?
3. What was the position of men, and what was the definition of masculinity, in Persian society?
4. What features of Persian society might explain the success of the Empire?
5. Judging by what Herodotus implies, what were some key differences between Persians and Greeks? Were the Persians more or less "civilized" than the Greeks, or is it possible to say?
6. What are the advantages and disadvantages of using an outside observer account to get at the characteristics of an early civilization?

6 ZOROASTRIANISM: THE MAJOR PERSIAN RELIGION

The religion of Zoroaster was spread in Persia by the Prophet Zarathustra (Zoroaster), probably around 600 B.C.E., though perhaps earlier. This seems to have been the first major religion founded by a particular, inspiring individual, though we know little about Zoroaster as a person beyond his influential writings. As an IndoEuropean people, Persians shared cultural roots with India and also with Greeks and Romans; Zoroastrianism however was a distinctive religious product, an ethical monotheism that can usefully be compared with Judaism, whose roots are somewhat earlier and seemingly quite separate. Zoroastrianism must also be treated in terms of change, away from the kinds of religions that had prevailed previously in Mesopotamia; not only ideas, but also practices (like animal sacrifice, of which Zoroaster firmly disapproved) were significantly challenged.

Zoroastrianism became deeply embedded in Iran, the Hymns or Gathas playing a role quite similar to the Old Testament's service for the Hebrews. Ultimately, the religion was eclipsed by the spread of Islam to Persia, but pockets survived; and it has also been argued that Zoroastrianism had significant influence on other religions that formed in the region, including Christianity.

HYMNS OF ZARATHUSTRA, VERSE 33

1

Towards the wicked man and the righteous one
And him in whom right and wrong meet
Shall the judge act in upright manner,
According to the laws of the present existence.

2

He who by word or thought or hands
Works evil to the wicked one,
Or he who converts his clansman to the good,
They please the Lord and fulfil his will.

From Jacques Duchesne-Guillemin, ed., *The Hymns of Zarathustra* (Boston: Beacon Press, 1952), pp. 49–51, 103–7.

3

He who, belonging to family or village or tribe, O Lord,
Is most good to the righteous man, or labours for the care of the herd,
He shall be in the pasture of Righteousness and of Good Mind.

• • •

4

I who by my prayer will keep from thee, O Wise One, disobedience and Bad Mind,
Discord from the family, from the village the evil that is very near,
The oppressors from the tribe, and from the herd's pasture the worst steward,

5

I who will invoke thy Discipline as the mightiest of all,
At the outcome, when I shall attain the long life,
The Dominion of the Good Mind and the straight paths of Right
Wherein dwells the Wise Lord,

6

I who, a priest, would learn through Righteousness,
Would learn from the Best Mind the straight paths,
Henceforth to practise husbandry in the sense in which it has been
   ordained,
I strive therefore to see thee and take counsel with thee, O Wise Lord!

Verse 30

1

Now will I speak to those who will hear
Of the things which the initiate should remember:
The praises and prayer of the Good Mind to the Lord
And the joy which he shall see in the light who has remembered them well.

2

Hear with your ears that which is the sovereign good;
With a clear mind look upon the two sides
Between which each man must choose for himself,
Watchful beforehand that the great test may be accomplished in our favour.

3

Now at the beginning the twin spirits have declared their nature,
The better and the evil,
In thought and word and deed. And between the two
The wise ones choose well, not so the foolish.

4

And when these two spirits came together,
In the beginning they established life and non-life,
And that at the last the worst existence should be for the wicked,
But for the righteous one the Best Mind.

5

Of these two spirits, the evil one chose to do the worst things;
But the Most Holy Spirit, clothed in the most steadfast heavens,
Joined himself unto Righteousness;
And thus did all those who delight to please the Wise Lord by honest deeds.

6

Between the two, the false gods also did not choose rightly,
For while they pondered they were beset by error,
So that they chose the Worst Mind.
Then did they hasten to join themselves unto Fury,
That they might by it deprave the existence of man.

7

And to him came Devotion, together with Dominion, Good Mind and
    Righteousness:
She gave endurance of body and the breath of life,
That he may be thine apart from them,
As the first by the retributions through the metal.

8

And when their punishment shall come to these sinners,
Then, O Wise One, shall thy Dominion, with the Good Mind,
Be granted to those who have delivered Evil into the hands of Righteousness, O
    Lord!

9

And may we be those that renew this existence!
O Wise One, and you other Lords, and Righteousness, bring your alliance,
That thoughts may gather where wisdom is faint.

10

Then shall Evil cease to flourish,
While those who have acquired good fame
Shall reap the promised reward
In the blessed dwelling of the Good Mind, of the Wise One, and of Righteousness.

11

If you, O men, understand the commandments which the Wise One has given,
Well-being and suffering—long torment for the wicked and salvation for
    the righteous—
All shall hereafter be for the best.

STUDY QUESTIONS

1. What were the distinctive features of Zoroastrianism as a religion? What features were similar to other major Middle Eastern and Indian religions?
2. What major changes did Zoroastrianism bring to the traditional religions in Mesopotamia?
3. What are some reasons that explain why Persians might convert to this new religion?
4. What are the similarities and differences between Zoroastrianism and Judaism? Between Zoroastrianism and early Hinduism in India?
5. What similarities exist between Christianity and Zoroastrianism, but why would early Christians worry about specific Zoroastrian influences?
6. What does this document reveal about the nature of Persian society and economy? How can the document be used as social evidence?

SECTION TWO

THE CLASSICAL PERIOD, 1000 B.C.E. to 500 C.E.

Basic political, cultural, and social traditions developed in China, India, and the Mediterranean world during the centuries between 1000 B.C.E. to 500 C.E. The key features of classical civilizations were *expansion* and *integration*. Each civilization expanded in territory and population, using the advantages of iron weaponry and tools. Expansion required new systems to hold larger territories together, including cultures (both religious and political beliefs) that could be widely shared, at least among elites. Political capacities expanded, allowing great empires. So did systems of internal trade. Nonetheless, each classical civilization defined its own distinctive beliefs and institutions, setting up enduring cultural and political differences that would affect later periods as well. But there was also new contact, particularly trade along the "Silk Road." Contacts brought opportunities for exchanges ranging from ideas to diseases, and this development had its own rich implications for the classical period and beyond.

CHINA

7 KEY CHINESE VALUES: CONFUCIANISM

Many Chinese beliefs were formed early, as civilization emerged along the Yellow River before 1000 B.C.E. One such belief stressed the importance of harmony in and with nature around the concept of the Way. More formal systems of thought developed later, in the 6th and 5th centuries B.C.E., during a divided and troubled period of Chinese politics. Various thinkers sought means to shore up a strong political system or live without one. Of the resulting philosophies or religions, Confucianism proved the most durable and significant.

Deemed by students a "Divine Sage," Confucius (Kong Fuzi) (ca. 551–479 B.C.E.) was founder of a humanistic school of philosophy that offered Zhou China a social and political ethos derived from idealized values of the past. As a remedy for the political chaos of his age, the famous teacher abandoned the decadent aristocratic code and offered in its place an ethical system focused on individual moral conduct, propriety, ritual, and benevolence. Arguing that the foundations of good government and the well-being of society rested on individual ethical behavior, Confucius urged the emperor and his assistants, the *junzi* (gentlemen), to provide moral examples for society at large. Confucius believed the appointment of modest, wise, polite, and virtuous gentlemen scholars was essential for good government and that this was the best means for eliminating the immorality and amorality that undermined law and order. Idealistic gentlemen could restore the conditions prevailing under the early Zhou dynasty, whose government Confucius viewed as a perfect form. In the selection from the *Analects,* which is a collection of sayings attributed to the "Master" and set down long after his death, one finds his views of gentlemen. Because scholars doubt that Confucius put his ideas into writing, it is impossible to determine whether these views are authentically his own or those of later Confucianists.

Confucian theories of government were adopted as state ideology during the Han dynasty [200 B.C.E.–220 C.E.], and many of his concepts proved fundamental to Chinese philosophy more generally. From the following passages, consider what the main interests and values of Confucianism were. Compare these with leading value systems—typically religious systems—in other ancient and classical civilizations. How do they

From Confucians, *The Analects of Confucius,* translated and annotated by Arthur Waley (London: George Allen and Unwin, Ltd., 1938), pp. 85, 90–91, 104–106, 121, 131, 152, 163, 167, 177–178, 181, 187–188, 197, 199, 200, 205–207, 233. Permission granted by the Arthur Waley Estate.

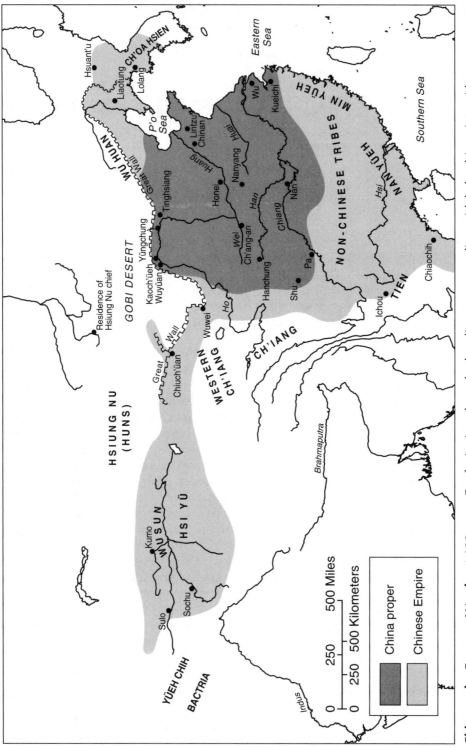

China under Emperor Wu about 100 B.C.E. Confucianism, launched earlier, was spreading widely by this point, with government backing.

compare with Judaism, or with Hindu or Buddhist concepts developing during the same time period in India?

THE SMALL ANALECTS

The Master said, If a gentleman is frivolous, he will lose the respect of his inferiors and lack firm ground upon which to build up his education. First and foremost he must learn to be faithful to his superiors, to keep promises, to refuse the friendship of all who are not like him. And if he finds he has made a mistake, then he must not be afraid of admitting the fact and amending his ways.

Zigong asked about the true gentleman. The Master said, He does not preach what he practises till he has practised what he preaches.

The Master said, A gentleman can see a question from all sides without bias. The small man is biased and can see a question only from one side.

The Master said, A gentleman in his dealings with the world has neither enmities nor affections; but wherever he sees Right he ranges himself beside it.

The Master said, A gentleman takes as much trouble to discover what is right as lesser men take to discover what will pay.

The Master said, A gentleman covets the reputation of being slow in word but prompt in deed.

The Master said, A gentleman who is widely versed in letters and at the same time knows how to submit his learning to the restraints of ritual is not likely, I think, to go far wrong.

The Master said, A true gentleman is calm and at ease; the Small Man is fretful and ill at ease.

At home in his native village his manner is simple and unassuming, as though he did not trust himself to speak. But in the ancestral temple and at Court he speaks readily, though always choosing his words with care.

At Court when conversing with the Under Ministers his attitude is friendly and affable; when conversing with the Upper Ministers, it is restrained and formal. When the ruler is present it is wary, but not cramped.

When the ruler summons him to receive a guest, a look of confusion comes over his face and his legs seem to give beneath his weight. When saluting his colleagues he passes his right hand to the left, letting his robe hang down in front and behind; and as he advances with quickened step, his attitude is one of majestic dignity.

When the guest has gone, he reports the close of the visit, saying, "The guest is no longer looking back."

On entering the Palace Gate he seems to shrink into himself, as though there were not room. If he halts, it must never be in the middle of the gate, nor in going through does he ever tread on the threshold. As he passes the Stance a look of confusion comes over his face, his legs seem to give way under him and words seem to fail him. While, holding up the hem of his skirt, he ascends the Audience Hall, he seems to double up and keeps in his breath, so that you would think he was not breathing at all. On coming out, after descending the first step his expression relaxes into one of satisfaction and relief. At the bottom of the steps he quickens his pace, advancing with an air of majestic dignity. On regaining his place he resumes his attitude of wariness and hesitation.

When carrying the tablet of jade, he seems to double up, as though borne down by its weight. He holds it at the highest as though he were making a bow, at the lowest, as though he were proffering a gift. His expression, too, changes to one of dread and his feet seem to recoil, as though he were avoiding something. When presenting ritual-presents, his expression is placid. At the private audience his attitude is gay and animated.

A gentleman does not wear facings of purple or mauve, nor in undress does he use pink or roan. In hot weather he wears an unlined gown of fine thread loosely woven, but puts on an outside garment before going out-of-doors. With a black robe he wears black lambskin; with a robe of undyed silk, fawn. With a yellow robe, fox fur. On his undress robe the fur cuffs are long; but the right is shorter than the left. His bedclothes must be half as long again as a man's height. The thicker kinds of fox and badger are for home wear. Except when in mourning, he wears all his girdle-ornaments. Apart from his Court apron, all his skirts are wider at the bottom than at the waist. Lambskin dyed black and a hat of dark-dyed silk must not be worn when making visits of condolence. At the Announcement of the New Moon he must go to Court in full Court dress.

When preparing himself for sacrifice he must wear the Bright Robe, and it must be of linen. He must change his food and also the place where he commonly sits. But there is no objection to his rice being of the finest quality, nor to his meat being finely minced. Rice affected by the weather or turned he must not eat, nor fish that is not sound, nor meat that is high. He must not eat anything discoloured or that smells bad. He must not eat what is overcooked nor what is undercooked, nor anything that is out of season. He must not eat what has been crookedly cut, nor any dish that lacks its proper seasoning. The meat that he eats must at the very most not be enough to make his breath smell of meat rather than of rice. As regards wine, no limit is laid down; but he must not be disorderly. He may not drink wine bought at a shop or eat dried meat from the market. He need not refrain from such articles of food as have ginger sprinkled over them; but he must not eat much of such dishes.

After a sacrifice in the ducal palace, the flesh must not be kept overnight. No sacrificial flesh may be kept beyond the third day. If it is kept beyond the third day, it may no longer be eaten. While it is being eaten, there must be no conversation, nor any word spoken while lying down after the repast. Any article of food, whether coarse rice, vegetables, broth or melon, that has been used as an offering must be handled with due solemnity.

He must not sit on a mat that is not straight.

When the men of his village are drinking wine he leaves the feast immediately after the village-elders have left. When the men of his village hold their Expulsion Rite, he puts on his Court dress and stands on the eastern steps.

When sending a messenger to enquire after someone in another country, he prostrates himself twice while speeding the messenger on his way. When K'ang-tzu sent him some medicine he prostrated himself and accepted it; but said, As I am not acquainted with its properties, I cannot venture to taste it.

When the stables were burnt down, on returning from Court, he said, Was anyone hurt? He did not ask about the horses.

When his prince sends him a present of food, he must straighten his mat and be the first to taste what has been sent. When what his prince sends is a present of uncooked meat, he must cook it and make a sacrificial offering. When his prince sends a live animal, he must rear it. When he is waiting upon his prince at meal-times, while his prince is making the sacrificial offering, he (the gentleman) tastes the dishes. If he is ill and his prince comes to see him, he has himself laid with his head to the East with his Court robes thrown over him and his sash drawn across the bed. When the prince commands his presence he goes straight to the palace without waiting for his carriage to be yoked.

On entering the Ancestral Temple, he asks about every detail.

If a friend dies and there are no relatives to fall back on, he says, "The funeral is my affair." On receiving a present from a friend, even a carriage and horses, he does not prostrate himself. He does so only in the case of sacrificial meat being sent.

In bed he avoids lying in the posture of a corpse. When at home he does not use ritual attitudes. When appearing before anyone in mourning, however well he knows him, he must put on an altered expression, and when appearing before anyone in sacrificial garb, or a blind man, even informally, he must be sure to adopt the appropriate attitude. On meeting anyone in deep mourning he must bow across the bar of his chariot; he also bows to people carrying planks. When confronted with a particularly choice dainty at a banquet, his countenance should change and he should rise to his feet. Upon hearing a sudden clap of thunder or a violent gust of wind, he must change countenance.

When mounting a carriage, he must stand facing it squarely and holding the mounting-cord. When riding he confines his gaze, does not speak rapidly or point with his hands.

(The gentleman) rises and goes at the first sign, and does not "settle till he has hovered." (A song) says:

The hen-pheasant of the hill-bridge,
Knows how to bide its time, to bide its time!
When Zilu made it an offering,
It sniffed three times before it rose.

Sima Niu asked about the meaning of the term Gentleman. The Master said, The Gentleman neither grieves nor fears. Sima Niu said, So that is what is meant by being a gentleman—neither to grieve nor to fear? The Master said, On looking within himself he finds no taint; so why should he either grieve or fear?

The Master said, The gentleman calls attention to the good points in others; he does not call attention to their defects. The small man does just the reverse of this.

The Master said, The true gentleman is conciliatory but not accommodating. Common people are accommodating but not conciliatory.

The Master said, The true gentleman is easy to serve, yet difficult to please. For if you try to please him in any manner inconsistent with the Way, he refuses to be pleased; but in using the services of others he only expects of them what they are capable of performing. Common people are difficult to serve, but easy to please. Even though you try to please them in a manner inconsistent with the Way, they will still be pleased; but in using the services of others they expect them (irrespective of their capacities) to do any work that comes along.

The Master said, The gentleman is dignified, but never haughty; common people are haughty, but never dignified.

The Master said, It is possible to be a true gentleman and yet lack Goodness. But there has never yet existed a Good man who was not a gentleman.

When the Master said, He who holds no rank in a State does not discuss its policies, Master Zeng said, "A true gentleman, even in his thoughts, never departs from what is suitable to his rank."

The Master said, A gentleman is ashamed to let his words outrun his deeds.

The Master said, The Ways of the true gentleman are three. I myself have met with success in none of them. For he that is really Good is never unhappy, he that is really wise is never perplexed, he that is really brave is never afraid. Zigong said, That, Master, is your own Way!

The Master said, (A gentleman) does not grieve that people do not recognize his merits; he grieves at his own incapacities.

The Master said, The gentleman who takes the right as his material to work upon and ritual as the guide in putting what is right into practice, who is modest in setting out his projects and faithful in carrying them to their conclusion, he indeed is a true gentleman.

The Master said, A gentleman is distressed by his own lack of capacity; he is never distressed at the failure of others to recognize his merits.

The Master said, A gentleman has reason to be distressed if he ends his days without making a reputation for himself.

The Master said, "The demands that a gentleman makes are upon himself; those that a small man makes are upon others."

The Master said, A gentleman is proud, but not quarrelsome, allies himself with individuals, but not with parties.

The Master said, A gentleman does not accept men because of what they say, nor reject sayings, because the speaker is what he is.

The Master said, A gentleman, in his plans, thinks of the Way; he does not think how he is going to make a living. Even farming sometimes entails times of shortage; and even learning may incidentally lead to high pay. But a gentleman's anxieties concern the progress of the Way; he has no anxiety concerning poverty.

The Master said, It is wrong for a gentleman to have knowledge of menial matters and proper that he should be entrusted with great responsibilities. It is wrong for a small man to be entrusted with great responsibilities, but proper that he should have a knowledge of menial matters.

The Master said, from a gentleman consistency is expected, but not blind fidelity.

Confucius said, There are three things against which a gentleman is on his guard. In his youth, before his blood and vital humours have settled down, he is on his guard against lust. Having reached his prime, when the blood and vital humours have finally hardened, he is on his guard against strife. Having reached old age, when the blood and vital humours are already decaying, he is on his guard against avarice.

Confucius said, There are three things that a gentleman fears: he fears the will of Heaven, he fears great men, he fears the words of the Divine Sages. The small man does not know the will of Heaven and so does not fear it. He treats great men with contempt, and scoffs at the words of the Divine Sages.

Confucius said, The gentleman has nine cares. In seeing he is careful to see clearly, in hearing he is careful to hear distinctly, in his looks he is careful to be kindly; in his manner to be respectful, in his words to be loyal, in his work to be diligent. When in doubt he is careful to ask for information; when angry he has a care for the consequences, and when he sees a chance of gain, he thinks carefully whether the pursuit of it would be consonant with the Right.

The Master said, He who does not understand the will of Heaven cannot be regarded as a gentleman. He who does not know the rites cannot take his stand. He who does not understand words, cannot understand people.

STUDY QUESTIONS

1. What were the proper goals of life according to Confucius?
2. What was the Confucian definition of a gentleman? Why did Confucianism place so much emphasis on manners and ceremony?
3. Did Confucius judge human nature to be good or bad? What was his attitude toward human emotions?
4. What social structure did Confucianism imply? What were the key social classes and how did they differ?
5. In what ways was Confucianism not a religion?
6. Why did Confucianism have such a deep impact on Chinese and East Asian history? What groups and institutions could benefit from it?
7. How does Confucianism compare with the political values and systems developed in Mesopotamia and Persia (Chapters 2 and 5)? What are the distinctive features of Confucianism as a basis for political life?

8 LEGALISM: AN ALTERNATIVE SYSTEM

A student of the Confucian Xunzi, Han Feizi (d. 233 B.C.E.) was the principal theoretician of Legalism, a school of philosophy adopted by the Qin after unifying China in 256 B.C.E. This former Confucian adopted the pragmatic view that the Chinese, perceived as antisocial and inherently evil, must be firmly controlled by an authoritative central government through strictly applied punitive laws. This harsh but effective solution for resolving the chaotic conditions that plagued the Zhou dynasty included the introduction of new managerial techniques, an improved bureaucracy, enhanced communications, land reforms, and standardization of weights, measures, and coinage. Han Feizi, who served as an official for the powerful but short-lived Qin dynasty (that gave China its name), died from poison at the hands of Li Si, a jealous Legalist rival. Han Feizi wrote 20 books and was honored by the grand historian, Sima Qian, with a biographical sketch.

How did Legalism differ from Confucianism in its view of human nature and the proper organization of the state? Officially, Legalism died with the demise of the Ch'in and the renewed interest in Confucian values. In fact, though, the Chinese state continued to combine Confucian ideals with the harsher police-like approach urged by Legalists—so this division of political approach was of more than passing importance. Both Legalism and Confucianism, somewhat ironically, promoted a strong state.

HAN FEIZI

If orders are made trim, laws never deviate; if laws are equable, there will be no culprit among the officials. Once the law is fixed, nobody can damage it by means of virtuous words. If men of merit are appointed to office, the people will have little to say; if men of virtue are appointed to office the people will have much to talk about. The enforcement of laws depends upon the method of judicial administration. Who administers judicial affairs with ease . . . attains supremacy. . . . Whoever procrastinates in creating order, will see his state dismembered.

Govern by penalties; wage war by rewards; and enlarge the bounties so as to put the principles of statecraft into practice. If so, there will be no wicked people in the state nor will there be any wicked trade at the market. If things are many and trifles are numerous, and if farming is relaxed and villainy prevails, the state will certainly be dismembered.

From Han Feizi, *The Complete Works*, 2 vols., translated by W. K. Liao (London: Arthur Probsthain, 1959), Vol. II, pp. 322–333. Copyright © 1959 by Arthur Probsthain. Reprinted by permission.

If the people have a surplus of food, make them receive rank by giving grain to the state. If only through their own effort they can receive rank, then farmers will not idle.

If a tube three inches long has no bottom, it can never be filled. Conferring office and rank or granting profit and bounty without reference to merit, is like a tube having no bottom.

If the state confers office and bestows rank, it can be said to devise plans with complete wisdom and wage war with complete courage. Such a state will find a rival. Again, if the state confers office and bestows rank according to merit, then rules will be simplified and opponents barred; this can be said to abolish government by means of government, abolish words by means of words, and bestow rank according to merit. Therefore the state will have much strength and none else in All-under-Heaven will dare to invade it. When its soldiers march out, they will take the objective and, having taken it, will certainly be able to hold it. When it keeps its soldiers in reserve and does not attack, it will certainly become rich.

The affairs of the government, however small, should never be abandoned. For instance, office and rank are always obtained according to the acquired merit; though there may be flattering words, it will be impossible thereby to make any interference in the state affairs. This is said to be "government by figures." For instance, in attacking with force, ten points are taken for every point given out; but in attacking with words, one hundred are lost for every one marched out. If a state is fond of force, it is called hard to attack; if a state is fond of words, it is called easy to attack.

If the ability of the official is equal to his post, if his duty is lightened and he never reserves any surplus energy in mind, and if he does not shift any responsibility of additional offices back to the ruler, then there will be no hidden grudge inside. If the intelligent ruler makes the state affairs never mutually interfere, there will be no dispute; if he allows no official to hold any kind of additional post, everybody will develop his talent or skill; and if he allows no two persons to share the same meritorious achievement, there will be no quarrel.

If penalties are heavy and rewards are few, it means that the superior loves the people, wherefore the people will die for rewards. If rewards are many and penalties are light, it means that the superior does not love the people, wherefore the people will never die for rewards.

If the profit issues from one outlet only, the state will have no rival; if it issues from two outlets, its soldiers will be half useful; and if the profit comes from ten outlets, the people will not observe the law. If heavy penalties are clear and if the people are always well disciplined and then if men are engaged in case of emergency, the superior will have all the advantage.

In inflicting penalties light offences should be punished severely; if light offences do not appear, heavy offences will not come. This is said to abolish penalties by means of penalties. And the state will certainly become strong. If crimes are serious but penalties are light, light penalties breed further troubles. This is said to create penalties through penalties, and such a state will infallibly be dismembered.

The sage in governing the people considers their springs of action, never tolerates their wicked desires, but seeks only for the people's benefit. Therefore, the penalty he inflicts is not due to any hatred for the people but to his motive of loving the people. If penalty triumphs, the people are quiet; if reward overflows, culprits appear. Therefore the triumph of penalty is the beginning of order; the overflow of reward, the origin of chaos.

Indeed, it is the people's nature to delight in disorder and detach themselves from legal restraints. Therefore, when the intelligent sovereign governs the state, if he makes rewards clear, the people will be encouraged to render meritorious services; if he makes penalties severe, the people will attach themselves to the law. If they are encouraged to render meritorious services, public affairs will not be obstructed; if they attach themselves to the law, culprits will not appear. Therefore, he who governs the people should nip the evil in the bud; he who commands troops, should inculcate warfare in the people's mind. If prohibitions can uproot causes of villainy, there will always be order; if soldiers can imagine warfare in mind, there will always be victory. When the sage is governing the people, he attains order first, wherefore he is strong; he prepares for war first, wherefore he wins.

Indeed, the administration of the state affairs requires the attention to the causes of human action so as to unify the people's mental trends; the exclusive elevation of public welfare so as to stop self-seeking elements; the reward for denunciation of crime so as to suppress culprits; and finally the clarification of laws so as to facilitate governmental procedures. Whoever is able to apply these four measures, will become strong; whoever is unable to apply these four measures, will become weak. Indeed, the strength of the state is due to the administration of its political affairs; the honour of the sovereign is due to his supreme power. Now, the enlightened ruler possesses the supreme power and the administrative organs; the ignoble ruler possesses both the supreme power and the administrative organs, too. Yet the results are not the same, because their standpoints are different. Thus, as the enlightened ruler has the supreme power in his grip, the superior is held in high esteem; as he unifies the administrative organs, the state is in order. Hence law is the origin of supremacy and penalty is the beginning of love.

Indeed, it is the people's nature to abhor toil and enjoy ease. However, if they pursue ease, the land will waste; if the land wastes, the state will not be in order. If the state is not orderly, it will become chaotic. If reward and penalty take no effect among the inferiors, government will come to a deadlock. Therefore, he who wants to accomplish a great achievement but hesitates to apply his full strength, can not hope for the accomplishment of the achievement; he who wants to settle the people's disorder but hesitates to change their traditions, can not hope to banish the people's disorder. Hence there is no constant method for the government of men. The law alone leads to political order. If laws are adjusted to the time, there is good government. If government fits the age, there will be great accomplishment. Therefore, when the people are naïve, if you regulate them with fame, there will be good government; when everybody in the world is intelligent, if you discipline them with penalties, they will obey. While time is moving on, if laws do not shift accordingly, there will be misrule; while abilities are diverse, if prohibitions are not changed, the state will be dismembered. Therefore, the sage in governing the people makes laws move with time and prohibitions change with abilities. Who can exert his forces to land-utilization, will become rich; who can rush his forces at enemies, will become strong. The strong man not obstructed in his way will attain supremacy.

Therefore, the way to supremacy lies in the way of shutting culprits off and the way of blocking up wicked men. Who is able to block up wicked men, will eventually attain supremacy. The policy of attaining supremacy relies not on foreign states' abstention from disturbing your state, but on their inability to disturb your state. Who has to rely on foreign powers' abstention from disturbing his state before he can maintain his own independence, will see his state dismembered; who relies on their inability to disturb his state and willingly enacts the law, will prosper.

Therefore, the worthy ruler in governing the state follows the statecraft of invulnerability. When rank is esteemed, the superior will increase his dignity. He will accordingly bestow rewards on men of merit, confer ranks upon holders of posts, and appoint wicked men to no office. Who devotes himself to practical forces, gets a high rank. If the rank is esteemed, the superior will be honoured. The superior, if honoured, will attain supremacy. On the contrary, if the state does not strive after practical forces but counts on private studies, its rank will be lowered. If the rank is lowered, the superior will be humbled. If the superior is humbled, the state will be dismembered. Therefore, if the way of founding the state and using the people can shut off foreign invaders and block up self-seeking subjects, and if the superior relies on himself, supremacy will be attained. . . .

In general, wherever the state is extensive and the ruler is honourable, their laws are so strict that whatever is ordered works and whatever is prohibited stops. Therefore, the ruler of men who distinguishes between ranks and regulates bounties, makes laws severe and thereby makes the distinction strict.

Indeed, if the state is orderly, the people are safe; if affairs are confused, the country falls into peril. Who makes laws strict, hits on the true nature of mankind; who makes prohibitions lenient, misses the apparent fact. Moreover, everybody is, indeed, gifted with desperate courage. To exert desperate courage to get what one wants, is human nature. Yet everybody's likes and dislikes should be regulated by the superior. Now the people like to have profit and bounty and hate to be punished; if the superior catches their likes and dislikes and thereby holds their desperate courage under control, he will not miss the realities of affairs.

However, if prohibitions are lenient and facts are missed, reward and penalty will be misused. Again, when governing the people, if you do not regard conformity to law as right, you will eventually observe no law. Therefore, the science and philosophy of politics should by all means emphasize the distinction between degrees of penalty and of reward.

Who governs the state, should always uphold the law. In life there are ups and downs. If any ruler goes down, it is because in regulating rewards and penalties he makes no distinction between different degrees. Who governs the state, always distinguishes between reward and punishment. Therefore, some people might regard the distinction between reward and punishment as distinction, which should not be called distinction in the strict sense.

As regards the distinction made by the clear-sighted ruler, it is the distinction between different grades of reward and of punishment. Therefore, his subjects respect laws and fear prohibitions. They try to avoid crime rather than dare to expect any reward. Hence the saying: "Without expecting penalty and reward the people attend to public affairs."

For this reason, the state at the height of order is able to take the suppression of villainy for its duty. Why? Because its law comprehends human nature and accords with the principles of government.

If so, how to get rid of delicate villainy? By making the people watch one another in their hidden affairs. Then how to make them watch one another? By implicating the people of the same hamlet in one another's crime. When everyone knows that the penalty or reward will directly affect him, if the people of the same hamlet fail to watch one another, they will fear they may not be able to escape the implication, and those who are evil-minded, will not be allowed to forget so many people watching them. Were such the law, everybody would mind his own doings, watch everybody else, and disclose the secrets of any culprit. For, whosoever denounces a criminal offence, is not held guilty but is given a reward; whosoever misses any culprit, is definitely censured and given the same penalty as the culprit. Were such the law, all types of culprits would be detected. If the minutest villainy is not tolerated, it is due to the system of personal denunciation and mutual implication.

Indeed, the most enlightened method of governing a state is to trust measures and not men. For this reason, the tactful state is never mistaken if it does not trust the empty fame of men. If the land within the boundary is always in order it is because measures are employed. If any falling state lets foreign soldiers walk all over its territory and can neither resist nor prevent them, it is because that state trusts men and uses no measures. Men may jeopardize their own country, but measures can invade others' countries. Therefore, the tactful state spurns words and trusts laws.

Broadly speaking, it is hard to uncover a crooked merit that appears to fulfill the promise; it is hard to disclose the feature of the fault that is ornamented with beautiful words. Therefore, penalty and reward are often misled by double-dealers. What is alleged to be fulfilling the promise but is hard to uncover, is a villainous merit. Any minister's fault is hard to disclose, because its motive is missed. However, if by following reason you can not disclose the false merit and by analyzing feelings you are still deceived by the villainous motive, then can both reward and punishment have no mistake respectively?

For such reasons, false scholars establish names inside, while itinerants devise plans outside, till the stupid and the coward mix themselves with the brave and the clever. Inasmuch as the false path is customary, they are tolerated by their age. Therefore, their law does not work and their penalty affects nobody. If so, both reward and penalty have to be double-dealings.

Therefore, concrete facts have their limits of extension, but abstract principles involve no accurate measures. The absence of such measures is due not to the law but to the abandonment of law and the dependence on cleverness. If the law is abandoned and cleverness is employed, how can the appointee to office perform his duty? If duty and office are not equivalent to each other, then how can the law evade mistakes and how can penalty evade troubles? For this reason reward and punishment will be thrown into confusion and disorder, and the state policy will deviate and err, because neither penalty nor reward has any clear distinction of degree as in the difference between black and white.

STUDY QUESTIONS

1. What was the purpose of government according to the Legalists? How did these views compare with Confucianism?
2. Did Legalists judge human nature to be good or bad?
3. Could Confucianists and Legalists agree on any major points? How might their views and recommendations be combined?
4. Can Legalism and Confucianism be explained by the different political contexts in which they arose?
5. Why was Legalism ultimately less successful than Confucianism in East Asian history?

9 DAOISM

Along with Confucianism, the religious philosophy of Daoism was a product of the chaotic period of the later Zhou dynasty. It also took deep roots in Chinese culture. It, too, probably reflected earlier Chinese beliefs including the references to a balanced Dao, or "Way," to which the religion gave a particular definition. Daoism attracted many in the upper classes, who found it spirituality appealing. Later, particularly as it additionally embraced beliefs in magical healing, it spread widely to the peasantry. After Buddhism began to reach China in the later Han dynasty, Daoists responded by more vigorous proselytizing efforts. Confucian officials recurrently attacked Daoism, but they never tried to proscribe it as they ultimately did with Buddhism, for although Daoism had different goals most Daoist leaders professed obedience to the emperor, which made the religion seem safe. Unlike most major religions, however, and unlike Confucianism itself, Daoism never spread significantly beyond its culture of origins, even to other parts of East Asia.

Daoism was attributed to Laozi, who probably lived in the 5th century B.C.E.—though his actual existence cannot be confirmed. Daoism stressed the divine impulse that directs all life, while urging a set of habits that would bring peace and harmony. The following passage is from the principal Daoist work, the *Dao de jing,* attributed to Laozi but which was probably compiled by Zhuangzi in the 4th or 3rd centuries B.C.E.

Assessing Daoist principles obviously invites comparison both with Confucianism (and Legalism) and with other major religions such as Hinduism and Buddhism. How could such a different set of ideas coexist with Chinese political philosophies without creating cultural disruption? How could some individuals be Confucianist and Daoist at the same time?

DAO DE JING

The Dao that can be told
is not the eternal Dao.
The name that can be named
is not the eternal Name.

The unnamable is the eternally real.
Naming is the origin
of all particular things.

Numbers 1–7, 20–25, 30–31, 56-57 from *Tao Te Ching* by Lao Tzu, *A New English Version, with Forward and Notes* by Stephen Mithcell. Translation Copyright © 1988 by Stephen Mitchell. Reprinted by permission of HarperCollins Publishers Inc.

Free from desire, you realize the mystery.
Caught in desire, you see only the manifestations.

Yet mystery and manifestations
arise from the same source.
This source is called darkness.

Darkness within darkness.
The gateway to all understanding.

When people see some things as beautiful,
other things become ugly.
When people see some things as good,
other things become bad.

Being and non-being create each other.
Difficult and easy support each other.
Long and short define each other.
High and low depend on each other.
Before and after follow each other.

Therefore the Master
acts without doing anything
and teaches without saying anything.
Things arise and she lets them come;
things disappear and she lets them go.
She has but doesn't possess,
acts but doesn't expect.
When her work is done, she forgets it.
That is why it lasts forever.

If you overesteem great men,
people become powerless.
If you overvalue possessions,
people begin to steal.

The Master leads
by emptying people's minds
and filling their cores,
by weakening their ambition
and toughening their resolve.
He helps people lose everything
they know, everything they desire,
and creates confusion
in those who think that they know.

Practice not-doing,
and everything will fall into place.

The Dao is like a well:
used but never used up.
It is like the eternal void:

filled with infinite possibilities.

It is hidden but always present.
I don't know who gave birth to it.
It is older than God. . . .

The Dao is called the Great Mother:
empty yet inexhaustible,
it gives birth to infinite worlds.

It is always present within you.
You can use it any way you want.

The Dao is infinite, eternal.
Why is it eternal?
It was never born;
thus it can never die.
Why is it infinite?
It has no desires for itself;
thus it is present for all beings.

The Master stays behind;
that is why she is ahead.
She is detached from all things;
that is why she is one with them.
Because she has let go of herself,
she is perfectly fulfilled. . . .

Stop thinking, and end your problems.
What difference between yes and no?
What difference between success and failure?
Must you value what others value,
avoid what others avoid?
How ridiculous!

Other people are excited,
as though they were at a parade.
I alone don't care,
I alone am expressionless,
like an infant before it can smile. . . .

If you want to accord with the Dao,
just do your job, then let go. . . .

Whoever relies on the Dao in governing men
doesn't try to force issues
or defeat enemies by force of arms.
For every force there is a counterforce.
Violence, even well intentioned,
always rebounds upon oneself.

The Master does his job
and then stops.

He understands that the universe
is forever out of control,
and that trying to dominate events
goes against the current of the Dao.
Because he believes in himself,
he doesn't try to convince others.
Because he is content with himself,
he doesn't need others' approval.
Because he accepts himself,
the whole world accepts him.
Weapons are the tools of violence;
all decent men detest them.

Weapons are the tools of fear;
a decent man will avoid them
except in the direst necessity
and, if compelled, will use them
only with the utmost restraint.
Peace is his highest value.
If the peace has been shattered,
how can he be content?
His enemies are not demons,
but human beings like himself.
[The Master] doesn't wish them personal harm.
Nor does he rejoice in victory.
How could he rejoice in victory
and delight in the slaughter of men?

He enters a battle gravely,
with sorrow and with great compassion,
as if he were attending a funeral. . . .

Those who know don't talk.
Those who talk don't know.

Close your mouth,
block off your senses,
blunt your sharpness,
untie your knots,
soften your glare,
settle your dust.
This is the primal identity.

Be like the Dao.
It can't be approached or withdrawn from,
benefited or harmed,
honored or brought into disgrace.
It gives itself up continually.
That is why it endures.
If you want to be a great leader,

you must learn to follow the Dao.
Stop trying to control.
Let go of fixed plans and concepts,
and the world will govern itself.

The more prohibitions you have,
the less virtuous people will be.
The more weapons you have,
the less secure people will be.
The more subsidies you have,
the less self-reliant people will be.

Therefore the Master says:
I let go of the law,
and people become honest.
I let go of economics,
and people become prosperous.
I let go of religion,
and people become serene.
I let go of all desire for the common good,
and the good becomes common as grass.

STUDY QUESTIONS

1. How is the Dao defined? How does it compare with a god or gods in other religions?
2. What kind of life should a Daoist lead, and why?
3. What might a Confucianist and a Daoist agree about? Where would they disagree? How would the two belief systems react to military activity?
4. Does the passage help explain why Daoism did not spread widely outside China?
5. How might Daoism affect other aspects of Chinese culture, such as artistic styles? Science and medicine?
6. As a major early religion, how does Daoism compare with Judaism?

10 WOMEN IN CLASSICAL CHINA: BAN ZHAO

Ban Zhao (ca. 45–120 C.E.), China's "foremost woman scholar," served unofficially as imperial historian to Emperor He (89–105 C.E.) while acting as an instructor in history, classical writing, astronomy, and mathematics to the Empress Deng and her ladies-in-waiting. Summoned to complete the historical books (*Han Shu*) of her deceased brother, Gu, the scholarly and talented widow is the only woman in China to have served in that capacity. Her success in overcoming contemporary restraints on women was due to an exceptional education, which she attributed to her scholarly parents. As a historian, moralist, and royal servant, Ban Zhao wrote numerous literary works, including narrative poems, commemorative verses, eulogies, and her famous *Lessons for Women*. This brief educational treatise, written expressly for women and the first of its kind in world history, offers interesting insights into the Chinese perceptions of the ideal woman as well as 1st-century Chinese customs. It contains advice in matters of customs and manners for girls in her family so that they might not "humiliate both your ancestors and your clan."

Ban Zhao's manual was the most successful and durable advice book for women in Chinese history, helping to support a firmly patriarchal gender system. The book was reprinted and widely used through the 19th century.

How does Ban Zhao define womanhood and women's roles? How do these definitions relate to other aspects of Chinese society such as Confucianism?

LESSONS FOR WOMEN

Introduction

I, the unworthy writer, am unsophisticated, unenlightened, and by nature unintelligent, but I am fortunate both to have received not a little favor from my scholarly father, and to have had a (cultured) mother and instructresses upon whom to rely for a literary education as well as for training in good manners. More than forty years have passed since at the age of fourteen I took up the dustpan and the broom in the Cao family. During this time with trembling heart I feared constantly that I might disgrace my parents, and that I might multiply difficulties for both the women and the men (of my husband's family). Day and night I was distressed in

From Nancy Lee Swann, Ban Zhao, "Lessons for Women," in *Pan Chao: Foremost Woman Scholar of China* (New York: The Century Co., 1932), pp. 82–87. Reprint permission granted by the American Historical Association.

heart, (but) I labored without confessing weariness. Now and hereafter, however, I know how to escape (from such fears).

Being careless, and by nature stupid, I taught and trained (my children) without system. Consequently I fear that my son Gu may bring disgrace upon the Imperial Dynasty by whose Holy Grace he has unprecedentedly received the extraordinary privilege of wearing the Gold and the Purple, a privilege for the attainment of which (by my son, I) a humble subject never even hoped. Nevertheless, now that he is a man and able to plan his own life, I need not again have concern for him. But I do grieve that you, my daughters, just now at the age for marriage, have not at this time had gradual training and advice; that you still have not learned the proper customs for married women. I fear that by failure in good manners in other families you will humiliate both your ancestors and your clan. I am now seriously ill, life is uncertain. As I have thought of you all in so untrained a state, I have been uneasy many a time for you. At hours of leisure I have composed in seven chapters these instructions under the title, "Lessons for Women." In order that you may have something wherewith to benefit your persons, I wish every one of you, my daughters, each to write out a copy for yourself.

From this time on every one of you strive to practise these (lessons).

Chapter I: Humility

On the third day after the birth of a girl the ancients observed three customs: (first) to place the baby below the bed; (second) to give her a potsherd with which to play; and (third) to announce her birth to her ancestors by an offering. Now to lay the baby below the bed plainly indicated that she is lowly and weak, and should regard it as her primary duty to humble herself before others. To give her potsherds with which to play indubitably signified that she should practise labor and consider it her primary duty to be industrious. To announce her birth before her ancestors clearly meant that she ought to esteem as her primary duty the continuation of the observance of worship in the home.

These three ancient customs epitomize a woman's ordinary way of life and the teachings of the traditional ceremonial rites and regulations. Let a woman modestly yield to others; let her respect others; let her put others first, herself last. Should she do something good, let her not mention it; should she do something bad, let her not deny it. Let her bear disgrace; let her even endure when others speak or do evil to her. Always let her seem to tremble and to fear. (When a woman follows such maxims as these,) then she may be said to humble herself before others.

Let a woman retire late to bed, but rise early to duties; let her not dread tasks by day or by night. Let her not refuse to perform domestic duties whether easy or difficult. That which must be done, let her finish completely, tidily, and systematically. (When a woman follows such rules as these,) then she may be said to be industrious.

Let a woman be correct in manner and upright in character in order to serve her husband. Let her live in purity and quietness (of spirit), and attend to her own affairs. Let her love not gossip and silly laughter. Let her cleanse and purify and arrange in order the wine and the food for the offerings to the ancestors. (When a woman observes such principles as these,) then she may be said to continue ancestral worship.

No woman who observes these three (fundamentals of life) has ever had a bad reputation or has fallen into disgrace. If a woman fail to observe them, how can her name be honored; how can she but bring disgrace upon herself?

Chapter II: Husband and Wife

The Way of husband and wife is intimately connected with *Yin* and *Yang,* and relates the individual to gods and ancestors. Truly it is the great principle of Heaven and Earth, and the great basis of human relationships. Therefore the "Rites" honor union of man and woman; and in the "Book of Poetry" the "First Ode" manifests the principle of marriage. For these reasons the relationship cannot but be an important one.

If a husband be unworthy then he possesses nothing by which to control his wife. If a wife be unworthy, then she possesses nothing with which to serve her husband. If a husband does not control his wife, then the rules of conduct manifesting his authority are abandoned and broken. If a wife does not serve her husband, then the proper relationship (between men and women) and the natural order of things are neglected and destroyed. As a matter of fact the purpose of these two (the controlling of women by men, and the serving of men by women) is the same.

Now examine the gentlemen of the present age. They only know that wives must be controlled, and that the husband's rules of conduct manifesting his authority must be established. They therefore teach their boys to read books and (study) histories. But they do not in the least understand that husbands and masters must (also) be served, and that the proper relationship and the rites should be maintained.

Yet only to teach men and not to teach women,—is that not ignoring the essential relation between them? According to the "Rites," it is the rule to begin to teach children to read at the age of eight years, and by the age of fifteen years they ought then to be ready for cultural training. Only why should it not be (that girls' education as well as boys' be) according to this principle?

Chapter III: Respect and Caution

As *Yin* and *Yang* are not of the same nature, so man and woman have different characteristics. The distinctive quality of the *Yang* is rigidity; the function of the *Yin* is yielding. Man is honored for strength; a woman is beautiful on account of her gentleness. Hence there arose the common saying: "A man though born like a wolf may, it is feared, become a weak monstrosity; a woman though born like a mouse may, it is feared, become a tiger."

Now for self-culture nothing equals respect for others. To counteract firmness nothing equals compliance. Consequently it can be said that the Way of respect and acquiescence is woman's most important principle of conduct. So respect may be defined as nothing other than holding on to that which is permanent; and acquiescence nothing other than being liberal and generous. Those who are steadfast in devotion know that they should stay in their proper places; those who are liberal and generous esteem others, and honor and serve (them).

If husband and wife have the habit of staying together, never leaving one another, and following each other around within the limited space of their own rooms, then they will lust after and take liberties with one another. From such action improper language will arise between the two. This kind of discussion may lead to licentiousness. Out of licentiousness will be born a heart of disrespect to the husband. Such a result comes from not knowing that one should stay in one's proper place.

Furthermore, affairs may be either crooked or straight; words may be either right or wrong. Straightforwardness cannot but lead to quarreling; crookedness cannot but lead to accusation. If there are really accusations and quarrels, then undoubtedly there will be angry affairs. Such a result comes from not esteeming others, and not honoring and serving (them).

(If wives) suppress not contempt for husbands, then it follows (that such wives) rebuke and scold (their husbands). (If husbands) stop not short of anger, then they are certain to beat (their wives). The correct relationship between husband and wife is based upon harmony and intimacy, and (conjugal) love is grounded in proper union. Should actual blows be dealt, how could matrimonial relationship be preserved? Should sharp words be spoken, how could (conjugal) love exist? If love and proper relationship both be destroyed, then husband and wife are divided.

Chapter IV: Womanly Qualifications

A woman (ought to) have four qualifications: (1) womanly virtue; (2) womanly words; (3) womanly bearing; and (4) womanly work. Now what is called womanly virtue need not be brilliant ability, exceptionally different from others. Womanly words need be neither clever in debate nor keen in conversation. Womanly appearance requires neither a pretty nor a perfect face and form. Womanly work need not be work done more skillfully than that of others.

To guard carefully her chastity; to control circumspectly her behavior; in every motion to exhibit modesty; and to model each act on the best usage, this is womanly virtue.

To choose her words with care; to avoid vulgar language; to speak at appropriate times; and not to weary others (with much conversation), may be called the characteristics of womanly words.

To wash and scrub filth away; to keep clothes and ornaments fresh and clean; to wash the head and bathe the body regularly, and to keep the person free from disgraceful filth, may be called the characteristics of womanly bearing.

With whole-hearted devotion to sew and to weave; to love not gossip and silly laughter; in cleanliness and order (to prepare) the wine and food for serving guests, may be called the characteristics of womanly work.

These four qualifications characterize the greatest virtue of a woman. No woman can afford to be without them. In fact they are very easy to possess if a woman only treasure them in her heart. The ancients had a saying: "Is Love afar off? If I desire love, then love is at hand!" So can it be said of these qualifications.

Chapter V: Whole-Hearted Devotion

Now in the "Rites" is written the principle that a husband may marry again, but there is no Canon that authorizes a woman to be married the second time. Therefore it is said of husbands as of Heaven, that as certainly as people cannot run away from Heaven, so surely a wife cannot leave (a husband's home).

If people in action or character disobey the spirits of Heaven and of Earth, then Heaven punishes them. Likewise if a woman errs in the rites and in the proper mode of conduct, then her husband esteems her lightly. The ancient book, "A Pattern for Women," . . . says: "To obtain the love of one man is the crown of a woman's life; to lose the love of one man is to miss the aim in woman's life." For these reasons a woman cannot but seek to win her husband's heart. Nevertheless, the beseeching wife need not use flattery, coaxing words, and cheap methods to gain intimacy.

Decidedly nothing is better (to gain the heart of a husband) than whole-hearted devotion and correct manners. In accordance with the rites and the proper mode of conduct, (let a woman) live a pure life. Let her have ears that hear not licentiousness; and eyes that see not depravity. When she goes outside her own home, let her not be conspicuous in dress and manners. When at home let her not neglect her dress. Women should not assemble in groups, nor gather together (for gossip and silly laughter). They should not stand watching in the gateways. (If a woman follows) these rules, she may be said to have whole-hearted devotion and correct manners.

If, in all her actions, she is frivolous, she sees and hears (only) that which pleases herself. At home her hair is dishevelled, and her dress is slovenly. Outside the home she emphasizes her femininity to attract attention; she says what ought not to be said; and she looks at what ought not to be seen. (If a woman does such as) these, (she may be) said to be without whole-hearted devotion and correct manners.

STUDY QUESTIONS

1. According to Ban Zhao, what were women's roles and purposes? How did Ban Zhao's approach fit the definition of patriarchalism?
2. What was Confucian about Ban Zhao's approach?
3. How good is this source as a means of determining women's situation in classical China? What social classes would this advice best describe, and why?
4. What was the relationship between these recommendations and Ban Zhao's own life?
5. How could women use Ban Zhao's ideas to some advantage, in winning certain protections and benefits within a patriarchal system?
6. How does Ban Zhao's version of patriarchy compare with Middle-Eastern patriarchy in the early civilization period, as suggested by the Hammurabi code and Jewish law?

PORTRAIT OF BAN ZHAO

曹大家班惠班

惠班名昭一名姬博學高才適曹世叔兄固著漢書

未及竟而卒和帝詔昭踵而成之數召入宮令皇后

諸貴人師事焉號曰大家

Portrait by Jim Guliang. The woodcut was published around 1690, early in the Qing dynasty and hundreds of years after Ban Zhao lived. The image is obviously the artist's invention, and illustrates not Ban Zhao herself, but her legacy. (Wan-go Weng Archive)

Ban Zhao's manual about women was reprinted frequently, all the way through the 19th century. Artists who sketched Ban Zhao reflected the author's ongoing importance, but since they had no idea what she actually looked like, they tried to convey what seemed suitable to them in light of her legacy.

STUDY QUESTIONS

1. Are there any features of this sketch that make it clear that this was *not* done during Ban Zhao's own lifetime? Any clear anachronistic elements?
2. What does the sketch suggest about the ongoing image of Ban Zhao?
3. Does the image correctly reflect Ban Zhao's own ideas about women?
4. Is this painting, created by a male artist, designed to illustrate women's inferiority?
5. Can you think of other important cases where we lack an original painting of a major historical figure, but where a rich portrait tradition developed later on?

11

THE ROLE OF THE STATE IN THE ECONOMY: THE SALT AND IRON DEBATES

Soon after taking office, Emperor Wu (reigned 140–87 B.C.E.), the greatest of the Han dynasty emperors, launched a major diplomatic and military offensive against China's most formidable adversary, the Xiongnu nomads of Mongolia. Beginning in the 120s B.C.E. the Chinese won a series of major battles against the Xiongnu, driving the nomads away from their northern and western borders. The Chinese victories over the nomads were important because they opened the way for increased trade and cultural interchange along the silk roads that soon stretched from China to the Mediterranean Sea.

The continuing battles with the Xiongnu were, however, a financial drain on the Han government. Single engagements sometimes involved over 100,000 soldiers, all of whom had to be clothed, fed, and provided with weapons. The army also required large numbers of cavalry horses, as well as huge herds of transport animals such as donkeys, mules, oxen, and camels. The expense necessary to fulfill these needs was enormous.

To meet the increasing demands on his treasury and ensure that the army would be adequately supplied, Emperor Wu introduced several new policies. As a way of raising more revenue, in 119 B.C.E. Wu authorized the establishment of governmental monopolies on the sale of salt and iron, two commodities that were essential to every Chinese household. A few years later he created the "equitable marketing" system, a policy that authorized officials to buy quantities of grain for the army when the price was low and then to sell some of it to civilian buyers when prices rose.

Wu's policies were successful in averting a fiscal crisis for the government and in providing for the army, but there was widespread opposition to them because they led to higher prices for necessities and opened the way for official malfeasance. After a group of Confucian scholars drafted a petition calling for the abolition of the salt and iron monopolies, Wu's successor, Emperor Zhao (reigned 86–74 B.C.E.), instructed his officials to meet with the scholars. The result was an extraordinary forum in 81 B.C.E., which must have lasted many days, in which Han officials and Confucian scholars exchanged views on the salt and iron monopolies, the marketing of grain, and a wide range of related issues. Although the scholars were unsuccessful in persuading the government to alter its policies, the arguments they made on this occasion lived on as a classic statement of Confucian values.

From Esson M. Gale, editor and translator, *Discourses on Salt and Iron* (Leiden, the Netherlands: E. J. Brill, 1931), pp. 1–7, 9–11.

After the meetings ended, Huan Kuan, a Han dynasty official, produced a written version of the discussions, casting them in the form of a debate. In the following excerpt from Huan Kuan's account, the Han officials are represented by the "Lord Grand Secretary" and the scholars are referred to as the "Literati." How does the debate illustrate both the power of the Chinese state and the nature of Confucian ideals?

ECONOMIC DEBATES

a. It so happened that in the sixth year of the *shiyuan* era an Imperial edict directed the Chancellor and the Imperial secretaries to confer with the recommended Worthies and Literati, and to enquire of them as to the rankling grievances among the people.

b. The Literati responded as follows: It is our humble opinion that the principle of ruling men lies in nipping in the bud wantonness and frivolity, in extending wide the elementals of virtue, in discouraging mercantile pursuits, and in displaying benevolence and righteousness. Let lucre never be paraded before the eyes of the people; only then will enlightenment flourish and folkways improve.

c. But now, with the system of the salt and iron monopolies, the liquor excise, and *equable marketing*, established in the provinces and the demesnes, the Government has entered into financial competition with the people, dissipating primordial candor and simplicity and sanctioning propensities to selfishness and greed. As a result few among our people take up the fundamental pursuits of life [agriculture], while many flock to the non-essential [industry and commerce]. Now sturdy natural qualities decay as artificiality thrives, and rural values decline when industrialism flourishes. When industrialism is cultivated, the people become frivolous; when the values of rural life are developed, the people are simple and unsophisticated. The people being unsophisticated, wealth will abound; when the people are extravagant, cold and hunger will follow. We pray that the salt, iron and liquor monopolies and the system of *equable marketing* be abolished so that the rural pursuits may be encouraged, people be deterred from entering the secondary occupations, and national agriculture be materially and financially benefited.

d. The Lord Grand Secretary said: When the Xiongnu rebelled against our authority and frequently raided and devastated the frontier settlements, to be constantly on the watch for them was a great strain upon the soldiery of the Middle Kingdom; but without measures of precaution being taken, these forays and depredations would never cease. The late Emperor [Wu], grieving at their long suffering of the denizens of the marches who live in fear of capture by the barbarians, caused consequently forts and seried signal stations to be built, where garrisons were held ready against the nomads. When the revenue for the defence of the frontier fell short, the salt and iron monopoly was established, the liquor excise and the system of *equable marketing* introduced; goods were multiplied and wealth increased so as to furnish the frontier expenses.

e. Now our critics here, who demand that these measures be abolished, at home would have the hoard of the treasury entirely depleted, and abroad would deprive the border of provision for its defence; they would expose our soldiers who defend the barriers and mount the walls to all the hunger and cold of the borderland. How else do they expect to provide for them? It is not expedient to abolish these measures!

f. The Literati: Confucius observed that *the ruler of a kingdom or the chief of a house is not concerned about his people being few, but about lack of equitable treatment; nor is he concerned about poverty, but over the presence of discontentment.* Thus the Son of Heaven should not speak about *much and little,* the feudal lords should not talk about *advantage and detriment,* ministers about *gain and loss,* but they should cultivate benevolence and righteousness, to set an example to the people, and extend wide their virtuous conduct to gain the people's confidence. Then will nearby folk lovingly flock to them and distant peoples joyfully submit to their authority. Therefore *the master conqueror does not fight; the expert warrior needs no soldiers; the truly great commander requires not to set his troops in battle array.* Cultivate virtue in the temple and the hall, then you need only to show a bold front to the enemy and your troops will return home in victory. The Prince who practices benevolent administration should be matchless in the world; for him, what use is expenditure?

g. The Lord Grand Secretary: The Xiongnu, savage and wily, boldly push through the barriers and harass the Middle Kingdom, massacring the provincial population and killing the keepers of the Northern Marches. They long deserve punishment for their unruliness and lawlessness. But Your Majesty graciously took pity on the insufficiency of the multitude and did not suffer his lords and knights to be exposed in the desert plains, yet unflinchingly You cherish the purpose of raising strong armies and driving the Xiongnu before You to their original haunts in the north. I again assert that the proposal to do away with the salt and iron monopoly and *equable marketing* would grievously diminish our frontier supplies and impair our military plans. I can not consider favorably a proposal so heartlessly dismissing the frontier question.

h. The Literati: The ancients held in honor virtuous methods and discredited resort to arms. Thus Confucius said: *If remoter people are not submissive, all the influences of civil culture and virtue are to be cultivated to attract them to be so; and when they have been so attracted, they must be made contented and tranquil?* Now these virtuous principles are discarded and reliance put on military force; troops are raised to attack the enemy and garrisons are stationed to make ready for him. It is the long drawn-out service of our troops in the field and the ceaseless transportation for the needs of the commissariat that cause our soldiers on the marches to suffer from hunger and cold abroad, while the common people are burdened with labor at home. The establishment of the salt and iron monopoly and the institution of finance officials to supply the army needs were not permanent schemes; it is therefore desirable that they now be abolished.

i. The Lord Grand Secretary: The ancient founders of the Commonwealth made open the ways for both fundamental and branch industries and facilitated equitable distribution of goods. Markets and courts were provided to harmonize various demands; there people of all classes gathered together and all goods collected, so that farmer, merchant, and worker could each obtain what he desired; the exchange completed, everyone went back to his occupation. *Facilitate exchange so that the people will be unflagging in industry* says the Book of Changes. Thus without artisans, the farmers will be deprived of the use of implements; without merchants, all prized commodities will be cut off. The former would lead to stoppage of grain production, the latter to exhaustion of wealth. It is clear that the salt and iron monopoly and *equable marketing* are really intended for the circulation of amassed wealth and the regulation of the consumption according to the urgency of the need. It is inexpedient to abolish them.

j. The Literati: Lead the people with virtue and the people will return to honest simplicity; entice the people with gain, and they will become vicious. Vicious habits would lead them away from righteousness to follow after gain, with the result that people will swarm on the road and throng at the markets. *A poor country may appear plentiful, not because it possesses abundant wealth, but because wants multiply and people become reckless,* said Laozi. Hence the true King promotes rural pursuits and discourages branch industries; he checks the people's desires through the principles of propriety and righteousness and provides a market for grain in exchange for other commodities, where there is no place for merchants to circulate useless goods, and for artisans to make useless implements. Thus merchants are for the purpose of draining stagnation and the artisans for providing tools; they should not become the principle concern of the government. . . .

m. The Lord Grand Secretary: Formerly the Princes in the provinces and the demesnes sent in their respective products as tribute. The transportation was vexatious and disorganized; the goods were usually of distressingly bad quality, often failing to repay their transport costs. Therefore Transportation Officers have been provided in every province to assist in the delivery and transportation and for the speeding of the tribute from distant parts. So the system came to be known as *equable marketing.* A Receiving Bureau has been established at the capital to monopolize all the commodities, buying when prices are low, and selling when prices are high, with the result that the Government suffers no loss and the merchants cannot speculate for profit. This is therefore known as the *balancing standard.* With the *balancing standard* people are safeguarded from unemployment; with the *equable marketing* people have evenly distributed labor. Both of these measures are intended to equilibrate all goods and convenience the people, and not to open the way to profit and provide a ladder to popular misdemeanor.

n. The Literati: The Ancients in levying upon and taxing the people would look for what the latter were skilled in, and not seek for those things in which they were not adept. Thus the farmers contributed the fruits of their labor, the weaving women, their products. Now the Government leaves alone what the people have and exacts what they have not, with the result that the people sell their products at a cheap price to satisfy demands from above. Recently in some of the provinces and demesnes they ordered the people to make woven goods. The officers then caused the producers various embarrassments and bargained with them. What was collected by the officers was not only the silk from Qi and Tao, or cloth from Shu and Han, but also other goods manufactured by the people which were mischievously sold at a standard price. Thus the farmers suffer twice over while the weaving women are doubly taxed. We have not yet seen that your marketing is "equable." As to the second measure under discussion, the government officers swarm out to close the door, gain control of the market and corner all commodities. With commodities cornered, prices soar; with prices rising, the merchants make private deals by way of speculation. Thus the officers are lenient to the cunning capitalists, and the merchants store up goods and accumulate commodities waiting for a time of need. Nimble traders and unscrupulous officials buy in cheap to get high returns. We have not yet seen that your standard is "balanced." For it seems that in ancient times *equable marketing* was to bring about equitable division of labor and facilitate transportation of tribute; it was surely not for profit or to make trade in commodities. . . .

STUDY QUESTIONS

1. What kind of society did the Confucian scholars seek to establish? According to them, what was wrong with the policies of the government? What did the scholars say, or imply, about the duties of governmental officials?
2. What were the secretary's arguments in defense of the government's policies? What did he think were the major responsibilities of the government?
3. Compare the attitudes of the scholars and the secretary toward the following groups: peasants, artisans, and merchants.
4. What does the debate suggest about the authority of Chinese emperors and their techniques of governing? What does it suggest about the importance of Confucian scholars and the teachings of Confucius?
5. Did the Han official who compiled the record of the debate present both sides fairly? Do you see any favoritism in the presentation? How do you explain this?
6. What do the views expressed in the debate reveal about the economy, about gender structures, and about the role of the government in the economy?
7. How does the debate illustrate the differences between Confucianism and Legalism?
8. How does the system of governance in classical China compare with that in India, Greece, and Rome?

CHINESE TOMB RUBBING

Visitors to major museums in the United States know that Chinese art can be a rich source of historical understanding. The paintings, sculptures, and other artifacts found in tombs dating from the Han dynasty are especially valuable in this regard. Many of these burial goods shed light on social and economic conditions.

The tomb rubbing depicts several important features of agricultural life during the Han era. Peasants are shown engaging in intensive hoeing, a technique they developed to conserve soil moisture on the arid Yellow River plain. The hoes the farmers are using doubtless have prongs made of cast iron, a metal produced in great quantity at this time only in China. Also noteworthy is the depiction of crops (probably millet or wheat) seeded in rows, another innovation of Chinese peasants during the Han period. Such methods helped to make Chinese farming one of the most productive agricultural systems in the classical world.

Agriculture in Northern China. Han Dynasty Rubbing. (MacQuitty International Photographic Collection/London)

STUDY QUESTIONS

1. Does the rubbing portray specific individuals, or generalized types?
2. How does the rubbing illustrate features of material life in Han China?
3. What does it suggest about social class in rural China? About gender relations?
4. In what ways does the rubbing illustrate aspects of Confucian teaching?
5. Why is the name of the sculptor unknown?

CLASSICAL INDIA

12 "To Fight in a Righteous War": *Varna* and Moral Duty in India

The system of social classes in India known as the caste system gradually took shape during the thousand years prior to the beginning of the Common Era. The Aryans, an Indo-European speaking people who may have come from the grasslands north of the Caspian Sea, took the lead in creating a four-part division of social classes in which lineal descent was significant, called *varnas* (a Sanskrit word meaning "color").

The new social system was strongly hierarchical. Priests (*brahmans*) ranked the highest and warriors (*kshatriyas*) came next. Merchants, artisans, and peasants (*vaishyas*) ranked third. The fourth *varna* was composed of the servants (*sudras*) of the three higher groups. A fifth category, made up of all those who were engaged in occupations defined as "unclean," stood outside the system of *varnas*; these people were known as "untouchables." (When the Portuguese arrived in India around 1500 C.E. they translated *varna* as "caste"; the "caste system" is thus a later European term used to describe Indian social realities.)

The *brahmans* taught that each *varna* had its own sacred or moral duty (*dharma*) to perform. The example we consider in this chapter is that of the warriors, whose sacred duty was to fight. A vivid illustration of the *dharma* of the warriors can be found in the famous literary text from early India, the *Bhagavad Gita (Song of God)*. The *Bhagavad Gita* is a portion of a much longer Indian classic, the *Mahabharata*, the epic tale of a war between two branches of the same family in the distant past. In its present form the *Bhagavad Gita* dates from the 2nd century B.C.E.

The central theme of the *Bhagavad Gita* is the dialogue between the warrior Arjuna, who is on the eve of a great battle, and his chariot driver Krishna, who is actually the Hindu god Vishnu. How do the following passages help us to understand the origins of the caste system?

From *The Bhagavad Gita*, translated by Juan Mascaro (Baltimore: Penguin Books, 1962), pp. 45–51. Copyright © 1962 by Juan Mascaro. Reproduced by permission of Penguin Books, Ltd.

BHAGAVAD GITA

CHAPTER 1

. . .

Arjuna

21 Drive my chariot, Krishna immortal, and place it between the two armies.
22 That I may see those warriors who stand there eager for battle, with whom I
     must now fight at the beginning of this war.
23 That I may see those who have come here eager and ready to fight, in their
     desire to do the will of the evil son of Dhritarashtra.

Sanjaya

24 When Krishna heard the words of Arjuna he drove their glorious chariot
     and placed it between the two armies.
25 And facing Bhishma and Drona and other royal rulers he said: "See, Arjuna,
     the armies of the Kurus, gathered here on this field of battle."
26 Then Arjuna saw in both armies fathers, grandfathers, sons,
27 grandsons; fathers of wives, uncles, masters;
28 brothers, companions and friends.
     When Arjuna thus saw his kinsmen face to face in both lines of battle, he was over-
     come by grief and despair and thus he spoke with a sinking heart.

Arjuna

When I see all my kinsmen, Krishna, who have come here on this field of battle,
29 Life goes from my limbs and they sink, and my mouth is sear and dry; a
     trembling overcomes my body, and my hair shudders in horror;
30 My great bow Gandiva falls from my hands, and the skin of my flesh is
     burning; I am no longer able to stand, because my mind is whirling and
     wandering.
31 And I see forebodings of evil, Krishna. I cannot foresee any glory if I kill my
     own kinsmen in the sacrifice of battle.
32 Because I have no wish for victory, Krishna, nor for a kingdom, nor for its
     pleasures. How can we want a kingdom, Govinda, or its pleasures or even
     life,
33 When those for whom we want a kingdom, and its pleasures, and the joys of
     life, are here in this field of battle about to give up their wealth and their
     life?
34 Facing us in the field of battle are teachers, fathers and sons; grandsons,
     grandfathers, wives' brothers; mothers' brothers and fathers of wives.
35 These I do not wish to slay, even if I myself am slain. Not even for the kingdom
     of the three worlds: how much less for a kingdom of the earth!
36 If we kill these evil men, evil shall fall upon us: what joy in their death could
     we have, O Janardana, mover of souls?

37   I cannot therefore kill my own kinsmen, the sons of king Dhritarashtra, the brother of my own father. What happiness could we ever enjoy, if we killed our own kinsmen in battle?

38   Even if they, with minds overcome by greed, see no evil in the destruction of a family, see no sin in the treachery to friends;

39   Shall we not, who see the evil of destruction, shall we not refrain from this terrible deed?

40   The destruction of a family destroys its rituals of righteousness, and when the righteous rituals are no more, unrighteousness overcomes the whole family.

41   When unrighteous disorder prevails, the women sin and are impure; and when women are not pure, Krishna, there is disorder of castes, social confusion.

42   This disorder carries down to hell the family and the destroyers of the family. The spirits of their dead suffer in pain when deprived of the ritual offerings.

43   Those evil deeds of the destroyers of a family, which cause this social disorder, destroy the righteousness of birth and the ancestral rituals of righteousness.

44   And have we not heard that hell is waiting for those whose familiar rituals of righteousness are no more?

45   O day of darkness! What evil spirit moved our minds when for the sake of an earthly kingdom we came to this field of battle ready to kill our own people?

46   Better for me indeed if the sons of Dhritarashtra, with arms in hand, found me unarmed, unresisting, and killed me in the struggle of war.

Sanjaya

47   Thus spoke Arjuna in the field of battle, and letting fall his bow and arrows he sank down in his chariot, his soul overcome by despair and grief.

CHAPTER 2

Sanjaya

1   Then arose the Spirit of Krishna and spoke to Arjuna, his friend, who with eyes filled with tears, thus had sunk into despair and grief.

Krishna

2   Whence this lifeless dejection, Arjuna, in this hour, the hour of trial? Strong men know not despair, Arjuna, for this wins neither heaven nor earth.

3   Fall not into degrading weakness, for this becomes not a man who is a man. Throw off this ignoble discouragement, and arise like a fire that burns all before it.

Arjuna

4   I owe veneration to Bhishma and Drona. Shall I kill with my arrows my grandfather's brother, great Bhishma? Shall my arrows in battle slay Drona, my teacher?

5   Shall I kill my own masters who, though greedy of my kingdom, are yet my sacred teachers? I would rather eat in this life the food of a beggar than eat royal food tasting of their blood.

6   And we know not whether their victory or ours be better for us. The sons of my uncle and king, Dhritarashtra, are here before us: after their death, should we wish to live?

7   In the dark night of my soul I feel desolation. In my self-pity I see not the way of righteousness. I am thy disciple, come to thee in supplication: be a light unto me on the path of my duty.

8   For neither the kingdom of the earth, nor the kingdom of the gods in heaven, could give me peace from the fire of sorrow which thus burns my life.

Sanjaya

9   When Arjuna the great warrior had thus unburdened his heart, "I will not fight, Krishna," he said, and then fell silent.

10   Krishna smiled and spoke to Arjuna—there between the two armies the voice of God spoke these words:

Krishna

11   Thy tears are for those beyond tears; and are thy words words of wisdom? The wise grieve not for those who live; and they grieve not for those who die—for life and death shall pass away.

12   Because we all have been for all time: I, and thou, and those kings of men. And we all shall be for all time, we all for ever and ever.

13   As the Spirit of our mortal body wanders on in childhood, and youth and old age, the Spirit wanders on to a new body: of this the sage has no doubts.

14   From the world of the senses, Arjuna, comes heat and comes cold, and pleasure and pain. They come and they go: they are transient. Arise above them, strong soul.

15   The man whom these cannot move, whose soul is one, beyond pleasure and pain, is worthy of life in Eternity.

16   The unreal never is: the Real never is not. This truth indeed has been seen by those who can see the true.

17   Interwoven in his creation, the Spirit is beyond destruction. No one can bring to an end the Spirit which is everlasting.

18   For beyond time he dwells in these bodies, though these bodies have an end in their time; but he remains immeasurable, immortal. Therefore, great warrior, carry on thy fight.

19   If any man thinks he slays, and if another thinks he is slain, neither knows the ways of truth. The Eternal in man cannot kill: the Eternal in man cannot die.

20   He is never born, and he never dies. He is in Eternity: he is for evermore. Never-born and eternal, beyond times gone or to come, he does not die when the body dies.

21   When a man knows him as never-born, everlasting, never-changing, beyond all destruction, how can that man kill a man, or cause another to kill?

22   As a man leaves an old garment and puts on one that is new, the Spirit leaves his mortal body and then puts on one that is new.

23   Weapons cannot hurt the Spirit and fire can never burn him. Untouched is he by drenching waters, untouched is he by parching winds.

24   Beyond the power of sword and fire, beyond the power of waters and winds, the Spirit is everlasting, omnipresent, never-changing, never-moving, ever One.

25   Invisible is he to mortal eyes, beyond thought and beyond change. Know that he is, and cease from sorrow.

26   But if he were born again and again, and again and again he were to die, even then, victorious man, cease thou from sorrow.

27   For all things born in truth must die, and out of death in truth comes life. Face to face with what must be, cease thou from sorrow.

28   Invisible before birth are all beings and after death invisible again. They are seen between two unseens. Why in this truth find sorrow?

29   One sees him in a vision of wonder, and another gives us words of his wonder. There is one who hears of his wonder; but he hears and knows him not.

30   The Spirit that is in all beings is immortal in them all: for the death of what cannot die, cease thou to sorrow.

31   Think thou also of thy duty and do not waver. There is no greater good for a warrior than to fight in a righteous war.

32   There is a war that opens the doors of heavens, Arjuna! Happy the warriors whose fate is to fight such war.

33   But to forgo this fight for righteousness is to forgo thy duty and honour: is to fall into transgression.

34   Men will tell of thy dishonour both now and in times to come. And to a man who is in honour, dishonour is more than death.

35   The great warriors will say that thou hast run from the battle through fear; and those who thought great things of thee will speak of thee in scorn.

36   And thine enemies will speak of thee in contemptuous words of ill-will and derision, pouring scorn upon thy courage. Can there be for a warrior a more shameful fate?

37   In death thy glory in heaven, in victory thy glory on earth. Arise therefore, Arjuna, with thy soul ready to fight. . . .

STUDY QUESTIONS

1. Why is Arjuna reluctant to fight?
2. What reasons does Krishna give for urging Arjuna into battle?
3. What clues regarding gender relations in India do you see in these passages? Do you see evidence of how masculinity and femininity were defined?

4. How did the *Bhagavad Gita* reinforce the system of *varnas*, or castes?

5. Why do you think the *Bhagavad Gita* has fascinated the people of India for 2,000 years? What other religions rely heavily on stories?

6. How would a Buddhist respond to Arjuna's ethical dilemma?

7. How does the advice from Krishna compare with the thinking of Confucius? What does this comparison suggest about how concepts of male "virtue" differed in classical India and China?

INDIAN PAINTING OF ARJUNA AND KRISHNA

An anonymous artist in the Himalayan foothills of northern India painted this colorful and stylized depiction of Arjuna and Krishna in their chariot, preparing to go (or not to go!) into battle. The painting dates from the early 19th century, i.e. about 3,000 years after the events that it ostensibly portrays. It is one of countless visual reminders by Indian painters and sculptors of the moment in the *Bhagavad Gita* when the two warriors debated the meaning of war, family, duty, and human life. Versions of this scene carved

Arjuna and Krishna. From Gordon Johnson, *Cultural Atlas of India* (Detail from Arjuna and his Charioteer Lord Krishna Confront Carna (1975–23–1), Indian, Darhwal School, Philadelphia Museum of Art: Purchased with the Edith H. Bell Fund, 1975)

in stone can be found embellishing Hindu temples throughout India and in many countries of Southeast Asia, notably Cambodia and Indonesia.

STUDY QUESTIONS

1. What techniques did the painter use to draw attention to Arjuna and Krishna?
2. To what extent does the painting seem to balance realism with deliberately stylized images?
3. How does the depiction of Krishna compare with that of the other figures?
4. What explains the enduring power of the *Bhagavad Gita* to Indian people? Are there Western counterparts to the *Gita*?

13 WHAT THE BUDDHA TAUGHT

Prince Gautama, the founder of Buddhism, was born around 560 B.C.E. in the foothills of the Himalayan Mountains near the present-day border of India and Nepal. His father was the ruler of one of the many small kingdoms in this region. According to Buddhist tradition, the young prince grew up in luxury and was much sheltered from life's problems. At age 29, however, he suddenly became aware of three causes of deep sorrow for all people: old age, illness, and death. Shocked by his discovery of humankind's suffering, the prince relinquished his royal privileges, left his wife and young son, and joined the ranks of India's many itinerant truth-seekers. Why, he wondered, is misery a part of every person's life?

After six years of wandering the roads of India's Ganges Plain in search of an answer to his question, the former prince entered into a state of deep meditation, an experience he underwent while seated under a fig tree in the village of present-day Bodh Gaya. When he emerged from this trance-like condition, he had achieved "enlightenment" and was henceforth known as the Buddha, the "Enlightened One." Leaving Bodh Gaya, he traveled west to Benares (present-day Varanasi), a major center of commerce and religious devotion on the Ganges River. At a deer park in nearby Sarnath, he delivered his first lecture (or sermon) to a small group of followers. Known as the Four Noble Truths, the lecture summarized the wisdom he had attained under the tree at Bodh Gaya and has traditionally been regarded by Buddhists as the core of the founder's teaching.

For the next 40 years or so, until his death around 483 B.C.E., the Buddha taught at various locations in northern India. He must have been a compelling teacher because he attracted many devoted followers. After his death they kept his teaching alive (and subtly changed it) by creating an organizational structure, a kind of Buddhist "church." They held conferences and formed the world's earliest monastic communities. The monks became effective missionaries on behalf of the new faith. Each year during the six months of dry weather they traveled India's dusty roads, carrying little more than a begging bowl, in quest of new converts. (During the rainy months the monks congregated in their monasteries and studied the teachings of the Buddha.) In the 3rd century B.C.E. the standing of Buddhism increased in India when Emperor Ashoka (reigned 268–233) became a lay Buddhist and gave support to the monks. Ashoka also sent one of his sons to Sri Lanka with a cutting from the tree at Bodh Gaya, now called the Bodhi (Wisdom) Tree, to introduce the faith to the South Asian island. By the beginning of the Common Era Buddhism had become an important part of Indian spiritual life and was beginning to spread to other Asian countries.

Reprinted with permission of the publishers from *Buddhism in Translations: Passages from the Buddhist Sacred Books,* translated by Henry Clarke Warren (Cambridge, MA.: Harvard University Press), pp. 368–374. Copyright © 1953 by the President and Fellows of Harvard College.

In studying the Four Noble Truths we journey back 2,500 years to the birth of one of the great world religions. How do the Four Noble Truths help us to understand why the impact of Buddhism has been so lasting?

FOUR NOBLE TRUTHS

1. The Truth Concerning Misery

And how, O priests, does a priest live, as respects the elements of being, observant of the elements of being in the four noble truths?

Whenever, O priest, a priest knows the truth concerning misery, knows the truth concerning the origin of misery, knows the truth concerning the cessation of misery, knows the truth concerning the path leading to the cessation of misery.

And what, O priests, is the noble truth of misery?

Birth is misery; old age is misery; disease is misery; death is misery; sorrow, lamentation, misery, grief, and despair are misery; to wish for what one cannot have is misery; in short, all the five attachment-groups are misery. . . .

This, O priests, is called the noble truth of misery.

2. The Truth of the Origin of Misery

And what, O priests, is the noble truth of the origin of misery?

It is desire leading to rebirth, joining itself to pleasure and passion, and finding delight in every existence,—desire, namely, for sensual pleasure, desire for permanent existence, desire for transitory existence.

But where, O priests, does this desire spring up and grow? Where does it settle and take root?

Where anything is delightful and agreeable to men, there desire springs up and grows, there it settles and takes root.

And what is delightful and agreeable to men, where desire springs up and grows, where it settles and takes root?

The eye is delightful and agreeable to men; there desire springs up and grows, there it settles and takes root.

The ear . . . the nose . . . the tongue . . . the body . . . the mind is delightful and agreeable to men; there desire springs up and grows, there it settles and takes root.

The Six Organs of Sense.

Forms . . . sounds . . . odors . . . tastes . . . things tangible . . . ideas are delightful and agreeable to men; there desire springs up and grows, there it settles and takes root.

The Six Objects of Sense.

Eye-consciousness . . . ear-consciousness . . . nose-consciousness . . . tongue-consciousness . . . body-consciousness . . . mind-consciousness is delightful and agreeable to men; there desire springs up and grows, there it settles and takes root.

The Six Consciousnesses.

Contact of the eye . . . ear . . . nose . . . tongue . . . body . . . mind is delightful and agreeable to men; there desire springs up and grows, there it settles and takes root.

The Six Contacts.

Sensation produced by contact of the eye . . . ear . . . nose . . . tongue . . . body . . . mind is delightful and agreeable to men; there desire springs up and grows, there it settles and takes root.

The Six Sensations.

Perception of forms . . . sounds . . . odors . . . tastes . . . things tangible . . . ideas is delightful and agreeable to men; there desire springs up and grows, there it settles and takes root.

The Six Perceptions.

Thinking on forms . . . sounds . . . odors . . . tastes . . . things tangible . . . ideas is delightful and agreeable to men; there desire springs up and grows, there it settles and takes root.

The Six Thinkings.

Desire for forms . . . sounds . . . odors . . . tastes . . . things tangible . . . ideas is delightful and agreeable to men; there desire springs up and grows, there it settles and takes root.

The Six Desires.

Reasoning on forms . . . sounds . . . odors . . . tastes . . . things tangible . . . ideas is delightful and agreeable to men; there desire springs up and grows, there it settles and takes root.

The Six Reasonings.

Reflection on forms . . . sounds . . . odors . . . tastes . . . things tangible . . . ideas is delightful and agreeable to men; there desire springs up and grows, there it settles and takes root.

The Six Reflections.

This, O priests, is called the noble truth of the origin of misery.

3. The Truth of the Cessation of Misery

And what, O priests, is the noble truth of the cessation of misery?

It is the complete fading out and cessation of this desire, a giving up, a losing hold, a relinquishment, and a nonadhesion.

But where, O priests, does this desire wane and disappear? where is it broken up and destroyed?

Where anything is delightful and agreeable to men; there desire wanes and disappears, there it is broken up and destroyed.

And what is delightful and agreeable to men, where desire wanes and disappears, where it is broken up and destroyed?

The eye is delightful and agreeable to men; there desire wanes and disappears, there it is broken up and destroyed.

[Similarly respecting the other organs of sense, the six objects of sense, the six consciousnesses, the six contacts, the six sensations, the six perceptions, the six thinkings, the six desires, the six reasonings, and the six reflections.]

This, O priests, is called the noble truth of the cessation of misery.

4. The Truth of the Path Leading to the Cessation of Misery

And what, O priests, is the noble truth of the path leading to the cessation of misery?

It is this noble eightfold path, to wit, right belief, right resolve, right speech, right behavior, right occupation, right effort, right contemplation, right concentration.

And what, O priests, is right belief?

The knowledge of misery, O priests, the knowledge of the origin of misery, the knowledge of the cessation of misery, and the knowledge of the path leading to the cessation of misery, this, O priests, is called "right belief."

And what, O priests, is right resolve?

The resolve to renounce sensual pleasures, the resolve to have malice towards none, and the resolve to harm no living creature, this, O priests, is called "right resolve."

And what, O priests, is right speech?

To abstain from falsehood, to abstain from backbiting, to abstain from harsh language, and to abstain from frivolous talk, this, O priests, is called "right speech."

And what, O priests, is right behavior?

To abstain from destroying life, to abstain from taking that which is not given one, and to abstain from immorality, this, O priests, is called "right behavior."

And what, O priests, is right occupation?

Whenever, O priests, a noble disciple, quitting a wrong occupation, gets his livelihood by a right occupation, this, O priests, is called "right occupation."

And what, O priests, is right effort?

Whenever, O priests, a priest purposes, makes an effort, heroically endeavors, applies his mind, and exerts himself that evil and demeritorious qualities not yet arisen may not arise; purposes, makes an effort, heroically endeavors, applies his mind, and exerts himself that evil and demeritorious qualities already arisen may be abandoned; purposes, makes an effort, heroically endeavors, applies his mind, and exerts himself that meritorious qualities not yet arisen may arise; purposes, makes an effort, heroically endeavors, applies his mind, and exerts himself for the preservation, retention, growth, increase, development, and perfection of meritorious qualities already arisen, this, O priest, is called "right effort."

And what, O priests, is right contemplation?

Whenever, O priests, a priest lives, as respects the body, observant of the body, strenuous, conscious, contemplative, and has rid himself of lust and grief; as respects sensations, observant of sensations, strenuous, conscious, contemplative, and has rid himself of lust and grief; as respects the mind, observant of the mind, strenuous, conscious, contemplative, and has rid himself of lust and grief; as respects the elements of being, observant of the elements of being, strenuous, conscious, contemplative, and has rid himself of lust and grief, this, O priests, is called "right contemplation."

And what, O priests, is right concentration?

Whenever, O priests, a priest, having isolated himself from sensual pleasures, having isolated himself from demeritorious traits, and still exercising reasoning, still exercising reflection, enters upon the first trance which is produced by isolation and characterized by joy and happiness; when, through the subsidence of reasoning and reflection, and still retaining joy and happiness, he enters upon the second trance, which is an interior tranquilization and intentness of the thoughts, and is produced by concentration; when, through the paling of joy, indifferent, contemplative, conscious, and in the experience of bodily happiness—that state which eminent men describe when they say, "Indifferent, contemplative, and living happily"—he enters upon the third trance; when, through the abandonment of happiness, through the abandonment of misery, through the disappearance of all antecedent gladness and grief, he enters upon the fourth trance, which has neither misery nor happiness, but is contemplation as refined by indifference, this, O priests, is called "right concentration."

This, O priests, is called the noble truth of the path leading to the cessation of misery.

STUDY QUESTIONS

1. According to the Four Noble Truths, what is the great problem that humans face? What is its solution?

2. Which steps in the eightfold path suggest the goal of social harmony? Which steps focus on the development of mental discipline? Which steps point toward the attainment of wisdom? How do you weigh the relative importance of these three aspects of the eightfold path?

3. What does the eightfold path suggest about the importance of ritual and a priesthood?

4. Does the eightfold path call for an ascetic life? How important is meditation to the eightfold path? What role does the exercise of reason have as one follows the eightfold path? Are the goals of the eightfold path attainable?

5. Is there a particular kind of social structure or set of gender relationships implied in the Four Noble Truths? Do the Four Noble Truths help us to understand why Buddhism in India seems to have appealed more to city-dwellers, especially merchants, rather than peasants? Why are there so many numbers in the Four Noble Truths?

6. How might the ideas represented by Krishna in the *Bhagavad Gita* have contributed to the waning of Buddhism in India?

7. How do the teachings in the Four Noble Truths compare with those of Confucianism and Daoism? What similarities and differences do you see?

8. How do the Four Noble Truths help us to understand why Buddhism spread so widely in Asia? What other evidence would be useful in this regard?

BUDDHIST CAVE PAINTING IN INDIA

Painting of *Bodhisattva* from Ajanta, India, 5th Century C.E.
(Photo by Stephen S. Gosch)

Around the beginning of the Common Era Buddhist monks in India began to establish temples in caves. The monks cut the caves out of hard rock, decorating the entrances and interiors with columns, statues and *stupas* (dome-shaped repositories for relics). They often painted the ceilings and walls with colorful scenes inspired by Buddhist teachings. A single cave temple could take generations to complete. Most of these sanctuaries were located near trade routes, so as to be accessible to the lay community and potential donors.

The group of 29 Buddhist cave temples at Ajanta in western India is one of the wonders of world art. Carved out of horseshoe-shaped cliffs above a river during the middle of the first millennium, the caves contain a splendid array of painting and sculpture. Many of the most vivid paintings illustrate themes from the *jataka* literature, the rich tradition of stories about the life of the Buddha that developed after his death.

This painting from Ajanta depicts a *bodhisattva* (a future Buddha and guide for others seeking salvation) engaged in teaching.

STUDY QUESTIONS

1. In what ways does the painting illustrate Buddhist ideals?
2. How does it suggest changes in Buddhist teachings from the time of the Buddha?
3. Why is most Buddhist art anonymous?
4. What other world religions have inspired traditions of great painting?

14 THE STATE AND THE ECONOMY IN INDIA

The classical period was extraordinarily creative regarding the development of political thinking in the major Eurasian civilizations. In China, the Confucians and the Legalists formulated ideas that have shaped political thinking in East Asia for the past 2,000 years. Similarly, Greek and Roman writers such as Plato, Aristotle, Cicero, and Plutarch pioneered ways of thinking about politics that, ever since they were formulated, have served as the baseline for discussions in the West.

India was also the home of innovative thinking about politics during the classical period. The pillar edicts of the Indian emperor Ashoka (reigned 268–232 B.C.E.), a fascinating blend of moral teaching and administrative measures, certainly qualify as creative thinking on the challenges of governing justly and effectively. Quite different in tone from Ashoka's edicts, but no less interesting, is the Indian political treatise called the *Arthashastra* (Precepts for Prosperity), which may have been written around 300 B.C.E.

Lost for many centuries, a copy of the *Arthashastra* written on palm leaves turned up in southern India shortly after 1900. Although there is some doubt regarding the authorship of the *Arthashastra*, most scholars think that it was written by Kautilya, the adviser of Chandragupta Maurya (reigned 321–297 B.C.E.). Chandragupta was the north Indian king who first unified most of the Indian subcontinent and established the Mauryan dynasty (321–184 B.C.E.), which reached its peak during the reign of Ashoka.

Scholars pounced on the *Arthashastra* immediately after it was discovered because of its richness as a source of evidence on India during the classical period, especially regarding techniques of governance, the economy and society. Because the *Arthashastra* seems to have been written as a manual of advice for a ruler, we cannot be sure of the extent to which its injunctions were implemented. Nonetheless, it is quite likely that at least some Indian rulers were influenced by the kind of thinking contained in the *Arthashastra*. How do the passages that follow shed light on Indian political, economic, and social life during the classical period?

From *Classical India*, edited by William H. McNeill and Jean W. Sedlar (New York: Oxford University Press, 1969), pp. 20–22, 24–27, 32–33, 35–36. Copyright © 1969 by Oxford University Press. Reprinted by permission.

THE ARTHASHASTRA

Chapter 10: On Spies

Advised and assisted by a tried council of officers, the ruler should proceed to institute spies.

Spies are in the guise of pseudo-student, priest, householder, trader, saint practising renunciation, classmate or colleague, desperado, poisoner and woman mendicant.

An artful person, capable of reading human nature, is a pseudo-student. Such a person should be encouraged with presents and purse and be told by the officer: "Sworn to the ruler and myself you shall inform us what wickedness you find in others."

One initiated in scripture and of pure character is a priest-spy. This spy should carry on farming, cattle culture and commerce with resources given to him. Out of the produce and profit accrued, he should encourage other priests to live with him and send them on espionage work. The other priests also should send their followers on similar errands.

A householder-spy is a farmer fallen in his profession but pure in character. This spy should do as the priest [above].

A trader-spy is a merchant in distress but generally trustworthy. This spy should carry on espionage, in addition to his profession.

A person with proper appearance and accomplishments as an ascetic is a saint-spy. He surrounds himself with followers and may settle down in the suburb of a big city and may pretend prayer and fasting in public. Trader-spies may associate with this class of spies. He may practise fortune-telling, palmistry, and pretend supernatural and magical powers by predictions. The followers will adduce proof for the predictions of their saint. He may even foretell official rewards and official changes, which the officers concerned may substantiate by reciprocating.

Rewarded by the rulers with money and titles, these five institutions of espionage should maintain the integrity of the country's officers.

Chapter 14: Administrative Councils

Deliberation in well-constituted councils precedes administrative measures. The proceedings of a council should be in camera and deliberations made top secret so that not even a bird can whisper. The ruler should be guarded against disclosure.

Whoever divulges secret deliberations should be destroyed. Such guilt can be detected by physical and attitudinal changes of ambassadors, ministers and heads.

Secrecy of proceedings in the council and guarding of officers participating in the council must be organised.

The causes of divulgence of counsels are recklessness, drink, talking in one's sleep and infatuation with women which [sic] assail councillors.

He of secretive nature or who is not regarded well will divulge council matters. Disclosure of council secrets is of advantage to persons other than the ruler and his high officers. Steps should be taken to safeguard deliberations. . . .

Chapter 20: Personal Security

The ruler should employ as his security staff only such persons as have noble and proven ancestry and are closely related to him and are well trained and loyal. No foreigners, or anonymous persons, or persons with clouded antecedents are to be employed as security staff for the ruler.

In a securely guarded chamber, the chief should supervise the ruler's food arrangements.

Special precautions are to be taken against contaminated and poisoned food. The following reveal poison: rice sending out deep blue vapour; unnaturally coloured and artificially dried-up and hard vegetables; unusually bright and dull vessels; foamy vessels; streaky soups, milk and liquor; white streaked honey; strange-tempered food; carpets and curtains stained with dark spots and threadbare; polishless and lustreless metallic vessels and gems.

The poisoner reveals himself by parched and dry mouth, hesitating talk, perspiration, tremour, yawning, evasive demeanour and nervous behaviour.

Experts in poison detection should be in attendance on the ruler. The physicians attending the ruler should satisfy themselves personally as to the purity of the drugs which they administer to the ruler. The same precaution is indicated for liquor and beverages which the ruler uses. Scrupulous cleanliness should be insisted on in persons in charge of the ruler's dress and toilet requisites. This should be ensured by seals. . . .

In any entertainment meant for the amusement of the ruler, the actors should not use weapons, fire and poison. Musical instruments and accoutrements for horses, elephants and vehicles should be secured in the palace.

The ruler should mount beasts and vehicles only after the traditional rider or driver has done so. If he has to travel in a boat, the pilot should be trustworthy and the boat itself secured to another boat. There should be a proper convoy on land or water guarding the ruler. He should swim only in rivers which are free of larger fishes and crocodiles and hunt in forests free from snakes, man-eaters and brigands.

He should give private audience only attended by his security guards. He should receive foreign ambassadors in his full ministerial council. While reviewing his militia, the ruler should also attend in full battle uniform and be on horseback or on the back of an elephant. When he enters or exits from the capital city, the path of the ruler should be guarded by staffed officers and cleared of armed men, mendicants and the suspicious. He should attend public performances, festivals, processions or religious gatherings accompanied by trained bodyguards. The ruler should guard his own person with the same care with which he secures the safety of those around him through espionage arrangements.

Chapter 21: Building of Villages

The ruler may form villages either on new sites or on old sites, either by shifting population from heavily populated areas in his own state or by causing population to immigrate into his state.

Villages should consist of not less than a hundred and not more than five hundred families of cultivators of the service classes. The villages should extend from about one and a half miles to three miles each [in circumference] and should be capable of defending each other. Village boundaries may consist of rivers, hills, forests, hedges, caves, bridges and trees.

Each eight hundred villages should have a major fort. There should be a capital city for every four hundred villages, a market town for every two hundred villages, and an urban cluster for every ten villages.

The frontiers of the state should have fortifications protected by internal guards, manning the entrances to the state. The interior of the state should be guarded by huntsmen, armed guards, forest tribes, fierce tribes and frontier men.

Those who do social service by sacrifices, the clergy, and the intellectuals should be settled in the villages on tax-free farms.

Officers, scribes, cattlemen, guards, cattle doctors, physicians, horse-trainers and news purveyors should be given life interest in lands.

Lands fit for cultivation should be given to tenants only for life. Land prepared for cultivation by tenants should not be taken away from them.

Lands not cultivated by the landholders may be confiscated and given to cultivators. Or they may be cultivated through hired labourers or traders to avoid loss to the state. If cultivators pay their taxes promptly, they may be supplied with grains, cattle and money.

The ruler should give to cultivators only such farms and concessions as will replenish the treasury and avoid denuding it.

A denuded exchequer is a grave threat to the security of the state. Only on rare occasions like settlement of new areas or in grave emergencies should tax-remissions be granted. The ruler should be benevolent to those who have conquered the crisis by remission of taxes.

He should facilitate mining operations. He should encourage manufacturers. He should help exploitation of forest wealth. He should provide amenities for cattle breeding and commerce. He should construct highways both on land and on water. He should plan markets.

He should build dikes for water either perennial or from other sources. He should assist with resources and communications those who build reservoirs or construct works of communal comfort and public parks.

All should share in corporate work, sharing the expenditure but not claiming profit.

The ruler should have suzerainty over all fishing, transport and grain trade, reservoirs and bridges.

Those who do not recognise the rights of their servants, hirelings and relatives should be made to do so.

The ruler should maintain adolescents, the aged, the diseased and the orphans. He should also provide livelihood to deserted women with prenatal care and protection for the children born to them. . . .

The ruler should abstain from taking over any area which is open to attack by enemies and wild tribes and which is visited by frequent famines and pests. He should also abstain from extravagant sports.

He should protect cultivation from heavy taxes, slave labour and severe penalties, herds of cattle from cattle lifters, wild animals, venomous creatures and diseases.

He should clear highways of the visitation of petty officials, workmen, brigands and guards. He should not only conserve existing forests, buildings and mines, but also develop new ones.

Chapter 41: Decay, Stabilisation, and Progress of States

A state should always observe such a policy as will help it strengthen its defensive fortifications and life-lines of communications, build plantations, construct villages, and exploit the mineral and forest wealth of the country, while at the same time preventing fulfillment of similar programmes in the rival state.

Any two states hostile to each other, finding that neither has an advantage over the other in fulfilment of their respective programmes, should make peace with each other.

When any two states which are rivals expect to acquire equal possessions over the same span of time, they should keep peace with each other.

A state can indulge in armed invasion only:

Where, by invasion, it can reduce the power of an enemy without in any way reducing its own potential, by making suitable arrangements for protection of its own strategic works. . . .

Chapter 54: Restoration of Lost Balance of Power

When an invader is assailed by an alliance of his enemies, he should try to purchase the leader of the alliance with offers of gold and his own alliance and by diplomatic camouflage of the threat of treachery from the alliance of powers. He should instigate the leader of the allied enemies to break up his alliance.

The invader should also attempt to break the allied enemies' formation by setting up the leader of the alliance against the weaker of his enemies, or attempt to forge a combination of the weaker allies against their leader. He may also form a pact with the leader through intrigue, or offer of resources. When the confederation is shattered, he may form alliances with any of his former enemies.

If a state is weak in treasury or in striking power, attention should be directed to strengthen both through stabilisation of authority. Irrigational projects are a source of agricultural prosperity. Good highways should be constructed to facilitate movements of armed might and merchandise. Mines should be developed, as they supply ammunition. Forests should be conserved, as they supply material for defence, communication and vehicles. Pasture lands are the source of cattle wealth.

Thus, a state should build up its striking power through development of the exchequer, the army and wise counsel; and, till the proper time, should conduct itself as a weak power towards its neighbours, to evade conflict or envy from enemy or allied states. If the state is deficient in resources, it should acquire them from related or allied states. It should attract to itself capable men from corporations, from wild and ferocious tribes, and foreigners, and organise espionage that will damage hostile powers.

STUDY QUESTIONS

1. According to the *Arthashastra,* what policies should a ruler adopt? What goals should one strive toward?
2. What does the advice to employ spies and to devote considerable attention to personal security suggest about political conditions in India during the classical period?

3. What do you learn from these passages about the economy and society in India? According to the *Arthashastra,* what should be the role of the state in the economy? Would a Legalist in China agree?

4. According to the *Arthashastra,* what should be the foreign policy goals of a ruler? What steps should be taken to realize those goals?

5. How might the attempts by Indian political leaders to establish strong and enduring states have been assisted or impeded by the values represented by Krishna in the *Bhagavad Gita* (Chapter 12)?

6. How do the goals suggested in the *Arthashastra* compare with those in Ashoka's edicts? How do you explain the contrasts?

7. What does the writing of the *Arthashastra* imply about the level of political thinking in India during the classical period?

8. Why was there so much creative political thinking during the classical period in India, China, Greece, and Rome?

15

EMPEROR ASHOKA
AND "RIGHT CONDUCT":
THE DOCTRINE OF *DHAMMA*

Emperor Ashoka (reigned 268–232 B.C.E.) was one of India's greatest rulers. Inheriting a huge empire from his Mauryan dynasty forebears, Ashoka won a hard-fought victory over the regional kingdom of Kaliṅga early in his reign. The violence required to defeat Kaliṅga left Ashoka shaken. He became a lay Buddhist, abjured further conquests, and devoted the remainder of his long reign to establishing political stability, fostering a prosperous economy, and promulgating the doctrine he called *Dhamma*.

The challenges Ashoka faced as the ruler of a large and diverse population were daunting. His direct authority was limited to the territory near the Mauryan dynasty capital of Pataliputra. Thickly settled regions located farther from the capital were either under the control of family members or political allies, neither of whom could be trusted to carry out the policies of the central government. The interior of the Indian subcontinent was largely in the hands of various unconquered tribal peoples. Among the Indian people as a whole, differences of ethnicity, caste, religion, and language were significant.

Dhamma is the Prakit form of the Sanskrit word *dharma* (see Chapter 10) and translates as moral duty, virtue or right conduct. Ashoka developed this concept to meet the challenge of governing his huge empire by persuasion rather than coercion. Urging, but not requiring, his subjects to embrace the tenets of the new doctrine, he had the main principles of *Dhamma* carved on rocks and pillars located in densely populated regions or along trade routes. As the earliest examples of writing in India that can be deciphered and dated with certainty, Ashoka's rock and pillar edicts are of extraordinary value to scholars.

In the edicts that follow, Ashoka refers to himself as Piyadassi ("of gracious demeanor"), an official name that he took after becoming emperor. How do the edicts help us to understand Ashoka and India during the 3rd century B.C.E.?

From Romila Thapar, *Ashoka and the Decline of the Mauryas,* new revised ed. (Delhi: Oxford University Press, 1997), pp. 250–257, 265.

ASHOKA'S EDICTS

1st Major Rock Edict

The Beloved of the Gods, Piyadassi the king, has had this inscription on *Dhamma* engraved. Here, no living thing having been killed, is to be sacrificed; nor is the holding of a festival permitted. For the Beloved of the Gods, the king Piyadassi, sees much evil in festivals, though there are some of which the Beloved of the Gods, the king Piyadassi, approves.

Formerly in the kitchens of the Beloved of the Gods, the king Piyadassi, many hundreds of thousands of living animals were killed daily for meat. But now, at the time of writing this inscription on *Dhamma,* only three animals are killed, two peacocks and a deer, and the deer not invariably. Even these three animals will not be killed in future.

2nd Major Rock Edict

Everywhere in the empire of the Beloved of the Gods, the king Piyadassi, and even in the lands on its frontiers, those of the Çolas, Pāṇḍyas, Satyāputras, Keralaputras [regions of India], and as far as Ceylon, and of the Greek king named Antiochus [of Syria] and of those [Hellenistic] kings who are neighbours of that Antiochus, everywhere the two medical services of the Beloved of the Gods, the king Piyadassi, have been provided. These consist of the medical care of man and the care of animals. Medicinal herbs whether useful to man or to beast, have been brought and planted wherever they did not grow; similarly, roots and fruits have been brought and planted wherever they did not grow. Along the roads wells have been dug and trees planted for the use of men and beasts.

3rd Major Rock Edict

Thus speaks the Beloved of the Gods, the king Piyadassi: When I had been consecrated twelve years I commanded as follows: Everywhere in my empire, the *yuktas* [subordinate officers] with the *rājūkas* [rural administrators] and the *prādeśikas* [heads of the districts], shall go on tour every five years, in order to instruct people in the *Dhamma* as well as for other purposes. It is good to be obedient to one's mother and father, friends and relatives, to be generous to brahmans and *śramanas* [Buddhist monks], it is good not to kill living beings, it is good not only to spend little, but to own the minimum of property. The council will instruct the officials to record the above, making it both manifest to the public and explaining why.

4th Major Rock Edict

In the past, the killing and injuring of living beings, lack of respect towards relatives, brahmans and *śramanas* had increased. But today, thanks to the practice of *Dhamma* on the part of the Beloved of the Gods, the king Piyadassi, the sound of the drum has become the sound of *Dhamma,* showing the people displays of heavenly chariots, elephants, balls of fire, and other divine forms. Through his instruction in *Dhamma* abstention from killing and non-injury to living beings, deference to relatives, brahmans and *śramanas,* obedience to mother and father, and obedience to elders have all increased as never before for many centuries. These and many other forms of the practice of *Dhamma* have increased and will increase. . . .

5th Major Rock Edict

Thus speaks the Beloved of the Gods, the king Piyadassi: It is hard to do good and he who does good, does a difficult thing. And I have done much good. And my sons, my grandsons and my descendants after them until the end of the world if they will follow my example, they too will do good. But he who neglects my reforms even in part will do wrong, for sin is easy to commit.

In the past there were no officers of *Dhamma*. It was I who first appointed them, when I had been consecrated for thirteen years. They are busy in all sects, establishing *Dhamma,* increasing interest in *Dhamma,* and attending to the welfare and happiness of those who are devoted to *Dhamma,* among the Greeks, the Kambojas, the Gandhāras, the Riṣṭhikas, the Pitinikas, and the other peoples of the west. Among servants and nobles, brahmans and wealthy householders, among the poor and the aged, they [the officers of *Dhamma*], are working for the welfare and happiness of those devoted to *Dhamma* and for the removal of their troubles. They are busy in promoting the welfare of prisoners should they have behaved irresponsibly, or releasing those that have children, are afflicted, or are aged. They are busy everywhere, here [at Pāṭaliputra] and in all the women's residences, whether my own, those of my brothers and sisters, or those of other relatives. Everywhere throughout my empire the officers of *Dhamma* are busy in everything relating to *Dhamma,* in the establishment of *Dhamma* and in the administration of charities among those devoted to *Dhamma.* For this purpose has this inscription of *Dhamma* been engraved. May it endure long and may my descendants conform to it.

6th Major Rock Edict

Thus speaks the Beloved of the Gods, the king Piyadassi: In the past the quick dispatch of business and the receipt of reports did not take place at all times. But I have now arranged it thus. At all times, whether I am eating, or am in the women's apartments, or in my inner apartments, or at the cattle-shed, or in my carriage, or in my gardens—wherever I may be, my informants should keep me in touch with public business. Thus everywhere I transact public business. And whatever I may order by word of mouth, whether it concerns a donation or a proclamation, or whatever urgent matter is entrusted to my officers, if there is any dispute or deliberation about it in the Council, it is to be reported to me immediately, at all places and at all times.

This I have commanded. In hard work and the dispatch of business alone, I find no satisfaction. For I consider that I must promote the welfare of the whole world, and hard work and the dispatch of business are the means of doing so. Indeed there is no better work than promoting the welfare of the whole world. And whatever may be my great deeds, I have done them in order to discharge my debt to all beings. I work for their happiness in this life, that in the next they may gain heaven. For this purpose has this inscription of *Dhamma* been engraved. May it endure long. May my sons, grandsons, and great grandsons strive for the welfare of the whole world. But this is difficult without great effort.

7th Major Rock Edict

The Beloved of the Gods, the king Piyadassi, wishes that all sects may dwell in all places, for all seek self-control and purity of mind. But men have varying desires and varying passions. They will either practise all that is required or else only a part. But even he who is generous, yet has no self control, purity of mind, gratitude, and firm faith, is regarded as mean.

8th Major Rock Edict

In the past, kings went on pleasure tours, which consisted of hunts and other similar amusements. The Beloved of the Gods, the king Piyadassi, when he had been consecrated ten years, went to the tree of Enlightenment. From that time arose the practice of tours connected with *Dhamma*, during which meetings are held with ascetics and brahmans, gifts are bestowed, meetings are arranged with aged folk, gold is distributed, meetings with the people of the countryside are held, instruction in *Dhamma* is given, and questions on *Dhamma* are answered. The Beloved of the Gods, the king Piyadassi, derives more pleasure from this, than from any other enjoyments.

9th Major Rock Edict

Thus speaks the Beloved of the Gods, the king Piyadassi: People practise various ceremonies. In illness, at the marriage of sons and daughters, at the birth of children, when going on a journey—on these and on other similar occasions people perform many ceremonies. Women especially perform a variety of ceremonies, which are trivial and useless. If such ceremonies must be performed they have but small results. But the one ceremony which has great value is that of *Dhamma*. This ceremony includes, regard for slaves and servants, respect for teachers, restrained behaviour towards living beings, and donations to *śramanas* and brahmans—these and similar practices are called the ceremony of *Dhamma*. So father, son, brother, master, friend, acquaintance, and neighbour should think, 'This is virtuous, this is the ceremony I should practice, until my object is achieved.' . . .

11th Major Rock Edict

Thus speaks the Beloved of the Gods, the king Piyadassi: There is no gift comparable to the gift of *Dhamma,* the praise of *Dhamma,* the sharing of *Dhamma,* fellowship in *Dhamma*. And this is—good behaviour towards slaves and servants, obedience to mother and father, generosity towards friends, acquaintances, and relatives and towards *śramanas* and brahmans, and abstention from killing living beings. Father, son, brother, master, friend, acquaintance, relative, and neighbour should say, 'this is good, this we should do'. By doing so, there is gain in this world, and in the next there is infinite merit, through the gift of *Dhamma*.

12th Major Rock Edict

The Beloved of the Gods, the king Piyadassi, honours all sects and both ascetics and laymen, with gifts and various forms of recognition. But the Beloved of the Gods does not consider gifts or honour to be as important as the advancement of the essential doctrine of all sects. This progress of the essential doctrine takes many forms, but its basis is the control of one's speech, so as not to extol one's own sect or disparage another's on unsuitable occasions, or at least to do so only mildly on certain occasions. On each occasion one should honour another man's sect, for by doing so one increases the influence of one's own sect and benefits that of the other man; while by doing otherwise one diminishes the influence of one's own sect and harms the other man's. Again, whosoever honours his own sect or disparages that of another man, wholly out of devotion to his own, with a view to showing it in a favourable light, harms his own sect even more seriously. Therefore, concord is to be commended, so that men may hear one another's principles and obey them. This is the desire of the Beloved of the Gods, that all sects should be well-informed, and should teach that which is good, and that everywhere their adherents should be told, 'The Beloved of the Gods does not consider gifts or honour to be as important as the progress of the essential doctrine of all sects.' Many are concerned with this matter—the officers of *Dhamma,* the women's officers, the managers of the state farms, and other classes of officers. The result of this is the increased influence of one's own sect and glory to *Dhamma.*

13th Major Rock Edict

When he had been consecrated eight years the Beloved of the Gods, the king Piyadassi, conquered Kaliṅga. A hundred and fifty thousand people were deported, a hundred thousand were killed and many times that number perished. Afterwards, now that Kaliṅga was annexed, the Beloved of the Gods very earnestly practised *Dhamma,* desired *Dhamma,* and taught *Dhamma.* On conquering Kaliṅga the Beloved of the Gods felt remorse, for, when an independent country is conquered the slaughter, death, and deportation of the people is extremely grievous to the Beloved of the Gods, and weighs heavily on his mind. What is even more deplorable to the Beloved of the Gods, is that those who dwell there, whether brahmans, *śramanas* or those of other sects, or householders who show obedience to their superiors, obedience to mother and father, obedience to their teachers and behave well and devotedly towards their friends, acquaintances, colleagues, relatives, slaves, and servants—all suffer violence, murder, and separation from their loved ones. Even those who are fortunate to have escaped, and whose love is undiminished [by the brutalizing effect of war], suffer from the misfortunes of their friends, acquaintances, colleagues, and relatives. This participation of all men in suffering, weighs heavily on the mind of the Beloved of the Gods. Except among the Greeks, there is no land where the religious orders of brahmans and *śramanas* are not to be found, and there is no land anywhere where men do not support one sect or another. Today if a hundredth or a thousandth part of those people who were killed or died or were deported when Kaliṅga was annexed were to suffer similarly, it would weigh heavily on the mind of the Beloved of the Gods.

The Beloved of the Gods believes that one who does wrong should be forgiven as far as it is possible to forgive him. And the Beloved of the Gods conciliates the forest tribes of his empire, but he warns them that he has power even in his remorse, and he asks them to repent, lest they be killed. For the Beloved of the Gods wishes that all beings should be unharmed, self-controlled, calm in mind, and gentle.

The Beloved of the Gods considers victory by *Dhamma* to be the foremost victory. And moreover the Beloved of the Gods has gained this victory on all his frontiers to a distance of six hundred *yojanas* [i.e. about 1500 miles], where reigns the Greek king named Antiochus, and beyond the realm of that Antiochus in the lands of the four [Hellenistic] kings named Ptolemy [of Egypt], Antiogonus, Magas, and Alexander; and in the south over the Çolas and Pāṇḍyas as far as Ceylon. Likewise here in the imperial territories among the Greeks and the Kambojas, Nābhakas and Nābhapanktis, Bhojas and Pitinikas, Andhras and Pārindas, everywhere the people follow the Beloved of the

Gods' instructions in *Dhamma*. Even where the envoys of the Beloved of the Gods have not gone, people hear of his conduct according to *Dhamma*, his precepts and his instruction in *Dhamma*, and they follow *Dhamma* and will continue to follow it.

What is obtained by this is victory everywhere, and everywhere victory is pleasant. This pleasure has been obtained through victory by *Dhamma*—yet it is but a slight pleasure, for the Beloved of the Gods only looks upon that as important in its results which pertains to the next world.

This inscription of *Dhamma* has been engraved so that any sons or great grandsons that I may have should not think of gaining new conquests, and in whatever victories they may gain should be satisfied with patience and light punishment. They should only consider conquest by *Dhamma* to be a true conquest, and delight in *Dhamma* should be their whole delight, for this is of value in both this world and the next.

7th Pillar Edict

Thus speaks the Beloved of the Gods, the king Piyadassi: On the roads I have had banyan trees planted, which will give shade to beasts and men, I have had mango-groves planted and I have had wells dug and rest houses built at every eight *kos*. And I have had many watering places made everywhere for the use of beasts and men. But this benefit is important, and indeed the world has enjoyed attention in many ways from former kings as well as from me. But I have done these things in order that my people might conform to *Dhamma*. . . .

STUDY QUESTIONS

1. How does Ashoka define *Dhamma*? Based on your reading of the edicts, what can you infer about Ashoka's reasons for issuing them? What do the edicts suggest about Ashoka's techniques for ruling his empire?
2. How do you respond to Ashoka's extraordinary confession in the 13 rock edict?
3. What do the edicts suggest about the economy of India? About literacy? About religious life? About contacts between India and other countries?
4. Was *Dhamma* a religion? What was Ashoka's attitude toward ritual? What was the relationship between *Dhamma* and Buddhism?
5. How do the ideas of Ashoka compare with those in the *Arthashastra* (see Chapter 14)? How do you explain the contrasts?
6. How do the ideas of Ashoka compare to those of Confucius? To those of Legalists like Han Feizi?
7. Do you see any similarities between Hammurabi's laws and *Dhamma*?
8. Can a ruler of a large state also be an ethical person?

16 GENDER RELATIONS IN INDIA: FOUR TYPES OF EVIDENCE

The sharp lines between social groups that were characteristic of the *varna* system as it developed in India during the first millennium B.C.E. had their counterpart in the system of strongly patriarchal gender relations that arose at about the same time. Although the documentary evidence regarding relationships between men and women in early India is extremely fragmentary and often indirect, a variety of written sources nonetheless suggest that well before the beginning of the Common Era the practice of subordinating females to males was well established.

In this chapter we look at three types of documentation that help us to grasp the character of gender relations in India during the classical period. First, we will examine a few songs from the *Therigatha,* a collection of more than 500 songs originally composed by Buddhist nuns (*theris*) who were contemporaries of the Buddha. Scholars think that the songs in the *Therigatha* were first put into writing in the 1st century B.C.E.

The second kind of evidence we consider comes from the *Laws of Manu,* an influential philosophical-legal treatise dating from the beginning of the Common Era. The anonymous authors of the *Laws of Manu* were *brahmans* whose purpose in writing the book was, in part, to outline prescribed modes of behavior. In the selections from the *Laws of Manu* that follow, the focus is on gender relations.

Finally, we draw for a second time from the great Indian epic, the *Mahabharata,* which, as we have seen in Chapter 12, was transformed from oral tradition into writing around the beginning of the Common Era. The selection that follows, "Savatri and the God of Death," has long been one of the most popular episodes in the *Mahabharata.* For a fourth type of evidence, see the Visual Source on page 114.

Selection I Susie Tharu and K. Lalita, selections from *Women Writing in India 600 B.C. to the Present: Volume 1: 600 B.C. to the Early Twentieth Century,* pp. 68–70. Copyright © 1991 by Susie Tharu and K. Lalita. Reprinted with the permission of The Feminist Press at the City University of New York, www.feministpress.org. Selection II from Barbara N. Ramusack, "Women in South and Southeast Asia," in *Restoring Women to History,* edited by Organization of American Historians (Bloomington, Ind.: Organization of American Historians, 1988), p. 9. Selection III from *Lustful Maidens and Ascetic Kings: Buddhist and Hindu Stories of Life* by Roy C. Amore and Larry D. Shinn. Copyright © 1981 by Oxford University Press, Inc. Used by permission of Oxford University Press, Inc.

INDIAN GENDER CULTURE

I. SONGS COMPOSED BY BUDDHIST NUNS

Mutta

[So free am I, so gloriously free]

So free am I, so gloriously free,
Free from three petty things—
From mortar, from pestle and from my twisted lord,
Freed from rebirth and death I am,
And all that has held me down
Is hurled away.

Ubbiri

["O Ubbiri, who wails in the wood"]

"O Ubbiri, who wails in the wood
'O Jiva! Dear daughter!'
Return to your senses, in this charnel field
Innumerable daughters, once as full of life as Jiva,
Are burnt. Which of them do you mourn?"
The hidden arrow in my heart plucked out,
The dart lodged there, removed.
The anguish of my loss,
The grief that left me faint all gone,
The yearning stilled,
To the Buddha, the Dhamma [Moral Law], and the Sangha [Community of
    Buddhists]
I turn, my heart now healed.

Sumangalamata

[A woman well set free! How free I am]

A woman well set free! How free I am,
How wonderfully free, from kitchen drudgery.
Free from the harsh grip of hunger,
And from empty cooking pots,
Free too of that unscrupulous man,
The weaver of sunshades.
Calm now, and serene I am,
All lust and hatred purged.
To the shade of the spreading trees I go
And contemplate my happiness.

Mettika

[Though I am weak and tired now]

Though I am weak and tired now,
And my youthful step long gone,

Leaning on this staff,
I climb the mountain peak.
My cloak cast off, my bowl overturned,
I sit here on this rock.
And over my spirit blows
The breath
Of liberty
I've won, I've won the triple gems [the Buddha, the Dhamma, and the Sangha]
The Buddha's way is mine.

II. THE LAWS OF MANU

In childhood a female must be subject to her father, in youth to her husband, and
    when her lord is dead, to her sons; a woman must never be independent
    [Manu, V, 184].

Though destitute of virtue, or seeking pleasure (elsewhere), or devoid of good
    qualities, (yet) a husband must be constantly worshipped as a god by a faithful
    wife [Manu, V, 154].

A virtuous wife who after the death of her husband constantly remains chaste, reaches
    heaven, though she have no son, just like those chaste men [Manu, V, 160].

But a woman who from a desire to have offspring violates her duty towards her
    dead husband, brings on herself disgrace in this world, and loses her place
    with her husband in heaven [Manu V, 161].

A wife, a son and a slave, these three are declared to have no property: the wealth
    which they earn is (acquired) for him to whom they belong [Manu, VIII, 416].

(When creating them) Manu allotted to women (a love of their) bed, (of their)
    seat and (of) ornament, impure desires, wrath, dishonesty, malice, and bad
    conduct [Manu, IX, 17].

In the sacred texts which refer to marriage the appointment (of widows) is
    nowhere mentioned, nor is the remarriage of widows prescribed in the rules
    concerning marriage [Manu, IX, 65].

A man, aged thirty years, shall marry a maiden of twelve who pleases him, or a man
    of twenty-four a girl eight years of age; if the performance of his duties would
    otherwise be impeded, he must marry sooner [Manu, IX, 94].

III. SAVATRI AND THE GOD OF DEATH

Ashvapati, the virtuous king of Madras, grew old without offspring to continue his
royal family. Desiring a son, Ashvapati took rigid vows and observed long fasts to
accumulate merit. It is said that he offered 10,000 oblations to the goddess Savatri
in hopes of having a son. After eighteen years of constant devotion, Ashvapati was
granted his wish for an offspring even though the baby born was a girl.

The king rejoiced at his good fortune and named the child Savatri in honor
of the goddess who gave him this joy to brighten his elder years.

Savatri was both a beautiful and an intelligent child. She was her father's
delight and grew in wisdom and beauty as the years passed. As the age approached
for Savatri to be given in marriage as custom demanded, no suitor came forward to

ask her father for her hand—so awed were all the princes by the beauty and intellect of this unusual maiden. Her father became concerned lest he not fulfill his duty as father and incur disgrace for his failure to provide a suitable husband for his daughter. At last, he instructed Savatri herself to lead a procession throughout the surrounding kingdoms and handpick a man suitable for her.

Savatri returned from her search and told her father that she had found the perfect man. Though he was poor and an ascetic of the woods, he was handsome, well educated, and of kind temperament. His name was Satyavan and he was actually a prince whose blind father had been displaced by an evil king. Ashvapati asked the venerable sage Narada whether Satyavan would be a suitable spouse for Savatri. Narada responded that there was no one in the world more worthy than Satyavan. However, Narada continued, Satyavan had one unavoidable flaw. He was fated to live a short life and would die exactly one year from that very day. Ashvapati then tried to dissuade Savatri from marrying Satyavan by telling her of the impending death of her loved one. Savatri held firm to her choice, and the king and Narada both gave their blessings to this seemingly ill-fated bond.

After the marriage procession had retreated from the forest hermitage of Savatri's new father-in-law, Dyumatsena, the bride removed her wedding sari and donned the ocher robe and bark garments of her ascetic family. As the days and weeks passed, Savatri busied herself by waiting upon the every need of her new family. She served her husband, Satyavan, cheerfully and skillfully. Satyavan responded with an even-tempered love which enhanced the bond of devotion between Savatri and himself. Yet the dark cloud of Narada's prophecy cast a shadow over this otherwise blissful life.

When the fateful time approached, Savatri began a fast to strengthen her wifely resolve as she kept nightly vigils while her husband slept. The day marked for the death of Satyavan began as any other day at the hermitage. Satyavan shouldered his axe and was about to set off to cut wood for the day's fires when Savatri stopped him to ask if she could go along saying, "I cannot bear to be separated from you today." Satyavan responded, "You've never come into the forest before and the paths are rough and the way very difficult. Besides, you've been fasting and are surely weak." Savatri persisted, and Satyavan finally agreed to take her along. Savatri went to her parents-in-law to get their permission saying she wanted to see the spring blossoms which now covered the forest. They too expressed concern over her health but finally relented out of consideration for her long period of gracious service to them.

Together Satyavan and Savatri entered the tangled woods enjoying the beauty of the flowers and animals which betoken spring in the forest. Coming to a fallen tree, Satyavan began chopping firewood. As he worked, he began to perspire heavily and to grow weak. Finally, he had to stop and lie down telling Savatri to wake him after a short nap. With dread in her heart, Savatri took Satyavan's head in her lap and kept a vigil knowing Satyavan's condition to be more serious than rest could assuage. In a short time, Savatri saw approaching a huge figure clad in red and carrying a small noose. Placing Satyavan's head upon the ground, Savatri arose and asked the stranger of his mission. The lord of death replied, "I am Yama and your husband's days are finished. I speak to you, a mortal, only because of your extreme merit. I have come personally instead of sending my emissaries because of your husband's righteous life."

Without a further word, Yama then pulled Satyavan's soul out of his body with the small noose he was carrying. The lord of death then set off immediately for the realm of the dead in the south. Grief stricken and yet filled with wifely devotion, Savatri followed Yama at a distance. Hours passed yet hunger and weariness could not slow Savatri's footsteps. She persisted through thorny paths and rocky slopes to follow Yama and his precious burden. As Yama walked south he thought he heard a woman's anklets tingling on the path behind him. He turned around to see Savatri in the distance following without pause. He called out to her to return to Satyavan's body and to perform her wifely duties of cremating the dead. Savatri approached Yama and responded, "It is said that those who walk seven steps together are friends. Certainly we have traveled farther than that together. Why should I return to a dead body when you possess the soul of my husband?"

Yama was impressed by the courage and wisdom of this beautiful young woman. He replied, "Please stop following me. Your wise words and persistent devotion for your husband deserve a boon. Ask of me anything except that your husband's life be restored, and I will grant it." Savatri asked that her blind father-in-law be granted new sight. Yama said that her wish would be granted, and then he turned to leave only to find that Savatri was about to continue following. Yama again praised her devotion and offered a second, and then a third boon. Savatri told Yama of the misfortune of her father-in-law's lost kingdom and asked that Yama assist in ousting the evil king from Dyumatsena's throne. Yama agreed. Then Savatri utilized her third boon to ask that her own father be given one hundred sons to protect his royal line, and that too was granted by Yama.

Yama then set off in a southerly direction only to discover after a short while that Savatri still relentlessly followed him. Yama was amazed at the thoroughly self-giving attitude displayed by Savatri and agreed to grant one last boon if Savatri would promise to return home. Yama again stipulated that the bereaved wife could not ask for her husband's soul. Savatri agreed to the two conditions and said, "I only ask for myself one thing, and that is that I may be granted one hundred sons to continue Satyavan's royal family." Yama agreed only to realize, upon prompting from Savatri, that the only way Satyavan's line could be continued would be for him to be restored to life. Although he had been tricked by the wise and thoughtful Savatri, Yama laughed heartily and said, "So it is! Auspicious and chaste lady, your husband's soul is freed by me." Loosening his noose Yama permitted the soul of Satyavan to return to its earthly abode and Savatri ran without stopping back to the place where Satyavan had fallen asleep. Just as Savatri arrived at the place where her husband lay, he awoke saying, "Oh, I have slept into the night, why did you not waken me?"

STUDY QUESTIONS

1. What are the main themes in the songs by the Buddhist nuns? How do the songs illustrate points in the Four Noble Truths?
2. What clues to the character of gender relations in India do you see in the songs? Might Buddhism have had a special appeal to women?
3. How do the Laws of Manu define womanhood and manhood? How do these definitions compare?

4. What is the attitude toward woman's sexuality in the Laws of Manu? How do you explain this attitude on the part of the authors?

5. How do men and women relate to one another in the story of Savatri? How does Savatri relate to Yama?

6. Are Savatri's actions consistent with the Laws of Manu?

7. Based on your reading of the documents in this chapter, what generalizations, however tentative, seem reasonable regarding gender relations in India around the beginning of the Common Era?

8. Compare the Laws of Manu with Hammurabi's Code.

9. Compare gender relations in India and China. Were both societies patriarchal? Were there significant differences between them? What other kinds of evidence would facilitate comparisons concerning the conditions of women?

GENDER IMAGERY IN INDIA

***Mithuna* at Karli, Western India, 2nd Century C.E.**
(Copyright Borromeo/Art Resources, NY)

To what extent can the study of art help us to understand how men and women related to one another in the past? The rich tradition of Buddhist and Hindu sculpture in India dating from the first millennium C.E. naturally provokes this tantalizing question. Of particular interest in this regard are the strongly sensual sculptures of loving couples known as *mithunas.* Symbolic of unity in Indian religions, *mithuna* couples have greeted worshippers at the entrances to Buddhist and Hindu temples for the past 2,000 years.

The amorous pair here is one of several that graces the façade of the large Buddhist cave temple dedicated around 100 C.E. at Karli, near Mumbai (formerly Bombay) in western India. Their fleshy bodies, revealing garments, and ornate jewelry recall an earlier tradition of Indian sculpture that featured statues of earth-spirits known as *yakshis* (females) and *yakshas* (males). Perhaps the open affection the figures demonstrate for each other and the rough equality suggested by their pose come from the same, ultimately Neolithic, tradition.

STUDY QUESTIONS

1. Do the figures seem to represent specific individuals or idealized general types? What features of the couple seem to be most important in answering this question? Does the couple seem to belong to a particular social class?
2. What aspects of the sculpture suggest equality between the two figures?
3. How does the suggestion of gender equality in the *mithuna* compare with other kinds of evidence regarding gender structures in India during the classical period?
4. What explains the sensuality in a work of art that decorates the entrance to a Buddhist temple? What does the *mithuna* have to do with the Four Noble Truths?

GREECE AND ROME

17 THE GREEK POLITICAL TRADITION

As with all the classical civilizations, the culture that developed along Europe's Mediterranean shores produced important political institutions and principles. The key political form, in Greece and later in republican Rome, was the city-state. Within its bounds, the portion of the population with political rights was supposed to participate actively in the affairs of state, to which it owed loyalty and service. Within this context, however, a variety of political structures arose. Some evolved toward democracy (though with many residents excluded from rights). As we will see in the next chapter, Athens led the way. Here it provided not only participant assemblies but also considerable support for individual freedom and legal rights. Other Greek city-states, however, stressed the power of government. Sparta, which would finally clash with Athens in the Peloponnesian War, set up a rigid militaristic regime designed to transform each male or female citizen into an absolute servant of the government. When Athens and Sparta warred at the end of the 5th century B.C.E., the conflict involved not only power, but also two clashing views of political life.

The Spartan system, described in this selection, was set up by the lawmaker Lycurgus after 650 B.C.E., in large part to keep a vast slave (helot) population under control. The description comes from the writings of Plutarch (ca. 45–125 C.E.), in a biography of Lycurgus. It is important to realize that most articulate Greeks esteemed Spartan values, preferring them to democracy. Why might this be so? What resulted, in classical Greece itself and in the later Greek heritage, from such sharply differentiated systems within a common culture?

PLUTARCH ON SPARTA

In order to [promote] the good education of their youth (which . . . he [Lycurgus] thought the most important and noblest work of a lawgiver), he went so far back as to take into consideration their very conception and birth, by regulating their marriages.

From Plutarch, *The Library of Original Sources*. Vol. II: *The Greek World*, edited by Oliver J. Thatcher (University Research Extension Co., Milwaukee, Wis.,: n.d.), pp. 118–119, 122, 128.

For Aristotle is wrong in saying, that, after he had tried all ways to reduce the women to more modesty and sobriety, he was at last forced to leave them as they were, because that, in the absence of their husbands, who spent the best part of their lives in the wars, their wives, whom they were obliged to leave absolute mistresses at home, took great liberties and assumed the superiority; and were treated with overmuch respect and called by the title of lady or queen. The truth is, he took in their case, also, all the care that was possible; he ordered the maidens to exercise themselves with wrestling, running, throwing and quoit [throwing game], and casting the dart, to the end that the fruit they conceived might, in strong and healthy bodies, take firmer root and find better growth, and withal that they, with this greater vigor, might be the more able to undergo the pains of childbearing. And to the end he might take away their over great tenderness and fear of exposure to the air, and all acquired womanishness, he ordered that the young women should go naked in the processions, as well as the young men, and dance, too, in that condition, at certain solemn feasts, singing certain songs, whilst the young men stood around, seeing and hearing them. On these occasions, they now and then made, by jests, a befitting reflection upon those who had misbehaved themselves in the wars; and again sang praises upon those who had done any gallant action, and by these means inspired the younger sort with an emulation of their glory. Those that were thus commended went away proud, elated, and gratified with their honor among the maidens; and those who were rallied were as sensibly touched with it as if they had been formally reprimanded; and so much the more, because the kings and the elders, as well as the rest of the city, saw and heard all that passed. Nor was there anything shameful in this nakedness of the young women; modesty attended them, and all wantonness was excluded. It taught them simplicity and a care for good health, and gave them some taste of higher feelings, admitted as they thus were to the field of noble action and glory. Hence it was natural for them to think and speak as Gorgo, for example, the wife of Leonidas, is said to have done, when some foreign lady, as it would seem, told her that the women of Lacedœmon were the only women of the world who could rule men; "With good reason," she said, "for we are the only women who bring forth men."

These public processions of the maidens, and their appearing naked in their exercises and dancings, were incitements to marriage, operating upon the young with the rigor and certainty, as Plato says, of love, if not of mathematics. But besides all this, to promote it yet more effectually, those who continued bachelors were in a degree disfranchised by law; for they were excluded from the sight of those public processions in which the young men and maidens danced naked, and, in wintertime, the officers compelled them to march naked themselves round the marketplace, singing as they went a certain song to their own disgrace, that they justly suffered this punishment for disobeying the laws. Moreover, they were denied that respect and observance which the younger men paid their elders; and no man, for example, found fault with what was said to Dercyllidas, though so eminent a commander; upon whose approach one day, a young man, instead of rising, retained his seat, remarking, "No child of yours will make room for me." . . .

Nor was it lawful, indeed, for the father himself to breed up the children after his own fancy; but as soon as they were seven years old, they were to be enrolled in certain companies and classes, where they all lived under the same order and discipline, doing their exercises and taking their play together. Of these, he who showed the most conduct and courage was made captain; they had their eyes always upon him, obeyed his orders, and underwent patiently whatsoever punishment he inflicted; so that the whole course of their education was one continued exercise of a ready and perfect obedience. The old men, too, were spectators of their performances, and often raised quarrels and disputes among them, to have a good opportunity of finding out their different characters, and of seeing which would be valiant, which a coward, when they should come to more dangerous encounters. Reading and writing they gave them, just enough to serve their turn; their chief care was to make them good subjects, and to teach them to endure pain and conquer in battle. To this end, as they grew in years, their discipline was proportionately increased; their heads were close-clipped, they were accustomed to go bare-foot, and for the most part to play naked.

After they were twelve years old, they were no longer allowed to wear any undergarment; they had one coat to serve them a year; their bodies were hard and dry, with but little acquaintance of baths and unguents; these human indulgences they were allowed only on some few particular days in the year. They lodged together in little bands upon beds made of the rushes which grew by the banks of the river Eurotas, which they were to break off with their hands without a knife; if it were winter, they mingled some thistle-down with their rushes, which it was thought had the property of giving warmth. By the time they were come to this age, there was not any of the more hopeful boys who had not a lover to bear him company. The old men, too, had an eye upon them, coming often to the grounds to hear and see them contend either in wit or strength with one another, and this as seriously and with as much concern as if they were their fathers, their tutors, or their magistrates; so that there scarcely was any time or place without some one present to put them in mind of their duty, and punish them if they had neglected it. . . .

Their discipline continued still after they were full-grown men. No one was allowed to live after his own fancy; but the city was a sort of camp, in which every man had his share of provisions and business set out, and looked upon himself not so much born to serve his own ends as the interest of his country. Therefore, if they were commanded nothing else, they went to see the boys perform their exercises, to teach them something useful, or to learn it themselves of those who knew better. And, indeed, one of the greatest and highest blessings Lycurgus procured his people was the abundance of leisure, which proceeded from his forbidding to them the exercise of any mean and mechanical trade. Of the money-making that depends on troublesome going about and seeing people and doing business, they had no need at all in a state where wealth obtained no honor or respect. The Helots tilled their ground for them, and paid them yearly in kind the appointed quantity, without any trouble of theirs. To this purpose there goes a story of a Lacedœmonian [Spartan] who, happening to be at Athens when the courts were sitting, was told of a citizen that had been fined for living an idle life, and was being escorted home in much distress of mind by his condoling friends; the Lacedœmonian was much surprised at it, and desired his friend to show him the man who was condemned for living like a freeman. So much beneath them did they esteem the frivolous devotion of time and attention to the mechanical arts and to money-making.

STUDY QUESTIONS

1. What was the nature of family regulation in Sparta? What were the reasons for it? Was the Spartan family system patriarchal?

2. What was the Spartan system of military recruitment and motivation for service?

3. Do you agree with historians who have argued that Sparta was a forerunner of contemporary government systems, or would this be a misleading assessment?

4. How do Spartan political principles compare with Confucian ideals and goals? Why was Confucianism more successful? How did Spartan values compare with Legalism? (See Chapters 7 and 8.)

18 ATHENIAN DEMOCRACY AND CULTURE

In 431 B.C.E. the Athenian leader Pericles (d. 429 B.C.E.) delivered a funeral oration for Greek military who died in the early stages of what became a long war with Sparta. This Peloponnesian War led ultimately to the defeat of Athens and to a political decline in classical Greece as a whole. The war involved rival ambitions between Athens and Sparta—for control of alliance systems or empires over smaller Greek city-states, but also a contrast between two political and cultural systems. Sparta ran an authoritarian state, under aristocratic control, with few cultural amenities. Athens, in contrast, was a commercial state, with many foreign residents, a proud cultural life featuring public art and theater, and a democratic political system.

Pericles' speech comes from the historian Thucydides (471–400 B.C.E.), whose *History of the Peloponnesian War* is one of the early masterpieces in the discipline. Thucydides invented the speeches he cites, and while they are probably close to the spirit of what was said, the practice has some drawbacks. Nevertheless, the Funeral Oration forms one of the great documents in Greek history, as it describes the glories Athens claimed for its system in tribute to the war dead.

Pericles, himself from an aristocratic family, had led Athens for several decades, often from behind the scenes. He describes, however, an active democracy and a vigorous, open cultural and economic life.

While accepting much of Pericles' description, certainly as a statement of ideals, to some extent as depiction of reality, it is important to read closely and tease out some important implications. Athenian democracy was not like modern democracy, as Pericles suggests in describing the rights and duties of citizens. The Athenian balance between individual rights and collective good was also distinctive.

Some groups were kept apart from the democratic system, as Pericles implies, for example, in his careful distinction between citizens and foreigners. Pericles also offers revealing comments on the cultural and political role of women. He makes some interesting remarks about Athens' empire, and these need to be considered in assessing Athens' overall role in Greece and the relationship between its internal democracy and its foreign policy.

This is of course a rallying speech, designed to honor the dead but also to motivate further military action against Sparta. Pericles was undoubtedly telling Athenians what they wanted to hear. Does this lead to any possible exaggerations or distortions?

From Thucydides, *The Peloponnesian War* (Crawley translation) (New York: Modern Library, 1934), pp. 102–109.

PERICLES

'Most of my predecessors in this place have commended him who made this speech part of the law, telling us that it is well that it should be delivered at the burial of those who fall in battle. For myself, I should have thought that the worth which had displayed itself in deeds, would be sufficiently rewarded by honours also shown by deeds; such as you now see in this funeral prepared at the people's cost. And I could have wished that the reputations of many brave men were not to be imperiled in the mouth of a single individual, to stand or fall according as he spoke well or ill. For it is hard to speak properly upon a subject where it is even difficult to convince your hearers that you are speaking the truth. On the one hand, the friend who is familiar with every fact of the story, may think that some point has not been set forth with that fullness which he wishes and knows it to deserve; on the other, he who is a stranger to the matter may be led by envy to suspect exaggeration if he hears anything above his own nature. For men can endure to hear others praised only so long as they can severally persuade themselves of their own ability to equal the actions recounted: when this point is passed, envy comes in and with it incredulity. However, since our ancestors have stamped this custom with their approval, it becomes my duty to obey the law and to try to satisfy your several wishes and opinions as best I may.

'I shall begin with out ancestors: it is both just and proper that they should have the honour of the first mention on an occasion like the present. They dwelt in the country without break in the succession from generation to generation, and handed it down free to the present time by their valour. And if our more remote ancestors deserve praise, much more do our own fathers, who added to their inheritance the empire which we now possess, and spared no pains to be able to leave their acquisitions to us of the present generation. Lastly, there are few parts of our dominions that have not been augmented by those of us here, who are still more or less in the vigour of life; while the mother country has been furnished by us with everything that can enable her to depend on her own resources whether for war or for peace. That part of our history which tells of the military achievements which gave us our several possessions, or of the ready valour with which either we or our fathers stemmed the tide of Hellenic [Greek] or foreign aggression, is a theme too familiar to my hearers for me to dilate on, and I shall therefore pass it by. But what was the road by which we reached our position, what the form of government under which our greatness grew, what the national habits out of which it sprang; these are questions which I may try to solve before I proceed to my panegyric [eulogy] upon these men; since I think this to be a subject upon which on the present occasion a speaker may properly dwell, and to which the whole assemblage, whether citizens or foreigners, may listen with advantage.

'Our constitution does not copy the laws of neighbouring states; we are rather a pattern to others than imitators ourselves. Its administration favours the many instead of the few; this is why it is called a democracy. If we look to the laws, they afford equal justice to all in their private differences; if to social standing, advancement in public life falls to reputation for capacity, class considerations not being allowed to interfere with merit; nor again does poverty bar the way, if a man is able to serve the state, he is not hindered by the obscurity of his condition. The freedom which we enjoy in our government extends also to our ordinary life. There, far from exercising a jealous surveillance over each other, we do not feel called upon to be angry with our neighbour for doing what he likes, or even to indulge in those injurious looks which cannot fail to be offensive, although they inflict no positive penalty. But all this ease in our private relations does not make us lawless as citizens. Against this fear is our chief safeguard, teaching us to obey the magistrates and the laws, particularly such as regard the protection of the injured, whether they are actually on the statute book, or belong to that code which, although unwritten, yet cannot be broken without acknowledged disgrace.

'Further, we provide plenty of means for the mind to refresh itself from business. We celebrate games and sacrifices all the year round, and the elegance of our private establishments forms a daily source of pleasure and helps to banish the spleen; while the magnitude of our city draws the produce of the world into our harbour, so that to the Athenian the fruits of other countries are as familiar a luxury as those of his own.

'If we turn to our military policy, there also we differ from our antagonists. We throw open our city to the world, and never by alien acts exclude foreigners from any opportunity of learning or observing, although the eyes of an enemy may occasionally profit by our liberality; trusting less in system and policy than to the native spirit of our citizens; while in education, where our rivals from their very cradles by a painful discipline seek after manliness, at Athens we live exactly as we please, and yet are just as ready to encounter every legitimate danger. In proof of this it may be noticed that the Lacedœmonians [Spartans] do not invade our country alone, but bring with them all their confederates; while we Athenians advance unsupported into the territory of a neighbour, and fighting upon a foreign soil usually vanquish with ease men who are defending their homes. Our united force was never yet encountered by any enemy, because we have at once to attend to our marine and to despatch our citizens by land upon a hundred different services; so that, wherever they engage with some such fraction of our strength, a success against a detachment is magnified into a victory over the nation, and a defeat into a reverse suffered at the hands of our entire people. And yet if with habits not of labour but of ease, and courage not of art but of nature, we are still willing to encounter danger, we have the double advantage of escaping the experience of hardships in anticipation and of facing them in the hour of need as fearlessly as those who are never free from them.

'Nor are these the only points in which our city is worthy of admiration. We cultivate refinement without extravagance and knowledge without effeminacy; wealth we employ more for use than for show, and place the real disgrace of poverty not in owning to the fact but in declining the struggle against it. Our public men have, besides politics, their private affairs to attend to, and our ordinary citizens, though occupied with the pursuits of industry, are still fair judges of public matters; for, unlike any other nation, regarding him who takes no part in these duties not as unambitious but as useless, we Athenians are able to judge at all events if we cannot originate, and instead of looking on discussion as a stumbling-block in the way of action, we think it an indispensable preliminary to any wise action at all. Again, in our enterprises we present the singular spectacle of daring and deliberation, each carried to its highest point, and both united in the same persons;

although usually decision is the fruit of ignorance, hesitation of reflexion. But the palm of courage will surely be adjudged most justly to those, who best know the difference between hardship and pleasure and yet are never tempted to shrink from danger. In generosity we are equally singular, acquiring our friends by conferring not by receiving favours. Yet, of course, the doer of the favour is the firmer friend of the two, in order by continued kindness to keep the recipient in his debt; while the debtor feels less keenly from the very consciousness that the return he makes will be a payment, not a free gift. And it is only the Athenians who, fearless of consequences, confer their benefits not from calculations of expediency, but in the confidence of liberality.

'In short, I say that as a city we are the school of Hellas [Greece]; while I doubt if the world can produce a man, who where he has only himself to depend upon, is equal to so many emergencies, and graced by so happy a versatility as the Athenian. And that this is no mere boast thrown out for the occasion, but plain matter of fact, the power of the state acquired by these habits proves. For Athens alone of her contemporaries is found when tested to be greater than her reputation, and alone gives no occasion to her assailants to blush at the antagonist by whom they have been worsted, or to her subjects to question her title by merit to rule. Rather, the admiration of the present and succeeding ages will be ours, since we have not left our power without witness, but have shown it by mighty proofs; and far from needing a Homer for our panegyrist, or other of his craft whose verses might charm for the moment only for the impression which they gave to melt at the touch of fact, we have forced every sea and land to be the highway of our daring, and everywhere, whether for evil or for good, have left imperishable monuments behind us. Such is the Athens for which these men, in the assertion of their resolve not to lose her, nobly fought and died; and well may every one of their survivors be ready to suffer in her cause.

'Indeed if I have dwelt at some length upon the character of our country, it has been to show that our stake in the struggle is not the same as theirs who have no such blessings to lose, and also that the panegyric of the men over whom I am now speaking might be by definite proofs established. That panegyric is now in a great measure complete; for the Athens that I have celebrated is only what the heroism of these and their like have made her, men whose fame, unlike that of most Hellenes, will be found to be only commensurate with their deserts. . . . For there is justice in the claim that steadfastness in his country's battles should be as a cloak to cover a man's other imperfections; since the good action has blotted out the bad, and his merit as a citizen more than outweighed his demerits as an individual. But none of these allowed either wealth with its prospect of future enjoyment to unnerve his spirit, or poverty with its hope of a day of freedom and riches to tempt him to shrink from danger. No, holding that vengeance upon their enemies was more to be desired than any personal blessings, and reckoning this to be the most glorious of hazards, they joyfully determined to accept the risk, to make sure of their vengeance and to let their wishes wait; and while committing to hope the uncertainty of final success, in the business before them they thought fit to act boldly and trust in themselves. Thus choosing to die resisting, rather than to live submitting, they fled only from dishonour, but met danger face to face, and after one brief moment, while at the summit of their fortune, escaped, not from their fear, but from their glory.

'So died these men as became Athenians. You, their survivors, must determine to have as unaltering a resolution in the field, though you may pray that it may have a happier issue. . . .'

STUDY QUESTIONS

1. How does Pericles describe the Athenian political system? How does he contrast it with Sparta?
2. What were the differences between Athenian and Spartan military systems (Chapter 17)?
3. Were there any similarities between Spartan and Athenian values and goals?
4. How did Athenian democracy differ from most modern democratic systems? Who were the citizens, and what were their obligations?
5. What does Pericles suggest about the position of women in Athenian politics and society?
6. What kind of balance does Pericles describe between individual expression and collective responsibility? Did individuals have definite rights against the state?
7. What was Athens' relation to its Greek empire? Does Pericles suggest reasons for the war between Sparta and Athens?
8. How did Athens deal with social and economic inequality?
9. How did Greek definitions of politics compare with Confucian definitions?

19

MEDITERRANEAN SOCIAL AND FAMILY STRUCTURE

In these selections, the philosopher Aristotle (384–322 B.C.E.) describes some widely accepted Greek principles of social organization that also came to be current in Rome. He is obviously intent on justifying a social hierarchy. How does he divide functions? Why does he prefer that manual labor (at least in agriculture) be done by slaves? The idea of hierarchy also extends to the family, with clear divisions between men and women. Were these unusual in classical civilizations? Does Aristotle's definition of the purposes of family organization differ from those in China and India?

Aristotle was an ardent defender of most Athenian political principles, including a degree of democracy as the Athenians defined it. How do his arguments for social and family hierarchy relate to Greek politics?

Social divisions existed in all the classical civilizations, of course. Were the kinds of divisions Aristotle described comparable to social structures elsewhere in the classical world—for example, in India's caste system?

ARISTOTLE

I. POLITICS

We stated above that the land ought to be possessed by those who have arms and enjoy full participation in the constitution, and why the cultivators should be different from the owners, also the nature and extent of the territory required. We must speak first about the division of the land for the purposes of cultivation and about those who will cultivate it, who and of what type they will be. We do not agree with those who have said that all land should be communally owned, but we do believe that there should be a friendly arrangement for sharing the usufruct [profits] and that none of the citizens should be without means of support. Next as to communal feeding, it is generally agreed that this is a very useful institution in a well-ordered society; why we too are of this opinion we will say later. In any case, where communal meals exist, all citizens should partake of them, though it is not easy for those who are badly off to pay the contribution fixed and keep a

Selection I from Aristotle, *The Politics,* translated by T. A. Sinclair (Harmmondsworth, England: Penguin Classics edition, 1962). Copyright © 1962 by the Estate of T. A. Sinclair. Reprinted by permission of Penguin Books Ltd. Selection II from Aristotle, *Economics,* Book I, in Vol. 10 of *The Oxford Translation of Aristotle,* edited by W. D. Ross (Oxford: Oxford University Press, 1921).

household going at the same time. Another thing that should be a charge on the whole community is the public worship of the gods. Thus it becomes necessary to divide the land into two parts, one publicly owned, the other privately. Each of these has to be further divided into two. One part of the public land will support the service of the gods, the other the communal feeding. Of the privately owned land one part will be near the frontier, the other near the city, so that every citizen will have two portions, one in each locality. This is not only in accordance with justice and equality but makes also for greater unity in the face of wars with bordering states. Without this dual arrangement some make too little of hostilities on the border, others too much, some underestimate the dangers of frontier quarrels, others take them too seriously, even sacrificing honour in order to avoid them. Hence in some countries it is the custom that when war against a neighbour is under consideration, those who live near to the border should be excluded from the discussion as being too closely involved to be able to give honest advice. It is therefore important that the territory should for the reasons given be divided in the manner stated. As for those who are to till the land, they should, if possible, be slaves (and we are building as we would wish). They should not be all of one stock nor men of spirit; this will ensure that they will be good workers and not prone to revolt. An alternative to slaves is foreigners settled on the countryside, men of the same type as the slaves just mentioned. They fall into two groups according to whether they work privately on the land of individual owners of property, or publicly on the common land. I hope later on to say how slaves ought to be used in agriculture and why it is a good thing that all slaves should have before them the prospect of receiving their freedom as a reward.

II. ECONOMICS

As regards the human part of the household, the first care is concerning a wife; for a common life is above all things natural to the female and to the male. For we have elsewhere laid down the principle that nature aims at producing many such forms of association, just as also it produces the various kinds of animals. But it is impossible for the female to accomplish this without the male or the male without the female, so that their common life has necessarily arisen. Now in the other animals this intercourse is not based on reason, but depends on the amount of natural instinct which they possess and is entirely for the purpose of procreation. But in the civilized and more intelligent animals the bond of unity is more perfect (for in them we see more mutual help and goodwill and co-operation), above all in the case of man, because the female and the male co-operate to ensure not merely existence but a good life. And the production of children is not only a way of serving nature but also of securing a real advantage; for the trouble which parents bestow upon their helpless children when they are themselves vigorous is repaid to them in old age when they are helpless by their children, who are then in their full vigour. At the same time also nature thus periodically provides for the perpetuation of mankind as a species, since she cannot do so individually. Thus the nature both of the man and of the woman has been preordained by the will of heaven to live a common life. For they are distinguished in that the powers which they possess are not applicable to purposes in all cases identical, but in some respects their functions are opposed to one another though they all tend to the same end. For nature has made the one sex stronger, the other weaker, that the latter through fear may be the more cautious, while the former by its courage is better able to ward off attacks; and that the one may acquire possessions outside the house, the other preserve those within. In the performance of work, she made one sex able to lead a sedentary life and not strong enough to endure exposure, the other less adapted for quiet pursuits but well constituted for outdoor activities; and in relation to offspring she has made both share in the procreation of children, but each render its peculiar service towards them, the woman by nurturing, the man by educating them.

First, then, there are certain laws to be observed towards a wife, including the avoidance of doing her any wrong; for thus a man is less likely himself to be wronged. This is inculcated by the general law, as the Pythagoreans say, that one least of all should injure a wife as being "a suppliant and seated at the hearth." Now wrong inflicted by a husband is the formation of connections outside his own house. As regards sexual intercourse, a man ought not to accustom himself not to need it at all nor to be unable to rest when it is lacking, but so as to be content with or without it. The saying of Hesiod is a good one:

A man should marry a maiden, that habits discreet he may teach her.

For dissimilarity of habits tends more than anything to destroy affection. As regards adornment, husband and wife ought not to approach one another with false affectation in their person any more than in their manners; for if the society of husband and wife requires such embellishment, it is no better than play-acting on the tragic stage.

Of possessions, that which is the best and the worthiest subject of economics comes first and is most essential—I mean, man. It is necessary therefore first to provide oneself with good slaves. Now slaves are of two kinds, the overseer and the worker. And since we see that methods of education produce a certain character in the young, it is necessary when one has procured slaves to bring up carefully those to whom the higher duties are to be entrusted. The intercourse of a master with his slaves should be such as not either to allow them to be insolent or to irritate them. To the higher class of slaves he ought to give some share of honour, and to the workers abundance of nourishment. And since the drinking of wine makes even freemen insolent, and many nations even of freemen abstain therefrom (the Carthaginians, for instance, when they are on military service), it is clear that wine ought never to be given to slaves, or at any rate very seldom. Three things make up the life of a slave, work, punishment, and food. To give them food but no punishment and no work makes them insolent; and that they should have work and punishment but no food is tyrannical and destroys their efficiency. It remains therefore to give them work and sufficient food; for it is impossible to rule over slaves without offering rewards, and a slave's reward is his food. And just as all other men become worse when they get no advantage by being better and there are no rewards for virtue and punishments for vice, so also is it with slaves. Therefore we must take careful notice and bestow or withhold everything, whether food or clothing or leisure or punishments, according to merit, in word and deed following the practice adopted by physicians in the matter of medicine, remembering at the same time that food is not medicine because it must be given continually.

The slave who is best suited for his work is the kind that is neither too cowardly nor too courageous. Slaves who have either of these characteristics are injurious to their owners; those who are too cowardly lack endurance, while the high-spirited are not easy to control. All ought to have a definite end in view; for it is just and beneficial to offer slaves their freedom as a prize, for they are willing to work when a prize is set before them and a limit of time is defined.

STUDY QUESTIONS

1. Why does Aristotle find slavery necessary? How does he define the proper treatment of slaves?
2. How does the discussion of slavery or the use of foreigners mesh with Athenian political values? Would Aristotle and Pericles have argued about these issues?
3. Are Aristotle's gender values patriarchal? How do they compare with the gender system of Sparta, described earlier by Lycurgus? (see Chapter 17.)
4. How do Greek gender values compare with those of classical India and China? Were they more or less severe?
5. How do Aristotle's views on social inequality compare with Confucian and Hindu views? What are the key similarities? How do all these social theories compare with characteristic modern discussions on the reasons and justifications for social inequality?

20

LEADERSHIP IN THE ROMAN REPUBLIC

This section contains three passages: two are from Plutarch's *Lives,* written during the early Roman Empire but looking back to earlier leaders. Plutarch first discusses Cato the Elder, who was elected censor in 184 B.C.E. This was a period when the Republic was expanding its conquests, acquiring new contacts with Greek culture, and developing a more prosperous upper class. Cato, using an office designed to oversee moral behavior, was obviously critical of many of these trends, regarding himself, and regarded by many others, as a bastion of traditional Roman republican values.

The second passage deals with Crassus, one of a triumvirate of leaders (along with the Generals Pompey and Julius Caesar) ruling the Republic in its later days. His leadership qualities are very different from those of Cato.

Finally, from essentially the same period, the great politician and orator Cicero writes in 63 B.C.E. to his brother about winning the election as consul, the highest executive office in the Republic, elected annually by a restricted group of voters. The Cicero family was not aristocratic, rather of business background, but there were opportunities to curry favor with the groups that wielded top power in the Republic. Cicero describes an active political system, but one increasingly divided between popular elements, often accused of demagoguery, and the aristocratic element.

The three passages taken together provide an opportunity to assess the changing nature of leadership in the Republic. Romans frequently discussed the importance of character in sustaining the political system, along with a number of institutions designed to prevent corruption and monitor executive power. Was this a distinctive approach? How do the values and realities of Roman leadership compare to qualities in other political societies, including our own?

1. PLUTARCH ON CATO

Cato grew more and more powerful by his eloquence, so that he was commonly called the Roman Demosthenes, but his manner of life was yet more famous and talked of. For oratorical skill was, as an accomplishment, commonly studied and sought after by all young men; but he was very rare who would cultivate the old habits of bodily labor,

Moralia Plutarch: Volume x, xv translated by Harold North Fowler and F.H. Sandbach. Reprinted by permission of the publishers and the Trustees of the Loeb Classical Library, Cambridge, Mass.: Harvard University Press, 1936, 1969. The Loeb Classical Library ® is a registered trademark of the President and Fellows of Harvard College.

or prefer a light supper, and a breakfast which never saw the fire; or be in love with poor clothes and a homely lodging, or could set his ambition rather on doing without luxuries than on possessing them. For now the state, unable to keep its purity by reason of its greatness, and having so many affairs, and people from all parts under its government, was fain to admit many mixed customs, and new examples of living.

With reason, therefore, everybody admired Cato, when they saw others sink under labors, and grow effeminate by pleasures; and yet beheld him unconquered by either, and that not only when he was young and desirous of honor, but also when old and grayheaded, after a consulship and triumph; like some famous victor in the games, persevering in his exercise and maintaining his character to the very last. He himself says, that he never wore a suit of clothes which cost more than a hundred drachmas; and that, when he was general and consul, he drank the same wine which his workmen did; and that the meat or fish which was bought in the market for his dinner did not cost above thirty *asses*. All of which was for the sake of the commonwealth, that so his body might be the hardier for the war.

Having a piece of embroidered Babylonian tapestry left him, he sold it; because none of his farmhouses were so much as plastered. Nor did he ever buy a slave for above fifteen hundred drachmas; as he did not seek for effeminate and handsome ones, but able, sturdy workmen, horse keepers and cowherds: and these he thought ought to be sold again, when they grew old, and no useless servants fed in a house. In short, he reckoned nothing a good bargain, which was superfluous; but whatever it was, though sold for a farthing, he would think it a great price, if you had no need of it; and was for the purchase of lands for sowing and feeding, rather than grounds for sweeping and watering.

Some imputed these things to petty avarice, but others approved of him, as if he had only the more strictly denied himself for the rectifying and amending of others. Yet certainly, in my judgment, it marks an overrigid temper, for a man to take the work out of his servants as out of brute beasts, turning them off and selling them in their old age, and thinking there ought to be no further commerce between man and man, than whilst there arises some profit by it. We see that kindness or humanity has a larger field than bare justice to exercise itself in; law and justice we cannot, in the nature of things, employ on others than men; but we may extend our goodness and charity even to irrational creatures; and such acts flow from a gentle nature, as water from an abundant spring. It is doubtless the part of a kind-natured man to keep even worn-out horses and dogs, and not only take care of them when they are foals and whelps, but also when they are grown old.

2. PLUTARCH ON CRASSUS

People were wont to say that the many virtues of Crassus were darkened by the one vice of avarice, and indeed he seemed to have no other but that; for it, being the most predominant, obscured others to which he was inclined. The arguments in proof of his avarice were the vastness of his estate, and the manner of raising it; for whereas at first he was not worth above three hundred talents, yet, though in the course of his political life he dedicated the tenth of all he had to Hercules, and feasted the people, and gave to every citizen corn enough to serve him three months, upon casting up his accounts, before he went upon his Parthian expedition, he found his possessions to amount to seven thousand one hundred talents; most of which, if we may scandal him with a truth, he got by fire and rapine, making his advantage of the public calamities. For when Sulla seized the city, and exposed to sale the goods of those that he had caused to be slain, accounting them booty and spoils, and, indeed, calling them so too, and was desirous of making as many, and as eminent men as he could, partakers in the crime, Crassus never was the man that refused to accept, or give money for them.

Moreover, observing how extremely subject the city was to fire, and to the falling down of houses, by reason of their height and their standing so near together, he bought slaves that were builders and architects, and when he had collected these to the number of more than five hundred, he made it his practice to buy houses that were on fire, and those in the neighborhood which, in the immediate danger and uncertainty, the proprietors were willing to part with for little or nothing; so that the greatest part of Rome, at one time or other, came into his hands.

Yet for all he had so many workmen, he never built anything but his own house, and used to say that those that were addicted to building would undo themselves soon enough without the help of other enemies. And though he had many silver mines, and much valuable land, and laborers to work in it, yet all this was nothing in comparison to his slaves, such a number and variety did he possess of excellent readers, amanuenses, silversmiths, stewards, and table waiters, whose instruction he always attended to himself, superintending in person while they learned, and teaching them himself, as counting it the main duty of a master to look over the servants, that are, indeed, the living tools of housekeeping. But it was surely a mistaken judgment, when he said "no man was to be accounted rich that could not maintain an army at his own cost and charges, for war". . . .

Crassus, however, was very eager to be hospitable to strangers; he kept open house, and to his friends he would lend money without interest, but called it in precisely at the time; so that his kindness was often thought worse than the paying the interest would have been. His entertainments were, for the most part, plain and citizenlike, the company general and popular; good taste and kindness made them pleasanter than sumptuosity would have done.

As for learning, he chiefly cared for rhetoric, and what would be serviceable with large numbers; he became one of the best speakers at Rome, and by his pains and industry outdid the best natural orators. For there was no trial how mean and contemptible soever that he came to unprepared; nay, several times he undertook and concluded a cause, when Pompey and Caesar and Cicero refused to stand up, upon which account particularly he got the love of the people, who looked upon him as a diligent and careful man, ready to help succor his fellow citizens. Besides, the people were pleased with his courteous and unpretending salutations and greetings; for he never met any citizen however humble and low, but he returned him his salute by name. He was also looked upon as a man well read in history, and pretty well versed in Aristotle's philosophy.

3. CICERO'S ADVICE

Almost every day as you go down to the Forum you must say to yourself, "I am a *novus homo*" [*i.e.* a new man without noble ancestry]. "I am a candidate for the consulship." "This is Rome." For the "newness" of your name you will best compensate by the brilliance of your oratory. This has ever carried with it great political distinction. See that all those aids to natural ability, which I know are your special gifts are ready for use . . . and finally take care that both the number and rank of your friends are unmistakable. For you have, as few new men have had,—all the tax-syndicate promoters, nearly the whole equestrian order, and many municipal towns, especially devoted to you, many people who have been defended by you, many trade guilds, and beside these a large number of the rising generation, who have become attached to you in their enthusiasm for public speaking, and who visit you daily in swarms, and with such constant regularity!

See that you retain these advantages by reminding these persons, by appealing to them, and by using every means to make them understand that this, and this only, is the time for those who are in your debt now, to show their gratitude, and for those who wish for your services in the future, to place you under an obligation. It also seems possible that a "new man" may be much aided by the fact that he has the good wishes of men of high rank, and especially of ex-consuls. It is a point in your favor that you should be thought worthy of this position and rank by the very men to whose position you are wishing to attain.

All these men must be canvassed with care, agents must be sent to them, and they must be convinced that we have always been at one with the Optimates (Aristocratic Party), that we have never been dangerous demagogues in the very least. . . . Also take pains to get on your side the young men of high rank, and keep the friendship of those whom you already have. They will contribute much to your political position. You have many already: make them feel how much you think depends on them; if you rouse to zeal those who are now only lukewarm friends, that will be a vast gain.

"Whosoever gives any sign of inclination to you, or regularly visits your house, you must put down in the category of friends. But yet the most advantageous thing is to be beloved and pleasant in the eyes of those who are friends on the more regular grounds of relationship by blood or marriage, the membership in the same club, or some close tie or other. You must take great pains that [these men] should love you and desire your highest honor—as, for example, your tribesmen, neighbors, clients, and finally your freedmen, yes even your slaves: for nearly all the gossip that forms public opinion emanates from your own servants' quarters. . . .

[As to people who crowd around you]: See that those who do so spontaneously understand that you regard yourself as forever obliged by their extreme kindness; from these on the other hand, who *owe* you the attention [for services rendered] frankly demand that so far as their age and business allow they should be constantly in attendance, and that those who are unable to accompany you in person, should find relatives to substitute in performing this duty. I am very anxious and think it most important that you should always be surrounded with numbers. Besides, it confers a great reputation, and great distinction to be accompanied by those whom you have defended and saved in the law courts. Put this demand fairly before them—that since by your means, and without any fee,—some have retained property, others their honor, or their civil rights, or their entire fortunes,—and since there will never be any other time when they can show their gratitude, they now should reward you by this service.

STUDY QUESTIONS

1. What were the main issues Cato faced as Censor? What kinds of values did he seek to uphold?
2. How did the leadership qualities of Crassus compare with those of Cato? Is it fair to see, in the comparison of the two men who lived over a century apart, a deterioration in Roman leadership? Or did the setting simply change, or both?
3. What do the tactics Cicero suggests imply about the nature of Roman institutions and about the Roman political process? Do these tactics resemble the qualities ascribed to Crassus? What kinds of tensions in the political system does Cicero imply, and how does he recommend overcoming them?
4. By implication, what would a traditionalist like Cato have thought of Cicero's advice?
5. Did the Roman republic have an unusual dependence on leadership qualities, compared to other classical societies? Is there a valid comparison with modern societies like the United States?
6. How would a Confucian judge the leadership qualities exemplified by Cato? By Crassus? How would a Confucian evaluate the political process implied by Cicero?

21

THE ROMAN MILITARY
AND THE EMPIRE

Roman legions formed one of the cornerstones of the Roman state. Developed under the republic, they played a vital role in the acquisition and defense of the empire. These selections, from the Roman historian Josephus (Flavius Josephus, 37–after 93 C.E.), discuss various aspects of the Roman military.

Military history is, obviously, a vital part of world history, and of any major society. Military history also commands wide interest among the general public—more than any other historical form. Historical presentations on American cable television, for example, feature military subjects and wars far more than any other topic. Yet historians do not always find it easy to integrate military history with other histories they treat.

Josephus' accounts provide opportunities for analyzing what the Roman military was all about. Josephus discusses how it was organized and how it prepared for action. He intended his account to flatter his fellow Romans, at the peak period of imperial glory. He also urged that it should console those whom the Romans had defeated, basically by showing how superior Roman military organization was, and discourage any attempts by subject peoples to challenge the empire.

The final passage from Josephus goes beyond discussion of the military, to an account of the celebration back in Rome of victory in the unusually bitter Jewish wars at the height of Rome's imperial power. Rome had defeated fierce Jewish resistance, and this victory ultimately led to the expulsion of the Jews from Palestine. The account of the celebrations makes it possible to see some of the reasons people might serve in the Roman military and the relationship among emperors, the army, and the Roman people. At the same time, the treatment of the Jews was unusually harsh. More commonly, Romans were more tolerant of the regions they conquered, allowing considerable autonomy even after military victory.

JOSEPHUS

I. DESCRIPTION OF THE ROMAN ARMIES AND ROMAN CAMPS

1. Now here one cannot but admire at the precaution of the Romans, in providing themselves of such household servants, as might not only serve at other times for the common offices of life, but might also be of advantage to them in their wars.

From *The Complete Works of Josephus*, Vol. 8 and Vol. 10: *The Wars of the Jews* (Cleveland: World Syndicate Publishing Company, n.d.), 8: Book III, Chap. V, pp. 12–18; Chap. VI, pp. 19–21; 10: Book VII, Chap. V, pp. 361–367.

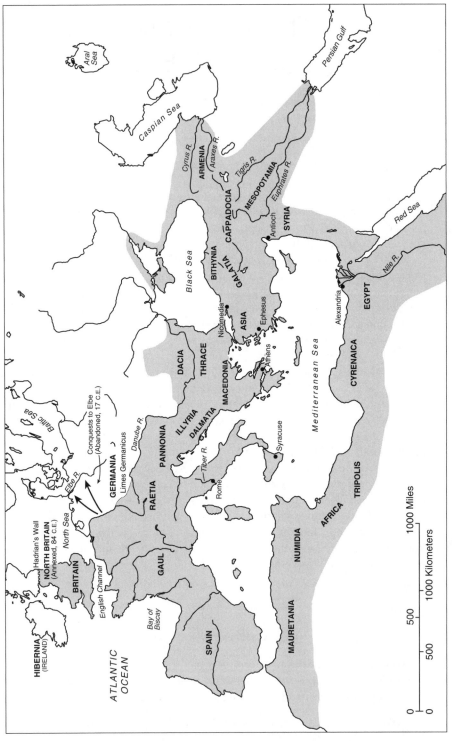

The Roman Empire at Its Greatest Extent, 98–117 C.E.

And, indeed, if any one does but attend to the other parts of their military discipline, he will be forced to confess that their obtaining so large a dominion hath been the acquisition of their valor, and not the bare gift of fortune; for they do not begin to use their weapons first in time of war, nor do they then put their hands first into motion, while they avoided so to do in times of peace; but, as if their weapons did always cling to them, they have never any truce from warlike exercises; nor do they stay till times of war admonish them to use them; for their military exercises differ not at all from the real use of their arms, but every soldier is every day exercised, and that with great diligence, as if it were in time of war, which is the reason why they bear the fatigue of battles so easily; for neither can any disorder remove them from their usual regularity, nor can fear affright them out of it, nor can labor tire them; which firmness of conduct makes them always to overcome those that have not the same firmness; nor would he be mistaken that should call those their exercises unbloody battles, and their battles bloody exercises. Nor can their enemies easily surprise them with the suddenness of their incursions; for as soon as they have marched into an enemy's land, they do not begin to fight till they have walled their camp about; nor is the fence they raise rashly made, or uneven; nor do they all abide ill it, nor do those that are in it take their places at random; but if it happens that the ground is uneven, it is first leveled: their camp is also four-square by measure, and carpenters are ready, in great numbers, with their tools, to erect their buildings for them.

2. As for what is within the camp, it is set apart for tents, but the outward circumference hath the resemblance to a wall, and is adorned with towers at equal distances, where between the towers stand the engines for throwing arrows and darts, and for slinging stones, and where they lay all other engines that can annoy the enemy, all ready for their several operations. They also erect four gates, one at every side of the circumference, and those large enough for the entrance of the beasts, and wide enough for making excursions, if occasion should require. They divide the camp within into streets, very conveniently, and place the tents of the commanders in the middle; but in the very midst of all is the general's own tent, in the nature of a temple, insomuch, that it appears to be a city built on the sudden, with its market-place, and place for handicraft trades, and with seats for the officers superior and inferior, where, if any differences arise, their causes are heard and determined. The camp, and all that is in it, is encompassed with a wall round about, and that sooner than one would imagine, and this by the multitude and the skill of the laborers; and, if occasion require, a trench is drawn round the whole, whose depth is four cubits, and its breadth equal.

3. When they have thus secured themselves, they live together by companies, with quietness and decency, as are all their other affairs managed with good order and security. Each company hath also their wood, and their corn, and their water brought them, when they stand in need of them; for they neither sup nor dine as they please themselves singly, but all together. Their times also for sleeping, and watching, and rising are notified beforehand by the sound of trumpets, nor is any thing done without such a signal; and in the morning the soldiery go every one to their centurions [officers], and these centurions to their tribunes, to salute them; with whom all the superior officers go to the general of the whole army, who then gives them of course the watchword and other orders, to be by them cared to all

that are under their command; which is also observed when they go to fight, and thereby they turn themselves about on the sudden, when there is occasion for making sallies, as they come back when they are recalled in crowds also.

4. Now when they are to go out of their camp, the trumpet gives a sound, at which time nobody lies still, but at the first intimation they take down their tents, and all is made ready for their going out; then do the trumpets sound again, to order them to get ready for the march; then do they lay their baggage suddenly upon their mules, and other beasts of burden, and stand, as at the place of starting, ready to march; when also they set fire to their camp, and this they do because it will be easy for them to erect another camp, and that it may not ever be of use to their enemies. Then do the trumpets give a sound the third time, that they are to go out, in order to excite those that on any account are a little tardy, that so no one may be out of his rank when the army marches. Then does the crier stand at the general's right hand, and asks them thrice, in their own tongue, whether they be now ready to go out to war or not? To which they reply as often, with a loud and cheerful voice, saying, "We are ready." And this they do almost before the question is asked them: they do this as filled with a kind of martial fury, and at the same time that they so cry out, they lift up their right hands also.

5. When, after this, they are gone out of their camp, they all march without noise, and in a decent manner, and every one keeps his own rank, as if they were going to war. The footmen are armed with breastplates and head-pieces, and have swords on each side; but the sword which is upon their left side is much longer than the other, for that on the right side is not longer than a span. Those foot-men also that are chosen out from the rest to be about the general himself have a lance and a buckler, but the rest of the foot soldiers have a spear and a long buckler, besides a saw and a basket, a pick-axe and an axe, a thong of leather and a hook, with provisions for three days, so that a footman hath no great need of a mule to carry his burdens. The horsemen have a long sword on their right sides, axed a long pole in their hand; a shield also lies by them obliquely on one side of their horses, with three or more darts that are borne in their quiver, having broad points, and not smaller than spears. They have also head-pieces and breastplates, in like manner as have all the footmen. And for those that are chosen to be about the general, their armor no way differs from that of the horsemen belonging to other troops; and he always leads the legions forth to whom the lot assigns that employment.

6. This is the manner of the marching and resting of the Romans, as also these are the several sorts of weapons they use. But when they are to fight, they leave nothing without forecast, nor to be done off-hand, but counsel is ever first taken before any work is begun, and what hath been there resolved upon is put in execution presently; for which reason they seldom commit any errors; and if they have been mistaken at any time, they easily correct those mistakes. They also esteem any errors they commit upon taking counsel beforehand to be better than such rash success as is owing to fortune only; because such a fortuitous advantage tempts them to be inconsiderate, while consultation, though it may sometimes fail of success, hath this good in it, that it makes men more careful hereafter; but for the advantages that arise from chance, they are not owing to him that gains them; and as to what melancholy accidents happen unexpectedly, there is this comfort in them, that they had however taken the best consultations they could to prevent them.

7. Now they so manage their preparatory exercises of their weapons, that not the bodies of the soldiers only, but their souls may also become stronger: they are moreover hardened for war by fear; for their laws inflict capital punishments, not only for soldiers running away from the ranks, but for slothfulness and inactivity, though it be but in a lesser degree; as are their generals more severe than their laws, for they prevent any imputation of cruelty toward those under condemnation, by the great rewards they bestow on the valiant soldiers; and the readiness of obeying their commanders is so great, that it is very ornamental in peace; but when they come to a battle, the whole army is but one body, so well coupled together are their ranks, so sudden are their turnings about, so sharp their hearing as to what orders are given them, so quick their sight of the ensigns, and so nimble are their hands when they set to work; whereby it comes to pass that what they do is done quickly, and what they suffer they bear with the greatest patience. Nor can we find any examples where they have been conquered in battle, when they came to a close fight, either by the multitude of the enemies, or by their stratagems, or by the difficulties in the places they were in; no, nor by fortune neither, for their victories have been surer to them than fortune could have granted them. In a case, therefore, where counsel still goes before action, and where, after taking the best advice, that advice is followed by so active an army, what wonder is it that Euphrates on the east, the ocean on the west, the most fertile regions of Libya on the south, and the Danube and the Rhine on the north, are the limits of this empire? One might well say that the Roman possessions are not inferior to the Romans themselves.

8. This account I have given the reader, not so much with the intention of commending the Romans, as of comforting those that have been conquered by them, and for the deterring others from attempting innovations under their government. This discourse of the Roman military conduct may also perhaps be of use to such of the curious as are ignorant of it, and yet have to mind to know it. I return now from this digression.

The Army on the March

2. But as Vespasian had a great mind to fall upon Galilee, he marched out of Ptolemais, having put his army into that order wherein the Romans used to march. He ordered those auxiliaries which were lightly armed, and the archers, to march first, that they might prevent any sudden insults from the enemy, and might search out the woods that looked suspiciously, and were capable of ambuscades. Next to these followed that part of the Romans which was completely armed, both footmen and horsemen. Next to these followed ten out of every hundred, carrying along with them their arms, and what was necessary to measure out a camp withal; and after them, such as were to make the road even and straight, and if it were any where rough and hard to be passed over, to plane it, and to cut down the woods that hindered their march, that the army might not be in distress, or tired with their march. Behind these he set such carriages of the army as belonged both to himself and to the other commanders, with a considerable number of their horsemen for their security. After these he marched himself, having with him a select body of footmen, and horsemen, and pikemen. After these came the peculiar cavalry of his own legion, for there were a hundred and twenty horsemen that peculiarly belonged to every legion. Next to these came the mules that carried the engines for sieges, and

other warlike machines of that nature. After these came the commanders of the cohorts and tribunes, having about them soldiers chosen out of the rest. Then came the ensigns encompassing the eagle, which is at the head of every Roman legion, the king, and the strongest of all birds, which seems to them a signal of dominion, and an omen that they shall conquer all against whom they march; these sacred ensigns are followed by the trumpeters. Then came the main army in their squadrons and battalions, with six men in depth, which were followed at last by a centurion, who, according to custom, observed the rest. As for the servants of every legion, they all followed the footmen, and led the baggage of the soldiers, which was borne by the mules and other beasts of burden. But behind all the legions came the whole multitude of the mercenaries; and those that brought up the rear came last of all for the security of the whole army, being both footmen, and those in their armor also, with a great number of horsemen.

II. TRIUMPH AFTER THE JEWISH WAR, 71 C.E., EMPEROR VESPASIAN AND HIS SON TITUS, WHO HAD BEEN COMMANDING GENERAL

4. Now all the soldiery marched out beforehand by companies, and in their several ranks, under their several commanders, in the night time, and were about the gates, not of the upper palaces, but those near the temple of Isis; for there it was that the emperors had rested the foregoing night. And as soon as ever it was day, Vespasian and Titus came out crowned with laurel, and clothed in those ancient purple habits which were proper to their family, and then went as far as Octavian's Walks; for there it was that the senate, and the principal rulers, and those that had been recorded as of the equestrian order, waited for them. Now a tribunal had been erected before the cloisters, and ivory chairs had been set upon it, when they came and sat down upon them. Whereupon the soldiery made an acclamation of joy to them immediately, and all gave them attestations of their valor; while they were themselves without their arms, and only in their silken garments, and crowned with laurel; then Vespasian accepted of these shouts of theirs; but while they were still disposed to go on in such acclamations, he gave them a signal of silence. And when every body entirely held their peace, he stood up, and covering the greatest part of his head with his cloak, he put up the accustomed solemn prayers; the like prayers did Titus put up also; after which prayers Vespasian made a short speech to all the people, and then sent away the soldiers to a dinner prepared for them by the emperors. Then did he retire to that gate which was called the Gate of the Pomp, because pompous shows do always go through that gate; there it was that they tasted some food, and when they had put on their triumphal garments, and had offered sacrifices to the gods that were placed at their gate, they sent the triumph forward, and marched through the theatres, that they might be more easily seen by the multitudes.

5. Now it is impossible to describe the multitude of the shows as they deserve, and the magnificence of them all; such indeed as a man could not easily think of as performed, either by the labor of workmen, or the variety of riches, or the rarities of nature; for almost all such curiosities as the most happy men ever get by piecemeal were here one heaped on another, and those both admirable and costly in their nature; and all brought together on that day demonstrated the vastness of the

dominions of the Romans; for there was here to be seen a mighty quantity of silver, and gold, and ivory, contrived into all sorts of things, and did not appear as carried along in pompous show only, but, as a man may say, running along like a river. Some parts were composed of the rarest purple hangings, and so carried along; and others accurately represented to the life what was embroidered by the arts of the Babylonians. There were also precious stones that were transparent, some set in crowns of gold, and some in other ouches, as the workmen pleased; and of these such a vast number were brought, that we could not but thence learn how vainly we imagined any of them to be rarities. The images of the gods were also carried, being as well wonderful for their largeness, as made very artificially, and with great skill of the workmen; nor were any of these images of any other than very costly materials; and many species of animals were brought, every one in their own natural ornaments. The men also who brought every one of these shows were great multitudes, and adorned with purple garments, all over interwoven with gold; those that were chosen for carrying these pompous shows having also about them such magnificent ornaments as were both extraordinary and surprising. Besides these, one might see that even the great number of the captives was not unadorned, while the variety that was in their garments, and their fine texture, concealed from the sight the deformity of their bodies. But what afforded the greatest surprise of all was the structure of the pageants that were borne along; for indeed he that met them could not but be afraid that the bearers would not be able firmly enough to support them, such was their magnitude; for many of them were so made, that they were on three or even four stories, one above another. The magnificence also of their structure afforded one both pleasure and surprise; for upon many of them were laid carpets of gold. . . . Moreover, there followed those pageants a great number of ships; and for the other spoils, they were carried in great plenty. But for those that were taken in the temple of Jerusalem, they made the greatest figure of them all; that is, the golden table, of the weight of many talents; the candlestick also, that was made of gold, though its construction were now changed from that which we made use of; for its middle shaft was fixed upon a basis, and the small branches were produced out of it to a great length, having the likeness of a trident in their position, and had every one a socket made of brass for a lamp at the tops of them. These lamps were in number seven, and represented the dignity of the number seven among the Jews; and the last of all the spoils, was carried the Law of the Jews. After these spoils passed by a great many men, carrying the images of Victory, whose structure was entirely either of ivory or of gold. After which Vespasian marched in the first place, and Titus followed him; Domitian also rode along with them, and made a glorious appearance, and rode on a horse that was worthy of admiration.

6. Now the last part of this pompous show was at the temple of Jupiter Capitolinus, whither when they were come, they stood still; for it was the Romans' ancient custom to stay till somebody brought the news that the general of the enemy was slain. This general was Simon, the son of Gioras, who had then been led in this triumph among the captives; a rope had also been put upon his head, and he had been drawn into a proper place in the forum, and had withal been tormented by those that drew him along; and the law of the Romans required that malefactors condemned to die should be slain there. Accordingly, when it was related that there was an end of him, and all the people had set up a shout for joy, they then began to offer those sacrifices which they had consecrated, in the prayers used in such

solemnities; which when they had finished, they went away to the palace. And as for some of the spectators, the emperors entertained them at their own feast; and for all the rest there were noble preparations made for feasting at home; for this was a festival day to the city of Rome, as celebrated for the victory obtained by their army over their enemies, for the end that was now put to their civil miseries, and for the commencement of their hopes of future prosperity and happiness.

STUDY QUESTIONS

1. What were the main features of Roman military preparation and organization?
2. Are there distinctively Roman features of military organization, or do you find this account fairly predictable, in terms of what you think of as standard military arrangements in any well-organized society?
3. What was life like for an ordinary soldier, and why might one wish to serve in the military?
4. What was the relationship between the imperial family, including the emperor himself, and the Roman army?
5. How did the Romans treat those whom they conquered, judging by this account?
6. What relationship does the document suggest between the Roman military and other facets of Roman society? How do military organizations compare to the political values described by Plutarch in the previous chapter?

22 WOMEN AND THE LAW IN ROME: LEGAL CODES

Rome was clearly a patriarchal society. In the early period of the republic, punishments against women, for example in cases of adultery, were very harsh, whereas men were treated much more leniently. By the time of the Empire (27 B.C.E. ff), however, legal protections began to improve. The inequalities of patriarchalism continued, but Roman women were far more protected in law than was common in patriarchal societies.

The following passages convey essential features of gender law during the Roman Empire. A first section comes from a speech attributed to the emperor Augustus in 9 C.E. Augustus was addressing some upper-class fathers, explaining why he had greatly increased protections for the family rights of women (protections for which he had been much criticized). The passage invited analysis toward explaining why Roman law began to treat women somewhat more fairly.

The second section contains laws pertaining to some of the key aspects of women's lives in Roman society, all associated with family life, which was the arena in which women were most involved. The laws come from various periods of the Empire, up to the Justinian Code in the early 6th century. The laws require fairly close reading to tease out two elements: first, ways in which women were receiving rather unusual protections; but second, ways in which they were still, even in family matters, treated as unequal to men.

Legal conditions were not, of course, the whole story. Women had no formal role in political life. Under the Empire they were allowed to testify in court, but with severe limitations. Individual upper-class women were sometimes educated, but men tended to scorn their capacities in this area.

Women's situation in the Roman Empire invites comparison with other classical societies, such as China, covered by other documents on the classical period.

WOMEN IN ROME

I. AUGUSTUS ON FAMILY

Though you are but few altogether . . . yet for this very reason I . . . praise you the more, and am heartily grateful to you because you have shown yourselves obedient and are helping to replenish the fatherland. For it is by lives so conducted that the Romans of later days will become a mighty multitude. We were at first a mere

From Seutonius, *The Twelve Caesars: Gaius Seutonius Tranquillus,* translated by Robert Graves (Baltimore: Penguin Books, 1957), Permission Granted by Carcanet Press Limited.

handful, you know, but when we had recourse to marriage and begot us children, we came to surpass all mankind not only in the manliness of our citizens but in the size of our population as well. Bearing this in mind, we must console the mortal side of our nature with an endless succession of generations that shall be like the torchbearers in a race, so that through one another we may render immortal the side of our nature in which we fall short of divine bliss. It was for this cause most of all that that first and greatest god, who fashioned us, divided the race of mortals in twain, making one half of it male and the other half female, and implanted in them love and compulsion to mutual intercourse, making their association fruitful, that by the young continually born he might render even mortality eternal. . . .

For is there anything better than a wife who is chaste, domestic, a good house-keeper, a rearer of children; one to gladden you in health, to tend you in sickness; to be your partner in good fortune, to console you in misfortune; to restrain the mad passion of youth, and to temper the unseasonable harshness of old age? And is it not a delight to acknowledge a child who shows the endowments of both parents, to nurture and educate it, at once the physical and spiritual image of yourself, so that in its growth another self lives again? . . . Those are the private advantages that accrue to those who marry and beget children; but for the State, for whose sake we ought to do many things that are even distasteful to us, how excellent and neces-sary it is, if cities and people are to exist, and if you are to rule others and all the world is to obey you, that there should be a multitude of men, to till the earth in time of peace, to make voyages, practice arts and follow handicrafts, and, in time of war, to protect what we already have with all the greater zeal because of family ties and to replace those that fall by others. Therefore men—for you alone may prop-erly be called men—and fathers. . . . I love and praise you for this; and I not only bestow the prizes I have already offered but will distinguish you still further by other honors and offices, so that you may not only reap great benefits yourselves but may also leave them to your children undiminished. . . .

II. LAWS OF MARRIAGE

A betrothal, like a marriage, is made with the consent of the contracting parties, and therefore, as in the case of a marriage, a son under paternal control must agree to it.

A girl who evidently does not resist the will of her father is understood to give her consent. A daughter is permitted to refuse to consent to her father's wishes only when he selects someone for her husband who is unworthy on account of his habits or who is of infamous character.

Widows under the age of twenty-five, even though they may have obtained the freedom of emancipation, still cannot marry a second time without the consent of their father. If, however, in the choice of a husband, the desire of the woman is opposed to that of her father and other relatives, it is established (just as has always been decreed with reference to the marriage of virgins), that judicial authority should be interposed for the purpose of examination, and if the parties are equal in family and in morals, he shall be considered preferable whom the woman has selected herself. . . . [371 C.E.]

The following law (326 C.E.) put an end to the activities of outside informers who must often have extorted blackmail.

III. ADULTERY ACCUSATIONS (TO PROTECT AGAINST OUTSIDE ACCUSATIONS AND BLACKMAIL)

Although adultery is considered a public crime, the right of accusation for which is granted to all persons in common, without any special interpretation of the law, still, lest the right of accusation be rashly entrusted to persons who wish to dishonor marriages, it is Our pleasure that the right of accusation shall be granted only to the nearest and closest of kin, that is, a father or cousins, and especially to consanguineous [blood] brothers who are driven by real indignation to accusation. But even upon those persons We impose the law that they shall have the right to suppress the accusation by annulment of the suit. The husband above all ought to be the avenger of the marriage bed, since to him the former Emperors of olden time granted the right to accuse the wife even on suspicion and not to be bound by the bond of inscription within the statutory time limits. [*Theodosian Code,* 326 C.E.]

IV. DIVORCE

It is our pleasure that no woman, on account of her own depraved desires, shall be permitted to send a notice of divorce to her husband on trumped-up grounds; as, for instance, that he is a drunkard or a gambler or a philanderer, nor indeed shall a husband be allowed to divorce his wife on every sort of pretext. But when a woman sends a notice of divorce, the following criminal charges only shall be investigated, that is, if she should prove that her husband is a homicide, a sorcerer, or a destroyer of tombs, so that the wife may thus earn commendation and at length recover her entire dowry. For if she should send a notice of divorce to her husband on grounds other than these three criminal charges, she must leave everything, even to her last hairpin, in her husband's home, and as punishment for her supreme self-confidence, she shall be deported to an island. In the case of a man also, if he should send a notice of divorce, inquiry shall be made as to the following three criminal charges, namely, if he wishes to divorce her as an adulteress, a sorceress, or a procuress [panderer]. For if he should cast off a wife who is innocent of these crimes, he must restore her entire dowry, and he shall not marry another woman. But if he should do this, his former wife shall be given the right to enter and seize his home by force and to transfer to herself the entire dowry of his later wife in recompense for the outrage inflicted upon her [*The Theodosian Code,* 331 C.E.]

On Property Rights

After the time of Augustus, the adulterous wife lost half her dowry.

It is to the interest of the state that women [in case of divorce] should have their dowries preserved in order that they can marry again.

The cause of the dowry always and everywhere takes precedence, for it is to the public interest for dowries to be preserved for wives, as it is absolutely necessary that women should be endowed for the procreation of progeny and to furnish the state with freeborn citizens.

When anyone desires to separate from a woman whom he married without a dowry, he shall not be permitted to do so, unless some fault is committed which is condemned by Our laws. If, however, he should reject her without her having been guilty of any fault, or he himself should commit such a fault . . . he shall be compelled to give her the fourth part of his own property [*Justinian Code,* 528 C.E.]

On Adultery

Although it is established by the contents of certain documents that you are consumed with the lust of immoderate desire, still, as it has been ascertained that you confined yourself to female slaves, and did not have intercourse with free women, it is clear that by a sentence of this kind your reputation suffers rather than that you become infamous [291 C.E.]

If any woman is discovered to have a clandestine love affair with her slave, she shall be subject to the capital sentence, and the rascally slave shall be delivered to the flames. All persons shall have the right to bring an accusation of this public crime. . . . [*Theodosian Code,* 326 C.E.]

STUDY QUESTIONS

1. What were some of the unusual legal protections offered to women in later Roman society?
2. What aspects of Roman law demonstrate that Rome was, at base, a patriarchal society?
3. How were men and women treated differently in cases of adultery?
4. What caused Rome's willingness to extend certain protections to women? What factors did Augustus suggest? Can you think of other factors?
5. How did women's conditions in Rome compare with those in other classical societies, such as China and India? How did the evaluation of women compare to that of Aristotle, in classical Greece (Chapter 19)?

23 THE FALL OF ROME

During the 4th and 5th centuries, the Roman Empire declined fairly steadily. By the late 5th century, the Empire in the West—Italy, Spain, part of North Africa, and also western Europe—had virtually disappeared. This was a huge development that broke the unity of the Mediterranean world and ushered in a period of considerable chaos in western Europe. The Empire in the eastern Mediterranean was less affected, and, transitioning into what became known as the Byzantine Empire, continued to operate effectively for many centuries.

People at the time, and scholars since, have tried to understand what caused this collapse of the western Empire. Some scholars have assumed that empires inevitably fall after a period of prosperity. A few have blamed sunspots, or the rise of Christianity that (it was claimed) sapped the fighting spirit of the Roman people. Explanations today focus on some combination of internal deterioration, probably furthered by the impact of extensive epidemic disease, plus the pressure of outside invasion, particularly by Germanic tribes.

It was obvious at the time that something was going badly wrong. People wondered how an empire that had attained such glory could fall to low estate. Some ordinary people had never been convinced of the merits of Roman rule or had become discouraged by long periods of high taxes and ineffective administration, so they welcomed the change. But others were more troubled.

The first of the following two passages written by a retired soldier, Ammianus Marcellinus, between 386 and 389 C.E. He wrote roughly 10 years after the battle of Adrianople, in the Balkans. There the Visigoths, a Germanic tribe, had defeated the Roman army under Emperor Valens, two years after they began pouring across the Danube River.

Marcellinus offers a pretty clear picture of what went wrong: Fierce Huns (a nomadic group pressing in from Central Asia) pressed the Germans, who in turn successfully pressed the Romans. His account attempts to describe what qualities of the Huns made them so hard to deal with. Is it credible? He also makes a stab at explaining why the Romans could not hold fast, which really offers a second causal explanation besides the more obvious focus on invasion.

Scholars today would not accept this explanation entirely, arguing that Marcellinus exaggerated on a number of points concerning the invaders, and simply missed some of the more basic trends that sapped Roman economic as well as political and military strength. The document raises obvious issues of interpretation. However, it is also important as evidence of ways that people who were at the time friendly to the Empire, could try to make sense of what was happening around them.

Selection I from James Harvey Robinson, *Readings in European History*, Vol. I (New York: Ginn and Company, 1904), pp. 35–39. Selection II from William Stearns Davis, *Readings in Ancient History*, Vol. I: *Rome and the West* (Boston: Allyn and Bacon, 1913), pp. 318–19.

The second passage was written by a Roman, Rutilus Numantius, who had been born in Gaul (France) but became the prefect (governor) of Rome in 413 C.E., as the empire was definitively falling apart. He was a pagan, probably hostile to Christianity. He was obviously highly enthusiastic about the qualities of Rome and its empire. Yet, writing in a time of obvious collapse, his passage invites interpretation: despite its obvious positive qualities does it unwittingly reflect Rome's decline? Certainly the passage invites analysis of what was being lost by Rome's fall in Western Europe, and of how loyal Romans might react when the Western empire disappeared entirely.

MARCELLINUS AND RUTILIUS NUMANTIUS

I. MARCELLINUS

The people called Huns, barely mentioned in ancient records, live beyond the sea of Azof, on the border of the Frozen Ocean, and are a race savage beyond all parallel. At the very moment of birth the cheeks of their infant children are deeply marked by an iron, in order that the hair, instead of growing in the proper season on their faces, may be hindered by the scars; accordingly the Huns grow up without beards, and without any beauty. They all have closely knit and strong limbs and plump necks; they are of great size, and low legged, so that you might fancy them two-legged beasts, or the stout figures which are hewn out in a rude manner with an ax on the posts at the end of bridges.

They are certainly in the shape of men, however uncouth, and are so hardy that they neither require fire nor well flavored food, but live on the roots of such herbs as they get in the fields, or on the half-raw flesh of any animal, which they merely warm rapidly by placing it between their own thighs and the backs of their horses.

They never shelter themselves under roofed houses, but avoid them, as people ordinarily avoid sepulchers as things not fit for common use. Nor is there even to be found among them a cabin thatched with reeds; but they wander about, roaming over the mountains and the woods, and accustom themselves to bear frost and hunger and thirst from their very cradles. . . .

There is not a person in the whole nation who cannot remain on his horse day and night. On horseback they buy and sell, they take their meat and drink, and there they recline on the narrow neck of their steed, and yield to sleep so deep as to indulge in every variety of dream.

And when any deliberation is to take place on any weighty matter, they all hold their common council on horseback. They are not under kingly authority, but are contented with the irregular government of their chiefs, and under their lead they force their way through all obstacles. . . .

None of them plow, or even touch a plow handle, for they have no settled abode, but are homeless and lawless, perpetually wandering with their wagons, which they make their homes; in fact, they seem to be people always in flight. . . .

This active and indomitable race, being excited by an unrestrained desire of plundering the possessions of others, went on ravaging and slaughtering all the nations in their neighborhood till they reached the Alani. . . .

[After having harassed the territory of the Alani and having slain many of them and acquired much plunder, the Huns made a treaty of friendship and alliance with those who survived. The allies then attacked the German peoples to the west.] In the meantime a report spread far and wide through the nations of the Goths, that a race of men, hitherto unknown, had suddenly descended like a whirlwind from the lofty mountains, as if they had risen from some secret recess of the earth, and were ravaging and destroying everything which came their way.

And then the greater part of the population resolved to flee and to seek a home remote from all knowledge of the new barbarians; and after long deliberation as to where to fix their abode, they resolved that a retreat into Thrace was the most suitable for these two reasons: first of all, because it is a district most fertile in grass, and secondly, because, owing to the great breadth of the Danube, it is wholly separated from the districts exposed to the impending attacks of the invaders.

Accordingly, under the command of their leader Alavivus, they occupied the banks of the Danube, and sent ambassadors to the emperor Valens, humbly entreating to be received by him as his subjects. They promised to live quietly, and to furnish a body of auxiliary troops if necessary.

While these events were taking place abroad, the terrifying rumor reached us that the tribes of the north were planning new and unprecedented attacks upon us; and that over the whole region which extends from the country of the Marcomanni and Quadi to Pontus, hosts of barbarians composed of various nations, which had suddenly been driven by force from their own countries, were now, with all their families, wandering about in different directions on the banks of the river Danube.

At first this intelligence was lightly treated by our people, because they were not in the habit of hearing of any wars in those remote districts till they were terminated either by victory or by treaty.

But presently the belief in these occurrences grew stronger and was confirmed by the arrival of ambassadors, who, with prayers and earnest entreaties, begged that their people, thus driven from their homes and now encamped on the other side of the river, might be kindly received by us.

The affair now seemed a cause of joy rather than of fear, according to the skillful flatterers who were always extolling and exaggerating the good fortune of the emperor. They congratulated him that an embassy had come from the farthest corners of the earth, unexpectedly offering him a large body of recruits; and that, by combining the strength of his own people with these foreign forces, he would have an army absolutely invincible. They observed further that the payment for military reïnforcements, which came in every year from the provinces, might now be saved and accumulated in his coffers and form a vast treasure of gold.

Full of this hope, he sent forth several officers to bring this ferocious people and their carts into our territory. And such great pains were taken to gratify this nation which was destined to overthrow the Empire of Rome, that not one was left behind, not even of those who were stricken with mortal disease. Moreover, so soon as they had obtained permission of the emperor to cross the Danube and to cultivate some districts in Thrace, they poured across the stream day and night, without ceasing, embarking in troops on board ships and rafts and on canoes made of the hollow trunks of trees. . . .

In this way, through the turbulent zeal of violent people, the ruin of the Roman Empire was brought about. This, at all events, is neither obscure nor uncertain, that the unhappy officers who were intrusted with the charge of conducting the multitude of the barbarians across the river, though they repeatedly endeavored to calculate their numbers, at last abandoned the attempt as hopeless. The man who would wish to ascertain the number might as well (as the most illustrious of poets says) attempt to count the waves in the African sea, or the grains of sand tossed about by the zephyrs. . . .

At that period, moreover, the defenses of our provinces were much exposed, and the armies of barbarians spread over them like the lava of Mount Etna. The imminence of our danger manifestly called for generals already illustrious for their past achievements in war; but nevertheless, as if some unpropitious deity had made the selection, the men who were sought out for the chief military appointments were of tainted character. The chief among them were Lupicinus and Maximus,— the one being count of Thrace, the other a leader notoriously wicked,—both men of great ignorance and rashness.

And their treacherous covetousness was the cause of all our disasters. . . . For when the barbarians who had been conducted across the river were in great distress from want of provisions, those detested generals conceived the idea of a most disgraceful traffic; and having collected dogs from all quarters with the most insatiable rapacity, they exchanged them for an equal number of slaves, among whom were several sons of men of noble birth. . . .

[After narrating the events which led up to the battle of Adrianople, and vividly describing the battle itself, Ammianus thus records the death of the emperor Valens:]

So now, with rage flashing in their eyes, the barbarians pursued our men, who were in a state of torpor [lethargy], the warmth of their veins having deserted them. Many were slain without knowing who smote them; some were overwhelmed by the mere weight of the crowd which pressed upon them; and some died of wounds inflicted by their own comrades. The barbarians spared neither those who yielded nor those who resisted. . . .

Just when it first became dark, the emperor, being among a crowd of common soldiers as it was believed,—for no one said either that he had seen him or been near him,—was mortally wounded with an arrow, and, very shortly after, died, though his body was never found. For as some of the enemy loitered for a long time about the field in order to plunder the dead, none of the defeated army or of the inhabitants ventured to go to them.

II. RUTILIUS NUMANTIUS

Give ear to me, Queen of the world which thou rulest, O Rome, whose place is amongst the stars! Give ear to me, mother of men, and mother gods!

Through thy temples we draw near to the very heaven. Thee do we sing, yea and while the Fates give us life, thee we *will* sing. For who can live and forget thee? Before thy image my soul is abased—graceless and sacrilegious, it were better for me to forget the sun, for thy beneficent influence shinest—even as his light—to the limits of the habitable world. Yea the sun himself, in his vast course, seems only to turn in thy behalf. He riseth upon thy domains; and on thy domains, it is again that he setteth.

As far as from one pole to the other spreadeth the vital power of nature, so far thy virtue hath penetrated over the earth. For all the scattered nations thou createst one common country. Those that struggle against thee are constrained to bend to thy yoke; for thou profferest to the conquered the partnership in thy just laws; thou hast made one city what was aforetime the wide world!

O Queen, the remotest regions of the universe join in a hymn to thy glory! Our heads are raised freely under thy peaceful yoke. For thee to reign, is less than to have so deserved to reign; the grandeur of thy deeds surpasses even thy might destinies.

STUDY QUESTIONS

1. What aspects of Marcellinus's account seem most accurate? What points seem least accurate, and what explains why Marcellinus would be prone to exaggerate?
2. How does Marcellinus explain Roman failure in the face of the barbarians? Are his explanations plausible? Do they suggest deeper internal weakness in Rome's state and society?
3. Does Marcellinus's account suggest some characteristic difficulties in explaining major disasters in a society?
4. Does the passage by Rutilius Numantius provide other kinds of evidence about Rome's decline, or should it be interpreted as a sign that things were not as bad as later historians have suggested?
5. What does Rutilius suggest about Rome's legacy, after the empire disappeared? How would loyal Romans of this sort react to the Germanic kingdoms that replaced Rome in the West?
6. What other kinds of evidence are necessary to figure out what went wrong during the later Roman Empire?
7. What do you think the main causes are that explain the frequent decline of once-great societies? Are there common patterns? Were the factors involved in western Rome unusual?

GLOBAL CONTACTS
AND WORLD RELIGION

24   GLOBAL CONTACTS: THE RISE OF THE PASTORAL NOMADS

One of the most important developments during the classical period was the rise of the pastoral nomads in Central Asia. From 500 B.C.E. onward, successive groups of horse riders dominated the wide swath of grasslands stretching from Mongolia to the region north of the Black Sea. For nearly two millennia the success or failure of rulers in China, India, Persia, and Russia often depended on their ability to mobilize effective defenses against—or trade with—the nomadic horse riders.

The first of the great nomadic confederations or "states" in eastern Central Asia was established around 200 B.C.E. by the people known to the Chinese as the Xiongnu. Based on the plains of present-day Mongolia, the Xiongnu were herders and hunters who occasionally engaged in trade with Chinese merchants. In times of hardship on the prairie, however, the Xiongnu frequently turned to raiding the storehouses of Chinese peasants to obtain grain and other necessities.

For the Xiongnu, the unification of China in 221 B.C.E. by Qin Shi Huangdi, also known as the First Emperor, was an ominous development. Soon after establishing his rule, the First Emperor had walls built along his northern frontier. (Much later, these separate walls were joined together to form the Great Wall.) The Chinese walls were built to fence out the nomads and, equally important to the First Emperor, to fence in potential Chinese allies of the nomads.

As the Chinese walls went up, the Xiongnu began to unite their traditionally fractious neighbors on the grasslands into a formidable military force. For the next 250 years, until the Xiongnu confederation unraveled in the 1st century C.E., the emperors of the Han dynasty were compelled to devote considerable attention to relations with the nomads. Indeed, relations with the successors of the Xiongnu on the grasslands of Central Asia remained a major priority for Chinese rulers until after 1700 C.E.

Because the Xiongnu did not have a system of writing, our richest sources of documentary evidence about them come from the writings of Chinese historians. The

Selections I, II, and III from *Records of the Grand Historian*, translated by Burton Watson. Copyright © 1993 Columbia University Press. Reprinted with permission of the publisher.

following account of the rise of the Xiongnu comes from the work of the greatest of the early Chinese historians, Sima Qian (ca. 145–90 B.C.E.), who probably relied on information obtained from Chinese officials, soldiers and merchants who had contacts with the nomads. How do the passages help us to understand the Xiongnu and their relations with the Chinese?

A CHINESE HISTORIAN DESCRIBES THE NOMADS

I. XIONGNU LIFEWAYS

The ancestor of the Xiongnu was a descendant of the rulers of the Xia dynasty [ca. 2000–1750 B.C.E.] by the name of Chunwei. As early as the time of Emperors Yao and Shun and before, we hear of these people, known as Mountain Barbarians, . . . living in the region of the northern barbarians and wandering from place to place pasturing their animals. The animals they raise consist mainly of horses, cows, and sheep, but include such rare beasts as camels, asses, mules, and wild horses. . . . They move about in search of water and pasture and have no walled cities or fixed dwellings, nor do they engage in any kind of agriculture. Their lands, however, are divided into regions under the control of various leaders. They have no writing, and even promises and agreements are only verbal. The little boys start out by learning to ride sheep and shoot birds and rats with a bow and arrow, and when they get a little older they shoot foxes and hares, which are used for food. Thus all the young men are able to use a bow and act as armed cavalry in time of war. It is their custom to herd their flocks in times of peace and make their living by hunting, but in periods of crisis they take up arms and go off on plundering and marauding expeditions. This seems to be their inborn nature. For long-range weapons they use bows and arrows, and swords and spears at close range. If the battle is going well for them they will advance, but if not, they will retreat, for they do not consider it a disgrace to run away. Their only concern is self-advantage, and they know nothing of propriety or righteousness.

From the chiefs of the tribe on down, everyone eats the meat of the domestic animals and wears clothes of hide or wraps made of felt or fur. The young men eat the richest and best food, while the old get what is left over, since the tribe honors those who are young and strong and despises the weak and aged. On the death of his father, a son will marry his stepmother, and when brothers die, the remaining brothers will take the widows for their own wives. . . .

Under the *Shanyu* [the Xiongnu leader] are the Wise Kings of the Left and Right, the left and right Luli kings, left and right generals, left and right commandants, left and right household administrators, and left and right Gudu marquises. The Xiongnu word for "wise" is "*tuqi*," so that the heir of the *Shanyu* is customarily called the "*Tuqi* King of the Left." Among the other leaders, from the wise kings on down to the household administrators, the more important ones command ten thousand horsemen and the lesser ones several thousand, numbering twenty-four leaders in all, though all are known by the title of "Ten Thousand Horsemen." The high ministerial offices are hereditary, being filled from generation to generation by the members of the Huyen and Lan families, and in more recent times by the Xubu family. These three families constitute the aristocracy of the nation. The kings and other leaders of the left live in the eastern sector, the region from Shanggu east to the lands of the Huimo and Chaoxian peoples. The kings and leaders of the right live in the west, the area from Shang Province west to the territories of the Yuezhi and Qiang tribes. The *Shanyu* has his court in the region north of Dai and Yunzhong. Each group has its own area, within which it moves about from place to place looking for water and pasture. The Left and Right Wise Kings and Luli kings are the most powerful, while the Gudu marquises assist the *Shanyu* in the administration of the nation. Each of the twenty-four leaders in turn appoints his own "chiefs of a thousand," "chiefs of a hundred," and "chiefs of ten," as well as his subordinate kings, prime ministers, chief commandants, household administrators, *zhuqu* officials, and so forth.

In the first month of the year the various leaders come together in a small meeting of the *Shanyu*'s court to perform sacrifices, and in the fifth month a great meeting is held at Longcheng at which sacrifices are conducted to the Xiongnu ancestors, Heaven and Earth, and the gods and spirits. In the autumn, when the horses are fat, another great meeting is held at the Dai Forest when a reckoning is made of the number of persons and animals.

According to Xiongnu law, anyone who in ordinary times draws his sword a foot from the scabbard is condemned to death. Anyone convicted of theft has his property confiscated. Minor offenses are punished by flogging and major ones by death. No one is kept in jail awaiting sentence longer than ten days, and the number of imprisoned men for the whole nation does not exceed a handful.

At dawn the *Shanyu* leaves his camp and makes obeisance to the sun as it rises, and in the evening he makes a similar obeisance to the moon. In seating arrangements the left side or the seat facing north is considered the place of honor. The days *wu* and *ji* of the ten-day week are regarded as most auspicious.

In burials the Xiongnu use an inner and an outer coffin, with accessories of gold, silver, clothing, and fur, but they do not construct grave mounds or plant trees on the grave, nor do they use mourning garments. When a ruler dies, the ministers and concubines who were favored by him and who are obliged to follow him in death often number in the hundreds or even thousands.

Whenever the Xiongnu begin some undertaking, they observe the stars and the moon. They attack when the moon is full and withdraw their troops when it wanes. After a battle those who have cut off the heads of the enemy or taken prisoners are presented with a cup of wine and allowed to keep the spoils they have captured. Any prisoners that are taken are made slaves. Therefore, when they fight, each man strives for his own gain. They are very skillful at using decoy troops to lure their opponents to destruction. When they catch sight of the enemy, they swoop down like a flock of birds, eager for booty, but when they find themselves hard pressed and beaten, they scatter and vanish like the mist. Anyone who succeeds in recovering the body of a comrade who has fallen in battle receives all of the dead man's property. . . .

II. THE RISE OF MODUN

At this time [around 210 B.C.E.] the Eastern Barbarians were very powerful and the Yuezhi were likewise flourishing. The *Shanyu* or chieftain of the Xiongnu was named Touman. Touman, unable to hold out against the Qin [Chinese] forces, had withdrawn to the far north, where he lived with his subjects for over ten years. After Mengtion died and the feudal lords revolted against the Qin, plunging China into a period of strife and turmoil, the convicts which the Qin had sent to the northern border to garrison the area all returned to their homes. The Xiongnu, the pressure against them relaxed, once again began to infiltrate south of the bend of the Yellow River until they had established themselves along the old border of China.

Touman's oldest son, the heir apparent to his position, was named Modun, but the *Shanyu* also had a younger son by another consort whom he had taken later and was very fond of. He decided that he wanted to get rid of Modun and set up his younger son as heir instead, and he therefore sent Modun as a hostage to the Yuezhi nation. Then, after Modun had arrived among the Yuezhi, Touman made a sudden attack on them. The Yuezhi were about to kill Modun in retaliation, but he managed to steal one of their best horses and escape, eventually making his way back home. His father, struck by his bravery, put him in command of a force of ten thousand cavalry.

Modun had some arrows made that whistled in flight and used them to drill his troops in shooting from horseback. "Shoot wherever you see my whistling arrow strike!" he ordered, "and anyone who fails to shoot will be cut down!" Then he went out hunting for birds and animals, and if any of his men failed to shoot at what he himself had shot at, he cut them down on the spot. After this, he shot a whistling arrow at one of his best horses. Some of his men hung back and did not dare shoot at the horse, whereupon Modun at once executed them. A little later he took an arrow and shot at his favorite wife. Again some of his men shrank back in

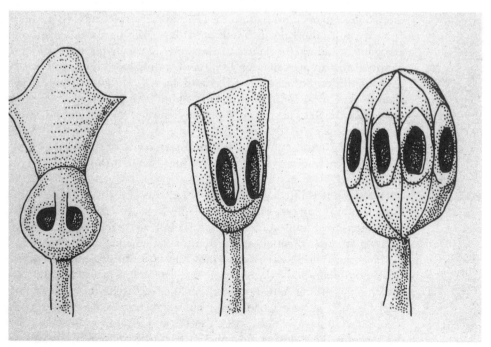

Whistling Arrowheads. (Gillian Jones from *The Mongols* by E.D. Phillips, Thames & Hudson Ltd., London)

terror and failed to discharge their arrows, and again he executed them on the spot. Finally he went out hunting with his men and shot a whistling arrow at one of his father's finest horses. All his followers promptly discharged their arrows in the same direction, and Modun knew that at last they could be trusted. Accompanying his father, the *Shanyu* Touman, on a hunting expedition, he shot a whistling arrow at his father and every one of his followers aimed their arrows in the same direction and shot the *Shanyu* dead. Then Modun executed his stepmother, his younger brother, and all the high officials of the nation who refused to take orders from him, and set himself up as the new *Shanyu*.

III. THE REIGN OF MODUN, 209–174 B.C.E.

At this time the Eastern Barbarians were very powerful and, hearing that Modun had killed his father and made himself leader, they sent an envoy to ask if they could have Touman's famous horse that could run 1,000 *li* in one day. Modun consulted his ministers, but they all replied, "The thousand-*li* horse is one of the treasures of the Xiongnu people. You should not give it away!"

"When a neighbouring country asked for it, why should I begrudge them one horse?" he said, and sent them the thousand-*li* horse.

After a while the Eastern Barbarians, supposing that Modun was afraid of them, sent an envoy to ask for one of Modun's consorts. Again Modun questioned his ministers, and they replied in a rage, "The Eastern Barbarians are unreasoning beasts to come and request one of the *Shanyu*'s consorts. We beg to attack them!"

But Modun replied, "If it is for a neighboring country, why should I begrudge them one woman?" and he sent his favorite consort to the Eastern Barbarians.

With this the ruler of the Eastern Barbarians grew more and more bold and arrogant, invading the lands to the west. Between his territory and that of the Xiongnu was an area of over 1,000 *li* of uninhabited land; the two peoples made their homes on either side of this wasteland [the Gobi Desert]. The ruler of the Eastern Barbarians sent an envoy to Modun saying, "The Xiongnu have no way of using this stretch of wasteland which lies between my border and yours. I would like to take possession of it!"

When Modun consulted his ministers, some of them said, "Since the land is of no use you might as well give it to him," while others said, "No, you must not give it away!"

Modun flew into a rage. "Land is the basis of the nation!" he said. "Why should I give it away?" And he executed all the ministers who had advised him to do so.

Then he mounted his horse and set off to attack the Eastern Barbarians, circulating an order throughout his domain that anyone who was slow to follow would be executed. The Eastern Barbarians had up until this time despised Modun and made no preparations for their defence; when Modun and his soldiers arrived, they inflicted a crushing defeat, killing the ruler of the Eastern Barbarians, taking prisoner his subjects, and seizing their domestic animals. Then he returned and rode west, attacking and routing the Yuezhi, and annexed the lands of the ruler of Loufan and the ruler of Boyang south of the Yellow River. Thus he recovered possession of all the lands which the Qin general Meng Tian had taken away from the Xiongnu; the border between his territory and that of the Han empire now followed the old line of defences south of the Yellow River, and from there he marched into the Chaona and Fushi districts and then invaded Yan and Dai. . . .

At this time Gaozu [reigned 202–195 B.C.E.], the founder of the Han, had just succeeded in winning control of the empire and had transferred Xin, the former king of Hann, to the rulership of Dai, with his capital at Mayi. The Xiongnu surrounded Mayi and attacked the city in great force, whereupon Hann Xin surrendered to them. With Hann Xin on their side, they then proceeded to lead their troops south across Mt. Juzhu and attack Taiyuan, marching as far as the city of Jinyang. Emperor Gaozu led an army in person to attack them, but it was winter and he encountered such cold and heavy snow that two or three out of every ten of his men lost their fingers from frostbite. Modun feigned a retreat to lure the Han soldiers on to an attack. When they came after him in pursuit, he concealed all of his best troops and left only his weakest and puniest men to be observed by the Han scouts. With this the entire Han force, supplemented by 320,000 infantry, rushed north to pursue him; Gaozu led the way, advancing as far as the city of Pingcheng.

Before the infantry had had a chance to arrive, however, Modun swooped down with 400,000 of his best cavalry, surrounded Gaozu on White Peak, and held him there for seven days. The Han forces within the encirclement had no way of receiving aid or provisions from their comrades outside, since the Xiongnu cavalry surrounded them on all sides, with white horses on the west side, greenish horses on the east, black horses on the north, and red ones on the south.

Gaozu sent an envoy in secret to Modun's consort, presenting her with generous gifts, whereupon she spoke to Modun, saying, "Why should the rulers of these two nations make such trouble for each other? Even if you gained possession of the Han lands, you could never occupy them, and the ruler of the Han may have his guardian deities as well as you. I beg you to consider the matter well!"

Modun had previously arranged for the troops of Wang Huang and Zhao Li, two of Hann Xin's generals, to meet with him, but though the appointed time had come, they failed to appear and he began to suspect that they were plotting with the Han forces. He therefore decided to listen to his consort's advice and withdrew his forces from one corner of the encirclement. Gaozu ordered his men to load their crossbows with arrows and hold them in readiness pointed toward the outside. These preparations completed, they marched straight out of the encirclement and finally joined up with the rest of the army.

Modun eventually withdrew his men and went away, and Gaozu likewise retreated and abandoned the campaign, dispatching Liu Jing to conclude a peace treaty with the Xiongnu instead. . . .

At this time a number of Han generals had gone over to the side of the Xiongnu, and for this reason Modun was constantly plundering the region of Dai and causing the Han great worry. Gaozu therefore dispatched Liu Jing to present a princess of the imperial family to the *Shanyu* to be his consort. The Han agreed to send a gift of specified quantities of silk floss and cloth, grain, and other food stuffs each year, and the two nations were to live in peace and brotherhood. After this Modun raided the frontier less often than before. Later Lu Wan, the king of Yan, revolted and led his party of several thousand followers across the border to surrender to the Xiongnu; they roamed back and forth in the region from Shanggu to the east, causing considerable disturbance. . . .

STUDY QUESTIONS

1. What do we learn from Sima Qian about the Xiongnu? What does the historian observe about the nomads' economy, political system, class structure, and religion?

2. According to Sima Qian, what seems to explain the rise of Modun as the Xiongnu *Shanyu*?

3. Based on your reading of Sima Qian, how would you characterize relations between the Xiongnu and the Chinese? What elements of accommodation between the two adversaries do you see? How did the Chinese attempt to manage relations with the nomads?

4. Does Sima Qian reveal a point of view toward the Xiongnu? Is he a Confucian (see Chapters 7, 10, and 11)? Is he hostile to the nomads?

5. How do the lifeways of the Xiongnu compare with those of the Huns (the two peoples were probably distantly related) as described by the Roman historian Marcellinus in the 4th century C.E. (see Chapter 23)? What similarities/ differences do you see in between the Xiongnu and the Huns? Do the two writers, one Chinese and the other Roman, differ in their descriptions of the barbarians? Which of the two accounts seems more realistic? How do you explain this?

25 GLOBAL CONTACTS: THE OPENING OF THE SILK ROAD

During the early Han dynasty (206 B.C.E.–220 C.E.) Chinese emperors began to send large amounts of silk—for both diplomatic and commercial reasons—to the nomads of Central Asia, especially the Xiongnu. Within a short time some of this silk found its way, by means of a type of relay trade, to Rome. Modern scholars refer to the East-West routes on which the fabric, and other commodities, moved as the Silk Road. By 100 C.E. the land routes linking China to Rome also had a maritime counterpart. Seaborne commerce flourished between Rome and India via the Red Sea and the Arabian Sea. Other routes farther east, connected Indian ports with harbors in Southeast Asia and China.

A great Afro-Eurasian commercial network had now come into being. Silk from China (the only country that produced it until after 500 C.E.), pepper and jewels from India, and incense from Arabia were sent to the Mediterranean region on routes that terminated in Roman cities such as Alexandria, Gaza, Antioch, and Ephesus. In exchange for the precious commodities, the Romans sent large amounts of silver and gold eastward to destinations in Asia.

Because the long-distance trade of the classical period was mainly in luxuries rather than in articles of daily use, its overall economic impact was probably limited. Most present-day historians think that the Rome-India-China trade was significant primarily because of its role in promoting the spread of religions, styles of art, technologies, and epidemic diseases.

The following selections are a mixture of Chinese and Roman evidence. How does the variety of materials in this chapter suggest the growth of long-distance contacts during the classical period?

Selection I from *Records of the Grand Historian by Sima Qian: Han Dynasty II*, revised ed. Translated by Burton Watson (New York: Columbia University Press, 1993), pp. 231–233. Selection II "Chinese Gifts of Silk to the Xiongnu" from *Trade and Expansion in Han China: A Study in the Structure of Sino-Barbarian Relations* by Ying-shih Yu (Berkeley: University of California Press, 1967), p. 47. Selection III. Reprinted by permission of the publishers and the Trustees of the Loeb Classical Library from *Seneca*: Volume III *Moral Essays*, LCL # 310, translated by John W. Basore, Cambridge Mass.: Harvard University Press, 1935. The Loeb Classical Library ® is a registered trademark of the President and Fellows of Harvard College. Selection III. from Suetonius, *The Twelve Caesars: Gaius Suetonius Tranquillus*, translated by Robert Graves (Baltimore: Penguin Books, 1957). Permission granted by Carcanet press limited. Selection IV from *The Travels of Fa-hsien (399–414 A.D.)*, or *Record of the Buddhistic Kingdoms*, translated by H. A. Giles (Cambridge University Press, 1923), pp. 76–79, 81.

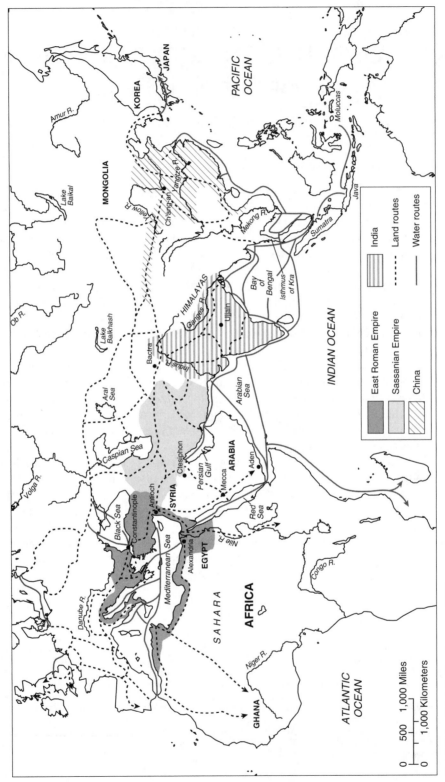

Established Trade Routes, ca. 600 C.E.

CHINESE AND ROMAN SOURCES

I. ZHANG QIAN'S JOURNEY WEST

[The description of Zhang Qian's mission to Central Asia comes from Sima Qian, the Chinese historian who authored the description of the Xiongnu nomads in Chapter 24. Although pinpointing the places early travelers visited is a notoriously difficult problem, modern researchers think that Zhang Qian probably journeyed as far as today's Kyrgyzstan (Chinese: Dayuan) and Afghanistan (Chinese: Daxia).]

Zhang Qian was the first person to bring back a clear accout of Dayuan [Kyrgyztan]. He was a native of Hanzhong and served as a palace attendant during the *jianyuan* era (140–135 B.C.E.). At this time the emperor [Han Wudi, reigned 140–87 B.C.E.] questioned various Xiongnu who had surrendered to the Han and they all reported that the Xiongnu had defeated the king of the Yuezhi people [also pastoral nomads] and made his skull into a drinking vessel. As a result the Yuezhi had fled and bore a constant grudge against the Xiongnu, though as yet they had been unable to find anyone to join them in an attack on their enemy.

The Han at this time was engaged in a concerted effort to destroy the Xiongnu, and therefore, when the emperor heard this, he decided to try to send an envoy to establish relations with the Yuezhi. To reach them, however, an envoy would inevitably have to pass through Xiongnu territory. The emperor accordingly sent out a summons for men capable of undertaking such a mission. Zhang Qian, who was a palace attendant at the time, answered the summons and was appointed as envoy to the Yuezhi.

He set out from Longxi, accompanied by Ganfu, a Xiongnu slave who belonged to a family in Tangyi. They travelled west through the territory of the Xiongnu and were captured by the Xiongnu and taken before the *Shanyu*. The *Shanyu* detained them and refused to let them proceed. "The Yuezhi people live north of me," he said. "What does the Han mean by trying to send an envoy to them! Do you suppose that if I tried to send an embassy to the kingdom of Yue in the southeast the Han would let my men pass through China?"

The Xiongnu detained Zhang Qian for over ten years and gave him a wife from their own people, by whom he had a son. Zhang Qian never once relinquished the imperial credentials that marked him as an envoy of the Han, however, and after he had lived in Xiongnu territory for some time and was less closely watched than at first, he and his party finally managed to escape and resume their journey toward the Yuezhi.

After hastening west for twenty or thirty days, they reached the kingdom of Dayuan. The king of Dayuan had heard of the wealth of the Han empire and wished to establish communication with it, though as yet he had been unable to do so. When he met Zhang Qian he was overjoyed and asked where Zhang Qian wished to go.

"I was dispatched as envoy of the Han to the Yuezhi, but the Xiongnu blocked my way and I have only just now managed to escape," he replied. "I beg Your Highness to give me some guides to show me the way. If I can reach my destination and return to the Han to make my report, the Han will reward you with countless gifts!"

The king of Dayuan trusted his words and sent him on his way, giving him guides and interpreters to take him to the state of Kangju [Uzbekistan]. From there he was able to make his way to the land of the Great Yuezhi.

Since the king of the Great Yuezhi had been killed by the Xiongnu, his son had succeeded him as ruler and had forced the kingdom of Daxia [Afghanistan] to recognize his sovereignty. The region he ruled was rich and fertile and seldom troubled by invaders, and the king thought only of his own enjoyment. He considered the Han too far away to bother with and had no particular intention of avenging his father's death by attacking the Xiongnu. From the court of the Yuezhi, Zhang Qian travelled on to the state of Daxia, but in the end he was never able to interest the Yuezhi in his proposals.

After spending a year or so in the area, he began to journey back along the Nanshan or Southern Mountains, intending to re-enter China through the territory of the Qiang barbarians, but he was once more captured by the Xiongnu and detained for over a year.

Just at this time the *Shanyu* died and the Luli King of the Left attacked the *Shanyu's* heir and set himself up as the new *Shanyu* (126 B.C.E.). As a result of this the whole Xiongnu nation was in turmoil and Zhang Qian, along with his Xiongnu wife and the former slave Ganfu, was able to escape and return to China. The emperor honoured Zhang Qian with the post of palace counsellor and awarded Ganfu the title of "Lord Who Carries Out His Mission".

Zhang Qian was a man of great strength, determination, and generosity. He trusted others and in turn was liked by the barbarians. Ganfu, who was a Xiongnu by birth, was good at archery, and whenever he and Zhang Qian were short of food he would shoot birds and beasts to keep them supplied. When Zhang Qian first set out on his mission, he was accompanied by over 100 men, but after thirteen years abroad, only he and Ganfu managed to make their way back to China.

Zhang Qian in person visited the lands of Dayuan, the Great Yuezhi, Daxia, and Kangju, and in addition he gathered reports on five or six other large states in the neighbourhood. All of his information he related to the emperor on his return. . . .

II. CHINESE "GIFTS" OF SILK TO THE XIONGNU

[Han Wudi used Zhang Qian's report to extend Chinese military power deep into Central Asia. A string of Chinese fortresses and checkpoints soon reached to Afghanistan. Diplomatic and commercial relations between the Chinese and the Central Asian nomads increased. At the heart of these contacts was the exchange of horses from Central Asia (called "tribute" by the Chinese) for silk from China (called "gifts" by the Chinese). The disguised trade of horses for silk along routes newly secured by the Chinese marks the opening of the Silk Road. One aspect of this trade is illustrated in the table.]

Year (B.C.E.)	Silk Floss (catties)	Silk Fabrics (pieces)
51	6,000	8,000
49	8,000	9,000
33	16,000	18,000
25	20,000	20,000
1	30,000	30,000

Note: 1 catty equals approximately 1/2 lb.

III. SILK IN ROME

A. Caesar's Canopies, ca. 50 B.C.E.

[The following passage from the historian Cassius Dio (164–224 C.E.) describes a huge celebration that Julius Caesar staged in his own honor around 50 B.C.E.]

If I mention one feature of his [Caesar's] extravagance at that time, I shall thereby give an idea of all the rest. In order that the sun might not annoy any of the spectators, he had curtains stretched over them made of silk, according to some accounts. Now this fabric is a device of barbarian luxury, and has come down from them even to us to gratify the fastidious taste of fine ladies.

B. Seneca on Silk and Gender

[The following passage from Seneca, a leading writer of the 1st century C.E., typifies much Roman writing about silk.]

I see there raiments of silk—if that can be called raiment, which provides nothing that could possibly afford protection for the body, or indeed modesty, so that, when a woman wears it, she can scarcely, with a clear conscience, swear that she is not naked. These are imported at vast expense from nations unknown even to trade, in order that our married women may not be able to show more of their persons, even to their paramours, in a bedroom than they do on the street.

C. An Emperor Wears Silk

[Suetonius, a leading historian of the 2nd century C.E., describes the clothing worn by Emperor Gaius (nicknamed "Caligula"), who reigned briefly in the 1st century.]

Caligula paid no attention to traditional or current fashions in his dress; ignoring male conventions and even the human decencies. Often he made public appearances in a cloak covered with embroidery and encrusted with precious stones, a long-sleeved tunic and bracelets; or in silk (which men were forbidden by law to wear) or even in a woman's robe; and came shod sometimes with slippers, sometimes with buskins, sometimes with military boots, sometimes with women's shoes. Occasionally he affected a golden beard and carried Jupiter's thunderbolt, Neptune's trident, or Mercury's serpent-twined staff. He even dressed up as Venus and, long before his expedition, wore the uniform of a triumphant general, often embellished with the breastplate which he had stolen from Alexander the Great's tomb at Alexandria. . . .

IV. SAILING FROM SRI LANKA TO CHINA: THE HOMEWARD JOURNEY OF A BUDDHIST MONK

[Around 400 C.E. a Chinese monk named Faxian traveled through Central Asia to India in order to visit the Buddhist holy places. After spending more than a decade away from home, the monk decided to return to China by sea. Departing from a port in Sri Lanka, he and his shipmates encountered stormy seas. Faxian's book about his travels is the earliest first-hand account of the sea route from India to China.]

Faxian remained in this country [Sri Lanka] for two years; and after repeated search he obtained a copy of the Disciplines according to the school of "The Faith Prevailing"; also copies of the long Agamas [Buddhist teachings] on cosmogony, and of the miscellaneous Agamas on ecstatic contemplation, and subsequently of a collection of extracts from the Canon, all of which China was without. When he had obtained these in Sanskrit, he took passage on board a large merchant-vessel, on which there were over two hundred souls, and astern of which there was a smaller vessel in tow, in case of accident at sea and destruction of the big vessel. Catching a fair wind, they sailed eastward for two days; then they encountered a heavy gale, and the vessel sprang a leak. The merchants wished to get aboard the smaller vessel; but the men on the latter, fearing that they would be swamped by numbers quickly cut the tow-rope in two. The merchants were terrified, for death was close at hand; and fearing that the vessel would fill, they promptly took what bulky goods there were and threw them into the sea. Faxian also took his pitcher and ewer, with whatever he could spare, and threw them into the sea; but he was afraid that the merchants would throw over his books and his images, and accordingly fixed his whole thoughts upon Guanyin, [the compassionate Bodhisattva], the Hearer of Prayers, and put his life into the hand of the Catholic [Buddhist] church in China, saying, "I have journeyed far on behalf of the Faith. Oh that by your awful power you would grant me a safe return from my wanderings."

The gale blew on for thirteen days and nights, when they arrived alongside of an island, and then, at ebb-tide, they saw the place where the vessel leaked and forthwith stopped it up, after which they again proceeded on their way.

This sea is infested with pirates, to meet whom is death. The expanse of ocean is boundless, east and west are not distinguishable; only by observation of the sun, moon, and constellations, is progress to be made. In cloudy and rainy weather, our vessel drifted at the mercy of the wind, without keeping any definite course. In the darkness of night nothing was to be seen but the great waves beating upon one another and flashing forth light like fire, huge turtles, sea-lizards, and such-like monsters of the deep. Then the merchants lost heart, not knowing whither they were going, and the sea being deep, without bottom, they had no place where they could cast their stone-anchor and stop. When the sky had cleared, they were able to tell east from west and again to proceed on their proper course; but had they struck a hidden rock, there would have been no way of escape.

And so they went on for more than ninety days until they reached a country named Java, where heresies and Brahmanism were flourishing, while the Faith of Buddha was in a very unsatisfactory condition.

After having remained in this country for five months or so, Faxian again shipped on board another large merchant-vessel which also carried over two hundred persons. They took with them provisions for fifty days and set sail on the 16th day of the 4th moon, and Faxian went into retreat on board the vessel.

A north-east course was set in order to reach Canton [today's Guangzhou in China]; and over a month had elapsed when one night in the second watch (9–11 p.m.) they encountered a violent gale with tempestuous rain, at which the travelling merchants and traders who were going to their homes were much frightened. However, Faxian once more invoked the Hearer of Prayers and the Catholic [Buddhist] Church in China, and was accorded the protection of their awful power until day broke. As soon as it was light, the Brahmans took counsel together and said, "Having this Shaman [monk] on board has been our undoing, causing us to get into this trouble. We ought to land the religious mendicant on some island; it is not right to endanger all our lives for one man." A "religious protector" of Faxian's replied, saying, "If you put this religious mendicant ashore, you shall also land me with him; if not, you had better kill me, for supposing that you land him, when I reach China I will report you to the king who is a reverent believer in the Buddhist Faith and honours religious mendicants." At this the merchants wavered and did not dare to land him just then.

Meanwhile, the sky was constantly darkened and the captain lost his reckoning. So they went of for seventy days until the provisions and water were nearly exhausted, and they had to use seawater for cooking, dividing the fresh water so that each man got about two pints. When all was nearly consumed, the merchants consulted together and said, "The ordinary time for the voyage to Canton is exactly fifty days. We have now exceeded that limit by many days; must we not have gone out of our course?"

Thereupon they proceeded in a northwesterly direction, seeking for land; and after twelve days and nights arrived south of the Lao mountain [on the Shandong Peninsula in China] at the boundary of the Prefecture of Changguang, where they obtained fresh water and vegetables.

And now, after having passed through much danger, difficulty, sorrow, and fear, suddenly reaching this shore and seeing the old familiar vegetables, they knew it was their fatherland. . . .

Faxian spent six years in travelling from Changan [today's Xi'an, the ancient Chinese capital] to Central India; he stayed there six years, and it took him three more to reach Qingzhou. The countries he passed through amounted to rather fewer than thirty. From the Sandy Desert westwards all the way to India, the dignified deportment of the priesthood and the good influence of the Faith were beyond all expression in detail. As, however, the ecclesiastics at home had had no means of hearing about these things, Faxian had given no thought to his own unimportant life, but came home across the sea, encountering still more difficulties and dangers. Happily, he was accorded protection by the divine majesty of the Precious [Buddhist] Trinity, and was thus preserved in the hour of danger. Therefore he wrote down on bamboo tablets and silk an account of what he had been through, desiring that the gentle reader should share this information.

STUDY QUESTIONS

1. What was the purpose of Zhang Qian's mission? Why were his diplomatic efforts unsuccessful? What is Sima Qian's overall judgment of the importance of Zhang Qian's travels?

2. How does the table illustrate the growth of contacts between the Chinese and the Xiongnu? What other kinds of evidence would be useful in documenting these contacts?

3. What are the main themes in the Roman writing about silk? How does silk seem to be related to Roman conceptions of masculinity and femininity? In what ways does the writing about silk suggest broader political, economic and social changes underway in Rome?

4. How did Faxian travel home? What does his mode of travel suggest about trade between India, Southeast Asia, and China in the late classical period? Who were the monk's shipmates? How does his voyage illustrate the connections between trade and religion?

5. How does Faxian's memoir illustrate the spread of Indian culture to Southeast Asia? How did Brahmanism and Buddhism get to Java?

6. Why do you think this chapter does not include an account of a Chinese traveler to Rome or an account of a Roman traveler to China?

7. In what sense did the process of "globalization" begin in the 1st century C.E.?

BUDDHIST *STUPA* IN SRI LANKA VISITED BY FAXIAN

When the Buddha died in 483 B.C.E., his body was cremated and its fragmentary remains were distributed to various locations in India where they were deposited in dome-shaped commemorative structures called *stupas*. Probably inspired by earlier traditions of interring kings in burial mounds, *stupas* gradually became one of the three main types of Buddhist architecture, the other two being prayer halls (*chaityas*) and monastic residential and lecture halls (*viharas*).

After Buddhism was introduced in Sri Lanka toward the end of the first millennium B.C.E., Sri Lankan kings sponsored the construction of monasteries and *stupas* in their capital at Anuradhapura. According to Sri Lankan tradition, one of these monasteries was home to a *bodhi* tree grown from a branch of the tree under which the Buddha had achieved enlightenment. A second monastery at Anuradhapura was thought to house, in great *stupa,* one of the Buddha's teeth.

The huge *stupa* shown here was one of many that the Chinese monk Faxian saw when he visited Anuradhapura in the early 5th century C.E. It illustrates features common to many *stupas:* a dome-shaped body (*anda*), a railed enclosure (*harmika*) at the top, and a spire (*yupa*) crowning the structure.

Buddhist *Stupa* at Anuradhapura, Sri Lanka, 3rd Century C.E. (Photo by Stephen S. Gosch)

STUDY QUESTIONS

1. What does the *stupa* suggest about the importance of Buddhism in Sri Lanka during the first millennium C.E.?
2. What does the *stupa* imply about the productivity of the Sri Lankan economy?
3. What do you think the key features of the *stupa* symbolize?
4. How does the *stupa* at Anuradhapura provide evidence of contacts between Sri Lanka and other countries?

26

MONKS AND MONARCHS: BUDDHISM SPREADS TO CHINA, KOREA, AND JAPAN

One of the most significant features of Buddhism during its 2,500-year history has been its extraordinary adaptability to diverse cultural and social settings. By the beginning of the Common Era Buddhism had spread widely in India, where its appeal seems to have been strongest among merchants and other urban groups, and in Sri Lanka, where it won favor from the peasants. In Central Asia, where it was introduced by monks and merchants from India, it caught on among pastoral nomads.

The Buddhist monks who gained new converts to their faith were divided into two great sects or "schools." Members of the older Theravada school were "conservative" in their understanding of Buddhism. They emphasized the humanity of the Buddha, the importance of the Four Noble Truths and the other doctrines attributed to the founder, and the need for Buddha-like mental discipline on the part of individuals seeking nirvana (salvation). Theravada Buddhism spread from India to Sri Lanka and then to numerous countries in Southeast Asia.

Mahayana Buddhists, on the other hand, were innovators. They taught that the Buddha of history was a god and emphasized the importance of faith in the Buddha (rather than mental discipline) as the means to attain nirvana. In addition, the Mahayanists taught that certain saint-like individuals known as *bodhisattvas* could assist ordinary lay people in their efforts to gain salvation. This was the type of Buddhism that spread to Central Asia and then, somewhat later, to China, Korea, and Japan.

Buddhism arrived in China during the 1st century C.E., in Korea during the 4th century, and in Japan during the 6th century. Because the political and cultural circumstances in these countries were quite different from those in India, there was a delay between the initial appearance of the new religion and the period of its widespread acceptance. In all three cases, the role of political elites in promoting Buddhism was significant. So too were the practice of magic and the belief in miracles.

The overall impact of Buddhism in the three East Asian countries was deep and lasting. A splendid tradition of Buddhist art and architecture flourished throughout East Asia during the postclassical centuries. In addition, the emphasis in the Mahayana tradition on

Section I from *Studies in Chinese Buddhism* by Arthur F. Wright, edited by Robert M. Somers (New Haven, Conn: Yale University Press, 1990), pp. 46–48, 52–53, 55–56, 58–59. Reprinted by permission of Yale University Press. Selection II from *Sources of Korean Tradition*, edited by Peter Lee and Theodore de Bary. Copyright © 1997. Columbia University Press. Reprinted with permission of the publisher. Selection III. "Japan Envoys and Emperors" from *Nihongi: Chronicles of Japan from the Earliest Times to A.D. 697*, translated by W.G. Aston (Rutland, VT: Charles E. Tuttle, 1972), pp. 65–68.

the virtue of compassion, personified by the *bodhisattvas,* seems to have resonated with special force on the beliefs and emotional life of Chinese, Koreans, and Japanese. Finally, Buddhist teachings (perhaps in a form that the founder would not have entirely approved) were frequently used to reinforce the authority of rulers in the three countries. Like Confucianism, Buddhism contributed to the formation of strong states. How do the following documents enable us to understand how Buddhism spread in East Asia?

BUDDHISM IN EAST ASIA

I. CHINA: FOTUDENG'S MISSION

[Fotudeng (d. 349 C.E.) was one of the most successful of the early Buddhist missionaries in China. He was born in Kucha, a Central Asian oasis community in today's western China. His proselytizing was centered in northern China near the former Han dynasty capital of Luoyang. In the 4th century this part of China was politically fragmented and ruled by various groups of nomad invaders. Fotudeng's biography appears in a history of China written in the 6th century.]

1. Zhu Fotudeng was a native of the Western Regions. His secular surname was Bo. When young he left lay life. He was pure and true and devoted to study. He knew by heart several million words of sūtras and was good at explaining the meaning of texts. Although he had not yet read the Confucian works and the histories of this country, when he discussed difficult points with scholars, all [his arguments] in a mysterious way fitted [with our Chinese traditions] like the two parts of a tally, and there was no one capable of humbling him [in debate].

2. He said of himself that he had gone twice to Jibin (Kashmir) and had there received instruction from famous masters. In the Western Regions, everyone called him the enlightened one.

3. In the fourth year of the Yungjia era of Huaidi of the Jin (310), he came to Luoyang with the purpose of spreading the Great Teaching. He was proficient at intoning magic spells and could make the spirits his servants. When he took sesame oil, mixed it with rouge, and smeared it on his palm, events more than 1,000 *li* [330 miles] distant were perfectly revealed in his palm as if he were face to face with them. He could also make those who kept the Buddhist regimen see [events as reflected in his palm]. Moreover, when he heard the sound of bells, he would foretell events therefrom, and [these prophecies] were never once unfulfilled.

4. He wished to establish a temple in Luoyang, but when there occurred the sack of Luoyang [in 310] by the invading armies of Liuyao, and the imperial capital was in turmoil, Deng's [i.e., Fotudeng's] plan to found a temple could not then be realized. He therefore retired to the country and thus watched from afar the political upheaval. At the time Shiluo encamped his army at Gebei where they devoted themselves entirely to the slaughter [of the people]. The śramaṇas [Buddhist monks] who met death were very numerous. Deng, out of his compassion for the people, wished to bring Luo under the influence of Buddhism. Thereupon, leaning on his priestly staff, he went to the headquarters. Luo's general, Guoheilüe, had long honored the Dharma [Buddhist teachings] so Deng went to stay at Lüe's house. Lüe, after accepting from him the Five Commandments, paid Deng the courtesies of a disciple. Afterwards, when on a punitive expedition under Luo, Lüeh always knew beforehand whether [an engagement] would be a victory or a

defeat. Luo marveled at this and asked him, "I was not aware that you had such extraordinary discernment, yet you know every time whether a military expedition will be a success or a failure. How is this?" Lüe replied, "General, your naturally extraordinary military prowess is being aided by supernatural influences. There is a certain śramaṇa whose knowledge of devices is exceptional. He said that you, my general, should conquer China and that he should be your teacher. All the things I have told you on various occasions were his words." Luo was delighted and said, "He is a gift from heaven." He summoned Deng and enquired, "What miraculous efficacy does Buddhism have?" Deng knew that Luo did not understand profound doctrines and would only be able to regard magic as evidence [of the power of Buddhism]. Accordingly he said, "Though the highest teachings are remote [from the general understanding], we can take nearby things as proof [of the efficacy of Buddhism]." Thereupon he took his begging bowl, filled it with water, burned incense, and said a spell over it. In a moment there sprang up blue lotus flowers whose brightness and color dazzled the eyes. Luo was convinced by this, and Deng accordingly admonished him, saying, "Now when a king's virtuous influence pervades the universe, the four sacred creatures [the unicorn, the phoenix, the tortoise, and the dragon] appear as good omens. When government is corrupt, and the Way is neglected, then comets will appear in the heavens. When heavenly signs manifest themselves, fortune and misfortune come in their wake. This is the constant testimony of ancient and modern times and the clear rule for Heaven and man." Luo was very pleased at this. Of those remaining who were to have been executed, 80 or 90 percent benefited from this [intervention on the part of Fotudeng]. Thereupon almost all the barbarians and Chinese in Zhongzhou worshipped the Buddha.

5. At this time there was a chronic illness which no one was able to cure. When Deng treated the disease, it was immediately cured. Those whom he secretly treated and who benefited in silence were uncountable.

6. Luo, returning to the north of the Yellow River from Gebei, passed through Fangtou. The people of Fangtou planned to raid the camp during the night. Deng said to Guoheilüe, "In a short time some brigands will arrive. I wanted to let you know." In fact it was as he had said, but since there were precautions taken, [the raid] did no damage. . . .

17. In the fourth month of the fourth year of Jianping (333), the sky was clear and there was no wind, yet on top of the pagoda a single bell sounded. Deng said to his followers, "The sound of the bell says, 'There will be a great mourning in the state, and it will not be later than this year.'" That year, in the seventh month, Luo died, and his son Hong succeeded to the throne. In a short time Shihu dethroned Hong and put himself on the throne. He moved the capital to Ye and named the era Jianwu (335–348).

18. Hu's wholehearted esteem for Deng was greater than that of Lo, so he sent down an edict which said, "The Heshang [a title given to Teng] is the great jewel of the state; honor and rank he will not accept, and great emoluments he will not receive. Since honors and emoluments are beneath his notice, with what shall we do honor to his virtue? Hereafter and henceforward it is fitting that he be clothed in silk brocade and that he ride in a carved palanquin. On the day of a court levee, when the Heshang ascends to the great hall, ministers from the Changshi down are all to help to carry up his Palanquin. The crown prince and the nobles are to assist

him in ascending. When the chamberlain announces the Daheshang [Great Heshang], all those who are seated are to rise to show their reverence." Moreover, Hu gave an order that the false Sikung, Linong, was morning and evening to enquire personally [as to Deng's health], that "the crown prince and the nobles are to pay Teng a visit once every five days as a mark of our reverence for him." . . .

24. Afterward a Jin army advanced to the Huai and the Si. The walled cities of Lang, Bi, and Fan were all raided. The three localities informed [Hu] of their distress. The people felt uneasy. Hu then said with an angry look, "I worship the Buddha and contribute to the monks; in spite of this I still draw foreign invaders. Buddha has no divine power!" Deng early the next morning went into [the palace]. Hu questioned Deng about the affair. Deng accordingly admonished him, saying, "Your Majesty, in ages past, was born as a great merchant. Coming to a temple in Jibin (Kashmir), he once provided for a great congregation [of monks]; in it were sixty arhats [monks of special merit]. I, my humble self, also took part in this meeting. At this time a man who had attained arhatship said to me, 'This merchant, when his life is ended, will take the body of a chicken, and after that he will be king of the land of Jin.' Now that you have become king, is that not a blessing? Armed raids on its border regions are usual for a state. Why revile the Three Treasures and allow evil thoughts to arise in the night?" Hu then believed and understood, knelt and gave thanks to him.

25. Hu once asked Deng, "Buddha's teaching is against the taking of life. I am the head of the empire, and without capital punishment, there is no means of keeping the country quiet. I have already violated the vows in putting living beings to death. Even though I still worship the Buddha, how shall I obtain blessings?" Deng said, "Worship of the Buddha on the part of emperors and kings lies in their being reverent in their persons and obedient in their hearts and in glorifying the Three Treasures [the Buddha, the Dharma, and the Sangha]. [It lies in] not making cruel oppressions and not killing the innocent. As to the rogues and irresponsibles whom the civilizing influence does not reform, when they are guilty of a crime, they must be put to death, and if they are guilty of an evil deed, they must be punished. You should execute only those who should be executed and punish only those who should be punished. If, cruelly and willfully, you put the innocent to death, then, even if you should pour out your wealth and devote yourself to the Dharma, there will be no escaping a bad end. I wish that the emperor might eliminate desire and cultivate compassion. If [your compassion] is broad and all pervading, then Buddhism will long prosper, and your good fortune will be prolonged." Although Hu was unable to comply entirely with this admonition, still benefits from it were not few. . . .

32. When Deng's program for bringing [the people] under the influence of Buddhism had been put into effect, many people worshiped Buddha; in every case they built temples and shrines or rushed to leave lay life. The true and the false were confused, and this gave rise to much misconduct. Hu issued an edict asking the opinions of the secretaries [zhongshu] saying, "The Buddha is called the world-honored one and is worshiped by the ruler. As for the lesser people of the villages and those without official rank, whether they should be allowed to worship the Buddha or not [is the question]. Moreover the śramaṇas should all be of the highest integrity and uprightness; their capabilities should be of the best. Only after that can they become proper devotees. At present the śramaṇas are very numerous. Some are troublemakers and avoid their state service. Many are not such men [as to meet the qualifications We have outlined above]. You may examine the matter

and advise as to [the distinctions to be made between] the true and the false." The *zhongshu zhuzuolang*, Wangdu, submitted a memorial saying, "That kings make the suburban sacrifices to Heaven and Earth and worship the myriad deities is recorded in the canons of sacrifice. The *Book of Rites* contains the regular sacrifices. Buddha, having been born in the Western Regions, is a foreign god. His merit does not help the people, and he is not one whom the emperor and the Chinese should sacrificially worship. Formerly when [the emperor] Ming of the Han had his dream and they first passed on this teaching, they only permitted men of the Western Regions to build temples in the capitals wherein to worship their god. No Chinese of this period were permitted to leave lay life. Wei adopted the Han regulations and followed the precedent. Now the Great Zhao has received the mandate and follows the ancient statutes. Institutions for Chinese and barbarians differ, and the spheres of men and of gods are different [among them]. What is alien differs from what is native, and sacrifices are different in ceremonial procedure [among them]. As to the clothing and ritual of the Chinese, it is not proper to intermingle them [with foreignisms]. The ruler should decide to forbid the people of Zhao from going to temples, burning incense and worshiping, and thereby he will conform to the ancient laws. From the lords and ministers down to the lowest classes, forbid them all by law. If there be those who transgress [this prohibition], let them be meted out the same punishment as those guilty of unauthorized worship. As for those men of Zhao who have become śramaṇas, let them return and follow the occupations of the four classes of civilians." The zhongshu ling, Wangbo, agreed with what Du had memorialized. Hu issued an edict, saying, "Du's argument is that Buddha is a deity of foreign lands and is not one whom it is proper for the emperor and the Chinese to worship. We were born out of the marches, and though We are unworthy, We have complied with our appointed destiny and govern the Chinese as their prince. As to sacrifices, we should follow our own customs, equally [with those of the Chinese]. Buddha being a barbarian god is the very one we should worship. Now regulations are carried into effect from above and for long ages serve as precepts [for posterity]. If a thing be truly without fault, why keep narrowly to the rules of former times? As for the I, the Zhao, and the myriad barbarians, if there are those who abandon their unauthorized worship and take pleasure in worshipping Buddha, We hereby permit all of them to become adherents." Thereupon the people who were lax in keeping the precepts were encouraged by this. . . .

II. KOREA: MONKS AND KINGS

[When Buddhism was first introduced into Korea, the peninsula was divided into three kingdoms: Koguryo controlled the north, Paekche ruled the southwest corner, and Silla, the unifier of the country in the 7th century, governed the central and eastern regions. The following mixture of early Korean documents (numbers 1 and 3) and an early Chinese source (number 2) record the coming of Buddhism to Paekche and Silla.].

A. The Monk Kyomik

In the fourth year, *pyŏngo*, of King Sŏng of Paekche [526], the monk Kyŏmik resolved to seek the rules of discipline and sailed to central India. He studied Sanskrit for five years at Great Vinaya Monastery in Saṇghāna [*this name and Vedatta, below, are unidentified reconstructions*] and acquired a sound knowledge of the language. He then studied the disciplinary texts thoroughly and solemnly embodied morality [*sīla*] in his heart. He returned together with an Indian monk, Tripiṭaka Master Vedatta, and brought with him the Sanskrit texts of the *Abhidharma Piṭaka* and five recensions of the Discipline. The king of Paekche welcomed the two at the outskirts of the capital with a plume-canopied carriage and drums and pipes and had them reside at Hŭngnyun Monastery. The king also summoned the country's twenty-eight famous monks and, together with Dharma Master Kyŏmik, had them translate seventy-two rolls of the rules of discipline. Thus Kyŏmik became the founder of the Disciplinary school in Paekche. Thereupon Dharma Masters Tamuk and Hyein wrote commentaries on the rules of discipline in thirty-six rolls and presented them to the king. The king composed a preface to the *Abhidharma* and this *New Vinaya*, treasured them in the T'aeyo Hall, and intended to have them carved on wood blocks for dissemination. The king died, however, before he could implement his plan.

B. The Monk Hyongwang (539–575)

The monk Hyŏngwang was a native of Ungju in Korea [Paekche]. As a youth—and one of marked intelligence—he abruptly abandoned the secular life and determined to gain access to a religious teacher of high repute. Thereafter he devoted himself to a pure and celibate existence and when fully grown, he resolved to cross the ocean in order to seek training in the meditative methods of China.

Accordingly, he made a journey to the state of Ch'en [in northern China], where to his good fortune, he visited Mount Heng and met the Reverend Teacher Hui-ssu, who opened his understanding to the transience of phenomena and brilliantly elucidated all the matters they discussed. . . .

Following his return to Korea, Hyŏngwang settled on Mount Ong in Ungju, where initially only a simple hermitage was constructed, but in time this was developed into a full monastery. It is written that "notes of the same key respond to each other," and so it was that those who wished to attain to the dharma clustered at his gate and opened themselves to his instruction. The carefree and young, those solemnly resolved to adhere to the true Path, even those who still craved the taste of flesh—they all, like ants in a line, sought him. Among these, there was one who ultimately ascended to a position of eminence and was designated as Hyŏngwang's successor. There was also one who achieved the "Fire Radiance Samādhi," two who achieved the "Water Radiance Samādhi," and even some who became proficient in both of these practices. Those who followed him and distinguished themselves were especially celebrated for their attainments in meditation. In fact, his disciples could be likened to the flocks of birds that haunt Mount Sumeru in that they all were of one color. While Hyŏngwang was yet living, he left Mount Ong and disappeared; where he went is not known.

When the patriarch of Nan-yüeh [in southern China] built an image hall, Hyŏngwang's likeness was one of the portraits of twenty-eight honored masters displayed there. His likeness is also to be seen in the Patriarchs' Hall at Kuo-ch'ing Monastery on Mount T'ien-t'ai [in China].

C. King Pophung of Silla

The monk Pŏpkong was the twenty-third king of Silla, Pŏphŭng [514–540]. His secular name was Wŏnjong; he was the first son of King Chijŭng [500–514] and Lady Yŏnje. He was seven feet tall. Generous, he loved the people, and they in turn regarded him as a saint or a sage. Millions of people, therefore, placed confidence in him. In the third year [516] a dragon appeared in the Willow Well. In the fourth year [517] the Ministry of War was established, and in the seventh year [520] laws and statutes were promulgated together with the official vestments. After his enthronement, whenever the king attempted to spread Buddhism, his ministers opposed him with much dispute. He felt frustrated, but remembering Ado's devout vow, he summoned all his officials and said unto them: "Our august ancestor, King Mich'u, together with Ado, propagated Buddhism, but he died before great merits were accumulated. That the knowledge of the wonderful transformation of Śākyamuni should be prevented from spreading makes me very sad. We think we ought to erect monasteries and recast images to continue our ancestor's fervor. What do you think?" Minister Kongal and others remonstrated with the king, saying, "In recent years the crops have been scarce, and the people are restless. Besides, because of frequent border raids from the neighboring state, our soldiers are still engaged in battle. How can we exhort our people to erect a useless building at this time?" The king, depressed at the lack of faith among his subordinates, sighed, saying, "We, lacking moral power, are unworthy of succeeding to the throne. The yin and the yang are disharmonious and the people ill at ease; therefore you opposed my idea and did not want to follow. Who can enlighten the strayed people by the wonderful dharma?" For some time no one answered.

In the fourteenth year [527] the Grand Secretary Pak Yŏmch'ok (Ich'adon or Kŏch'adon), then twenty-six years old, was an upright man. With a heart that was sincere and deep, he advanced resolutely for the right cause. Out of willingness to help the king fulfill his noble vow, he secretly memorialized the throne: "If Your Majesty desires to establish Buddhism, may I ask Your Majesty to issue a false decree to this officer, stating that the king desires to initiate Buddhist activities. Once the ministers learn of this, they will undoubtedly remonstrate. Your Majesty, declaring that no such decree has been given, will then ask who has forged the royal order. They will ask Your Majesty to punish my crime, and if their request is granted, they will submit to Your Majesty's will."

The king said, "Since they are bigoted and haughty, we fear they will not be satisfied even with your execution." Yŏmch'ok replied, "Even the deities venerate the religion of the Great Sage. If an officer as unworthy as myself is killed for its cause, miracles must happen between heaven and earth. If so, who then will dare to remain bigoted and haughty?" The king answered, "Our basic wish is to further the advantageous and remove the disadvantageous. But now we have to injure a loyal subject. Is this not sorrowful?" Yŏmch'ok replied, "Sacrificing his life in order to accomplish goodness is the great principle of the official. Moreover, if it means the eternal brightness of the Buddha Sun and the perpetual solidarity of the kingdom, the day of my death will be the year of my birth." The king, greatly moved, praised Yŏmch'ok and said, "Though you are a commoner, your mind harbors thoughts worthy of brocaded and embroidered robes." Thereupon the king and Yŏmch'ok vowed to be true to each other.

Afterward a royal decree was issued, ordering the erection of a monastery in the Forest of the Heavenly Mirror, and officials in charge began construction. The court officials, as expected, denounced it and expostulated with the king. The king remarked, "We did not issue such an order." Thereupon Yŏmch'ok spoke out, "Indeed, I did this purposely, for if we practice Buddhism the whole country will become prosperous and peaceful. As long as it is good for the administration of the realm, what wrong can there be in forging a decree?" Thereupon the king called a meeting and asked the opinion of the officials. All of them remarked, "These days monks bare their heads and wear strange garments. Their discourses are wrong and in violation of the Norm. If we unthinkingly follow their proposals, there may be cause for regret. We dare not obey Your Majesty's order, even if we are threatened with death." Yŏmch'ok spoke with indignation, saying, "All of you are wrong, for there must be an unusual personage before there can be an unusual undertaking. I have heard that the teaching of Buddhism is profound and arcane. We must practice it. How can a sparrow know the great ambition of a swan?" The king said, "The will of the majority is firm and unalterable. You are the only one who takes a different view. I cannot follow two recommendations at the same time." He then ordered the execution of Yŏmch'ok [15 September 527].

Yŏmch'ok then made an oath to Heaven: "I am about to die for the sake of the dharma. I pray that rightness and the benefit of the religion will spread. If the Buddha has a numen [divine power], a miracle should occur after my death." When he was decapitated, his head flew to Diamond Mountain, falling on its summit, and white milk gushed forth from the cut, soaring up several hundred feet. The sun darkened, wonderful flowers rained from heaven, and the earth trembled violently. The king, his officials, and the commoners, on the one hand terrified by these strange phenomena and on the other sorrowful for the death of the Grand Secretary who had sacrificed his life for the cause of the dharma, cried aloud and mourned. They buried his body on Diamond Mountain with due ceremony. At the time the king and his officials took an oath: "Hereafter we will worship the Buddha and revere the clergy. If we break this oath, may heaven strike us dead."

In the twenty-first year [534], trees in the Forest of the Heavenly Mirror were felled in order to build a monastery. When the ground was cleared, pillar bases, stone niches, and steps were discovered, proving the site to be that of an old monastery. Materials for beams and pillars came from the forest. The monastery being completed, the king abdicated and became a monk. He changed his name to Pŏpkong, mindful of the three garments and the begging bowl. He aspired to lofty conduct and had compassion for all. Accordingly, the monastery was named Taewang Hŭngnyun because it was the king's abode. This was the first monastery erected in Silla.

The queen, too, served Buddha by becoming a nun and residing at Yŏnghŭng Monastery. Since the king had patronized a great cause, he was given the posthumous epithet of Pŏphŭng (Promoter of Dharma), which is by no means idle flattery. Thereafter, at every anniversary of Yŏmch'ok's death, an assembly was held at Hŭngnyun Monastery to commemorate his martyrdom.

III. JAPAN: ENVOYS AND EMPERORS

[Buddhism came to Japan during the period when the earliest emperors were increasing their authority and constructing a strong state. The first of the following selections comes from the Nihongi, *the history of Japan that was compiled around 700 C.E.]*

A. From the Nihongi

Winter, 10th month [552 C.E.]. King Syŏng-myŏng of Pékché [also called King Syŏng] sent Kwi-si of the Western Division, and the Tal-sol, Nu-ri Sa-chhi-hyé, with a present to the Emperor of an image of Shaka Butsu [the Buddha] in gold and copper, several flags and umbrellas, and a number of volumes of "Sutras."

Separately he presented a memorial in which he lauded the merit of diffusing abroad religious worship, saying:—"This doctrine is amongst all doctrines the most excellent. But it is hard to explain, and hard to comprehend. Even the Duke of Chow and Confucius had not attained to a knowledge of it. This doctrine can create religious merit and retribution without measure and without bounds, and so lead on to a full appreciation of the highest wisdom. Imagine a man in possession of treasures to his heart's content, so that he might satisfy all his wishes in proportion as he used them. Thus it is with the treasure of this wonderful doctrine. Every prayer is fulfilled and naught is wanting. Moreover, from distant India it has extended hither to the three Han states [Chinese] where there are none who do not receive it with reverence as it is preached to them.

Thy servant, therefore, Myŏng, King of Pèkché, has humbly despatched his retainer, Nu-ri Sa-chhi, to transmit it to the Imperial Country [Japan], and to diffuse it abroad throughout the home provinces, so as to fulfil the recorded saying of Buddha: 'My law shall spread to the East.'"

This day the Emperor, having heard to the end, leaped for joy, and gave command to the Envoys, saying:—"Never from former days until now have we had the opportunity of listening to so wonderful a doctrine. We are unable, however, to decide of ourselves." Accordingly he inquired of his Ministers one after another, saying:—"The countenance of this Buddha which has been presented by the Western frontier State is of a severe dignity, such as we have never at all seen before. Ought it to be worshipped or not?" Soga no Oho-omi, Iname no Sukune, addressed the Emperor, saying:—"All the Western frontier lands without exception do it worship. Shall Akitsu Yamato [the Emperor] alone refuse to do so?" Okoshi, Mononobe no Oho-muraji, and Kamako, Nakatomi no Muraji, addressed the Emperor jointly, saying:—"Those who have ruled the Empire in this our State have always made it their care to worship in Spring, Summer, Autumn and Winter the 180 Gods of Heaven and Earth, and the Gods of the Land and of Grain. If just at this time we were to worship in their stead foreign Deities, it may be feared that we should incur the wrath of our National Gods."

The Emperor said:—"Let it be given to Iname no Sukune, who has shown his willingness to take it, and, as an experiment, make him to worship it."

The Oho-omi knelt down and received it with joy. He enthroned it in his house at Oharida, where he diligently carried out the rites of retirement from the world, and on that score purified his house at Muku-hara and made it a Temple. After this a pestilence was rife in the Land, from which the people died prematurely. As time went on it became worse and worse, and there was no remedy. Okoshi, Mononobe no Ohomuraji, and Kamako, Nakatomi no Muraji, addressed the Emperor jointly, saying:—"It was because thy servants' advice on a former day was not approved that the people are dying thus of disease. If thou dost now retrace thy steps before matters have gone too far, joy will surely be the result! It will be well promptly to fling it away, and diligently to seek happiness in the future."

The Emperor said:—"Let it be done as you advise." Accordingly officials took the image of Buddha and abandoned it to the current of the Canal of Naniha. They also set fire to the Temple, and burnt it so that nothing was left. Hereupon, there being in the Heavens neither clouds nor wind, a sudden conflagration consumed the Great Hall (of the Palace). . . .

Summer, 5th month, 7th day [553 C.E.]. The following report was received from the province of Kahachi:—"From within the sea at Chinu, in the district of Idzumi, there is heard a voice of Buddhist chants, which re-echoes like the sound of thunder, and a glory shines like the radiance of the sun." In his heart the Emperor wondered at this, and sent Unate no Atahe [here we have only Atahe, and the personal name is not given, probably owing to the error of some copyist] to go upon the sea and investigate the matter.

This month Unate no Atahe went upon the sea, and the result was that he discovered a log of camphor-wood shining brightly as it floated on the surface. At length he took it, and presented it to the Emperor, who gave orders to an artist to make of it two images of Buddha. These are the radiant camphor-wood images now in the Temple of Yoshino.

B. Emperor Temmu's Propagation of Buddhism, 676–685 C.E.

On this day [Autumn, eighth month, 17th day, fifth year of the reign of Temmu, or 676], the Emperor ordered all the provinces to release living things.

Winter, eleventh month, 20th day. Messengers were sent to all parts of the country to expound the *Sutra of the Golden Light* and the *Ninnō Sutra*.

Summer, fifth month, 1st day [680]. By the imperial command, a gift of varying amount consisting of coarse silk, floss silk, raw silk, and cloth was made to each of the twenty-four temples located within the capital.

The expounding of the *Sutra of the Golden Light* was begun this day in the imperial palace and in the temples.

Winter, eleventh month, 12th day. The Empress was taken ill. The Emperor in praying for her recovery made a vow on her behalf, and began the erection of the Yakushiji. He ordered the ordination of one hundred persons to enter the Buddhist priesthood. As a result the Empress recovered and an amnesty was proclaimed.

Spring, third month, 27th day [685]. The Emperor decreed that every household in every province should erect a family Buddhist shrine in which to place an image of Buddha along with Buddhist sutras. These shrines were to be worshipped and offerings of food were to be made to them.

C. Emperor Shomu Calls for the Building of Temples, 741 C.E.

In the thirteenth year of Tempyō [741], 24th day of the third month, the Emperor [Shōmu] decreed, saying, "We, even though lacking in virtue, have been entrusted with the responsibilities of governing the country. We have not been able to spread our beneficent rule, and day and night We are besieged with the feeling of inadequacies. Of old, enlightened kings carried on the work of former sovereigns, and brought peace to the nation and joy to the people. They eradicated calamities and brought about happiness. What was the secret behind their beneficent rule which enabled them to attain these goals? Lately, annual grain crops have not been abundant, and we have been visited by pestilence frequently. Remorse and trepidation are mixed in Our mind, and We work diligently to atone for Our sins.

"Seeking widely to benefit all sentient beings, and to gain happiness for all uniformly, We sent messengers in past years on fast horses to shrines everywhere in our country and increased their stipends. Last year We ordered that every province should erect one golden image of Buddha Shakamuni, sixteen feet in height, and write out one copy of the *Daihannyakyō*.

"From the past spring until the harvest time in the fall, the wind and rain were orderly and the five crops grew abundantly. It happened in this manner, as if the spirit, the seer, has answered Our supplications, recognizing Our sincerity. With fear and trembling, and without engaging in Our own speculations, We have consulted the scriptures. It is said that in the countries where the *Sutra of the Golden Light* was explained, read and propagated devoutly, the Four Deva Kings would always come to protect them. Thus all calamities would be eradicated and fear and pestilence would be extinguished. The hearts' desires would be fulfilled, and there would be continuous joy.

"Thus We command that each of the provinces shall with reverence erect a seven-storied pagoda, and write out a copy each of the *Sutra of the Golden Light* and the *Sutra of the Lotus of the Wonderful Law*. We also plan to make special copies of the *Sutra of the Golden Light* in golden characters, and deposit a copy in each of the pagodas. It is Our desire that the Sacred Law prosper, and be transmitted eternally, coeval with heaven and earth. The benefit of the protection of the Sacred Law encompasses both this world and the world on the other shore. It must be made known to all. The building of a temple is, at the same time, the finest decoration for the state. Thus a good location must be found, which must be made permanent. If the location is too near a population center, unwittingly it may acquire the undesirable stench. If it is too far away from a population center, unwittingly it may make the gathering of the people a burdensome chore.

"Ye, provincial governors must perform your duties diligently, and make yourselves pure. Let the heaven know of your sincerity that it may abide by you and protect you. Let the people near and afar know Our august wishes."

STUDY QUESTIONS

1. How did Fotudeng win support for Buddhism in China? What seems to have been his strategy for winning converts?
2. Why did Chinese rulers support the Fotudeng? How did the monk demonstrate the value of Buddhism to them?
3. How did Buddhism begin in Silla? What evidence do you see of the importance of Confucianism in Silla? Of traditional folk religion?
4. How did Buddhism reach Japan? According to the *Nihongi,* how did the emperor's advisers react to the gifts from Paekche? Were the advisers Confucians? Why was Buddhism initially rejected by the Japanese? Why did later emperors support Buddhism?
5. What similarities or differences do you see in the spread of Buddhism in the three East Asian countries?
6. What is the relationship between the Buddhism depicted in these documents and the Four Noble Truths (see Chapter 13)? How do you explain the differences? Have other religions changed in similar ways?
7. What do these documents suggest about contacts and exchanges between East Asian countries? Why did Buddhism not spread west to the Mediterranean region?
8. How does the spread of Buddhism compare to that of Christianity and Islam (see Chapter 27 for Christianity)? Were the same forces at work in all three cases?

BUDDHIST SCULPTURE IN CHINA

Vairocana Buddha at Longmen, Northern China, 7th century. (Photo by Stephen S. Gosch)

The practice of sculpting images of the Buddha began in northern India and Gandhara (present-day northern Pakistan and Afghanistan) during the early centuries of the Common Era. As Buddhism spread eastward along Central Asian trade routes to China and neighboring countries, so also did the tradition of making statues of the Buddha.

Around 500 C.E. the ex-nomads who governed most of northern China as the Northern Wei dynasty (439–534) sponsored the construction of a great Buddhist cave complex—featuring more than 100,000 images of the Buddha—near their new capital at Luoyang. As at Ajanta in India, the caves near Luoyang (known as the Longmen caves) were carved out of cliffs that rise above a riverbed. Work at the site continued long after the fall of the Northern Wei regime, culminating during the first half of the Tang dynasty (618–906).

The huge (35 feet tall) Vairocana Buddha shown here was commissioned by Emperor Gaozong (reigned 650–683) and completed in 675. According to Mahayanist tradition, the Vairocana Buddha is the ultimate cosmic Buddha, the original creative spirit. The Vairocana Buddha at Longmen sits Indian-style on a lotus throne and wears the type of clingy garment characteristic of Gandharan Buddhas (and also of Greco-Roman statues). A flaming halo, which may be an echo of Zoroastrian fire worship in Persia, adds to his majesty. Perhaps the sculptors at Longmen worked from sketches brought back from Gandhara by pilgrims and other travelers.

STUDY QUESTIONS

1. What features of the statue might have strengthened the faith of Buddhists in China?
2. How does the statue suggest changes in Buddhist teaching from the time of the historic Buddha?
3. What type of relationship between religious authority and political authority is suggested by the statue?
4. In what way does the statue indicate contacts between China and other countries?

27   THE SPREAD OF CHRISTIANITY: JUSTIN, ANONYMOUS DOCUMENTS

In the two centuries after the death of Christ, Christianity spread widely in the Roman Empire and in other parts of the Middle East. An early decision by St. Paul was crucial, as Christians moved away from attention only to Jewish converts toward a belief that the religion was open to all believers. By the 4th century, probably about 10 percent of all people in the Roman Empire had become Christian, and there were also centers in Armenia and Ethiopia, beyond Rome's borders. Christianity was on its way to becoming one of the major world religions. Its growth came despite the lack of support and occasional persecution from the Roman state.

The following documents, all from the early church and mostly by anonymous writers, treat two of the key issues involved in the spread of Christianity. The first two passages deal with some of the motivations to convert to Christianity, along with the basic Christian message of salvation in a heavenly afterlife. The second two passages deal with issues of setting up a government for the church that would be more stable than individual local religious communities in a situation where the state was sometimes hostile. Christianity managed to construct a solid organizational tradition, even in difficult times, that would be one of its hallmarks in world history from that point onward.

The first document probably dates from the late 2nd century. Called the "Acts of John" it was not in fact written by any of the apostles. As Christianity spread, legends about the powers of Christ and the apostles, such as John, spread widely. In this account, John deals first with a paralyzed woman, then calls on Christ's backing to confront the pagan idols in the major Middle-Eastern city of Ephesus. The narrative is not necessarily factual except in the sense of showing how Christians in the period understood the process of conversion.

The second document was written by a Roman intellectual, Justin, in the mid-2nd century. It discusses the relationship between Christianity and Greco-Roman philosophy, showing how the religion was superior to the philosophy but could be cast in terms that made sense to those steeped in the classical philosophical tradition. The passage is constructed as a dialogue between Justin and another philosopher who helps show him the way.

The third document was probably written around 95 C.E. It was attributed to Clement, the third bishop of Rome, but in fact it is not known who wrote it. The topic is clear: the need for firm principles of church government and loyalty to church leaders.

The occasion was a split in the church of Corinth (a city in Greece). The document proposes a clear way to defend church leadership and avoid damaging divisions.

Finally, another document on church government, the Didache, probably written around 100 C.E., deals with another obvious problem, sorting out the authenticity of wandering Christian prophets. The tests follow from basic Christian precepts, but then a later passage suggests some more structural remedies.

CHRISTIAN RECORDS

I. THE "ACTS OF JOHN"

And when John saw the great multitude [outside the house of Cleopatra, a sick woman in Ephesus], he prayed to the Lord, "Now the time of refreshing and confidence has come with you. O Christ; now is the time for us weary ones to have help from you, physician, who heal freely. Keep my entrance here free from derision! I beseech you, Jesus, help such a great multitude to come to the Lord of the universe. Behold the affliction, behold those who lie here! Even those who came here, make holy instruments for your service, after they have seen your gift. For you have said yourself, O Christ, 'Ask and it shall be given you.' We therefore beseech you, O King, not for gold, not for silver, not for riches, not for possession, nor for any transient, earthly goods, but for two souls through whom you will convert those present to your way, to your knowledge, to your confidence, and to your infallible promise. For many of them shall be saved, after they have known your power through the resurrection of the departed. Give us, therefore, hope in you! I will go to Cleopatra and say, 'Arise, in the name of Jesus Christ.'"

And he went, touched her face, and said, "Cleopatra, he whom every ruler fears, and every creature, power, abyss, and darkness and unsmiling death and the heights of heaven and the caverns of the lower world and the resurrection of the dead and the sight of the blind and the whole power of the ruler of the world, and the pride of its prince, says, 'Rise up and become not a pretext for many who will not believe, and an affliction for souls who hope and could be saved.'" And Cleopatra cried out at once, "I will rise, master, save your handmaiden!" When she had risen after the seven days, the whole city of Ephesus was stirred by the miraculous sight. . . .

After two days the birthday of the idol's temple was celebrated. While everybody was dressed in white garments, John wore black and went to the temple. They laid hold of him and tried to kill him. But John said, "Men, you are mad to lay hold of me, the servant of the only God." And climbing on to the platform he spoke to them:

"Men of Ephesus, you are in danger of behaving like the sea. Every discharging river and every precipitating spring, downpours and incessant waves and torrents rushing from the rock, and permeated by the bitter salt which is in the sea. Thus to this day you are unchangeably hostile to true piety, and you perish in your old idolatry. How many miraculous deeds did you see me perform, how many cures! And still you are hardened in the heart and cannot see clearly. What now, men of Ephesus? I have ventured now to come up to this idol's temple, to convince you that you are wholly without God and dead to human reasoning. Behold, here I stand. You all assert that Artemis [Greek goddess] is powerful. Pray to her, that I alone die! Or if you cannot accomplish this, I alone will call upon my God to kill you all because of your unbelief."

Since they already knew him and had seen the dead raised, they cried aloud, "Do not treat us so and kill us, we beseech you, John; we know indeed that you can do it." And John answered them, "If you do not wish to die, let me convince you of your idolatry. Any why? So that you may desist from your old error. Be now converted by my God or I will die at the hands of your goddess. For I will pray in your presence to my God, and ask him to have mercy upon you."

After these words he prayed, "God, who are God above all so-called gods, who to this day have been despised at Ephesus, you induced me to come to this place, which I never had in view. You have abrogated every form of worship through conversion to you. In your name every idol, every demon, and every unclean spirit is banished. May the deity of this place, which has deceived so many, now also give way to your name, and thus show your mercy on this place! For they walk in error."

And with these words of John the altar of Artemis suddenly split into many parts, and the oblations put up in the temple suddenly fell to the ground, and its glory broke, and so did more than seven of the idols. And half of the temple fell down, so that when the roof came down, the priest also was killed at one stroke. And the people of the Ephesians cried, "There is only one God, that of John, only one God who has compassion for us; for you alone are God; now we have become converted, since we saw your miraculous deeds. Have mercy upon us, God, according to your will, and deliver us from our great error." And some of them lay on their faces and cried; others bent their knees and prayed; others rent their garments and lamented; still others tried to escape.

And John stretched out his hands and prayed with uplifted soul to the Lord, "Glory be to you, my Jesus, the only God of truth, who procure your servants in manifold ways!" And after these words he said to the people, "Rise up from the ground, people from Ephesus, pray to my God, and know how his invisible power was made manifest and his miraculous deeds took place before your eyes! Artemis herself should have helped. Her servant should have received help from her and not have died. Where is the power of the deity? Where are the sacrifices? Where the birthday? Where the festivals? Where the garlands? Where the great enchantment and the poison allied to it?"

And the people rose up from the ground and made haste to destroy the remainder of the temple, crying, "We know that the God of John is the only one, and henceforth we worship him, since we have obtained mercy from him." And as John came down, many of the people touched him, saying, "Help us, John, help us who die in vain! You see our intention; you see how the multitude following you cleaves to hope in your God. We have seen the way in which we have gone astray when we were lost. We have seen that our gods were erected in vain. We have seen their great and disgraceful derision. But give us, we beseech you, help without hindrance, when we have come to your house! Receive us, who are desperate!"

II. JUSTIN, A CHRISTIAN PHILOSOPHER

The majority of the philosophers have simply neglected to inquire whether there is one or even several gods, and whether or not a divine providence takes care of us, as if this knowledge were unnecessary to our happiness. Moreover, they try to convince us that God takes care of the universe with its genera and species, but not of me and you and of each individual, for otherwise there would be no need of our praying to him night and day. It is not difficult to see where such reasoning leads them. It imparts a certain immunity and freedom of speech to those who hold these opinions, permitting them to do and to say whatever they please, without any fear of punishment or hope of reward from God. How could it be otherwise, when they claim that things will always be as they are now, and that you and I shall live in the next life just as we are now, neither better or worse. . . .

"Philosophy is indeed one's greatest possession, and is most precious in the sight of God, to whom it alone leads us and to whom it unites us, and they in truth are holy who have applied themselves to philosophy. But, many have failed to discover the nature of philosophy, and the reason why it was sent down to men; otherwise, there would not be Platonists, or Stoics, or Peripatetics, or Theoretics, or Pythagoreans, since the science of philosophy is always one and the same. Now, let me tell you why it has at length become so diversified. They who first turned to philosophy, and, as a result, were deemed illustrious, were succeeded by others who gave no time to the investigation of truth, but, amazed at the courage and self-control of their teachers as well as with the novelty of their teachings, held that to be the truth which each had learned from his own teacher. And they in turn transmitted to their successors such opinions, and others like them, and so they became known by the name of him who was considered the father of the doctrine. When I first desired to contact one of these philosophers, I placed myself under the tutelage of a certain Stoic. After spending some time with him and learning nothing new about God, (for my instructor had no knowledge of God, nor did he consider such knowledge necessary), I left him and turned to a Peripatetic who considered himself an astute teacher. After a few days with him, he demanded that we settle the matter of my tuition fee in such a way that our association would not be unprofitable to him. Accordingly, I left him, because I did not consider him a real philosopher. Since my spirit still yearned to hear the specific and excellent meaning of philosophy, I approached a very famous Pythagorean, who took great pride in his own wisdom. In my interview with him, when I expressed a desire to become his pupil, he asked me, 'What? Do you know music, astronomy, and geometry? How do you expect to comprehend any of those things that are conducive to happiness, if you are not first well acquainted with those studies which draw your mind away from objects of the senses and render it fit for the intellectual, in order that it may contemplate what is good and beautiful?' He continued to speak at great length in praise of those sciences, and of the necessity of knowing them, until I admitted that I knew nothing about them; then he dismissed me. As was to be expected, I was downcast to see my hopes shattered, especially since I respected him as a man of considerable knowledge. But, when I reflected on the length of time that I would have to spend on those sciences, I could not make up my mind to wait such a long time. In this troubled state of mind the thought occurred to me to consult the Platonists, whose reputation was great. Thus it happened that I spent as much time as possible in the company of a wise man who was highly esteemed by the Platonists and who had but recently arrived in our city. Under him I forged ahead in philosophy and day by day I improved. The perception of incorporeal things quite overwhelmed me and the Platonic theory of ideas added wings to my mind, so that in a short time I imagined myself a wise man. So great was my folly that I fully expected immediately to gaze upon God, for this is the goal of Plato's philosophy." . . .

Chapter 6

"'I don't care,' [my acquaintance] answered, 'if Plato or Pythagoras or anyone else held such views. What I say is the truth, and here is how you may learn it. The soul itself either is life or it possesses life. If it is life, it would cause something else to exist, not itself, just as motion causes something other than itself to move. Now, no one would deny that the soul lives; and if it lives, it does not live as life itself, but as a partaker of life. But, that which partakes of anything is different from that of which it partakes. Now, the soul partakes of life because God wishes it to live; it will no longer partake of life whenever God doesn't wish it to live. For the power to live is not an attribute of the soul as it is of God. As one does not live forever, and one's body is not forever united to one's soul, since, whenever this union must be discontinued, the soul leaves the body and one no longer exists, so also, whenever the soul must cease to live, the spirit of life is taken from it and it is no more, but it likewise returns to the place of its origin.' . . .

Chapter 8

"When he said these and many other things . . . my spirit was immediately set on fire, and an affection for the prophets, and for those who are friends of Christ, took hold of me; while pondering on his words, I discovered that his was the only sure and useful philosophy. Thus it is that I am now a philosopher. Furthermore, it is my wish that everyone would be of the same sentiments as I, and never spurn the Savior's words; for they have in themselves such tremendous majesty that they can instill fear into those who have wandered from the path of righteousness, whereas they ever remain a great solace to those who heed them. Thus, if you have any regard for your own welfare and for the salvation of your soul, and if you believe in God, you may have the chance, since I know you are no stranger to this matter, of attaining a knowledge of the Christ of God, and, after becoming a Christian, of enjoying a happy life."

III. CHURCH GOVERNMENT

The apostles received the gospel for us from the Lord Jesus Christ; Jesus, the Christ, was sent from God.

Thus Christ is from God and the apostles from Christ. In both instances the orderly procedure depends on God's will.

And so the apostles, after receiving their orders and being fully convinced by the resurrection of our Lord Jesus Christ and assured by God's word, went out in the confidence of the Holy Spirit to preach the good news that God's Kingdom was about to come.

They preached in country and city, and appointed their first converts, after testing them by the Spirit, to be the bishops and deacons of future believers.

Nor was this any novelty, for Scripture had mentioned bishops and deacons long before. For this is what Scripture says somewhere: "I will appoint their bishops in righteousness and their deacons in faith." . . .

Now our apostles, thanks to our Lord Jesus Christ, knew that there was going to be strife over the title of bishop.

It was for this reason and because they had been given an accurate knowledge of the future, that they appointed the officers we have mentioned. Furthermore, they later added a codicil to the effect that, should these die, other approved men should succeed to their ministry.

In the light of this, we view it as a breach of justice to remove from their ministry those who were appointed either by them [the apostles] or later on and with the whole church's consent, by others of the proper standing, and who, long enjoying everybody's approval, have ministered to Christ's flock faultlessly, humbly, quietly, and unassumingly.

For we shall be guilty of no slight sin if we eject from the episcopate men who have offered the sacrifices with innocence and holiness.

Happy, indeed, are those presbyters who have already passed on, and who ended a life of fruitfulness with their task complete. For they need not fear that anyone will remove them from their secure positions.

But you, we observe, have removed a number of people, despite their good conduct, from a ministry they have fulfilled with honor and integrity. . . .

It is disgraceful, exceedingly disgraceful, and unworthy of your Christian upbringing, to have it reported that because of one or two individuals the solid and ancient Corinthian Church is in revolt against its presbyters.

This report, moreover, has reached not only us, but those who dissent from us as well. The result is that the Lord's name is being blasphemed because of your stupidity, and you are exposing yourselves to danger.

We must, then, put a speedy end to this. We must prostrate ourselves before the Master, and beseech him with tears to have mercy on us and be reconciled to us and bring us back to our honorable and holy practice of brotherly love. . . .

IV. THE DIDACHE: MORE ON CHURCH GOVERNMENT

Now, you should welcome anyone who comes your way and teaches you all we have been saying.

But if the teacher proves himself a renegade and by teaching otherwise contradicts all this, pay no attention to him. But if his teaching furthers the Lord's righteousness and knowledge, welcome him as the Lord.

Now about the apostles and prophets: Act in line with the gospel precept.

Welcome every apostle on arriving, as if he were the Lord.

But he must not stay beyond one day. In case of necessity, however, the next day too. If he stays three days, he is a false prophet.

On departing, an apostle must not accept anything save sufficient food to carry him till his next lodging. If he asks for money, he is a false prophet.

While a prophet is making ecstatic utterances, you must not test or examine him. For "every sin will be forgiven," but this sin "will not be forgiven."

However, not everybody making ecstatic utterances is a prophet, but only if he behaves like the Lord. It is by their conduct that the false prophet and the [true] prophet can be distinguished

For instance, if a prophet marks out a table in the Spirit, he must not eat from it. If he does, he is a false prophet.

Again, every prophet who teaches the truth but fails to practice what he preaches is a false prophet. . . .

You must, then, elect for yourselves bishops and deacons who are a credit to the Lord, men who are gentle, generous, faithful, and well tried. For their ministry to you is identical with that of the prophets and teachers.

You must not, therefore, despise them, for along with the prophets and teachers they enjoy a place of honor among you.

Furthermore, do not reprove each other angrily, but quietly, as you find it in the gospel. Moreover, if anyone has wronged his neighbor, nobody must speak to him, and he must not hear a word from you, until he repents.

Say your prayers, give your charity, and do everything just as you find it in the gospel of our Lord.

STUDY QUESTIONS

1. What were some of the motivations to convert to Christianity?
2. How could Christianity relate to Greco-Roman culture?
3. What kinds of people might be attracted to early Christianity?
4. What were some of the principles of early church government? How did Christian leaders work to prevent local divisions?
5. How does document 3 relate to Catholic beliefs in church organization and the priesthood? What were the problems that this document tries to resolve?
6. What were some of the problems of early Christian communities? How did emerging church government deal with these problems?
7. How does the spread of Christianity compare to that of Buddhism discussed in the previous chapter?

SECTION THREE

THE POSTCLASSICAL PERIOD, 500–1500 C.E.: EXPANSIONS AND CONTACTS

After the collapse of key classical dynasties or empires, new influences arose in many older centers—particularly with the rise of Islam and the spread of Buddhism. Civilization also expanded from older centers—thus the rise of a Japanese form of East Asian culture and the development of civilization in northwestern Europe and in Russia, linked, however, to earlier Mediterranean forms. Civilizations also expanded in portions of the Americas and sub-Saharan Africa.

During most of the postclassical period, Islamic civilization, centered in the Middle East and North Africa, became the leading force. Other themes included the sheer spread of major religions—particularly Islam, Christianity, and Buddhism—and the resultant impact on the arts and politics. International trade expanded rapidly, as did imitation of older centers by regions solidifying forms of civilization for the first time, such as northern Europe and Japan. The expansion of trade led to new kinds of questions about merchants and merchants' motives, although different societies offered different resolutions. Toward the end of the period, Mongol conquests and a brief flurry of Chinese trading expeditions intensified international contacts, including technology exchange from Asia and the spread of epidemic disease.

The chapters in this section focus on developments within major civilizations, as the roster expanded. Several chapters then deal with growing trade and the Mongol conquests as sources of change; and several final chapters take up various aspects of the expanding range of international contacts.

28 THE KORAN AND THE FAMILY

The canonical source of Islam (*al-Islâm, meaning "surrender"*) is the Koran [Qur'ān], which contains revelations from Allah, "the God of Abraham, Ishamael, Isaac, and Jacob, and the Tribes [of Israel] . . . and Jesus," to the Prophet Muhammad [ca. 570–632 C.E.]. Transmitted through the intermediary of the angel Gabriel during the 20 years of Muhammad's apostolate, these full and complete revelations embodied Allah's "eternal knowledge and judgement of all things" and a perfection of all previous religions. As the ultimate authority in Islam and the "supreme self-manifestation of God to His creatures," the Koran was early reduced to writing. Yet an official, authoritative edition did not appear until after the Prophet's death in 632 C.E. Divided into 114 chapters *(suras)* and containing 77,639 words, the text of the Koran is arranged in order of decreasing length with complete disregard for chronology. Internally each *sura* consists of verses [*ayāt*, meaning "signs" or "tokens"] with post-Muhammad headings derived from key terms in the text. Written in classical Arabic, the Koran adheres to a metrical style and was designed to be heard. In the following selections from Sura IV ("Women") the focus is on women, children, orphans, and inheritances, with injunctions to males in the Islamic patriarchal society regarding them.

The following passages obviously invite judgments about what kind of family life and gender relations were urged in Islamic society. We can compare these with other versions of a patriarchal system in classical China and India (see Chapters 7 and 12). These passages also show how Islamic religion developed specific regulations, not just general ethics, for personal and family behavior, harking back to older Middle Eastern traditions in this area (see Chapters 2 and 4). Finally, the passages also show something of the Islamic view of God, in whose name men and women were to regulate their relationships.

From "Koran" from *The Koran Interpreted*, 2 vols. from Arthur J. Arberry. Copyright © 1955 by George Allen. Reprinted by permission of HarperCollins Publishers Ltd.

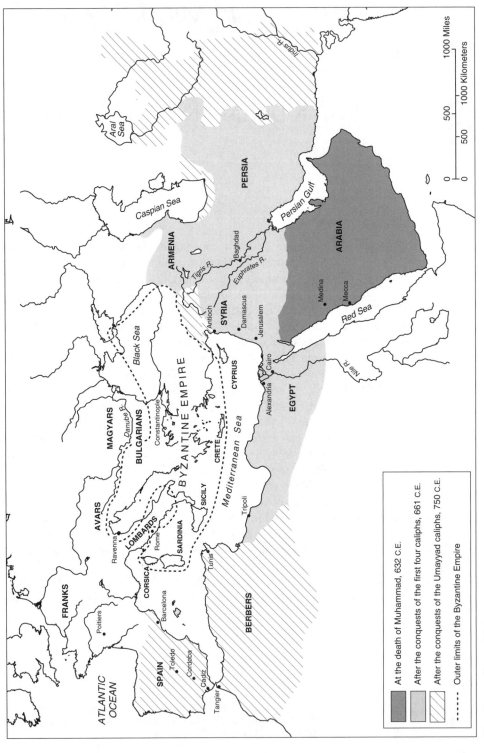

The Expansion of Islam.

THE KORAN

In the Name of God, the Merciful, the Compassionate

• • •

Give the orphans their property, and do not
exchange the corrupt for the good; and devour
not their property with your property; surely that is a great crime.
If you fear that you will not act justly
toward the orphans, marry such women
as seem good to you, two, three, four;
but if you fear you will not be equitable,
then only one, or what your right hands own;
so it is likelier you will not be partial.
And give the women their dowries as a gift
spontaneous; but if they are pleased
to offer you any of it, consume it with wholesome appetite.
But do not give to fools their property
that God has assigned to you to manage;
provide for them and clothe them out of it,
and speak to them honourable words.
Test well the orphans, until they reach
the age of marrying; then, if you perceive
in them right judgment, deliver to them
their property; consume it not wastefully and hastily
ere they are grown. If any man is rich,
let him be abstinent; if poor, let him consume in reason.
And when you deliver to them their property,
take witnesses over them; God suffices for a reckoner.

To the men a share of what parents and kinsmen
leave, and to the women a share of what
parents and kinsmen leave, whether it be
little or much, a share apportioned;
and when the division is attended by
kinsmen and orphans and the poor,
make provision for them out of it,
and speak to them honourable words.
And let those fear who, if they left
behind them weak seed, would be afraid
on their account, and let them fear
God, and speak words hitting the mark.
Those who devour the property of orphans
unjustly, devour Fire in their bellies,
and shall assuredly roast in a Blaze.
God charges you, concerning your children:
to the male the like of the portion

of two females, and if they be women
above two, then for them two-thirds
of what he leaves, but if she be one
then to her a half; and to his parents
to each one of the two the sixth
of what he leaves, if he has children;
but if he has no children, and his
heirs are his parents, a third to his
mother, or, if he has brothers, to his
mother a sixth, after any bequest
he may bequeath, or any debt.
Your fathers and your sons—you know not
which out of them is nearer in profit
to you. So God apportions; surely God is
  All-knowing, All-wise.

And for you a half of what your wives
leave, if they have no children; but
if they have children, then for you of what
they leave a fourth, after any bequest
they may bequeath, or any debt.
And for them a fourth of what you leave,
if you have no children; but if you
have children, then for them of what
you leave an eighth, after any bequest
you may bequeath, or any debt.
If a man or a woman have no heir
direct, but have a brother or a sister,
to each of the two a sixth; but if they
are more numerous than that, they share
equally a third, after any bequest
he may bequeath, or any debt not
prejudicial; a charge from God. God is
  All-knowing, All-merciful.

Those are God's bounds. Whoso obeys God
and His Messenger, He will admit him
to gardens underneath which rivers flow,
therein dwelling forever; that is the mighty triumph.
But whoso disobeys God, and His Messenger,
and transgresses His bounds, him He will
admit to a Fire, therein dwelling
forever, and for him there awaits a humbling chastisement.

Such of your women as commit indecency,
call four of you to witness against them;
and if they witness, then detain them
in their houses until death takes them

or God appoints for them a way.
And when two of you commit indecency,
punish them both; but if they repent
and make amends, then suffer them to be;
God turns, and is All-compassionate.
God shall turn only towards those who do
evil in ignorance, then shortly repent;
God will return towards those; God is
    All-knowing, All-wise.
But God shall not turn towards those
who do evil deeds until, when one of them
is visited by death, he says, "Indeed
now I repent," neither to those who die
disbelieving; for them We have prepared a painful chastisement.

O believers, it is not lawful for you
to inherit women against their will;
neither debar them, that you may go off
with part of what you have given them,
except when they commit a flagrant indecency.
Consort with them honourably; or if
you are averse to them, it is possible
you may be averse to a thing, and God set in it much good.
And if you desire to exchange a wife
in place of another, and you have given
to one a hundredweight, take of it nothing.
What, will you take it by way of calumny and manifest sin?
How shall you take it, when each of you has been
privily with the other, and they have taken from you a solemn compact?
And do not marry women that your fathers
married, unless it be a thing of the past;
surely that is indecent and hateful, an evil way.

Forbidden to you are your mothers and daughters,
your sisters, your aunts paternal and maternal,
your brother's daughters, your sister's daughters,
your mothers who have given suck to you,
your suckling sisters, your wives' mothers,
your stepdaughters who are in your care
being born of your wives you have been in to—
but if you have not yet been in to them
it is no fault in you—and the spouses
of your sons who are of your loins,
and that you should take to you two sisters
together, unless it be a thing of the past;
God is All-forgiving, All compassionate;
and wedded women, save what your right hands own.
So God prescribes for you. Lawful for you,

beyond all that, is that you may seek,
using your wealth, in wedlock and not
in licence. Such wives as you enjoy thereby,
give them their wages apportionate; it is no
fault in you in your agreeing together,
after the due apportionate. God is
    All-knowing, All-wise.

Any one of you who has not the affluence
to be able to marry believing freewomen
in wedlock, let him take believing handmaids
that your right hands own; God knows very well
your faith; the one of you is as the other.
So marry them, with their people's leave,
and give them their wages honourably
as women in wedlock, not as in licence or taking lovers.
But when they are in wedlock, if they
commit indecency, they shall be liable
to half the chastisement of freewomen.
That provision is for those of you who fear
fornication; yet it is better for you
to be patient. God is All-forgiving
    All-compassionate.
God desires to make clear to you, and to
guide you in the institutions of those
before you, and to turn towards you; God is
    All-knowing, All-wise;
and God desires to turn towards you, but
those who follow their lusts desire you
to swerve away mightily. God desires
to lighten things for you, for man was created a weakling. . . .
Do not covet that whereby God in bounty
has preferred one of you above another.
To the men a share from what they have earned,
and to the women a share from what they
have earned. And ask God of his bounty;
    God knows everything.

To everyone We have appointed heirs
of that which parents and kinsmen leave,
and those with whom you have sworn compact.
So give to them their share; God is witness over everything.

Men are the managers of the affairs of women
for that God has preferred in bounty
one of them over another, and for that
they have expended of their property.
Righteous women are therefore obedient,

guarding the secret for God's guarding.
And those you fear may be rebellious
admonish; banish them to their couches,
and beat them. If they then obey you,
look not for any way against them; God is
   All-high, All-great.
And if you fear a breach between the two,
bring forth an arbiter from his people
and from her people an arbiter, if they
desire to set things right; God will
compose their differences; surely God is
   All-knowing, All-aware. . . .

If a woman fear rebelliousness or aversion
in her husband, there is no fault in them
if the couple set things right between them;
right settlement is better; and souls are very
prone to avarice. If you do good
and are godfearing, surely God is aware of
   the things you do.
You will not be able to be equitable
between your wives, be you ever so eager;
yet do not be altogether partial
so that you leave her as it were suspended.
If you set things right, and are godfearing,
God is All-forgiving, All-compassionate.
But if they separate, God will enrich
each of them of His plenty; God is
   All-embracing, All-wise.

STUDY QUESTIONS

1. Did Islam enforce a patriarchal gender system?
2. What were the key protections for women, and how did they compare with protective features in the earlier classical and river-valley civilizations?
3. Were women spiritually equal to men in Islam? How was this reconciled with patriarchal traditions?
4. What kinds of concerns did Islam emphasize concerning sexuality?
5. Why did Muhammad believe he had improved conditions for women in Arab society?
6. How did Islamic beliefs and practices concerning women compare with Confucian and Hindu systems?

29

THE ISLAMIC RELIGION

The Hadith (which means a story, tale, or report) supplements the Koran as a source for Islamic religious, social, and legal precepts. These are collections of traditions attributed to Muhammad, his companions, and early caliphs. Consisting of rules and practical social norms (*sunnah*) formulated by the prophet and enforced by early leaders in the Islamic community, the Hadith contains prescribed rules and behaviors that guide Muslims but are not offered in the Koran. Proclaimed in sermons or informally before witnesses, the apostolic traditions remained unwritten until the beginning of the 7th century. In response to Caliph Oman II's orders for a formal collection of extant traditions, an Iranian savant, Abū 'Abdallah Muhammad (b. Ismāil al-Bukhārī, 810–870), traveled throughout the Islamic World, where he uncovered more than 600,000 rulings. Joined by other collectors, al-Bukhārī devised a critical scientific method to separate authentic traditions from the spurious. From this, he produced an authoritative Hadith consisting of 7,397 authentic traditions. His collection, along with those by 'Abul Husain Muslim (819–874) and four less reliable collectors, acquired canonical status among the orthodox Sunnis and is known as the *Sahīh* ("The Genuine").

In the Hadith selections that follow, you can get a sense of what the main religious duties of a Muslim are and how the individual relates to Allah. What is distinctive about Muslim religious life? Why do so many people find Islam such a satisfactory religion, often converting to it from other faiths?

THE HADITH

Said the Apostle of Allah—upon whom be Allah's blessing and peace—: "The [true] Muslim is he from whose tongue and whose hand [other] Muslims are safe, and the [true] Muhājir is he who has fled from those things Allah has forbidden."

Islam is built upon five things: on testifying that there is no deity save Allah and that Muhammad is his Apostle, on performing prayer, on paying the legal alms (*zakāt*), on the pilgrimage [to Mecca], and on the fast of Ramadān.

The Apostle of Allah—upon whom be Allah's blessing and peace—was asked which [good] work was the most excellent, and he answered: "Belief in Allah and in His Apostle." He was asked: "And then which?" He replied: "Jihād in the way of Allah." He was again asked: "and then what?" and he replied: "An acceptable pilgrimage."

From *A Reader on Islam*, edited by Arthur Jeffery (New York: Books for Libraries, A Division of Arno Press, 1980), pp. 81–86. Copyright © Arno Press, 1980. Reprinted by permission.

No one ever bears witness that there is no deity save Allah and that Muhammad is the Apostle of Allah, [testifying to it] sincerely from his heart, but Allah will preserve him from Hell-fire.

There is no Muslim who plants a tree or cultivates a plot from which birds of man or domestic beasts [may gather food to] eat, but has therein an act of charitable alms [recorded to his merit].

If a man seizes the property of others with intent to restore it, Allah will settle with him, but if he seizes it with intent to waste it Allah will make waste of him.

If a slave serves honestly his [earthly] master and worships earnestly his [heavenly] Lord, he will have a double recompense.

He who shows concern for the widows and the unfortunate [ranks as high] as one who goes on Jihād in the way of Allah, or one who fasts by day and who rises at night [for prayer].

A [true] believer views his sins as though he were sitting beneath a mountain which he fears may fall on him, but an evil-doer views his sins as a fly that moves across his nose.

In this world be as a stranger, or as one who is just passing along the road.

In two things an old man's heart never ceases to be that of a youth, in love of this world and in hoping long.

Were a man to possess two valleys full of gold he would be wanting a third, for nothing will ever really fill man's belly but the dust.

To look at a woman is forbidden, even if it is a look without desire, so how much the more is touching her.

Said he—upon whom be Allah's blessing and peace—: "Avoid seven pernicious things." [His Companions] said: "And what are they, O Apostle of Allah?" He answered: "Associating anything with Allah, sorcery, depriving anyone of life where Allah has forbidden that save for just cause, taking usury, devouring the property of orphans, turning the back on the day of battle, and slandering chaste believing women even though they may be acting carelessly."

No one who enters Paradise will ever want to return to this world, even could he possess the earth and all that is on it, save the martyrs who desire to return to this world and be killed ten times so great is the regard in which they find themselves held.

To be stationed on the frontier for one day during Holy War is better than [to possess] this world and all that is on it. A place in Paradise the size of one of your whip-lashes is better than this world and all that is on it. A night or a day that a man spends on Holy War is better than this world and all that is on it.

The similitude of a stingy man and a generous giver of alms is that of two men wearing cloaks of mail in which the hand-pieces are fastened to the collar-piece. Whenever the generous giver starts to give an alms it stretches for him so that it is as though it were not, but when the stingy man starts to give an alms every link clings to the one next it so contracting that his hands are kept tight by his collar-bone and however much he strives it will not stretch.

It is right to "hearken and obey" so long as one is not bidden disobey [Allah], but should the command be to disobedience let there be no "hearken and obey."

Traveling is part of one's punishment, for one is deprived of one's sleeping, one's eating, one's drinking thereby, so whenever any one of you has finished what he had to do let him hurry home.

Allah desires to meet those who desire to meet with Him, but is disinclined to meet those who are disinclined to meet with Him.

The man who has the lightest punishment on the Day will be the one who has live coals placed under the soles of his feet [so hot that] his brains will boil from the heat thereof.

If a man sees something in [the conduct of] his ruler which he dislikes let him put up with it patiently, for there is no one who separates himself even a span from the community and dies [in that separation], but dies a pagan death.

When Friday comes angels take their seat over every mosque gate and write down in order those who come in, but when the prayer-leader sits they fold their sheets and come to hearken to the words.

Said the Prophet—upon whom be Allah's blessing and peace—: "I had a look into Paradise and I saw that the poor made up most of its inhabitants, and I had a look into Hell and saw that most of its inhabitants were women."

When [the month of] Ramadān begins the gates of heaven are set open, the gates of Hell are locked shut, and the satans are chained.

Treat women-folk kindly for woman was created of a rib. The crookedest part of a rib is its upper part. If you go to straighten it out you will break it, and if you leave it alone it will continue crooked. So treat women in kindly fashion.

Whosoever testifies that there is no deity save Allah, that Muhammad is His servant and His Apostle, that Jesus is His servant and His Apostle and His word which He cast to Mary and a Spirit from Him, that Paradise is a reality and Hell-fire a reality, him will Allah bring into Paradise in accordance with his works.

Only two men are really to be envied, namely, a man to whom Allah has given Scripture and who sits up at nights with it, and a man to whom Allah has given wealth which he distributes in charitable alms day and night.

Said the Apostle of Allah—upon whom be Allah's blessing and peace: "O band of youths, let him among you who is able to make a home get married, and let him who is not able betake himself to fasting for he will find in that a quencher [of his passions]."

The worst of foods is that of a feast to which the rich have been invited and the poor overlooked, yet anyone who overlooks an invitation is in rebellion against Allah and His Apostle.

Said the Apostle of Allah—upon whom be Allah's blessing and peace—: "Do not wear silks and satins, and do not drink from gold and silver vessels nor eat from dishes made thereof, for these things are theirs in this world but ours in the world to come."

Said the Apostle of Allah—upon whom be Allah's blessing and peace—: "Gabriel said to me: 'Whosoever of your community dies without ever having associated any other with Allah will enter Paradise' (or perhaps he said: 'will not enter Hell-fire'). Someone said: 'Even if he is an adulterer or a thief?' He replied: 'Even if.'"

The similitude of a good companion and a bad one is [that of] a man who carries musk and one who blows a blacksmith's bellows, for one who is carrying musk may give you a share, or you may purchase some of it, or in any case enjoy the delightful smell, but one who blows the blacksmith's bellows will either set your clothes on fire or accost you with an evil smell.

Said the Prophet—upon whom be Allah's blessing and peace—: "The first group to enter Paradise will have faces like the moon on the night of its fullness, will neither spit nor blow their noses or defecate therein, their utensils there will be of gold, their combs of gold and silver, their censers of aloes wood, their sweat will be musk, and each of them will have two spouses so beautiful that the marrow of their leg-bones will be visible through the flesh. There will be no differences or disputings among them for they will all be of one heart, glorifying Allah morning and evening."

"Ā'isha said: "I was stuffing a pillow for the Prophet—upon whom be Allah's blessing and peace—on which were images like those on a saddle-cushion, when he came and stood on the doorway. His countenance started to alter, so I said: 'What is it, O Apostle of Allah?' He said: 'What are you doing with this pillow?' 'It is a pillow,' I answered, 'that I have made for you on which you may recline.' Said he: 'Do you not know that angels will not enter a house in which there is a picture? On the Day makers of [such] pictures will be punished, for [Allah] will say to them: 'Give life to that which you have created.'"

Among the signs of the coming of the Hour are these: ignorance will be apparent and learning inconspicuous, fornication will be rampant and the drinking of wine, men will be few but women many so that fifty women will have but one husband between them.

Said the Prophet—upon whom be Allah's blessing and peace—: "He who drinks wine in this world and repents not of it will be forbidden it in the world to come."

There is no misfortune befalls a Muslim but Allah will atone for some sin of his thereby, even if it be only [so small a misfortune as] his being pricked by a thorn.

Said the Prophet—upon whom be Allah's blessing and peace—: "Visions are from Allah but dreams are from Satan, so if any one of you sees anything disagreeable [during sleep] let him spit three times when he wakens up and take refuge [with Allah] from its evil, and then it will do him no harm."

Said the Apostle of Allah—upon whom be Allah's blessing and peace—: "Among the greatest of mortal sins is that a man curse his parents." They said: "O Apostle of Allah, how could a man curse his parents?" He replied: "The man who reviles another man's parents is reviling his own father and mother." . . .

The Apostle of Allah—on whom be Allah's blessing and peace—once kissed al-Hasan the son of 'Alī while al-Aqra' b. Hābis of Tamīm was sitting there. Al-Aqra' said: "I have ten sons but never have kissed any one of them." The Apostle of Allah—upon whom be Allah's blessing and peace—looked at him, and then said: "He who does not show tenderness will not have tenderness shown him."

Said the Prophet—upon whom be Allah's blessing and peace—: "Whoever casts himself down from a mountain so as to kill himself will be in Hell continually casting himself down thus for ever and ever. Whoever sips poison so as to kill himself will in Hell have poison in his hand which he will go on sipping there for ever and ever. Whoever kills himself with a knife will in Hell have a knife in his hand which he will go on continually plunging into his bowels for ever and ever."

Said he—upon whom be Allah's blessing and peace—: "Let none of you wish for death because of any hardship that has befallen him. If he needs must say something, let him say: 'Allahumma! let me live so long as life is best for me, and let me pass away when passing away is the best thing for me.'"

Said the Prophet—upon whom be Allah's blessing and peace—: "Allah made mercy in a hundred parts. Ninety-nine of these parts He kept with Himself and one single part He sent down on earth. It is by reason of this one part that creatures show mercy to one another, so that a mare carefully lifts her hoof fearing lest with it she harm her foal."

Said the Apostle of Allah—on whom be Allah's blessing and peace—: "Let him who believes in Allah and the Last Day refrain from doing harm to his neighbour. Let him who believes in Allah and the Last Day see to it that he properly honours his guest. Let him who believes in Allah and the Last Day either speak what is good or hold his tongue."

Said the Prophet—upon whom be Allah's blessing and peace—: "No one will ever experience the sweetness of faith till he loves a man solely for the sake of Allah, till he feels that he would rather be cast into Hell-fire then return to unbelief once Allah has delivered him from it, till Allah and His Apostle are dearer to him than anything besides."

Muhammad b. Muqātil Abū'l-Hasan has related to me [saying]: 'Abdallah informed us on the authority of Humaid b. 'Abd ar-Rahmān, on the authority of Abū Huraira—with whom may Allah be pleased—that a man came to the Apostle of Allah—upon whom be Allah's blessing and peace—saying: "O Apostle of Allah, there is no hope for me." He replied: "Too bad for you." Said [the man]: "I had intercourse with my wife during Ramadān." [The Prophet] answered: "Then set free a slave." Said he: "I have none." [The Prophet] answered: "Then fast for two months on end." Said he: "But I could not." [The Prophet] answered: "Then feed sixty poor people." Said he: "I have not the wherewithall." Just then there was brought to [the Prophet] a basket of dates, so he said to the man: "Take this and distribute it as charitable alms [in expiation for your sin]." Said he: "O Apostle of Allah, [am I to distribute it] to other than my own family? when by Him in whose hand is my soul there is no one between the gateposts of the city more needy than I am." Thereat the Prophet laughed till his canine teeth showed, and he said: "Go along and take it."

STUDY QUESTIONS

1. What are some of the main religious obligations of Muslims, according to these passages? What were the goals of a proper religious life?
2. How do the gender values in these passages compare with the previous selections from the Koran? What might account for any differences?
3. What was the Islamic approach to social and economic inequality? To slavery? How did this approach compare with the social theories of the classical Mediterranean period? (See Chapter 19.)
4. What were some of the major offenses against Islamic rules?
5. Do these passages suggest some of the reasons for Islam's striking success as a world religion?

30

RELIGIOUS AND POLITICAL ORGANIZATION IN THE ISLAMIC MIDDLE EAST

The office of imam, or leader, dates from Muhammad's death in 632, when a successor, or caliph, was elected. The word *imam* is also applied to local leaders of worship within a mosque. The following passage, from Al-Mawārdī's (d. 1058) *Ordinance of Government,* describes the central leadership of Islam during the centuries of Arab dominance in the office most commonly known as the caliphate. The statement of the duties and eligibility of the caliph comes from the majority, or Sunni Muslims. Minority Shiite Muslims split away in their belief that the caliphate was a divinely designated office inherited by descendants of Muhammad.

The orthodox Sunni view held that the imam or caliph was an elected and secular office that did, however, involve strict religious as well as political duties. The authority of the office was absolute so long as its holder adhered to the Koran and Hadith. Early elective procedures gave way to inheritance of the office in the Umayyad and Abbasid dynasties (661–750 and 750–1378), but the concept of the caliph's duties remained consistent. This office, then, was the chief political legacy of Islam during the centuries of Arab rule in the Middle East. In what sense was the caliphate a religious office? In what sense did it embrace nonreligious functions? What kind of government structure did the powers of the caliphate imply?

AL MAWĀRDĪ

The office of Imam was set up in order to replace the office of Prophet in the defense of the faith and the government of the world. By general consensus [*ijmā'*], from which only al-Asamm dissents, the investiture of whichsoever member of the community exercises the functions of Imam is obligatory. But there is disagreement as to whether this obligation derives from reason or from Holy Law. One group says it derives from reason, since it is in the nature of reasonable men to submit to a leader who will prevent them from injuring one another and who will settle quarrels and disputes, for without rulers men would live in anarchy and heedlessness like benighted savages. . . .

Another group says that the obligation derives from the Holy Law and not from reason, since the Imam deals with matters of Holy Law to which, in reason, he would be allowed not to devote himself, since reason does not make them obligatory. All that reason requires is that a reasonable man should refrain from mutual injury and conflict with his neighbor and act equitably in mutual fairness and good relations, conducting himself in accordance with his own reason, and not with someone else's. But it is the Holy Law which intervenes to entrust these affairs to its religious representative. . . .

The obligation of the Imamate, which is thus confirmed, is a collective duty, like the Holy War and the pursuit of knowledge, so that when it is performed by those whose charge it is, the general obligation of the rest of the community lapses. If no one discharges it, then two groups of people must be distinguished from the rest; first, the electors, who choose an Imam for the community; and second, those eligible for the Imamate, one of whom must be made Imam. The rest of the community, who belong neither to the one nor to the other group, commit no sin or offense if there is a delay in filling the Imamate. When these two groups are constituted and take over the collective obligation, each group must conform to the prescribed conditions. The conditions required in the electors are three:

1. Rectitude [*'adāla*] in all respects.
2. The knowledge to recognize the required qualifications for the Imamate.
3. The discernment and wisdom to choose the candidate best suited to the Imamate, the most capable and the best informed of the conduct of public affairs.

He who is in the city of the Imam has no privilege or precedence, because of this, over those in other places. That those who are present in the city of the Imam undertake the appointment of the new Imam is custom, not law; this happens because they are the first to hear of his death and because those who are best qualified to succeed him are usually to be found in his city.

The conditions of eligibility for the Imamate are seven:

1. Rectitude in all respects.
2. The knowledge to exercise personal judgment [*ijtihād*] in cases and decisions.
3. Soundness of hearing, sight, and tongue so that he may deal accurately with those matters which can only be attained by them.
4. Soundness of limb so that he has no defect which would prevent him from moving freely and rising quickly.
5. The discernment needed to govern the subjects and conduct public affairs.
6. The courage and vigor to defend the lands of Islam and to wage holy war against the enemy.
7. Descent, that is to say, he must be of the tribe of Quraysh, as is prescribed by a text and accepted by consensus. . . .

The Imamate is conferred in two ways: one is by the choice of the electors [literally, those competent to bind and to loosen], and the other is by the nomination of the previous Imam. . . .

When the electors meet, they scrutinize the qualified candidates and proceed to appoint that one among them who is the most worthy, who best meets the required conditions, and to whom the people are most willing to give obedience. They recognize him without delay. If the exercise of their judgment leads them to choose a particular person from the community, they offer him the Imamate. If he accepts, they swear allegiance to him, and the Imamate is vested in him by this procedure. Allegiance to him and obedience to him then become binding on the entire community. If he holds back and refuses an Imamate, it cannot be imposed upon him, since it is a contract by consent and choice and may not involve compulsion or constraint. In such case the Imamate is offered to another qualified candidate.

If two candidates are equally well qualified, the elder takes precedence in choice; however, seniority, where the parties are of age, is not a necessary condition, and if the younger is appointed, it is still valid. If one is wiser and the other braver, the choice should be determined by the needs of the time. If the need for courage is more urgent because of the disorder of the frontiers and the appearance of rebels, then the braver has a better claim. If the need for wisdom is more urgent because of the quiescence of the populace and the appearance of heretics, then it is the wiser who has a better claim. . . .

The duties of the Imam in the conduct of public affairs are ten:

1. To maintain the religion according to established principles and the consensus of the first generation of Muslims. If an innovator appears or if some dubious person deviates from it, the Imam must clarify the proofs of religion to him, expound that which is correct, and apply to him the proper rules and penalties so that religion may be protected from injury and the community safeguarded from error.

2. To execute judgments given between litigants and to settle disputes between contestants so that justice may prevail and so that none commit or suffer injustice.

3. To defend the lands of Islam and to protect them from intrusion so that people may earn their livelihood and travel at will without danger to life or property.

4. To enforce the legal penalties for the protection of God's commandments from violation and for the preservation of the rights of his servants from injury or destruction.

5. To maintain the frontier fortresses with adequate supplies and effective force for their defense so that the enemy may not take them by surprise, commit profanation there, or shed the blood, either of a Muslim or an ally [*mu'āhad*].

6. To wage holy war [*jihād*] against those who, after having been invited to accept Islam, persist in rejecting it, until they either become Muslims or enter the Pact [*dhimma*] so that God's truth may prevail over every religion [cf. Koran, ix, 33].

7. To collect the booty and the alms [*sadaqa*] in conformity with the prescriptions of the Holy Law, as defined by explicit texts and by independent judgment [*ijtihād*], and this without terror or oppression.

8. To determine the salaries and other sums due from the treasury, without extravagance and without parsimony, and to make payment at the proper time, neither in advance nor in arrears.

9. To employ capable and trustworthy men and appoint sincere men for the tasks which he delegates to them and for the money which he entrusts to them so that the tasks may be competently discharged and the money honestly safeguarded.

10. To concern himself directly with the supervision of affairs and the scrutiny of conditions so that he may personally govern the community, safeguard the faith, and not resort to delegation in order to free himself either for pleasure or for worship, for even the trustworthy may betray and the sincere may deceive. God said, "O David, we have made you our vicegerent [*khalīfa*] on earth; therefore, judge justly among men and do not follow your caprice, which will lead you astray from God's path." [Koran, xxxviii, 25]. In this, God was not content with delegation, but required a personal performance and did not excuse the following of passions, which, He says, lead astray from His path, and this, though He considered David worthy to judge in legion and to hold His viceregency [*khalīfa*]. This is one of the duties of government of any shepherd. The Prophet of God, may God bless and save him, said, "You are all shepherds, and you are all answerable for your flocks."

. . .

The rules of the Imamate and its general jurisdiction over the interests of religion and the governance of the community, as we have described them, being established, and the investiture of an Imam being duly confirmed, the authority which comes from him to his deputies is of four kinds:

1. Those who have unlimited authority of unlimited scope. These are the viziers [high executives], for they are entrusted with all public affairs without specific attribution.

2. Those who have unlimited authority of limited scope. Such are the provincial and district governors, whose authority is unlimited within the specific areas assigned to them.

3. Those who have limited authority of unlimited scope. Such are the chief *qādī*, the commander of the armies, the commandant of the frontier fortresses, the intendant of the land tax, and the collector of the alms, each of whom has unlimited authority in the specific functions assigned to him.

4. Those with limited authority of limited scope, such as the *qādī* of a town or district, the local intendant of the land tax, collector of tithes, the frontier commandment, or the army commander, every one of whom has limited authority of limited scope.

STUDY QUESTIONS

1. How would a Muslim distinguish between good and bad government?
2. What kind of enforcement for good government does this document suggest?

3. What should a Muslim do when a ruler did not live up to his obligations?
4. What was the power, in principle, of a Muslim ruler? What kind of bureaucratic system did Al-Māwardī suggest?
5. How did Islamic political principles compare with those of Christianity?
6. Why do scholars disagree about the political implications and flexibility of Islam? Are there potential tensions about appropriate political behavior, in cases of a less than ideal government, embedded in this document?

RELIGIOUS LEADERSHIP IN ISLAM: THE IMAM

Islamic Imam or Caliph. This illustration comes from a Persian literary text, "Al Maquamat," or "the Meetings," in the second half of the 13th century. The illustrator was named Nariri. The scene depicts an Imam, Abou Zayd, preaching in the Mosque of Samarkand. The great trading city in Central Asia (in what is now Uzbekistan) was of the center of silk road commerce. (From "Al Maquamat", "The Meetings"), Illustrated by Hariri, second quarter of 13th century, Persian library texts. (Bibliothéque National, Paris/www.bridgeman.co.uk)

The style is Persian. Persian art by this point reflected not only earlier traditions, but also Chinese influences, suggested in some of the stylized poses of the people shown. It was also, of course, Muslim. The Qu'ran offered no justification for art, and strict Muslims shunned any representation of human or animal figures lest they promote false worship. Art developed nevertheless, focused on decorative motifs and Arab calligraphy. This allowed rulers and cities to display artistic achievement and splendor without violating the strictest religious provisions. Persian artists, obviously, went further, using Arab motifs but also adding human figures. One result is some visual knowledge of how Muslim religious services were organized.

STUDY QUESTIONS

1. What does this scene suggest about the relationship between Muslim religious leadership and ordinary faithful? What was an Imam?
2. How does this picture correspond to texts, like the Ordinances of Government, that described an Imam's duties?
3. What are the characteristic Arab artistic themes in this picture?
4. What Persian and other Asian influences show in the picture?

CHINA AND JAPAN

31
PEASANT LIFE IN TANG AND SONG CHINA: EVIDENCE FROM POETRY AND LEGAL DOCUMENTS

During the postclassical period most Chinese people, perhaps 85 percent of the population, were peasants working small plots of land, as had been true for the previous several thousand years. The contributions of the peasants to the country were essential: They grew the grain, bred the animals, made the cloth, mined the coal, built the roads and dug the canals. They also made up the great majority of the soldiers in the army.

What was it like to be a peasant in China during the postclassical period? This basic question has been the focus of much research by scholars during the past several decades. One line of inquiry has studied the material standards of the peasants. How much land did they possess? What techniques did they employ in cultivating the land? How onerous was their tax burden? A second subject of investigation has been the beliefs of the peasants. To what extent did Confucianism, Daoism, and Buddhism shape their thinking? How influential on the peasants was traditional folk religion?

Although the paucity of documentation regarding the peasants makes it impossible, at least for the present, to fully answer many of these questions, the poems and legal

Selection I.A, "Recruiting Officer of Shih-Hao" Tang Poem by Dufu from *Sunflower Splendor*, translated by Irving Y. Lo, Wu-chi Lu and Irving Yucheng Lo. Copyright © 1990 by Indiana University Press. Reprinted by permission of Indiana University Press. Selection I.B, "Watching the Wheat Reapers" Tang Poem by Bo Zhuyi from *Sunflower Splendor*, translated by Irving Y. Lo, Wu-chi Lu and Irving Yucheng Lo. Copyright © 1990 by Indiana University Press. Reprinted by permission of Indiana University Press, and "The Old Man of Hsin-feng" pages 203-205 by Liu Zongyuan, translated by Eugene Eoyang from *Sunflower Splendor*, translated by Irving Y. Lo, Wu-chi Lu and Irving Yucheng Lo. Reprinted by permission of Eugene Eoyang. Selection I.C, "Farmers" pages 214 by Bi Rixiu, translated by Jan W. Walls from *Sunflower Splendor*, translated by Irving Y. Lo, Wu-chi Liu and Irving Yucheng Lo. Reprinted by permission of Dr. Jan W. Walls. Selection I.D, "Lament of a Woman Acorn Gatherer" by Bi Rixiu, translated by William H. Nienhauser, Jr. from *Sunflower Splendor*, translated by Iriving Y. Lo, Wu-chi Lu and Irving Yucheng Lo. Reprinted by permission of William H. Nienhauser, Jr. Selections II.A and II.B from Jacques Gernet, *Daily Life in China on the Eve of the Mongol Invasion, 1250–1276*, translated by H.M. Wright (Stanford, Calif.: Stanford University Press, 1970), pp. 103–104. Selection III.A, "Lament of the Farm Wife of Wu," translated by Burton Watson, and III.C, from *The Columbia Anthology of Traditional Chinese Literature*, edited by Victor Mair. Copyright © 1996 Columbia University Press. Reprinted with permission of the publisher. Selection III.B from *Science and Civilization in China, 5.IX: Textile Technology: Spinning and Reeling*, by Dieter Kuhn (Cambridge, Mass.: Cambridge University Press, 1988), Frontspiece.

documents in this chapter enable us to make a beginning. Most of the poets whose verse appears in this chapter were governmental officials who, in order to obtain their positions, had passed rigorous examinations testing their mastery of Confucian teachings. Some of the officials, notably Dufu, are regarded as among China's greatest poets. Of course, the social origins, rich literary learning, and standard of living of the officials set them apart from the peasants. However, as they moved from posting to posting, the officials had an opportunity to closely observe rural life in many of China's regions and this is reflected in the poems that follow.

The two legal documents sandwiched between the Tang and Song poems date from the 9th and 10th centuries and were found, together with many similar records, in the western Chinese town of Dunhuang about a hundred years ago. From 400–1000 Dunhuang was one of the most important rest stops for caravans traveling on the Silk Roads to and from China. It was also a huge Buddhist monastic complex, featuring worship centers in about 500 splendidly decorated caves, some of which were also libraries. Around the year 1000 the monks and merchants abandoned Dunhuang, probably because of invasions by nomads from the north. Owing to the extremely arid climate in this region, the contents of the caves—statues, paintings, and documents of various kinds—were preserved in amazingly good condition until discovered by a British archaeologist in the early 20th century.

How do the poems and legal records help us to understand the lives of the peasants?

PEASANTS IN CHINESE CULTURE

I. TANG POEMS

A. From Dufu (712–770)

Recruiting Officer of Shihao

At dusk I sought lodging at Shihao village,
When a recruiting officer came to seize men at night.
An old man scaled the wall and fled,
His old wife came out to answer the door.

How furious was the officer's shout!
How pitiable was the woman's cry!
I listened as she stepped forward to speak:
"All my three sons have left for garrison duty at Ye;
From one of them a letter just arrived,
Saying my two sons had newly died in battle.
Survivors can manage to live on.
But the dead are gone forever.
Now there's no other man in the house,
Only a grandchild at his mother's breast.
The child's mother has not gone away;
She has only a tattered skirt for wear.
An old woman, I am feeble and weak,
But I will gladly leave with you tonight
To answer the urgent call at Heyang—
I can still cook morning gruel for your men."

The night drew on, but talking stopped;
It seemed I heard only half-concealed sobs.
As I got back on the road at daybreak,
Only the old man was there to see me off.

B. From Bo Zhuyi (772–846)

Watching the Wheat-Reapers

Farm families have leisure months,
In the fifth month chores double up.
When south wind rises at night,
Fields and dikes are covered with golden wheat.

Women old and young carry baskets of food,
Children and toddlers bring out porridge in pots,
Following each other with food for the farmhands,
Those stout fellows on the southern knoll.

Their feet steamed by the sultry vapor from the soil,
Their backs scorched by the sun's burning light;
Drained of all strength to feel any heat,
Their only regret, summer days are too short.

Then there are those poor womenfolk,
Their children clinging to their side.
With their right hand they pick up leftover grains;
On their left arm dangles a broken basket.

To hear their words of complaint—
All who listen will grieve for them:
Their family land stripped clean to pay tax,
They now glean the field to fill their stomach.

What deeds of merit have I done?
I've neither farmed nor raised silkworms;
My official's salary, three hundred piculs of rice,
And at year's end there is surplus grain to eat.

Thinking of this, I feel guilty and ashamed;
All day long I cannot keep it out of my mind.

The Old Man of Xinfeng with the Broken Arm

An old man from Xin'feng, eighty-eight years old,
Hair on his temples and his eyebrows white as snow.
Leaning on his great-great-grandson, he walks to the front of the inn,
His left arm on the boy's shoulder, his right arm broken.
I ask the old man how long has his arm been broken,
And how it came about, how it happened.
The old man said he grew up in the Xinfeng district.
He was born during blessed times, without war or strife,

And he used to listen to the singing and dancing in the Pear Garden,
Knew nothing of banner and spear, or bow and arrow.
Then, during the Tianbao period, a big army was recruited:
From each family, one was taken out of every three,
And of those chosen, where were they sent?
Five months, ten thousand miles away, to Yunnan,
Where, it is said, the Lu River runs,
Where, when flowers fall from pepper trees, noxious fumes rise;
Where, when a great army fords the river, with its seething eddies,
Two or three out of ten never reach the other side.

The village, north and south, was full of the sound of wailing,
Sons leaving father and mother, husbands leaving wives.
They all said, of those who went out to fight the barbarians,
Not one out of a thousand lived to come back.
At the time, this old man was twenty-four,
And the army had his name on their roster.

"Then, late one night, not daring to let anyone know,
By stealth, I broke my arm, smashed it with a big stone.
Now I was unfit to draw the bow or carry the flag,
And I would be spared the fighting in Yunnan.
Bone shattered, muscles ached, it wasn't unpainful,
But I could count on being rejected and sent home.

"This arm has been broken now for over sixty years:
I've lost one limb, but the body's intact.
Even now, in cold nights, when the wind and rain blow,
Right up to daybreak, I hurt so much I cannot sleep,
But I have never had any regrets.
At least, now I alone have survived
Or else, years ago at the River Lu,
I would have died, my spirit fled, and my bones left to rot:
I would have wandered, a ghost in Yunnan looking for home,
Mourning over the graves of ten thousands."
So the old man spoke: I ask you to listen.
Have you not heard the Prime Minister of the Kaiyuan period, Song Kaifu?
How he wouldn't reward frontier campaigns, not wanting to glorify war?
And, have you not heard of Yang Guozhong, the Prime Minister of the
    Tianbao period,
Wishing to seek favor, achieved military deeds at the frontier,
But, before he could pacify the frontier, the people became disgruntled:
Ask the old man of Xinfeng with the broken arm!

C. From Liu Zongyuan (773–819)

Farmers

Beyond the bamboo fence, cooking fire and smoke,
An evening when neighboring farmers chat.

From courtyard's edge autumn insects chirrup,
scattered hempstalks, now desolate and alone.
Silk from the worms all surrendered as tax,
loom and shuttle lean idly on the wall.
An officer passes through one night,
and is served a feast of fowl and millet.
Everyone says the official is harsh,
his language full of reprimands.
East villagers are behind in their rent
and wagon wheels sink in mire and bog.
Officials' residences are short on mercy;
where whips and rods are given fiendish rein.
We must attend cautiously to our work,
for flesh and skin are to be pitied.
We welcome now the new year's arrival,
fearing only to tread on the former tracks.

D. From Bi Rixiu (CA. 833–883)

Lament of a Woman Acorn-Gatherer

Deep into autumn the acorns ripen,
Scattering as they fall into the scrub on the hill.
Hunched over, a hoary-haired crone
Gathers them, treading the morning frost.
After a long time she's got only a handful,
An entire day just fills her basket.
First she suns them, then steams them,
To use in making late winter provisions.

At the foot of the mountain she has ripening rice,
From its purple spikes a fragrance pervades.
Carefully she reaps, then hulls the grain,
Kernel after kernel like a jade earring.
She takes the grain to offer as government tax,
In her own home there are no granary bins.
How could she know that well over a picul of rice
Is only five pecks in official measurement?

Those crafty clerks don't fear the law,
Their greedy masters won't shun a bribe.
In the growing season she goes into debt,
In the off season sends grain to government bin.
From winter even into spring,
With acorns she tricks her hungry innards.

• • •

Aah, meeting this old woman acorn-gatherer,
Tears come uncalled to moisten my robe.

II. TWO CONTRACTS FROM DUNHUANG, CA. 900

A. Fan Huaidong Borrows a Piece of Silk

'On the first day of the third moon of the year [marked by the cyclical signs] *jiazi*, Fan Huaidong and his brothers, whose family is in need of a little cloth, have borrowed from the monk Li a piece of white silk 38 feet long and two feet and half an inch wide. In the autumn, they will pay as interest 40 bushels of corn and millet. As regards the capital, they will repay it [in the form of a piece of silk of the same quality and size] before the end of the second moon of the following year. If they do not repay it, interest equivalent to that paid at the time of the loan [that is, 40 bushels of cereals] shall be paid monthly. The two parties having agreed to this loan in presence of each other shall not act in any way contrary to their agreement. The borrowers: Wenda, Huaida, Huaizhu and their elder brother Huaidong.'

B. Zhao Sengzi Pawns His Son, Jiuzi

'Contract agreed on the third day of the 11th moon of the year *yiuei*. The monumental-stonemason Zhao Sengzi, because . . . he is short of commodities and cannot procure them by any other means, sells today, with the option of repurchase, his own son Jiuzi to his relation [by agreement] the lord Li Qianding. The sale price has been fixed at 200 bushels of corn and 200 bushels of millet. Once the sale has been concluded, there will neither be anything paid for the hire of the man, nor interest paid on the commodities. If it should happen that the man sold, Jiuzi, should fall ill and die, his elder brother will be held responsible for repaying the part of the goods [corresponding to the period of hire which had not been completed]. If Jiuzi should steal anything of small or great value from a third person, either in the country or in town, it is Jiuzi himself [and not his employer] from whom reparation will be demanded . . . The earliest time-limit for the repurchase of Jiuzi has been fixed at the sixth year. It is only when this amount of time has elapsed that his relations are authorized to repurchase him. Lest a higher price should then be asked for him, this contract has been drawn up to establish proof of the agreement.'

III. SONG POEMS

A. From Sushi (1037–1101)

Lament of the Farm Wife of Wu

Rice this year ripens so late!
We watch, but when will frost winds come?
They come—with rain in bucketfuls;
the harrow sprouts mold, the sickle rusts.
My tears are all cried out, but rain never ends;
it hurts to see yellow stalks flattened in the mud.
We camped in a grass shelter for a month by the fields;
then it cleared and we reaped the grain, followed the wagon home,
sweaty, shoulders sore, carting it to town—
the price it fetched, you'd think we came with chaff.
We sold the ox to pay taxes, broke up the roof for kindling;

we'll get by for the time, but what of next year's hunger?
Officials demand cash now—they won't take grain;
the long northwest border tempts invaders.
Wise men fill the court—why do things get worse?
I'd be better off bride to the River Lord!

B. From Zhengda (1126–1193)

*[Zhengda, also known as the "Recluse of Stone Lake," is the one poet in this chapter who may
not have been a governmental official.]*

[Untitled Poem]

When the wheat is green and luxuriant
    and the barley yellow,
Every morning at sunrise
    when the air is still cool,
The girls and women exchange few words,
    they have much work to do;
The odour of cocoons boiling behind the shed
    comes through to the front of the gate.
The reeling-frame creaks
    like rain spattering in the wind.
The cocoons are fat and their long filaments
    reel unbroken threads.
How shall we find the time this year
    to weave silk clothes?
Tomorrow we will go to the Western Gate
    and sell the raw silk.

C. From Yang Wanli (1127–1206)

Watching a Village Festival

The village festival is really worth seeing—
mountain farmers praying for a good harvest.

Flute players, drummers burst forth from nowhere;
laughing children race after them.
Tiger masks, leopard heads swing from side to side.
Country singers, village dancers perform for the crowd.

I'd rather have one minute of this wild show
than all the nobility of kings and generals.

STUDY QUESTIONS

1. What do the poems suggest about the material standards of the peasants? How
   did the peasants provide for their material needs? What did they produce?
   What kinds of tools did they use?

2. What did Chinese governments require from the peasants? How would you describe the relationship of the peasants to the government?
3. Do the poems provide any evidence of peasant protest?
4. Were the peasants economically self-sufficient? Did they depend on markets?
5. Do the poems suggest that the lives of the peasants were changing over time?
6. Do the poems provide any clues to the beliefs of the peasants? Do you see any indications of Confucianism, Daoism, Buddhism, or folk traditions? What do the poems reveal about the attitudes of Tang and Song officials toward the peasants? Do you see evidence of the officials' Confucian learning?
7. How do the two contracts from Dunhuang add to our understanding of how the peasants lived? What do the contracts suggest about the role of Buddhism in China?
8. What other kinds of evidence would enable us to add to our understanding of the peasants?
9. Do you think Chinese peasants were poorer or better off than peasants elsewhere in the postclassical world?

CHINESE WOODBLOCK PRINT

More than 300 treatises on agriculture were published in China during the Song dynasty. Emperors sponsored the publication of many of the books and most of the authors were governmental officials. The books were printed from blocks of wood on which the text had been cut, a technique invented by Buddhist monks in western China during the Tang dynasty. Some of the books contained meticulously drawn illustrations depicting key aspects of agricultural life.

In the scene depicted here, which comes from a book first published in 1145, a peasant hands a basket of rice seeds to his son to soak prior to sprouting. Behind the peasant an elderly man, probably his father, observes the action. Standing at the door-way of the family dwelling are the peasant's wife and two daughters. An empty chain-pump sits on the bank next to the irrigation canal. Behind the pump, carefully diked paddies stretch out in the distance.

Chinese Peasant Family, Woodblock Print, Song Dynasty.

STUDY QUESTIONS

1. What aspects of rice cultivation are illustrated in the scene?
2. What does the print suggest about family life and gender relations among Chinese peasants?
3. How might the print be viewed, in part, as an attempt to promote Confucian teachings?
4. Why did Chinese emperors sponsor the publication of farming manuals?
5. What does the publication of numerous agricultural books suggest about the extent of literacy in Song China?

32 "THE NOBLE AND MAGNIFICENT CITY OF HANGZHOU": MARCO POLO IN CHINA

The Chinese economy grew rapidly during the three centuries from 950 to 1250 C.E. There was a great increase in coal mining and in the manufacture of iron tools and weapons. The production of silk and porcelain also expanded. In southern China the amount of rice harvested shot upward. In addition, major new overseas ports emerged on China's southeast coast. Chinese ships, making use of the mariner's compass (a Chinese invention), began to ply the waters of the South China Sea and the eastern half of the Indian Ocean as never before.

Marco Polo, a Venetian merchant, traveled to China near the end of this great economic boom. Polo, who had journeyed eastward via the overland routes across Central Asia, arrived in China during the 1270s just as the Mongols were completing their long campaign of conquest in China. He remained in China for 20 years and traveled widely in the country; during part of his time in China Polo may have been employed by the Mongols as an official. In the 1290s Polo decided to return home and chose the maritime route, setting sail from the (then) great Chinese port of Quanzhou.

Scholars have long regarded Marco Polo's book, if used carefully, as an important historical document. Polo's account of his travels, which he dictated to a professional writer shortly after returning home, is a mixture of careful observation, a traveler's tendency to exaggerate (especially in regard to numbers), and fantastic "wonder" stories. In the following passages Polo reports on the city of Hangzhou. What impressed him about Hangzhou?

THE TRAVELS OF MARCO POLO

Upon leaving Va-giu you pass, in the course of three days' journey, many towns, castles and villages, all of them well-inhabited and opulent. The people have an abundance of provisions. At the end of three days you reach the noble and magnificent city of Hangzhou, a name that signifies "The Celestial City." This name it merits from its preeminence, among all others in the world, in point of grandeur and

From *The Travels of Marco Polo,* edited by Milton Rugoff (New York: NAL Penguin Inc., 1961), pp. 208–212, 214–217, 220. Copyright © 1961 by Milton Rugoff. Reprinted by arrangement with NAL Penguin Inc.

beauty, as well as from its many charms, which might lead an inhabitant to imagine himself in paradise.

This city was frequently visited by Marco Polo, who carefully and diligently observed and inquired into every aspect of it, all of which he recorded in his notes, from which the following particulars are drawn. According to common estimate, this city is a hundred miles around. Its streets and canals are extensive, and there are squares or market places, which are frequented by a prodigious number of people and are exceedingly spacious. It is situated between a fresh, very clear lake and a river of great magnitude, the waters of which run via many canals, both large and small, through every quarter of the city, carrying all sewage into the lake and ultimately to the ocean. This furnishes communication by water, in addition to that by land, to all parts of the town, the canals being of sufficient width for boats and the streets for carriages.

It is commonly said that the number of bridges amounts to twelve thousand. Those which cross the principal canals and are connected with the main streets have arches so high and are built with so much skill that the masts of vessels can pass under them. At the same time, carts and horses can pass over them, so gradual is the upward slope of the arch. If they were not so numerous, there would be no way of crossing from one part to another.

Beyond the city, and enclosing it on that side, there is a moat about forty miles in length, very wide, and issuing from the river mentioned before. This was excavated by the ancient kings of the province so that when the river overflowed its banks, the floodwater might be drawn off into this channel. This also serves for defense. The earth dug from it was thrown to the inner side, and forms a mound around the place.

There are within the city ten principal squares or market places, besides innumerable shops along the streets. Each side of these squares is half a mile in length, and in front of them is the main street, forty paces in width and running in a straight line from one end of the city to the other. It is crossed by many low and convenient bridges. These market squares are four miles from each other. Parallel to the main street, but on the opposite side of the square, runs a very large canal. On the nearer bank of this stand large stone warehouses provided for merchants who arrive from India and other parts with their goods and effects. They are thus situated conveniently close to the market squares. In each of these, three days in every week, from forty to fifty thousand persons come to the markets and supply them with every article that could be desired.

There is a great deal of game of all kinds, such as roebuck, stags, fallow deer, hares, and rabbits, together with partridges, pheasants, quail, hens, capon, and ducks and geese beyond number, for so easily are they bred on the lake that, for the value of a Venetian silver groat, you may purchase a pair of geese and two pair of ducks. There, too, are the houses where they slaughter cattle, such as oxen, calves, kids, and lambs, to furnish the tables of the rich and of leading citizens. . . .

At all seasons there is in the markets a great variety of herbs and fruits, especially pears of an extraordinary size, weighing ten pounds each, that are white inside and very fragrant. There are also peaches in season, both the yellow and white kinds, and of a delicious flavor. . . . From the sea, fifteen miles distant, a vast quantity of fish is each day brought up the river to the city. There is also an abundance of fish in the lake, which gives employment at all times to a group of fisherman. . . .

Each of the ten market squares is surrounded with high dwelling houses, in the lower part of which are shops where every kind of manufacture is carried on and every article of trade is offered, including spices, drugs, trinkets, and pearls. In certain shops nothing is sold but the wine of the country, which they make continually and serve out fresh to their customers at a moderate price. Many streets connect with the market squares, and in some of them are many cold baths, attended by servants of both sexes. The men and women who frequent them have been accustomed from childhood to wash in cold water, which they consider highly conducive to health. At these baths, however, they have rooms provided with warm water for the use of strangers who cannot bear the shock of the cold. All are in the habit of washing themselves daily, and especially before their meals. . . .

On each side of the principal street mentioned earlier, which runs from one end of the city to the other, there are great houses and mansions with their gardens, and near these, the dwellings of the artisans who work in the shops of the various trades. At all hours you see such multitudes of people passing to and fro on their personal affairs that providing enough food for them might be thought impossible. But one notes that on every market day the squares are crowded with tradespeople and with articles brought by cart and boat—all of which they sell out. From the sale of a single article such as pepper, some notion may be formed of the vast quantity of meat, wine, groceries, and the like, required by the inhabitants of Hangzhou. From an officer in the Great Khan's customs, Marco Polo learned that the amount of pepper bought daily was forty-three loads, each load being 243 pounds.

The inhabitants of the city are idolaters [Buddhists, Daoists, and Confucians]. They use paper money as currency. The men as well as the women are fair-skinned and handsome. Most of them always dress themselves in silk, as a result of the vast quantity of that material produced in Hangzhou, exclusive of what the merchants import from other provinces.

Among the handicrafts in the city, twelve [which are not identified] are considered superior to the rest as being more generally useful. For each of these there are a thousand workshops, and each shop employs ten, fifteen, or twenty workmen, and in a few instances as many as forty, under their respective masters. . . .

There are on the lake a great number of pleasure vessels or barges that can hold ten, fifteen, or twenty persons. They are from fifteen to twenty paces in length, broad-beamed, and not liable to rock. Men who want to enjoy this pastime in the company either of women friends or other men can hire one of these barges, which are always kept in excellent order, and have suitable seats and tables and every other furnishing needed for a party. The cabins have a flat roof or upper deck, where the boatmen stand; and by means of long poles, which they thrust to the bottom of the lake (which is not more than one or two fathoms in depth), shove the barges along. These cabins are painted inside with various colors and figures; all parts of the vessel are likewise adorned with painting. There are windows on either side, which may be opened to allow the company, as they sit at table, to look out in every direction and feast their eyes on the variety and beauty of the passing scene. The pleasure of this exceeds any that can be derived from amusements on land; for as the lake extends the whole length of the city, you have a distant view, as you stand in the boat, of all its grandeur and beauty, its palaces, temples, large convents, and gardens with great trees growing down to the water's edge, while at the same time you can enjoy the sight of other similar boats continually passing you, filled in like manner with parties in pursuit of amusement. . . .

It must be observed . . . that the streets of Hangzhou are all paved with stone and brick, and so too are all the principal roads running from there through the province of Manzi [south China]. By means of these, travelers can go to every part without muddying their feet. But as his Majesty's couriers go on horseback in great haste and cannot ride on pavement, a strip of road is left unpaved for their benefit.

The main street of the city is paved with stone and brick to the width of ten paces on each side, the center strip being filled with gravel and having curved drains for carrying off rain water into nearby canals so that it remains always dry. On this gravel, carriages continually pass to-and-fro. . . .

In every street of this city there are stone buildings or towers. In case a fire breaks out in any quarter, which is by no means unusual since the houses are mostly made of wood, the inhabitants may move their possessions to the safety of these towers.

By a regulation of his Majesty, there is a guard of ten watchmen, stationed under cover on all the principal bridges, five on duty by day and five by night. Each of these guards is provided with a drumlike wooden instrument as well as one of metal, together with a water clock which tells the hours of the day and night. When the first hour of the night has passed, one of the watchmen strikes once on the wooden instrument, and also upon the gong. At the end of the second hour he strikes twice, and so on as the hours advance. The guard is not allowed to sleep and must be always on the alert. In the morning as soon as the sun rises, they strike a single stroke again, as in the evening before, and so on from hour to hour. . . .

In cases of rioting or insurrection among the citizens, this police guard is also utilized; but independently of them, his Majesty always keeps on hand a large body of troops, both infantry and cavalry, under the command of his ablest officers.

For the purposes of the nightly watch, towers of earth have been thrown up at a distance of more than a mile from each other. On top of these is a wooden drum, which, when struck with a mallet by the guard stationed there, can be heard at a great distance. If precautions of this nature were not taken there would be a danger that half the city would be consumed. The usefulness of these guards in case of a popular uprising is obvious. . . .

Every father, or head of a household, is required to list on the door of his house the names of each member of his family, as well as the number of his horses. When any person dies, or leaves the dwelling, the name is struck out; similarly, when anyone is born, the name is added to the list. Thus the authorities know at all times the exact number of inhabitants. The same practice is followed throughout the province of Cathay [north China] as well as Manzi. In like manner, all the keepers of inns and public hotels inscribe the names of those who stay with them, noting the day and the hour of their arrival and departure. A copy of this record is transmitted daily to the magistrates stationed in the market squares.

STUDY QUESTIONS

1. What does Marco Polo report about the size and layout of Hangzhou?
2. How important was commerce in Hangzhou? What evidence do you see of the role of Hangzhou in long-distance trade?

3. What evidence in Marco Polo's report do you see regarding the standard of living of the residents of Hangzhou?

4. What evidence is there that fire was a serious problem in Hangzhou? What provisions were made for detecting and suppressing fires?

5. What evidence is there to suggest that the Hangzhou authorities were worried about the possibility of riot or insurrection? What steps were taken to prevent such occurrences? What does Polo's report suggest about the role of the state in China?

6. Were clocks important in Hangzhou?

7. How did the lives of Hangzhou residents compare with the lives of the peasants in the Chinese poems and legal documents? Are the differences attributable to changes over time or to the quality of urban life as opposed to rural life?

8. How does Marco Polo's report on Hangzhou provide us with evidence regarding the condition of the Chinese economy during the 13th century?

9. In Polo's observations about Hangzhou, is there an implied comparison with western European cities such as his hometown of Venice?

10. How does Polo's report illustrate the importance of cross-cultural contacts during the Mongol era?

33 VALOR AND FAIR TREATMENT: THE RISE OF THE SAMURAI

In 794 C.E. the Japanese emperor Kammu (reigned 781–806) established a new capital in Kyoto, a city that he built to look very much like Changan, the home of the Tang emperors in China. For the next two centuries the successors of Kammu governed Japan in accordance with precepts borrowed from their Chinese mentors. Gradually, however, the Chinese style of rule began to weaken in Japan. Emperors began to lose power to landowners and warriors who lived in the countryside far from the capital. Rural military groups formed lord-vassal relationships with one another that resembled the feudal ties then being established in Western Europe. As these long-term political and social changes unfolded, a new class of warriors emerged in the Japanese provinces—the samurai (literally, "those who serve").

By the 12th century the effective authority of the court in Kyoto had almost disappeared. Two great coalitions of samurai battled for control of the country. A turning point was reached when Minamoto Yoritomo (1147–1199) led one of the warrior coalitions to victory over its rivals. However, instead of deposing the emperor, as would likely have happened in China, Yoritomo allowed the emperor to remain in Kyoto and to continue to reign as the symbolic head of state. Yoritomo established a second capital at Kamakura, near present-day Tokyo, becoming Japan's first shogun or supreme military ruler. As in China, Japanese emperors continued to succeed one another in the capital, but unlike the situation in China, Japan was now effectively ruled by its warrior class. The samurai established a distinctive pattern of governance in Japan that lasted for the next seven centuries. Even today the memory of samurai rule remains part of the political culture in Japan.

The first of the following selections is taken from the *Tale of the Heike,* the most famous literary account of the rise of the samurai. Inspired by the wars that gave rise to the Kamakura shoguns, the *Tale of the Heike* took shape shortly after the events that it describes. In the selection here, Yoshinaka, a leader of the Minamoto forces, is killed by other Minamotos who are jealous of his success. The second reading comes from the set of instructions that Hojo Shigetoki, a leading samurai, gave to his 18-year-old son in

Selection I from *The Tale of the Heike,* translated by Hiroshi Kitagawa and Bruce T. Tsuchida (Tokyo: University of Tokyo Press, 1975), pp. 519–523. Copyright © 1975, The University of Tokyo Press. Reprinted by permission. Selection II from *A History of Japan to 1334* by George Sansom. Copyright © 1958 by the Board of Trustees of the Leland Stanford Junior University. All rights reserved. Used with permission of Stanford University Press, www.sup.org.

1247, following the latter's appointment to a key post in the shogunal administration. How do these selections help us to understand the rise of the samurai?

SAMURAI VALUES

I. FROM THE *TALE OF THE HEIKE*

Yoshinaka had brought with him from Shinano Province two beautiful women, Tomoe and Yamabuki. Of the two, Yamabuki had become ill and had remained in the capital.

Tomoe was indescribably beautiful; the fairness of her face and the richness of her hair were startling to behold. Even so, she was a fearless rider and a woman skilled with the bow. Once her sword was drawn, even the gods and devils feared to fight against her. Indeed, she was a match for a thousand. Thus it was that whenever a war broke out, she armed herself with a strong bow and a great sword, and took a position among the leaders. In many battles she had won matchless fame. This time too she had survived, though all her companions had been killed or wounded. Tomoe was among the seven last riders.

At first the men of Yoritomo's force had thought that Yoshinaka would take the Tamba Road through Nagasaka or would cross over the Ryūge Pass toward the north. Instead, taking neither of these, Yoshinaka urged his horse toward Seta in search of Kanehira. Kanehira had held his position at Seta until Noriyori's repeated assaults had reduced his eight hundred men to fifty. He then ordered his men to roll up their banners and rode back toward the capital to ascertain his master's fate. He was galloping along the lakeshore of Uchide when he caught sight of Yoshinaka ahead of him at a distance of one chō. Recognizing each other, master and retainer spurred their horses to join each other. Seizing Kanehira's hands, Yoshinaka said: "I would have fought to the death on the banks of the Kamo at Rokujō. Simply because of you, however, I have galloped here through the enemy swarms."

"It was very kind of you, my lord," replied Kanehira. "I too would have fought to the death at Seta. But in fear of your uncertain fate, I have come this way."

"We are still tied by karma," said Yoshinaka. "There must be more of my men around here, for I have seen them scattered among the hills. Unroll the banner and raise it high!"

As soon as Kanehira unfurled the banner, many men who had been in flight from the capital and Seta saw it and rallied. They soon numbered more than three hundred.

"Since we still have so many men, let us try one last fight!" shouted Yoshinaka jubilantly. "Look! That band of soldiers over there! Whose army is that?"

"I hear," replied one of Yoshinaka's men, "that is Tadayori's army, my lord."

"How many men are there in his army?"

"About six thousand, my lord."

"Just right!" cried out Yoshinaka. "Since we are determined to fight to the death, let us ride neck and neck with our valiant foes and die gallantly in their midst. Forward!"

Shouting, Yoshinaka dashed ahead. That day he wore armor laced with twilled silk cords over a red battle robe. His helmet was decorated with long golden horns. At his side hung a great sword studded with gold. He carried his quiver a lit-tle higher than usual on his back. Some eagle-feathered arrows still remained. Grip-ping his rattan-bound bow, he rode his famous horse, Oniashige [Gray Demon].

Rising high in his stirrups, he roared at the enemy: "You have often heard of me. Now take a good look at the captain of the Imperial Stables of the Left and governor of Iyo Province—Rising-Sun General Minamoto no Yoshinaka, that is who I am! I know that among you is Kai no Ichijōjirō Tadayori. We are fit opponents for each other. Cut off my head and show it to Yoritomo!"

At this challenge, Tadayori shouted to his men: "Now, hear this! He is the commander of our enemy. Let him not escape! All men—to the attack!"

Tadayori tried to seize Yoshinaka by surrounding him with his many men. Yoshinaka fought desperately, urging his horse into the six thousand, galloping back and forth, left and right, like a spider's legs. When he had dashed through the enemy, he found that his three hundred men had been cut down to fifty. Then he encountered another army of two thousand led by Sanehira. He continued on, attacking several other small bands of one or two hundred here and there, until at last his men were reduced to four. Tomoe was among the survivors.

Yoshinaka called her to his side and said: "You are a woman—leave now for wherever you like, quickly! As for me, I shall fight to the death. If I am wounded, I will kill myself. How ashamed I would be if people said that Yoshinaka was accom-panied by a woman in his last fight."

Tomoe would not stir. After repeated pleas, however, she was finally con-vinced to leave.

"I wish I could find a strong opponent!" she said to herself. "Then I would show my master once more how well I can fight." She drew her horse aside to wait for the right opportunity.

Shortly thereafter, Moroshige of Musashi, a warrior renowned for his great strength, appeared at the head of thirty horsemen. Galloping alongside Moroshige, Tomoe grappled with him, pulled him against the pommel of her saddle, and giv-ing him no chance to resist, cut off his head. The fight concluded, she threw off her armor and fled to the eastern provinces.

Among the remaining retainers of Yoshinaka, Tezuka no Tarō was killed, and his uncle, Tezuka no Bettō, took flight, leaving only Kanehira. When Yoshinaka found himself alone with Kanehira, he sighed: "My armor has never weighed upon me before, but today it is heavy."

"You do not look tired at all, my lord," replied Kanehira, "and your horse is still fresh. What makes it feel so heavy? If it is because you are discouraged at having none of your retainers but me, please remember that I, Kanehira, am a match for a thousand. Since I still have seven or eight arrows left in my quiver, let me hold back the foe while you withdraw to the Awazu pine wood. Now I pray you to put a peace-ful end to yourself."

No sooner had he spoken to his master than another band of soldiers con-fronted them. "Please go to the pine wood, my lord," said Kanehira again. "Let me fight here to keep them away from you."

"I would have died in the capital!" replied Yoshinaka. "I have come this far with no other hope but to share your fate. How can I die apart from you? Let us fight until we die together!"

With these words, Yoshinaka tried to ride neck and neck with Kanehira. Now Kanehira alighted from his horse, seized the bridle of his master's mount, and pleaded in tears: "Whatever fame a warrior may win, a worthless death is a lasting shame for him. You are worn out, my lord. Your horse is also exhausted. If you are surrounded by the enemy and slain at the hand of a low, worthless retainer of some unknown warrior, it will be a great shame for you and me in the days to come. How disgraceful it would be if such a nameless fellow could declare, 'I cut off the head of Yoshinaka, renowned throughout the land of Japan!'"

Yoshinaka finally gave in to Kanehira's entreaty and rode off toward the pine wood of Awazu. Kanehira, riding alone, charged into the band of some fifty horsemen. Rising high in his stirrups, he cried out in a thunderous voice: "You have often heard of me. Now take a good look. I am Imai no Shirō Kanehira, aged thirty-three, a foster brother of Lord Yoshinaka. As I am a valiant warrior among the men of Lord Yoshinaka, your master, Yoritomo, at Kamakura must know my name well. Take my head and show it to him!"

Kanehira had hardly uttered these words when he let fly his remaining eight arrows one after another without pause. Eight men were shot from their horses, either dead or wounded. He then drew his sword and brandished it as he galloped to and fro. None of his opponents could challenge him face to face, though they cried out: "Shoot him down! Shoot him down!"

Sanehira's soldiers let fly a shower of arrows at Kanehira, but his armor was so strong that none of them pierced it. Unless they aimed at the joints of his armor, he could never be wounded.

Yoshinaka was now all alone in the pine wood of Awazu. It was the twenty-first day of the first month. Dusk had begun to fall. Thin ice covered the rice fields and the marsh, so that it was hard to distinguish one from the other. Thus it was that Yoshinaka had not gone far before his horse plunged deep into the muddy slime. Whipping and spurring no longer did any good. The horse could not stir. Despite his predicament, he still thought of Kanehira. As Yoshinaka was turning around to see how he fared, Tamehisa, catching up with him, shot an arrow under his helmet. It was a mortal wound. Yoshinaka pitched forward onto the neck of his horse. Then two of Tamehisa's retainers fell upon Yoshinaka and struck off his head. Raising it high on the point of his sword, Tamehisa shouted: "Kiso no Yoshinaka, renowned throughout the land of Japan as a valiant warrior, has been killed by Miura no Ishida Jirō Tamehisa!"

Kanehira was fighting desperately as these words rang in his ears. At that moment he ceased fighting and cried out: "For whom do I have to fight now? You, warriors of the east, see how the mightiest warrior in Japan puts an end to himself!" Thrusting the point of his sword into his mouth, he flung himself headlong from his horse so that the sword pierced his head.

Yoshinaka and Kanehira died valiant deaths at Awazu. Could there have been a more heroic battle?

II. HOJO SHIGETOKI: A SAMURAI INSTRUCTS HIS SON

The men under your command . . . must be carefully chosen for your service. Do not take "difficult" fellows. If men under your orders, however loyal, are wanting in intelligence, you must not trust them with important duties, but rely upon experienced older men. If you are in doubt refer to me, Shigetoki.

In dealing with subordinates do not make an obvious distinction between good and not-good. Use the same kind of language, give the same kind of treatment to all, and thus you will get the best out of the worst. But you yourself must not lose sight of the distinction between good character and bad character, between capable and incapable. You must be fair, but in practice you must not forget the difference between men who are useful and men who are not. Remember that the key to discipline is fair treatment in rewards and in punishments. But make allowance for minor misdeeds in young soldiers and others, if their conduct is usually good.

Do not be careless or negligent in the presence of subordinates, especially of older men. Thus do not spit or snuffle or lounge about on a chest with your legs dangling. This only gives men the impression that you do not care for their good opinion. Preserve your dignity. If you behave rudely, they will tell their families and gossip will spread. You must treat all servants with proper consideration and generosity, not only your own people but also those of your parents and other superiors. If you do not, they will scorn you and say to one another: "He thinks he is very important, but he doesn't amount to much."

Remember, however, that there are times when a commander must exercise his power of deciding questions of life or death. In those circumstances since human life is at stake you must give most careful thought to your action. Never kill or wound a man in anger, however great the provocation. Better get somebody else to administer the proper punishment. Decisions made in haste before your feelings are calm can only lead to remorse. Close your eyes and reflect carefully when you have a difficult decision to make.

When accusations are brought to you, always remember that there must be another side to the question. Do not merely indulge in anger. To give fair decisions is the most important thing not only in commanding soldiers but also in governing a country.

STUDY QUESTIONS

1. What virtues do the warriors in the *Tale of the Heike* display?
2. What is the nature of the relationship between Yoshinaka and Kanehira? How strong is the emotional bond between them?
3. In what ways is Tomoe important in the *Tale of the Heike*? What does the role of Tomoe suggest about gender relations among the early samurai?
4. What advice does the samurai father give to his son?
5. To what extent did the virtues displayed by the samurai warriors conflict with the requirements of becoming effective administrators?
6. To what extent does the *Tale of the Heike* romanticize both the reality of war and the character of the samurai class? Compare the *Tale of the Heike* with the Chinese poems from the Tang dynasty on the issue of war. What differencs do you see?
7. How did Japanese feudal values compare with Confucian political principles, which also influenced postclassical Japan?
8. In what ways did Japan become different from China in the 12th and 13th centuries?
9. What similarities do you see between the samurai and the Mongols? What are the important differences?

34

THE EARLY STAGES
OF THE BYZANTINE EMPIRE

Two selections by the Palestinian historian Procopius deal with the formative period of the Byzantine Empire under the Emperor Justinian. Justinian ruled in the 6th century, becoming one of the Empire's leading historical figures though offering an interesting mixture of failure and success. Procopius, a Christian and a subject of the Emperor, obviously wrote to please but maintained a critical sense: he admired Justinian's ambition but did not find him terribly intelligent and, in other writing, noted Justinian's subjection to the will of his wife, Theodora.

Justinian eagerly attempted to recover many of the Western territories of the Roman Empire, and the first passage deals with some of his negotiations with Germanic and religious leaders in Italy toward this end. The complications suggest some of the aftermath of the fall of the Empire in the West, as well as Justinian's own ambitions. But the effort failed, after a few brief conquests in parts of Italy and North Africa.

More important was the tone Justinian set for the vigorous eastern portion of the empire, centered around Constantinople (Byzantium) in southeastern Europe and Asia Minor. Justinian codified the Roman legal system, introduced financial and administrative reforms, and tightened imperial control of the Eastern Orthodox Church. His desire to recapture Roman splendor prompted great expenditure on a public building program, particularly at Constantinople. Fearing that "posterity, beholding the enormous size and number of [buildings], should deny their being the work of one man," Justinian ordered a Palestinian historian, Procopius, to compose a treatise on his new program.

Selection II is taken from Procopius's *On Justinian's Buildings*. Written in 555 C.E., it predictably exaggerated Justinian's prowess, but it did capture the emperor's ambition. Procopius focused on the Church of the Holy Wisdom (Hagia Sophia) in Constantinople, completed in 537 as Christendom's largest and most beautiful edifice. (The church would later be converted to a mosque, when Turks captured Constantinople [Istanbul] in 1453; it is now a museum.) Justinian is said to have boasted of the great church, "Solomon, I have surpassed you!" Like the Byzantine Empire itself, the new building

Selection I from Procopius, *History of the Wars*, translated by H.B. Dewing, v. III (London: William Heinemann, 1919); pp. 23–33. Selection II from Procopius, *Of the Buildings of Justinian*, translated by Aubrey Stewart (London: Palestine Pilgrims' Text Society, 1888), pp. 2–5, 9–11.

combined Roman and Middle Eastern (particularly Persian) styles, setting up a new culture closely related to that of the late Roman Empire.

The second selection suggests key elements of the political as well as artistic program of early Byzantium. How does Byzantium compare with ancient Rome (see Chapter 18)? Why would Byzantium prove to be such an important cultural and political example to other East European peoples, particularly the Slavs as they established their civilization to the north? What elements of Byzantine civilization would these imitators be most likely to copy?

PROCOPIUS

SELECTION I: PROCOPIUS, THE HISTORY

There was among the Goths (Germanic tribe) one Theodatus, a man already of mature years, versed in the Latin literature and the teachings of Plato but without any experience whatsoever in war and taking no part in active life, and yet extraordinarily devoted to the pursuits of money. This Theodatus had gained possession of (many lands in the Tuscan region of Italy) and he was eager by violent methods to wrest the remainder from their owners. (The ruler) Amalasuntha was exerting herself to curb this desire of his, and consequently he was always vexed with her and resentful. He formed the plan, therefore, of handing over Tuscany to the Emperor Justinian, in order that, on receiving from him a great sum of money and an office in the Senate, he might pass the rest of his life in Byzantium. After Theodatus had formed this plan, two envoys from Byzantium came to the chief priest of Rome . . . to confer about a doctrine of faith, which is the subject of disagreement and controversy among the Christians. As for the points in dispute . . . I shall by no means make mention of them; for I consider it a sort of insane folly to invesitage the nature of God, enquiring of what sort it is. For man cannot, I think, apprehend even human affairs with accuracy, much less those things which pertain to the nature of God . . . For I will say nothing whatever about God save that He is altogether good and has all things in His power . . . As for Theodatus, he met these envoys secretly and directed them to report to the Emperor Justinian what he had planned.

(But at this juncture Amalasuntha lost confidence in her son, now drunk and diseased, and worried that other Goths would attack her.) For this reason she was desirous of handing over the power of the Goths and Italians to the Emperor Justinian, in order that she herself might be saved. (But Justinian was angry with Amalasuntha, whom he accused of supporting troops fighting him in North Africa. Responding to his envoy, Amalasuntha claimed that she had not interfered when the Emperor was fighting the Vandals, another Germanic tribe, and also let his fleet resupply in Sicily). "Therefore (she wrote to Justinian) thou art indebted to us for the chief cause of thy victory . . . and now that art claiming the right to despoil us of our territory in Sicily, which has belonged to the Goths from ancient times." Such was the message which Amalasuntha wrote openly to the emperor; but secretly she agreed to put the whole of Italy into his hands . . . And the emperor, overjoyed at this situation, immediately sent (an envoy) to Italy, a discreet and gentle person and fitted by nature to persuade men.

But while these things were going on, Theodatus was denounced before Amalasuntha by many Italians, who stated that he had done violence to all the people of Tuscany and had without cause seized their estates. (Amalsuntha found him guilty) and compelled him to pay back everything which he has wrongfully seized and then dismissed him. And since in this way she had given the greatest offense to the man, from that time she was on hostile terms with him, exceedingly vexed as he was by reason of his fondness for money, because he was unable to continue his unlawful and violent practices . . .

(Later, Amalsuntha had to make Theodotus king, because her son was no longer able to perform these duties; she did not realize his hatred of her. He allied with relatives of prominent Goths she had earlier killed, and ultimately killed her himself. Though Theodotus claimed that other Goths had done this, against his will, the emperor decided to send a force of 7,000 men to try to conquer Sicily.) And if it should be possible to reduce it to subjection without any trouble, they were to take possession and not let it go again; but if they should meet with any obstacle, they were to sail with all speed to North Africa . . .

And he also sent a letter to the leaders to the Franks (another Germanic tribe) as follows: "The Goths, having seized Italy by violence, which was ours, have not only refused absolutely to give it back, but have committed further acts of injustice against us which are unendurable and pass beyond all founds. For this reason we have been compelled to take the field against them, and it is proper that you should join with us in waging this war, which is rendered yours as well as ours not only by the orthodox faith, which reject the current heresies, but also by the enmity we both feel toward the Goths." Such was the emperor's letter; and making a gift of money to them, he agreed to give more as soon as they should take an active part. . . .

II. ON JUSTINIAN'S BUILDINGS

The lowest dregs of the people in Byzantium once assailed the Emperor Justinian in the rebellion called Nika, which I have clearly described in my "History of the Wars." To prove that it was not merely against the Emperor, but no less against God that they took up arms, they ventured to burn the church of the Christians. (This church the people of Byzantium call Sophia, *i.e.,* . . . *Wisdom;* a name most worthy of God.) God permitted them to effect this crime, knowing how great the beauty of this church would be when restored. Thus the church was entirely reduced to ashes; but the Emperor Justinian not long afterwards adorned it in such a fashion, that if anyone had asked the Christians in former times if they wished their church to be destroyed and thus restored, showing them the appearance of the church which we now see, I think it probable that they would have prayed that they might as soon as possible behold their church destroyed, in order that it might be turned into its present form.

· · ·

The Emperor Justinian was born in our time, and succeeding to the throne when the state was decayed, added greatly to its extent and glory by driving out from it the barbarians, who for so long a time had forced their way into it, as I have briefly narrated in my "History of the Wars." They say that Themistocles, the son of Neocles, prided himself on his power of making a small state great, but our Emperor has the power of adding others states to his own, for he has annexed to the Roman Empire many other states which at his accession were independent, and has founded innumerable cities which had no previous existence. As for religion, which he found uncertain and torn by various heresies, he destroyed everything which could lead to error, and securely established the true faith upon one solid foundation. Moreover, finding the laws obscure through their unnecessary multitude, and confused by their conflict with one another, he firmly established them by reducing the number of those which were unnecessary, and in the case of those that were contradictory, by confirming better ones. He forgave of his own accord those who plotted against him, and, by loading with wealth those who were in want, and relieving them from the misfortunes which had afflicted them, he rendered the empire stable and its members happy. By increasing his armies he strengthened the Roman Empire, which lay everywhere exposed to the attacks of barbarians, and fortified its entire frontier by building strong places.

· · ·

Now, as I said before, we must turn our attention to the buildings of this monarch, lest posterity, beholding the enormous size and number of them, should deny their being the work of one man; for the works of many men of former times, not being confirmed by history, have been disbelieved through their own excessive greatness.

· · ·

It is, indeed, a proof of the esteem with which God regarded the Emperor, that He furnished him with men who would be so useful in effecting his designs, and we are compelled to admire the intelligence of the Emperor, in being able to choose the most suitable of mankind to carry out the noblest of his works.

The church consequently presented a most glorious spectacle, extraordinary to those who beheld it, and altogether incredible to those who are told of it. In height it rises to the very heavens, and overtops the neighbouring buildings like a ship anchored among them: it rises above the rest of the city, which it adorns, while it forms a part of it, and it is one of its beauties that being a part of the city, and growing out of it, it stands so high above it, that from it the whole city can be beheld as from a watchtower. Its length and breadth are so judiciously arranged that it appears to be both long and wide without being disproportioned. It is distinguished by indescribable beauty, for it excels both in its size and in the harmony of its proportion, having no part excessive and none deficient; being more magnificent than ordinary buildings, and much more elegant than those which are out of proportion. It is singularly full of light and sunshine; you would declare that the place is not lighted by the sun from without, but that the rays are produced within itself, such an abundance of light is poured into this church. . . . Thus far I imagine the building is not incapable of being described, even by a weak and feeble tongue. As the arches are arranged in a quadrangular figure, the stonework between them takes the shape of a triangle; the lower angle of each triangle, being compressed between the shoulders of the arches, is slender, while the upper part becomes wider as it rises in the space between them, and ends against the circle which rises from thence, forming there its remaining angles. A spherical-shaped dome standing upon this circle makes it exceedingly beautiful; from the lightness of the building it does not appear to rest upon a solid foundation, but to cover the place beneath as though it were suspended from heaven by the fabled golden chain. All these parts surprisingly joined to one another in the air, suspended one from another, and resting only on that which is next to them, form the work into one admirably harmonious whole, which spectators do not care to dwell upon for long in the mass, as each individual part attracts the eye and turns it to itself. The sight causes men to constantly change their point of view, and the spectator can nowhere point to any part, which he admires more than the rest, but having viewed the art which appears everywhere, men contract their eyebrows as they look at each point, and are unable to comprehend such workmanship, but always depart thence stupified through their incapacity to comprehend it.

· · ·

The entire ceiling is covered with pure gold, which adds glory to its beauty, though the rays of light reflected upon the gold from the marble surpass it in beauty; there are two porticos on each side, which do not in any way dwarf the size of the church, but add to its width. In length they reach quite to the ends, but in height they fall short of it; these also have a domed ceiling and are adorned with gold. Of these two porticos, the one is set apart for male, and the other for female worshippers; there is no variety in them, nor do they differ in any respect from one another, but their very equality and similarity add to the beauty of the church. Who could describe the galleries of the portion set apart for women, or the numerous porticos and cloistered courts with which the church is surrounded? who could tell of the beauty of the columns and marbles with which the church is adorned? One would think that one had come upon a meadow full of flowers in bloom: who would not admire the purple tints of some and the green of others, the glowing red and glittering white, and those, too, which nature, like a painter, has marked with the strongest contrasts of colour? Whoever enters there to worship perceives at once that it is not by any human strength or skill, but by the favour of God that this work has been perfected; his mind rises sublime to commune with God, feeling that He cannot be far off, but must especially love to dwell in the place which He has chosen; and this takes place not only when a man sees it for the first time, but it always makes the same impression upon him, as though he had never beheld it before. No one ever became weary of this spectacle, but those who are in the Church delight in what they see, and, when they leave it, magnify it in their talk about it; moreover, it is impossible accurately to describe the treasure of gold and silver plate and gems, which the Emperor Justinian has presented to it; but by the description of one of them, I leave the rest to be inferred. That part of the church which is especially sacred, and where the priests alone are allowed to enter, which is called the Sanctuary, contains forty thousand pounds' weight of silver.

STUDY QUESTIONS

1. What were some of the complications in Justinian's efforts to recapture Italy? Why was it even possible to envisage a reconquest?

2. What does Procopius' history suggest about the nature of Germanic rule in Italy? What does it suggest about religious issues beginning to emerge between eastern and western Christianity, as well as about his own reactions?

3. Does Procopius' description of the situation in Italy help explain why Justinian and his eastern empire could not reconquer the Western Mediterranean?

4. What were the main architectural features of Justinian's great church? What did the building suggest about religious attitudes among Byzantine leaders? Why would such a church be built?

5. How did Procopius link the cathedral's opulence to true Christian values?

6. What relationship between church and state does the passage suggest?

7. What was the relationship of the Byzantine Empire to the Roman Empire? In what sense was it a continuation, and in what sense did it change?

THE GREATEST CATHEDRAL IN BYZANTIUM

Ottoman Turks captured Constantinople in 1453, and renamed it Istanbul. They converted the great cathedral to a mosque, and copied this kind of design in other mosque buildings (such as the great Blue Mosque, also in Istanbul). After the Ottoman Empire collapsed and a more secular government took over in Turkey, in the 1920s, Saint Sophia became a museum, an obvious tourist attraction from that point onward.

Interior of Saint Sophia. This is the great cathedral built by the Early Byzantine Emperor Justinian, described in the passage by Procopius. It was built in the domed style characteristic of Orthodox churches and cathedrals. It was one of the great wonders of East European Christianity, sure to strike awe in visitors, including merchants and travelers from Slavic regions like Russia, who would later convert to Orthodox Christianity. The style was also quite different from characteristic church buildings in Western Europe, at least until the Renaissance reintroduced a passion for classical styles including great domes and ornate decoration. (Giraudon/ Art Resource, NY)

STUDY QUESTIONS

1. How did Saint Sophia reflect earlier Roman architectural styles?
2. Why would an emperor like Justinian want to build a structure like this?
3. What does the cathedral suggest about Byzantine attitudes toward God?
4. What does it suggest about the Byzantine state and economy, and about the power of the Emperor?
5. How do the basic architectural features compare with Procopius' description?
6. What impression would this cathedral make on visitors?
7. What changes in the cathedral were needed to convert it to a mosque?

35 RUSSIA CONVERTS TO CHRISTIANITY

The conversion of the Slavs to Orthodox Christianity was one of the formative steps in the development of Slavic civilization, as the Orthodox Church assumed a major role in the transmission and assimilation of Byzantine culture into Eastern Europe. Byzantine emperors employed judicious diplomacy, international trade, and the church to transform their hostile and barbaric neighbors into cultural satellites. Kievan Russia, following King Vladimir's conversion to Orthodox Christianity in the late 10th century C.E., proved especially receptive to Byzantine culture and used the empire as a prototype in evolving its own governmental institutions. Provided with a modified Greek alphabet (Glagolithic or Cyrillic), created expressly in about 863 for the translation of biblical and liturgical works into Slavic by Saint Cyril (also known as Constantine), Russian scholars began to record their history and to produce a remarkable native literature. Having no need to master the Greek and Latin languages, which proved essential for full reception of Byzantium's classical heritage, Russian scholars remained somewhat outside the mainstream of traditional classical thought.

The following selections appear in the *Russian Primary Chronicle* ("The Tale of Bygone Years"), our principal historical source for the history of Kievan Russia during the 10th to 12th centuries. Originally compiled in about 1110, the earliest surviving copy is a 1377 version (Laurentian). The account of the conversion of the Slavs by Saints Cyril and Methodius in the 9th century is probably of Moravian origin and may be dependent on old texts and the oral tradition. The account of Vladimir's conversion and baptism in 988 is undoubtedly a Russian legend.

Although the conversion to Christianity was certainly a major step in the Slavic civilization, it also raises questions: Why, according to the *Chronicle* account, did most Slavs pick Orthodox Christianity? Why did they bother to convert to a new religion at all, and what impact would this new religion have on their culture?

RUSSIAN PRIMARY CHRONICLE

There was at that time but one Slavic race, including the Slavs who settled along the Danube and were subjugated by the Magyars, as well as the Moravians, the Czechs, the Lyakhs [Poles], and the Polianians, the last of whom are now called Russians. It was for these Moravians that Slavic books were first written, and this writing prevails also among the Russians and the Danubian Bulgarians.

From *A Source Book for Russian History from Early Times to 1917,* 2 vols., edited by George Vernadsky, (New Haven, Conn.: Yale University Press, 1972), Vol. I, pp. 12–13, 25–26. Copyright © Yale University Press, 1972. Reprinted by permission.

When the Moravian Slavs and their princes were living in baptism, the Princes Rostislav, Sviatopolk, and Kotsel sent messengers to the [Byzantine] emperor Michael, saying, "Our nation is baptized, and yet we have no teacher to direct and instruct us and to interpret the Sacred Scriptures. We understand neither Greek nor Latin. Some teach us one thing and some another. Furthermore, we do not understand written characters nor their meaning. Therefore send us teachers who can make known to us the words of the Scriptures and their sense." The Emperor Michael, upon hearing their request, called together all the scholars and reported to them the message of the Slavic princes. . . . The emperor prevailed upon them [Constantine and Methodius] to undertake the mission and sent them into the Slavic country to Rostislav, Sviatopolk, and Kotsel. When they arrived [in 863], they undertook to compose a Slavic alphabet and translated the Acts and the Gospels. The Slavs rejoiced to hear the greatness of God extolled in their native tongue. The apostles afterward translated the Psalter, the Oktoechos, and other books.

Now some zealots began to condemn the Slavic books, contending that it was not right for any other nation to have its own alphabet, apart from the Hebrews, the Greeks, and the Latins, according to Pilate's superscription, which he composed for the Lord's cross. When the pope at Rome heard of this situation, he rebuked those who murmured against the Slavic books. . . . Constantine then returned again and went to instruct the people of Bulgaria, but Methodius remained in Moravia.

Prince Kotsel appointed Methodius bishop of Pannonia in the see of Saint Andronicus, one of the Seventy, a disciple of the holy apostle Paul. Methodius chose two priests who were very rapid writers and translated the whole Scriptures in full from Greek into Slavic in six months. . . . Now Andronicus is the apostle of the Slavic race. He traveled among the Moravians, and the apostle Paul taught there likewise. . . . Since Paul is the teacher of the Slavic race, from which we Russians too are sprung, even so the apostle Paul is the teacher of us Russians, for he preached to the Slavic nation and appointed Andronicus as bishop and successor to himself among them. But the Slavs and the Russians are one people, for it is because of the Varangians that the latter became known as Russians, though originally they were Slavs. While some Slavs were termed Polianians, their speech was still Slavic, for they were known as Polianians because they lived in the fields [*pole* means "field" in Russian]. But they had the same Slavic language.

· · ·

[In the year 980] Vladimir began to reign alone in Kiev, and he set up idols on the hills outside the castle: one of Perun, made of wood with a head of silver and a moustache of gold, and others of Khors, Dazh'bog, Stribog, Simar'gl, and Mokosh'. The people sacrificed to them, calling them gods, and brought their sons and their daughters to sacrifice them to these devils. They desecrated the earth with their offerings, and the Russian land and this hill were defiled with blood.

· · ·

In the year 6495 [987] Vladimir summoned together his boyars [nobles] and the city elders and said to them, "Behold, the Bulgars came before me, saying,

'Accept our religion.' Then came the Germans and praised their own faith. After them came the Jews. Finally the Greeks appeared, disparaging all other faiths but praising their own, and they spoke at length, telling the history of the whole world from its beginning. Their words were wise, and it was marvelous to listen and pleasant for anyone to hear them. They preached about another world. 'Anyone,' they said, 'who adopts our religion and then dies shall arise and live forever. But anyone who embraces another faith shall in the next world be consumed by fire.' What is your opinion on this subject, and what do you answer?" The boyars and the elders replied, "You know, Prince, that no man condemns what is his own but praises it instead. If you desire to make certain, you have servants at your disposal. Send them to inquire about the ritual of each and how he worships God."

Their counsel pleased the prince and all people, so that they chose ten good and wise men.

[They visited foreign lands, and] then they returned to their country. The prince called together his boyars and the elders, and he said: "The envoys who were sent out have returned. Let us hear what took place." He said, "Speak in the presence of my retinue." The envoys then reported, "When we journeyed among the Bulgars, we observed how they worship in their temple. . . . Their religion is not good. Then we went among the Germans and saw them performing many ceremonies in their temples, and we saw no beauty there. Then we went to Greece, and the Greeks led us to where they worship their God, and we did not know whether we were in heaven or on earth. For on earth there is no such splendor or such beauty, and we are at a loss to describe it. We know only that God dwells there among men, and their service is better than the ceremonies of other nations. For we cannot forget that beauty. Every man, after tasting something sweet, is afterward unwilling to accept that which is bitter, and therefore we can no longer remain here [in paganism]." Then the boyars said in reply, "If the Greek faith were evil, it would not have been adopted by your grandmother Olga, who was wiser than anyone else." Vladimir then responded, asking, "Where shall we accept baptism?" and they replied, "Wherever you wish." . . .

After a year had passed, in 6496 [988], Vladimir proceeded with an armed force against Kherson, a Greek city [by the Black Sea]. . . . [After a siege] the inhabitants . . . surrendered.

Vladimir and his retinue entered the city, and he sent messages to the emperors Basil and Constantine, saying, "Behold, I have captured your glorious city. I have also heard that you have an unwedded sister. Unless you give her to me in marriage, I shall deal with your own city as I have with Kherson." When the emperors heard this message they were troubled, and they issued this statement: "It is not proper for Christians to give women in marriage to pagans. If you are baptized, you shall have her for your wife, inherit the kingdom of God, and be our co-believer. If you do not do so, however, we cannot give you our sister in marriage." When Vladimir learned of their response, he said to the emperors' envoys, "Tell the emperors I will accept baptism, since I have already given some study to your religion, and the Greek faith and ritual, as described by the emissaries I sent to examine it, has pleased me well." When the emperors heard this report they rejoiced and persuaded their sister Anna [to consent to the match]. They then sent word to Vladimir, "Be baptized, and then we shall send you our sister." But Vladimir said,

"Let your sister herself come [with the priests] to baptize me." The emperors complied with his request and sent their sister, accompanied by some dignitaries and priests. . . . The bishop [episkop] of Kherson, together with the princess's priests . . . baptized Vladimir. . . .

As a bride price in exchange for the princess, he gave Kherson back to the Greeks and then went back to Kiev.

When the prince arrived at his capital, he directed that the idols should be overturned and that some should be cut to pieces and others burned up. . . .

Thereupon Vladimir sent heralds throughout the whole city, proclaiming, "If anyone, whether rich or poor, beggar or slave, does not come tomorrow to the river, he will be an enemy of mine." When the people heard this they went gladly, rejoicing and saying, "If this were not good, the prince and his boyars would not have accepted it." On the morrow the prince went forth to the Dnieper with the priests of the princess and those from Kherson, and a countless multitude assembled. They all went into the water; some stood up to their necks, others to their breasts, and the younger up to their breasts near the bank, some people holding children in their arms, while the adults waded farther out. The priests stood by and offered prayers. There was joy in heaven and upon earth at the sight of so many souls saved. But the Devil groaned, "Woe is me! They are driving me out of here!" . . .

He [Vladimir] ordered that wooden churches should be built and established where [pagan] idols had previously stood. He founded the Church of Saint Basil on the hill where the idol of Perun and the other images had been set, and where the prince and the people had offered their sacrifices. He began to found churches, to assign priests throughout the cities and towns, and to bring people in for baptism from all towns and villages. He began to take the children of the best families and send them for instruction from books.

STUDY QUESTIONS

1. What kinds of causes for historical change does this account emphasize?
2. How is Vladimir's conversion explained?
3. What relationship is suggested between king and nobles? Between king and ordinary subjects?
4. What church-state relationship is implied by this account?
5. Given obvious distortions and simplifications in this account, what is its value as a historical source? What does it say about Russian politics, religion, and society at this time?
6. How did Russian conversion compare with earlier Christian conversions, and the issues they involved as discussed in Chapter 27?

36

FEUDALISM:
CONTEMPORARY DESCRIPTIONS
AND THE MAGNA CARTA

Although imperial or royal rule received great attention in post-classical Eastern Europe, feudalism was more characteristic in Western Europe. Western feudalism, evolving in turbulent 8th-century France, offered aristocratic landowners potential security in the absence of law and order. By concession or usurpation, major landowners assumed substantial legal and governmental powers from the central government and proceeded through private arrangements with lesser landowners (their vassals) to create local militias for defensive purposes. Inherently particularistic and initially undisciplined, feudalism enveloped the monarchy itself. Feudalism evolved its own system of law and code of ethics for its members as it spread throughout Europe to assume a dominant role in the political and cultural history of the Middle Ages. Introduced to England in 1066 by William the Conqueror—who substantially curbed the powers of all feudal vassals while retaining considerable central authority—feudalism emphasized mutual obligations within the military elite, often including the king. All members, including the monarchs who headed the feudal system, enjoyed specific rights but were also bound by feudal law to perform fixed obligations.

The first document was written by a well-known French bishop, who offers a general description—obviously somewhat idealized—of what feudalism involved. The second, from a 9th-century feudal contract, describes conditions of separation; these should be compared with the ideal statement and also with the less legalistic values in Japanese feudalism. The third document shows how the contractual emphases in Western feudalism—I'll live up to my obligations if you live up to yours—could lead to innovations in the system of monarchy, innovations that would have durable importance in the Western political tradition. The only available means for feudal vassals to force an obstinate royal overlord to observe the binding feudal law was to resort to arms. Such means were used in 1215 by secular and ecclesiastical vassals under the leadership of Stephen Langton,

Selections I and II from Brian Tierney, *Sources of Medieval History* (New York: Alfred A. Knopf, 1978), Vol. I, pp. 131, 133. Permission granted by the McGraw-Hill Companies. Selection III from *Documents Illustrating the History of Civilization in Medieval England* (1066–1600), edited by R. Trevor Davis (New York: Dutton & Co., 1926) pp. 39–52. Reprinted from *Statutes of the Realm*, 1810, Vol. 1, pp. 5ff.

archbishop of Canterbury, against King John of England. John was forced to place his seal on the Magna Carta, a charter of 60 chapters listing arbitrary royal encroachments on the feudal law as well as violations against traditional rights and liberties. Although the charter exerted little real impact on medieval English law and government because John died nine weeks after signing the document, its rediscovery and use by 17th-century opponents of royal absolutism allowed it to take a fundamental position in the English constitution. Contrary to popular belief, the original charter did not establish the individual right to trial by jury.

The Magna Carta must be interpreted as a feudal document: How does it define rights and government, and who participates in what kind of rights? Feudalism was a political response to the extremely chaotic conditions of the early Middle Ages in Western Europe. The feudal system could be bent toward more centralized rule only with difficulty, and the Magna Carta reveals some of the resulting tensions. Feudalism did, however, generate the beginnings of political principles, based on the concept of mutuality, that would be used in later political systems, as the subsequent revival of the Magna Carta attests (see Volume II for later concepts of limited government). The Western feudal concept must also be compared with that of Japan (see Chapter 33).

FEUDAL DOCUMENTS

I. FULBERT, BISHOP OF CHARTRES, ON FEUDAL OBLIGATIONS [1020]

To William most glorious duke of the Aquitanians, bishop Fulbert the favor of his prayers.

Asked to write something concerning the form of fealty [fidelity], I have noted briefly for you on the authority of the books the things which follow. He who swears fealty to his lord ought always to have these six things in memory; what is harmless, safe, honorable, useful, easy, practicable. Harmless, that is to say that he should not be injurious to his lord in his body; safe, that he should not be injurious to him in his secrets or in the defenses through which he is able to be secure; honorable, that he should not be injurious to him in his justice or in other matters that pertain to his honor; useful, that he should not be injurious to him in his possessions; easy or practicable, that that good which his lord is able to do easily, he make not difficult, nor that which is practicable he make impossible to him.

However, that the faithful vassal should avoid these injuries is proper, but not for this does he deserve his holding: for it is not sufficient to abstain from evil, unless what is good is done also. It remains, therefore, that in the same six things mentioned above he should faithfully counsel and aid his lord, if he wishes to be looked upon as worthy of his benefice and to be safe concerning the fealty which he has sworn.

The lord also ought to act toward his faithful vassal reciprocally in all these things. And if he does not do this he will be justly considered guilty of bad faith, just as the former, if he should be detected in the avoidance of or the doing of or the consenting to them, would be perfidious [disloyal] and perjured.

I would have written to you at greater length, if I had not been occupied with many other things, including the rebuilding of our city and church which was lately entirely consumed in a great fire; from which loss though we could not for a while be diverted, yet by the hope of the comfort of God and of you we breathe again.

II. LORDS AND VASSALS [816]

If anyone shall wish to leave his lord (*seniorem,*) and is able to prove against him one of these crimes, that is, in the first place, if the lord has wished to reduce him unjustly into servitude; in the second place, if he has taken counsel against his life; in the third place, if the lord has committed adultery with the wife of his vassal; in the fourth place, if he has wilfully attacked him with a drawn sword; in the fifth place, if the lord has been able to bring defence to his vassal after he has commended his hands to him, and has not done so; it is allowed to the vassal to leave him. If the lord has perpetrated anything against the vassal in these five points it is allowed the vassal to leave him.

III. THE MAGNA CARTA

John, by the grace of God, king of England, lord of Ireland, duke of Normandy and Aquitaine, and count of Anjou, to the archbishops, bishops, abbots, earls, barons, justiciars, foresters, sheriffs, stewards, servants, and to all his bailiffs and loyal persons, greeting. Know that, having regard to God and for the salvation of our souls, and those of all our predecessors and heirs, and unto the honour of God and the advancement of Holy Church, and for the reform of our realm, by the counsel of our venerable fathers . . . we have granted:

I. In the first place we have granted to God, and by this our present charter confirmed for us and our heirs for ever that the English Church shall be free, and shall have her rights entire and her liberties inviolate; and we will that it be thus observed; which is apparent from this, that the freedom of elections, which is reckoned most important and very essential to the English Church, we, of pure and unconstrained will, did grant, and did by our charter confirm and did obtain the ratification of the same from our Lord, Pope Innocent III., before the quarrel arose between us and our barons: and this we will observe, and our will is that it be observed in good faith by our heirs for ever. We have also granted to all freemen of our kingdom, for us and our heirs for ever, all the underwritten liberties, to be had and held by them and their heirs, of us and our heirs for ever.

• • •

XII. No scutage [tax] or aid shall be imposed on our kingdom, unless by common counsel of our kingdom, except for ransoming our person, for making our eldest son a knight, and for marrying our eldest daughter once; and for them there shall not be levied more than a reasonable aid. In like manner it shall be done concerning aids from the city of London.

XIII. And the city of London shall have all its ancient liberties and free customs, as well by land as by water; furthermore we decree and grant that all other cities, boroughs, and towns, and ports shall have all their liberties and free customs.

XIV. And for obtaining the common counsel of the kingdom about the assessing of an aid (except in the three cases aforesaid) or of a scutage, we will cause to be summoned the archbishops, bishops, abbots, earls, and greater barons, individually by our letters; and we will moreover cause to be summoned generally through our sheriffs and bailiffs, all others who hold of us in chief, for a definite date, namely after the expiry of at least forty days, and at a definite place; and in all letters of such summons we will specify the reason of the summons. And when the summons has thus been made, the business shall proceed on the day appointed, according to the counsel of such as are present, although not all who are summoned have come.

. . .

XXIII. No village or individual shall be compelled to make bridges at river banks, except those who were from old times rightfully compelled to do so.

XXIV. No sheriff, constable, coroners, or others of our bailiffs, shall hold pleas of our crown.

. . .

XXVIII. No constable or other bailiff of ours shall take corn or other provisions from anyone without immediately tendering money in exchange, unless by permission of the seller he is allowed to postpone payment.

XXIX. No constable shall compel any knight to give money in stead of castle guard, when he is willing to perform it in his own person, or (if he himself cannot do it from any reasonable cause) then by another reliable man; and if we have led him or sent him upon military service, he shall be quit of guard, in proportion to the time during which he has been on service because of us.

XXX. No sheriff or bailiff of ours, or other person, shall take the horses or carts of any freeman for transport duty, against the will of the said freeman.

XXXI. Neither we nor our bailiffs shall take for our castles or for any other work of ours, timber which is not ours, against the will of the owner of that timber.

XXXII. We will not retain beyond one year and one day, the lands of those who have been convicted of felony, and the lands shall thereafter be handed over to the lords of the fiefs.

. . .

XXXVIII. No bailiff for the future shall, upon his own unsupported complaint, put anyone to his "law" without reputable witnesses brought for this purpose.

XXXIX. No freeman shall be taken or imprisoned or disseised or exiled or in anyway destroyed, nor will we go upon him nor send upon him, except by the lawful judgement of his peers or by the law of the land.

XL. To no one will we sell, to no one will we refuse right or justice.

XLI. All merchants shall have safe and secure exit from England, and entry to England, with right to tarry there and to move about as well by land as by water, for buying and selling by the ancient and right customs, quit from all evil tolls, except, in time of war, such merchants as are of the land at war with us. And if such are found in our land at the beginning of the war, they shall be detained, without injury to their bodies or goods, until information be received by us or by our chief justiciar how the merchants of our land found in the land at war with us are treated; and if our men are safe there the others shall be safe in our land.

XLII. It shall be lawful in future for anyone to leave our kingdom and to return safe and secure by land and water, except for a short period in time of war on grounds of public policy—reserving always the allegiance due to us—excepting always those imprisoned or outlawed in accordance with the law of the kingdom, and natives of any country at war with us, and merchants, who shall be treated as is above provided.

. . .

XLV. We will appoint as justices, constables, sheriffs, or bailiffs only such as know the law of the kingdom and mean to observe it well.

. . .

LII. If anyone has been dispossessed or removed by us, without the legal judgement of his peers, from his lands, castles, franchises, or from his right, we will immediately restore them to him; and if a dispute arise over this, then let it be decided by the five-and-twenty barons, of whom mention is made below in the clause for securing the peace. Moreover, for all those possessions, from which any-one has, without the lawful judgement of his peers been disseised or removed, by our father, King Henry, or by our brother, King Richard, and which we retain in our hand—or which are possessed by others, to whom we are bound to warrant them— we shall have respite until the usual term of crusaders; excepting those things about which a plea has been raised, or an inquest made by our order, before our taking of the cross; but as soon as we return from our pilgrimage—or if by chance we desist from our pilgrimage—we will immediately grant full justice therein.

. . .

LV. All fines made by us unjustly and against the law of the land, shall be entirely remitted, or else it shall be done concerning them according to the deci-sion of the five-and-twenty barons of whom mention is made below in (the clause for) securing the peace, or according to the judgement of the majority of the same, along with the aforesaid Stephen, archbishop of Canterbury, if he can be present, and such others as he may wish to bring with him for this purpose; and if he cannot be present the business shall nevertheless proceed without him, provided always that if any one or more of the aforesaid five-and-twenty barons are in a similar suit, they shall be removed as far as shall concern this particular judgement, others being substituted in their places after having been selected by the rest of the five-and-twenty for this purpose only, and after having been sworn.

. . .

LX. Moreover, all these aforesaid customs and liberties, the observance of which we have granted in our kingdom as far as pertains to us towards our men, shall be observed by all of our kingdom, as well clergy as laymen, as far as pertains to them towards their men.

      LXI. Since, moreover, for God and the amendment of our kingdom and for the better allaying of our quarrel that has arisen between us and our barons, we have granted all these concessions, desirous that they should enjoy them in complete and firm stability for ever, we give and grant to them the underwritten security, namely, that the barons choose five-and-twenty barons of the kingdom, whomsoever they will, who shall be obliged, to observe and hold, and cause to be observed, with all their might, the peace and liberties which we have granted and confirmed to them by this our present Charter, so that if we, or our justiciar, or our bailiffs or any one of our officers, shall in anything be at fault towards anyone, or shall have broken any one of the articles of the peace or of this security, and the offence be notified to four barons of the aforesaid five-and-twenty, the said four barons shall come to us (or to our justiciar, if we are out of the realm) and, laying the transgression before us, petition to have that transgression redressed without delay. And if we shall not have corrected the transgression (or, in event of our being out of the kingdom, if our justiciar shall not have corrected it) within forty days, reckoning from the time it has been notified to us (or to our justiciar, if we should be out of the kingdom), the four barons aforesaid shall refer the matter to the rest of the five-and-twenty barons, and those five-and-twenty barons shall, together with the community of the whole land, distrain and distress us in all possible ways, namely, by seizing our castles, lands, possessions, and in any other way they can, until redress has been obtained as they deem fit, saving our own person and the persons of our queen and children; and when redress has been obtained, they shall resume their former relations toward us. . . .

STUDY QUESTIONS

1. What were the basic characteristics of European feudalism? What did lords and vassals gain from a feudal tie? What were their respective obligations?
2. In what ways is it clear that vassals, although required to be loyal to their lords, were basically in the same social class?
3. In what ways was the Magna Carta a feudal document? How had the king violated feudalism, and what remedies were proposed?
4. Why were the Magna Carta's principles (though not the document itself) important in Western political history? How did feudal ideas about restrictions on a king compare with more modern ideas of limited government?
5. What were the main differences between Japanese and European feudalism? What was the long-term significance of these differences? Would Japanese vassals have approved of an approach such as that suggested in the Magna Carta?
6. What would a Confucian bureaucrat have thought of the feudal system? Would he have preferred the European or the Japanese version?

37

MEDIEVAL THEOLOGY:
ANSELM OF CANTERBURY BLENDS
FAITH AND REASON

The dominant role of the Christian religion in all aspects of European civilization during the Middle Ages had led some historians to label the period an "age of faith." A hierarchical society appointed by God and governed by his vice-regents, the pope and king, focused concern on preparation for life after death and devoted considerable energy toward the honor and glorification of God. By the mid-12th century C.E. the theological rationale of the nature of God, man, and the universe—based on revelation and patristic traditions—encountered a serious challenge from the previously unknown logical and philosophical works of Aristotle, which offered a conflicting worldview including the primacy of reason as a means for establishing truth. Western thinkers eagerly recaptured Greek learning, and also Arab and Jewish philosophies about nature and reason. Leading theologians successfully met the challenge by applying Aristotelian methodology and by incorporating many of Aristotle's philosophical concepts to construct a Christian theological and philosophical system, called scholasticism, which brought their views into agreement.

The reconciliation of Christian faith and Aristotelian logic was a major concern of St. Anselm (1033–1109). Born in northern Italy, Anselm became a monk and ultimately rose to the leading post of the Catholic church in England, with the office of Archbishop of Canterbury; he was ultimately sainted. Anselm believed that logic could and should be used to demonstrate Christian truths, though he in no sense wished to challenge key Christian beliefs. His insistence that reason and faith were compatible is indeed the essence of his approach. Anselm was one of many Western churchmen and intellectuals between the 11th and the 13th centuries to work in this vein. His arguments allow us to grasp a distinctive moment in Western cultural history, when at the same time two powerful currents, Christianity and rationalism, were being advanced in ways that would affect later periods as well.

Ultimately called scholasticism, this rationalistic theology as put forth by Anselm was a striking creation that allowed its supporters to believe that they possessed a comprehensive framework through which everything that could be understood, was understood—and yet faith was at the same time affirmed. Scholasticism was a special achievement, differ-

Excerpt from *Anselm of Canterbury: Volume One, Mongolian Proslogion.* Debate with Guanilo. A Meditation on Human Redemption. Translated and edited by Jasper Hopkins, & Herbert W. Richardson (Toronto: Edwin Mellen Press, 1974), pp. 89, 91–97, 98–99. Reprinted by permission of Edwin Mellen Press.

ent from philosophical work either before or since (though it resembled debates occurring in Islam at about the same point, and it borrowed from these debates). It was also, however, a key point in a larger intellectual history that ran from the ancient Greeks to modern Western science. How did Anselm's system resemble, as well as differ from later Western intellectual assumptions? (See Volume II, chapter 2).

ANSELM OF CANTERBURY, MONOLOGION

I began to ask myself whether perhaps a single argument could be found which would constitute an independent proof and would suffice by itself to demonstrate that (1) God truly [really] exists, that (2) He is the Supreme Good, needing no one else yet needed by all else in order to exist and to fare well, and that (3) He is whatever else we believe about the Divine Substance. I often and earnestly turned my attention to this goal. At times what I was in quest of seemed to me to be apprehensible; at other times it completely eluded my mental powers. At last, despairing, I wanted to give up my pursuit of an argument which I supposed could not be found. But when I wanted to shut out the very thought [of such an argument], lest by engaging my mind in vain, it would keep me from other projects in which I could make headway—just then this argument began more and more to force itself insistently upon me, unwilling and resisting as I was. Then one day when I was tired as a result of vigorously resisting its entreaties, what I had despaired of finding appeared in my strife-torn mind in such way that I eagerly embraced the reasoning I had been anxiously warding off. Supposing, then, that to record what I had joyously discovered would please its readers, I wrote the following short work on this subject (and on various others) in the role of someone endeavoring to elevate his mind toward contemplating God and seeking to understand what he believes.

O the wretched fate of man when he lost that end for which he was made! O that hard and ominous fall! Alas, what he lost and what he found, what vanished and what remained! He lost the happiness for which he was created and found a wretchedness for which he was not created. The necessary condition for happiness vanished and the sufficient condition for wretchedness remained. Man then ate the bread of angels for which he now hungers; and now he eats the bread of sorrows, which then he did not know. Alas, the common mourning of all men, the universal lament of the sons of Adam! Adam burped with satiety; we sigh with hunger. He abounded; we go begging. He happily possessed and wretchedly deserted; we unhappily lack and wretchedly desire, while, alas, remaining empty. Why did he not, when easily able, keep for us that of which we have been so gravely deprived? Why did he shut us out from the light and enshroud us in darkness? Why did he take life away from us and inflict death? Wretched creatures that we are, expelled from that home, impelled to this one; cast down from that abode, sunken to this one! [We have been banished] from our homeland into exile, from the vision of God into our own blindness, from the delight of immortality into the bitterness and horror of death. O miserable transformation from such great good into such great evil! What a grievous loss, a heavy sorrow, an unmitigated plight! . . .

O Lord, I acknowledge and give thanks that You created in me Your image so that I may remember, contemplate, and love You. But this image has been so effaced by the abrasion of transgressions, so hidden from sight by the dark billows of sin, that unless You renew and refashion it, it cannot do what it was created to do. Lord, I do not attempt to comprehend Your sublimity, because my intellect is not at all equal to such a task. But I yearn to understand some measure of Your truth, which my heart believes and loves. . . .

God cannot be thought not to exist. Assuredly, this being exists so truly [really] that it cannot even be thought not to exist. For there can be thought to exist something whose non-existence is inconceivable; and this thing is greater than anything whose non-existence is conceivable. Therefore, if that than which a greater cannot be thought could be thought not to exist, then that than which a greater cannot be thought would not be that than which a greater cannot be thought—a contradiction. Hence, something than which a greater cannot be thought exists so truly [really] that it cannot even be thought not to exist.

And You are this being, O Lord our God. Therefore, Lord my God, You exist so truly [really] that You cannot even be thought not to exist. And this is rightly the case. For if any mind could conceive of something better than You, the creature would rise above the Creator and would sit in judgment over the Creator—an utterly preposterous consequence. Indeed, except for You alone, whatever else exists can be conceived not to exist. Therefore, You alone exist most truly [really] of all and thus most greatly of all; for whatever else there is does not exist as truly [really] as You and thus does not exist as much as do You. Since, then, it is so readily clear to a rational mind that You exist most greatly of all, why did the Fool say in his heart that God does not exist? Why indeed except because he is foolish and simple!

God is whatever it is better to be than not to be. He alone, existing through Himself, creates all else from nothing. What, then, are You, Lord God, than whom nothing greater can be thought? What in fact are You except that which—as highest of all things, alone existing through Himself—created all else from nothing? For whatever is not this is less great than can be conceived. But You cannot be thought to be less great than can be conceived. Consequently, You are just, truthful, blessed, and whatever it is better to be than not to be. For it is better to be just than not just, blessed than not blessed.

How He is omnipotent although there are many things which He cannot do. But how are You omnipotent if You cannot do all things? Or how can You do all things if You are not able to be corrupted or to tell a lie or to make what is true be false—for example, to make what has already happened not to have happened—and the like? Or is the "ability" to do these things not power but lack of power? For anyone who is able to do these things is able to do what is disadvantageous to himself and what he ought not to do. And the more he is able to do these things, the more powerful are adversity and perversity over him and the less powerful he is against them. Therefore, anyone who in this sense is able, is able not by a power but by a lack of power. For it is not the case that he is called able because he himself is able; rather [he is called able] because his own lack of power causes something else to be powerful over him—or [for some other reason coinciding] with some other way of speaking. For we say many things improperly—for example, when we substitute "to be" for "not to be" and substitute "to do" for "not to do" or for "to do nothing." Indeed, we often say to someone who denies that something is the case, "Yes, it's as you say it is," although we would say more properly, "It's not, as you say it's not." Likewise, we say, "This man is sitting even as that man is also doing" or "This man is resting even as that man is also doing"—although sitting is not doing anything and resting is doing nothing. Thus, when someone is said to have the ability to cause or to experience what is disadvantageous to himself or what he ought not to cause or experience, this so-called ability is understood to be an inability. For the more he has the alleged ability, the more powerful are adversity and perversity over him and the more powerless he is against them. Therefore, Lord God, . . .

How He who is completely and supremely just spares the wicked. He is justly merciful to the wicked. But how can You spare the wicked if You are completely and supremely just? For how can He who is completely and supremely just do something which is not just? Or how is it just to give eternal life to one deserving eternal death? How, then, good Lord—good both to those who are good and to those who are wicked—how can You save the wicked if it is not just for them to be saved and if You do only what is just? Inasmuch as Your goodness is incomprehensible, is this reason hidden in the inaccessible light in which You dwell? Truly in the deepest and inmost seat of Your goodness is hidden a fount from which the stream of Your mercy flows. For although You are completely and supremely just, nevertheless because You are completely and supremely good You are also beneficent to the wicked. Indeed, You would be less good if You were beneficent to none of the wicked. For someone who is good both to those who are good and to those who are wicked is better than someone who is good only to those who are good. And someone who is good by virtue of both punishing and sparing the wicked is better than someone who is good by virtue of merely punishing the wicked. Therefore, if You are merciful because You are supremely good, and if You are supremely good only because You are supremely just, then surely You are merciful because You are supremely just. Help me, just and merciful God, whose light I seek; help me to understand what I am saying. Truly, then, You are merciful because You are just.

STUDY QUESTIONS

1. What is Anselm trying to accomplish? Why was this kind of work important in Western European intellectual history?
2. What kinds of arguments does Anselm use to prove God's existence and key attributes? Why did Anselm believe that reason should be used, along with faith?
3. What were some of the key principles of the Christian faith at this point in Western history?
4. How did this kind of intellectual approach compare with philosophical approaches in other major religions?
5. What were some potential weaknesses in Anselm's approach? Why might other Christian thinkers criticized the reliance on reason?
6. Why is scholastic philosophy, of the sort Anselm furthered, viewed as important in the larger Western intellectual tradition? Can you see any relationship to the later advancement of science?

38 CHRISTINE DE PIZAN: WOMEN AND SOCIETY IN THE LATE MIDDLE AGES

Christine de Pizan was born in Venice around 1365. (She died about 1431.) She lived most of her life in Paris, however, where her father had traveled to serve as physician and astrologer in the royal court. Christine married a university graduate and had three children, but her husband died young, leaving her to support her family. She chose the admittedly unusual course for that time—for anyone, but particularly for a woman—of making her living as a writer, earning support not from manuscript sales directly—though many copies were made of her principal works—but through patronage from noble families. She wrote the *Mirror of Honor: The Treasury of the City of Ladies* in 1405, partly as a guide to educating young women and partly to refute some recent writings that had been very derogatory toward women.

Current historians usually regard Christine de Pizan as something of a feminist, eager to demonstrate women's capacity in an age admittedly dominated by men. They acknowledge, at the same time, that (quite understandably, particularly for someone dependent on the support of others) Christine de Pizan carefully reflected dominant beliefs of the time in many ways—and there's no reason to think she did not accept most of them herself. Interpreting her work thus requires an understanding of the value systems of the time, as well as some criteria to assessing what "feminism" usefully conveys in premodern historical settings.

It is also important to look at this work in terms of how women may actually have lived—particularly those in the upper classes, about which Christine de Pizan was best informed. This involves some sense of daily activities and demands, and a larger evaluation of their power position in the household.

Finally, of course, Christine de Pizan deliberately evokes a clear social hierarchy. The document invites an assessment of how this hierarchy was defined, how the major groups differed from each other, and how the hierarchy was justified.

MIRROR OF HONOR

Here is set forth the way the good princess, counseled by God, will decide to follow.

You must then decide which of these two ways you will follow. So the good princess inspired by God speaks to herself. Discretion truly is called the mother of Virtue. Why the mother? Because she conducts and leads, and the one who fails to

From Christine de Pizan, *A Medieval Woman's Mirror of Honor: The Treasury of the City of Ladies.* C.C. Willard, tr. New York: Persea Books, 1989.

follow her finds that enterprises without her come to nothing and are worthless. Therefore, I must work discreetly. Why discretion? Before I undertake anything, I consider first of all the strength or weakness of my own body and my fragility. Then I weigh the demands I must balance in this human state to which God has committed me. Considering these things honestly, I know that however excellent my will, I have a very weak body for suffering great abstinence or intense pain, and a feebleness of spirit from that fragility and inconstancy. Knowing myself thus, I do not deceive myself into imagining that I am of such great virtue to act when God says, "You will leave father and mother for my sake." I could not. I could not leave husband, children, my worldly state, and all earthly preoccupations with the intention of serving God completely in the contemplative life, as the most perfect human beings have done. I must not try to do what I know would be inadequate for the demands.

What then should I do? Should I follow the active life? Happy are those who can fulfill its demands successfully. Good Lord, why didn't You create me poor, so that I could at least serve You more perfectly for love of You? I cannot leave everything to devote myself only to good work. Good Lord, advise me and inspire me! Tell me what I must do for salvation. Though I know well enough that I should not love or desire anything but You alone, and though I know all other joy is meaningless, still I don't find the strength in myself to relinquish the world completely. So I am troubled. For You say that it is impossible for the rich to be saved.

Holy Information then comes to the rescue of the good princess and says: "Here is what you will do. God does not insist that you leave everything to follow Him except for those who wish to devote themselves to a perfect life. Rather, each can save herself according to her own state. When God says that it is impossible for the rich to be saved, he means the rich without virtue; those who do not distribute their wealth in alms; those whose only pleasure is in their possessions. Truly God hates them, so they never will enter the Kingdom of Heaven.

"Surely you can see this for yourself. Haven't there been kings and princes who now are saints in Paradise? <u>Saint Louis</u> and others like him did not abandon the world but rather reigned and governed their lands in a manner pleasing to God. Similarly, many queens and princesses now are saints in Paradise, such as <u>Saint Elizabeth</u>, the Queen of Hungary; and others. God doubtlessly is willing to be served by people of any estate. Any who wish it can be saved; for it isn't the position which brings damnation but not knowing how to use it wisely."

Therefore, since I conclude that I am not strong enough to follow either of these paths, at least I will try the middle way, as Saint Paul advises, and select from each path as much of the best as I am able.

WHEREIN IT IS EXPLAINED HOW THE GOOD AND WISE PRINCESS WILL ATTEMPT TO MAKE PEACE BETWEEN THE PRINCE AND HIS BARONS IF THERE IS ANY DIFFICULTY BETWEEN THEM

If any neighboring or foreign prince wars for any grievance against her lord, or if her lord wages war against another, the good lady will weigh the odds carefully. She will balance the great ills, infinite cruelties, losses, deaths, and destruction to property and people against the war's outcome, which is usually unpredictable. She will seriously consider whether she can preserve the honor of her lord and yet prevent the war. Working wisely and calling on God's aid, she will strive to maintain peace. So also, if any prince of the realm or the country, or any baron, knight, or powerful subject should hold a grudge against her lord, or if he is involved in any such quarrel and she foresees that for her lord to take a prisoner or make a battle would lead to trouble in the land, she will strive toward peace. In France the discontent of an insignificant baron (named <u>Bouchart</u>) against the King of France, the great prince, has recently resulted in great trouble and damage to the kingdom. The *Chronicles of France* recount the tale of many such misadventures. Again, not long ago, in the case of Lord <u>Robert of Artois</u>, a disagreement with the king harmed the French realm and gave comfort to the English.

Mindful of such terrible possibilities, the good lady will strive to avoid destruction of her people, making peace and urging her lord (the prince) and his council to consider the potential harm inherent in any martial adventure. Furthermore, she must remind him that every good prince should avoid shedding blood, especially that of his subjects. Since making a new war is a grave matter, only long thought and mature deliberation will devise the better way toward the desired result. Thus, always saving both her own honor and her lord's, the good lady will not rest until she has spoken, or has had someone else speak to those who have committed the misdeed in question, alternately soothing and reproving them. While their error is great and the prince's displeasure reasonable, and though he ought to punish them, she would always prefer peace. Therefore, if they would be willing to correct their ways or make suitable amends, she gladly would try to restore them to her lord's good graces.

With such words as these, the good princess will be peacemaker. In such manner, Good <u>Queen Blanche</u>, mother of Saint Louis, always strove to reconcile the king with his barons, and, among others, the Count of Champagne. The proper role of a good, wise queen or princess is to maintain peace and concord and to avoid wars and their resulting disasters. Women particularly should concern themselves with peace because men by nature are more foolhardy and headstrong, and their overwhelming desire to avenge themselves prevents them from foreseeing the resulting dangers and terrors of war. But woman by nature is more gentle and circumspect. Therefore, if she has sufficient will and wisdom she can provide the best possible means to pacify man. . . .

WHEREIN IS DESCRIBED THE LIFESTYLE OF THE WISE PRINCESS ACCORDING TO THE ADMONITIONS OF PRUDENCE.

Prudence will suggest that the wise princess order her life according to such a regime as this. Rising early every morning, her first words will be addressed to God. She will pray: "Lord, keep me free this day from mortal sin, from sudden death, and from all misfortunes. So be it with my family and friends. Grant pardon to the dead. Grant peace and tranquility to our subjects. Amen." She would end with a <u>Pater Noster</u> and any additional prayers her devotion might suggest.

She will prefer not to surround herself with an elaborate morning service. Such was the habit of Good Queen Joan, formerly wife of King Charles V of France. During her lifetime she arose every morning before daybreak and lighted her own candle to recite her <u>Hours</u>, thus not permitting her serving women to rise up and lose necessary sleep. When ready, the wise princess will go to chapel to hear morning <u>Mass</u> either as often as her devotion dictates or her time allows. The lady with great responsibilities in government has little time free from ruling. Lords often give over their rule to their ladies when they know them to be wise and good and when they themselves are obliged to be absent. Such women have enormous responsibility and authority to govern their lands and serve as council chief. These ladies should be excused even by God if they do not spend so much time in lengthy prayers as those with greater leisure. Certainly they merit no less for attending to the public good and welfare of all in their power than if they spent more time in prayer.

Of course, a lady might elect total dedication to the contemplative life, completely renouncing the active life. However, while that contemplative life can exist without the active, the active cannot endure without some portion of the contemplative. Therefore, the active lady leaving her chapel will personally, with humility and devotion, give alms with her own hands, showing by her actions that she does not despise the poor. Any requests for mercy or aid she will listen to kindly, replying graciously, and immediately attending to those which can be fulfilled. By so doing, she will enhance not only the gift but her own reputation. If time will not allow her to hear all the requests, she will refer the rest to virtuous men accompanying her who have been charged with listening to them and who by nature and character are charitable, efficient, and honorable.

After this, the lady who governs will go to her council on those days when it meets. There she will carry herself with such presence, such bearing, and such a countenance that, seated on her high throne of office, she will indeed appear to be the ruler of them all. Everyone will revere her as a wise mistress of great authority. She will listen diligently to all propositions and to the opinions of everyone present. Carefully remembering the principal points of each problem and the suggested conclusions, she scrupulously will note which members speak the best, with most due consideration, and which offer the finest possible advice. Then she will weigh the wisest, most lively, most honorable opinions. Naturally, she will consider the causes and reasons inspiring the speakers' diversity of opinions, instructing herself on the cause of each effect. When her own time comes for speaking or replying, her reasoning will be so wise that nothing could be further from simplicity or ignorance. Moreover, she will be informed in advance of what will be proposed in the council. Such preparation for important matters by wise advice will permit her to speak and act to her own advantage.

HERE BEGINS THE DISCUSSION OF PRUDENCE'S PRINCIPAL TEACHINGS WHICH SHOULD BE OBSERVED BY EVERY PRINCESS WHO LOVES AND DESIRES HONOR. THE FIRST OF THESE CONCERNS HER ATTITUDE TOWARD HER LORD AND MASTER.

The first of the rules is: A lady loving honor, or any woman in the estate of marriage, must love her husband and live with him in peace. Otherwise she already has encountered the torments of Hell, where storms rage perpetually. Although doubtlessly women of all sorts may love their husbands dearly, either they do not know all of these rules or, because of their youth, do not know how to demonstrate their love. This lesson will teach them how.

The noble princess wishing to love according to the rules of honor will conduct herself toward her lord, whether he is young or old, in all ways expected for good faith and true love. She will be humble toward him in deed, word, and attitude. She will obey him without complaint and will keep her peace as punctiliously as did Good <u>Queen Esther</u> in the Bible's first chapter of her book, where her lord so loved and honored her that she had no wish he would not grant. The lady will show her love by lavishing care and attention on all matters pertaining to his welfare, that of his soul as well as of his body. In order to attend to his soul she will win the confidence of his confessor, to whom she can turn if she sees in her lord any indication of sin whose practice could lead to his perdition. She might hesitate to mention such frailty to her husband for fear of displeasing him; instead, she will have his confessor admonish him, begging him to serve Our Lord faithfully. And, when giving alms and doing good works, she always will say: "Pray God for my lord and me."

Parallel to her concern for her lord's soul is the lady's concentration on his bodily needs. She must assure that his health is maintained and his life preserved from threat. Therefore she will wish to talk frequently with his physicians, inquiring about the state of his health, sometimes being present at their consultations, and wisely heeding their opinions. Similarly, she will want to be sure her husband's servants serve him well. If need be, she will not hesitate to take personal charge, no matter who has been appointed to this duty. Because it is not customary for royal ladies to be in such close contact with their <u>husbands</u> as other women are with theirs, the lady frequently will inquire for information about him from chamberlains and others of his suite. She will see him as often as possible, always expressing joy at their meeting. In his presence she will show a joyful face and say things which she knows will please him.

WHICH SPEAKS OF ARTISANS' WIVES AND HOW THEY SHOULD CONDUCT THEMSELVES.

Now we must speak of the lifestyle of women married to the artisans who live in the cities and good towns, both in Paris and elsewhere. Of course, these women will find valuable the good advice already given to others if they so wish. However, although certain trades are more highly regarded than others (for instance, goldsmiths, embroiderers, armorers, and tapestry weavers are thought more distinguished than masons and shoemakers), we address the wives of all craftsmen. All of them should be attentive and diligent.

If they wish to earn money honorably, they should urge their husbands and their workmen to take up their trade early in the morning and leave it late. No trade is so good that if one is not hard-working one barely lives from one crust of bread to the next. Urging the others to action, she herself should put her hand to the task, making sure that she knows the craft so well that she can direct the workmen if her husband is not there and reprove them if they do not work well. She must admonish them against laziness; a master often is deserted by irresponsible, lethargic workmen. When her husband gets a commission for some difficult and unusual task, she firmly must convince him not to accept any work through which he might suffer a loss. If he does not personally know his client, she should advise him to produce as little work as possible on <u>credit</u>. Several already have been ruined by this. Sometimes greed to earn more or the importance of the tendered offer tempts one to such risks.

The artisan's wife should keep her husband attracted to her by love, so that he will stay at home the more willingly, not tempted to join those foolish bands of <u>young men in taverns</u> and not likely to dissipate his earnings with superfluous, outrageous expenses, as many young artisans do, especially in Paris. Rather, treating him with tenderness, she should keep him nearby. Common wisdom has it that three things drive a man from his home: a quarrelsome wife, a smoking hearth, and a leaking roof.

Furthermore, she should be willing to stay home, not running here and there every day, gossiping in the neighborhood to find out what everybody else is doing, nor frequenting her cronies. All this makes for poor housekeeping. Neither is it good for her to go to so many gatherings across town, nor to go traveling off needlessly on pilgrimages, which invariably would cause unnecessary expense.

She also should encourage her husband to let them live within their income so that their expenses will not be greater than their earnings, which would force them into debt at the year's end. If she has children, she first should have them taught at school so that they will better know how to serve God; then she ought to have them apprenticed to some trade so that they can earn their living. For a great gift to one's child is knowledge, a skill, or a trade. Beyond these, the mother above all must protect the child from affectation and indulgence. These greatly discredit children of the good towns—and reflect badly on their fathers and mothers, otherwise expected to be the source of virtue and good habits.

WHICH SPEAKS TO THE WIVES OF LABORERS.

Now drawing close to the end of our discussion—for which the time has come—we will speak to the simple wives of village workers. For them it is hardly necessary to forbid expensive ornaments and extravagant clothes; for they are well protected from all that. Nevertheless, though commonly they are nourished with black bread, milk, bacon, and soup, their thirst quenched with water, and though they have heavy enough burdens to bear, still their lives often are more secure and better nourished than the lives of those seated in high places. Because all creatures, no matter what their estate, need instruction in living well, we wish these women to participate in our lessons.

Humble women living in the village, on the plains, or in the mountains! You often cannot hear what the church preaches about salvation except from your priest or chaplain in his brief Sunday instruction. If our lesson should reach your ears, remember it so that the ignorance which could mislead you will not hinder your salvation.

Know, first of all, that there is a single God: all powerful, completely good, just, wise, from whom nothing is hidden, and who rewards every being for good or evil according to what she deserves. He alone should be perfectly loved and served.

Whole-heartedly and willingly, as you love Him, you must be sure that you do not do unto your neighbors or others what you would not have them do unto you. You must admonish your husbands to do likewise. If working the land for others, they must do it well and loyally, as if for yourselves. At harvest time, they should pay the master with wheat that has been grown on the land, if such is the agreement, and not mix in oats, pretending that nothing else was grown there, not hide the good ewes or the best rams at their neighbor's in order to pay the master with inferior animals, and not pretend that his best ones are dead by showing him the skins of other animals, nor pay him with the worst fleeces. Nor should they give the master a dishonest accounting of his carts or other property, nor of his poultry.

WHICH SPEAKS OF THE SITUATION OF THE POOR.

We began with the rich, subsequently speaking to all classes of women; now we will end our work by addressing the poor, beloved by God yet despised by the world. We urge them to patience in hope of the promised crown after life.

Blessed poor, so called by the word of God in the Scriptures, awaiting the possession of Heaven merited by poverty patiently borne! Rejoice in that mighty promise of all-surpassing joy to which no other can compare. It is not promised to kings or princes or to the rich unless they can equal you in spirit, that is, if they are voluntarily poor, disdaining all riches and all worldly vanities.

Dear friends, beloved of God: Let our admonitions enter your understanding to remind you to protect yourselves against the arrows of impatience. They may prick you because of your various, overwhelming afflictions such as hunger, thirst, cold poor lodgings, helplessness, friendlessness, old age, illness without comfort, and, topping all, the world's deprecation, unkindness, and rejection of you as if you were not Christians at all but some other species of being.

Of course you are wounded by the world's despising you and casting you out. But for God's sake, consider how trivial are honors given to kings and rich men, now dead, in their lifetime. Such temporal rewards have caused the damnation of many who would have been far better off in your situation.

But if you accept your poverty, firmly trusting in God and not coveting things other than those which please Him, you can acquire more noble possessions and greater riches than a hundred thousand worlds can hold and these can endure forever. All things considered, if you know how to benefit from it, you have reason to praise God for the estate to which He has called you.

Good poor women, you should comfort your husbands with our advice and help one another. Poor widows, you must take comfort in God, awaiting the endless joy God will grant you.

STUDY QUESTIONS

1. Is feminism a useful label for Christine de Pizan (understanding that it was not at all a term used at the time)? How would you define the more feminist aspects of her writings? How does she implicitly compare women with men?
2. Judging by this document, what were the principal results of Christianity for women? Did Christianity promote women's capacities compared to those of men?
3. How does Christine de Pizan compare with writers from other societies who offered advice to women—for example, Ban Zhao in China's classical period?

Do differences outweigh similarities, or vice versa? How would you explain the differences?

4. Many historians have argued that, overall, women's conditions were deteriorating in the later Middle Ages, compared to men's prerogatives. Does this document reflect any such trend? What other kinds of materials would be needed to assess this trend?

5. What kind of social hierarchy is implied by this document? How do Christine de Pizan's views of social hierarchy compare to her views about inequality between men and women?

39

MERCHANTS AND
THE RISE OF COMMERCE

The development of more extensive trade, and cities built on trade, was a key development during the post-classical period in Western Europe. From very low levels after the collapse of Rome, trade began to increase in the 10th century. Internal trade within Europe was vital, but wider international activities developed as well. With trade came urban government and a new merchant class, vital innovations in social and political structure.

The rise of trade at this point raises a crucial analytical problem. The temptation is strong to say: aha, trade, merchants therefore modern, the seeds of Western capitalism. There is a bit of truth in this because some merchants did invest capital, and growing trade would ultimately help lead to commercial forms more familiar in the modern world. It is important, in other words, to recognize the significance of the development and its ultimate role in generating further economic and social change.

But the merchants involved were not modern, not even primarily capitalistic. They had distinctive values and institutions that fit well into the larger context of Western Europe at that point. Among other things, they formed guilds, which stressed cooperation and association, rather than competition.

The following document, from Southampton, a seaport in England, is fairly typical, in discussing the arrangements merchants made. It allows explicit exploration of what was commercial yet not modern about the patterns involved. It also deserves close reading for the light it also sheds on the impact of religious values and the implications for political life. Merchant activity was not just economic, but had broader connections with the community.

ORDINANCES OF THE GUILD MERCHANT
OF SOUTHAMPTON

In the first place, there shall be elected from the guild merchant, and established, an alderman [magistrate], a steward, a chaplain, four skevins, and an usher. And it is to be known that whosoever shall be alderman shall receive from each one entering into the guild fourpence, the steward, twopence; the chaplain, twopence; and the usher, one penny. And the guild shall meet twice a year; that is to say, on the Sunday next after St. John the Baptist's day, and on the Sunday next after St. Mary's day.

From Department of History of the University of Pennsylvania, *Original Sources of European History*, Vol. II [Philadelphia: University of Pennsylvania Press, 1902], pp. 12–17.

And when the guild shall be sitting no one of the guild is to bring in any stranger, except when required by the alderman or steward. . . .

And when the guild shall sit, the lepers of La Madeleine shall have of the alms of the guild, two sesters [eight gallons] of ale, and the sick of God's House and of St. Julian shall have two sesters of ale. And the Friars Minors shall have two sesters of ale and one sester of wine. And four sesters of ale shall be given to the poor wherever the guild shall meet.

And when the guild is sitting, no one who is of the guild shall go outside of the town for any business, without the permission of the steward. And if any one does so, let him be fined two shillings, and pay them.

And when the guild sits, and any guildsman is outside of the city so that he does not know when it will happen, he shall have a gallon of wine, if his servants come to get it. And if a guildsman is ill and is in the city, wine shall be sent to him, two loaves of bread and a gallon of wine and a dish from the kitchen; and two approved men of the guild shall go to visit him and look after his condition.

And when a guildsman dies, all those who are of the guild and are in the city shall attend the service of the dead, and guildsmen shall bear the body and bring it to the place of burial. And whoever will not do this shall pay according to his oath, two pence, to be given to the poor. And those of the ward where the dead man shall be ought to find a man to watch over the body the night that the dead shall lie in his house. And so long as the service of the dead shall last, that is to say the vigil and the mass, there ought to burn four candles of the guild, each candle of two pounds weight or more, until the body is buried. And these four candles shall remain in the keeping of the steward of the guild.

The steward ought to keep the rolls and the treasure of the guild under the seal of the alderman of the guild.

And when a guildsman dies, his eldest son or his next heir shall have the seat of his father, or of his uncle, if his father was not a guildsman, and of no other one; and he shall give nothing for his seat. No husband can have a seat in the guild by right of his wife, nor demand a seat by right of his wife's ancestors.

And no one has the right or power to sell or give his seat in the guild to any man; and the son of a guildsman, other than his eldest son, shall enter into the guild on payment of ten shillings, and he shall take the oath of the guild. . . .

And if any guildsman strikes another with his fist; and is convicted thereof, he shall lose the guild until he shall have bought it back for ten shillings, and taken the oath of the guild again like a new member. And if a guildsman strikes another with a stick, or a knife, or any other weapon, whatever it may be, he shall lose the guild and the franchise, and shall be held as a stranger until he shall have been reconciled to the good men of the guild and has made recompense to the one whom he has injured, and has paid a fine to the guild of twenty shillings; and this shall not be remitted.

If any one does an injury, who is not of the guild, and is of the franchise or strikes a guildsman and is reasonably convicted he shall lose his franchise and go to prison for a day and a night.

And if any stranger or any other who is not of the guild nor of the franchise, strikes a guildsman, and is reasonably convicted thereof, let him be in prison two days and two nights, unless the injury is such that he should be more severely punished. . . .

And no one of the city of Southampton shall buy anything to sell again in the same city, unless he is of the guild merchant or of the franchise. And if anyone shall do so and is convicted of it, all which he has so bought shall be forfeited to the king; and no one shall be quit of custom unless he proves that he is in the guild or in the franchise, and this from year to year.

And no one shall buy honey, fat, salt herrings, or any kind of oil, or millstones, or fresh hides, or any kind of fresh skins, unless he is a guildsman: nor keep a tavern for wine, nor sell cloth at retail, except in market or fair days; not keep grain in his granary beyond five quarters, to sell at retail, if he is not a guildsman; and whoever shall do this and be convicted, shall forfeit all to the king.

No one of the guild ought to be partner or joint dealer in any of the kinds of merchandise before mentioned with anyone who is not of the guild, by any manner of coverture, or art, or contrivance, or collusion, or any other manner. And whosoever shall do this and be convicted, the goods in such manner bought shall be forfeited to the king, and the guildsman shall lose the guild.

If any guildsman falls into poverty and has not the wherewithal to live, and is not able to work or to provide for himself, he shall have one mark from the guild to relieve his condition when the guild shall sit. . . .

And no private man nor stranger shall bargain for or buy any kind of merchandise coming into the city before a burgess of the guild merchant, so long as the guildsman is present and wishes to bargain for and buy this merchandise; and if anyone does so and is convicted, that which he buys shall be forfeited to the king.

And anyone who is of the guild merchant shall share in all merchandise which another guildsman shall buy or any other person, whosoever he is, if he comes and demands part and is there where the merchandise is bought, and also if he gives satisfaction to the seller and gives security for his part. But no one who is not a guildsman is able or ought to share with a guildsman, without the will of the guildsman.

And if any guildsman or other of the city refuse a part to the guildsman in the manner above said, he shall not buy or sell in that year in the town, except his victuals [food]. . . .

Every year, on the morrow of St. Michael, shall be elected by the whole community of the town, assembled in a place provided, to consider the estate and treat of the common business of the town—then shall be elected by the whole community, twelve discreet men to execute the king's commands, together with the bailiffs, and to keep the peace and protect the franchise, and to do and keep justice to all persons, as well poor as rich, natives or strangers, all that year; and to this they shall be sworn in the form provided. And these twelve discreet men shall choose the same day two discreet men from among themselves and the other profitable and wise men to be bailiffs for the ensuing year, who shall take care that the customs shall be well paid; and they shall receive their jurisdiction the day after Michaelmas, as has been customary. And this shall be done from year to year, so that the bailiffs shall be renewed every year, and the twelve aforesaid, if there is occasion. The same shall be done as to clerk and sergeants of the city, in making and removing. . . .

No one shall go out to meet a ship bringing wine or other merchandise coming to the town, in order to buy anything, before the ship be arrived and come to anchor for unloading; and if any one does so and is convicted, the merchandise which he shall have bought shall be forfeited to the king.

STUDY QUESTIONS

1. What were the main goals of guild merchants, and how did they organize to achieve these goals?
2. How were the guild organizations effective in promoting trade and the general increase in commercial activity?
3. How did the structures and values of these merchants differ from those associated with modern capitalism? Are there any connections?
4. How did the guild relate to Christian religious values?
5. What were the political implications of the guild? What did the guild organization imply about relations between the merchants and the king, and about the power of central government in the growing towns?

40 EAST AFRICA AND ARAB TRADERS

This document is an early account—a sea story, really—of Arab contact with East Africa. Buzurg ibn Shahriyar was a Persian Gulf sailor who wrote his collection of sailors' tales in the middle of the 10th century. The story refers to some part of East Africa, probably Somalia or northern Kenya on the present-day map. Parts of it are surely fanciful, but it describes some real contacts as well. Ultimately, Arabs and Africans mixed in the coastal cities and islands of this region, setting up Swahili language and culture. This story refers to a point at which these connections were just beginning.

BUZURG IBN SHAHRIYAR

Ismailawaih told me, and several sailors who were with him, that in the year A.H. 310 [= C.E. 922] he left Oman in his ship to go to Kanbalu [Persian Gulf]. A storm drove him towards Sofala on the Zanj coast. 'Seeing the coast where we were, the captain said, and realizing that we were falling among cannibal negroes and were certain to perish, we made the ritual ablutions and turned our hearts towards God, saying for each other the prayers for the dead. The canoes of the negroes surrounded us and brought us into the harbour; we cast anchor and disembarked on the land. They led us to their king. He was a young negro, handsome and well made. He asked us who we were, and where we were going. We answered that the object of our voyage was his own land.

'You lie, he said. It was not in our land that you intended to disembark. It is only that the winds have driven you thither in spite of yourselves.

'When we had admitted that he spoke the truth, he said: Disembark your goods. Sell and buy, you have nothing to fear.

'We brought all our packages to the land and began to trade, a trade which was excellent for us, without any obstacles or customs dues. We made the king a number of presents to which he replied with gifts of equal worth or ones even more valuable. When the time to depart came, we asked his permission to go, and he

Excerpt from *The East African Coast: Select Documents from the First to the Nineteenth Century* (London: Rex Collings, 1975), pp. 9–12. Reprinted by permission of GSP Freeman-Grenville.

agreed immediately. The goods we had bought were loaded and business was wound up. When everything was in order, and the king knew of our intention to set sail, he accompanied us to the shore with several of his people, got into one of the boats and came out to the ship with us. He even came on board with seven of his companions.

'When I saw them there, I said to myself: In the Oman market this young king would certainly fetch thirty dinars, and his seven companions sixty dinars. Their clothes alone are not worth less than twenty dinars. One way and another this would give us a profit of at least 3,000 dirhams, and without any trouble. Reflecting thus, I gave the crew their orders. They raised the sails and weighed anchor.

'In the meantime the king was most agreeable to us, making us promise to come back again and promising us a good welcome when we did. When he saw the sails fill with the wind and the ship begin to move, his face changed. You are off, he said. Well, I must say good-bye. And he wished to embark in the canoes which were tied up to the side. But we cut the ropes, and said to him: You will remain with us, we shall take you to our own land. There we shall reward you for all the kindnesses you have shown us.

'Strangers, he said, when you fell upon our beaches, my people wished to eat you and pillage your goods, as they have already done to others like you. But I protected you, and asked nothing from you. As a token of my goodwill I even came down to bid you farewell in your own ship. Treat me then as justice demands, and let me return to my own land.

'But no one paid any heed to his words; no notice was taken of them. As the wind got up, the coast was not slow to disappear from sight. Then night enfolded us in its shrouds and we reached the open sea.

'When the day came, the king and his companions were put with the other slaves whose number reached about 200 head. He was not treated differently from his companions in captivity. The king said not a word and did not even open his mouth. He behaved as if we were unknown to him and as if we did not know him. When he got to Oman, the slaves were sold and the king with them. . . .

(Years later the sailors return to the region and to their horror, find the king back on his throne. He offers them mercy and freedom to trade. They in turn asked how he escaped.)

'He answered: After you had sold me in Oman, my purchaser took me to a town called Basrah [in Iraq],—and he described it. There I learnt to pray and to fast, and certain parts of the Koran. My master sold me to another man who took me to the country of the king of the Arabs, called Baghdad—and he described Baghdad. In this town I learnt to speak correctly. I completed my knowledge of the Koran and prayed with the men in the mosques. I saw the Caliph, who is called al-Muqtadir [908–32]. I was in Baghdad for a year and more, when there came a party of men from Khorasan mounted on camels. Seeing a large crowd, I asked where all these people were going. I was told: To Mecca. What is Mecca? I asked. There, I was answered, is the House of God to which Muslims make the Pilgrimage. And I was told the history of the temple. I said to myself that I should do well to follow the caravan. My master, to whom I told all this, did not wish to go with them or to let me go. But I found a way to escape his watchfulness and to mix in the crowd of pilgrims. On the road I became a servant to them. They gave me food to eat and got for me the two cloths needed for the *ihram* [the ritual garments used for the pilgrimage]. Finally, they instructing me, I performed all the ceremonies of the pilgrimage.

'Not daring to go back to Baghdad, for fear that my master would take away my life, I joined up with another caravan which was going to Cairo. I offered my services to the travellers, who carried me on their camels and shared their provisions with me. When I got to Cairo I saw the great river which is called the Nile. I asked: Where does it come from? They answered: Its source is in the land of the Zanj. On which side? On the side of a large town called Aswan, which is on the frontier of the land of the blacks.

'With this information, I followed the banks of the Nile, going from one town to another, asking alms, which was not refused me. . . .

'When the day came [when I reached my own land], I went into the town and walked towards my palace. I found my family just as I had left them, but plunged into grief. My people listened to the account of my story, and it surprised them and filled them with joy. Like myself, they embraced the religion of Islam. Thus I returned into possession of my sovereignty, a month before you came. And here I am, happy and satisfied with the grace God has given me and mine, of knowing the percepts of Islam, the true faith, prayers, fasting, the pilgrimage, and what is permitted and what is forbidden: for no man else in the land of the Zanj has obtained a similar favour. And if I have forgiven you, it is because you were the first cause of the purity of my religion.

STUDY QUESTIONS

1. What is the moral of the story? How is the moral illustrated?
2. Why were Arab traders interested in East Africa?
3. What were some key differences between Arabs and East Africans?
4. What were African reactions to Arabs, and what were some probable causes of these attitudes?
5. What kind of cultural contacts formed along the Swahili coast?
6. What were the main attitudes of Arab Muslims toward East Africans, when the whole story is taken into account?
7. How did Arab trade and Arab attitudes compare with later European patterns in Africa (see volume II)?

41   Al-Bakrí on West Africa

'Abd al-'Aziz al-Bakrí is one of the most important sources available on West African history in the postclassical period, including the great empire of Ghana. He focused on the Sudanic region, the vast stretches of West Africa below the Sahara desert—not the contemporary nation called Sudan, which is farther east. al-Bakrí was a Muslim scholar in Spain, who died at an advanced age in 1094 (487 by the Muslim calendar). Of his many writings, two major geographies have survived. al-Bakrí never traveled in Africa, but he had extensive historical sources from 10th-century work on Africa (work that has since been lost), and he also met many travelers and merchants coming from the Sudan.

Although not a travelogue, al-Bakrí's account is primarily descriptive, and thus forces the reader to recombine information to make generalizations about the leading features of postclassical West Africa. There is extensive discussion of African government and the policies of kings, including their uses and adaptations of Islam. Important information also relates to the leading features of the African economy, and how the economy supported state building. Understandably, al-Bakrí was particularly interested in the position of Islam and its relationship to more traditional African religions.

al-Bakrí was remarkably nonjudgmental. He is noticeably more tolerant, for example concerning evidence about women, than Ibn Battuta, the more famous Arab traveler of Africa, whose selection follows this one. But al-Bakrí could be gullible, as was (is?) common among people writing about strange places. He clearly accepts a preposterous story about goats. Does he make any other mistakes as a result of credulousness?

Accounts like al-Bakrí's are vital for the information they provide about African history. They also explain the impressions people in the Middle East and Western Europe formed about Africa in a period when contact was important but not yet routine.

AL-BAKRÍ

[There is a people in] Sūdān who worship a certain snake, a monstrous serpent with a mane and a tail and a head shaped like that of the Bactrian camel. It lives in a cave in the desert. At the mouth of the cave stands a trellis and stones and the habitation of the adepts of the cult of that snake. They hang up precious garments

From J. R. P. Hopkins, tr., N. Levtzion, and J. F. P. Hopkins, eds., *Corpus of Early Arabic Sources for West African History* (Cambridge: Cambridge University Press, 1981), pp. 78–83, 85–87.

and costly objects on the trellis and place plates of food and cups of milk and intoxicating drink (*sharāb*) there. When they want the serpent to come out to the trellis they pronounce certain formulas and whistle in a particular way and the snake emerges. When one of their rulers dies they assemble all those whom they regard as worthy of kingship, bring them near the cave, and pronounce known formulas. Then the snake approaches them and smells one man after another until it prods one with its nose. As soon as it has done this it turns away towards the cave. The one prodded follows as fast as he can and pulls from its tail or its mane as many hairs as he is able. His kingship will last as many years as he has hairs, one hair per year. This, they assert, is an infallible prediction.

Their country adjoins the land of the Farwiyyūn. This is the independent kingdom of the Farwiyyūn. Among the strange things found there is a pool where water collects and in it a plant grows of which the roots are the surest means of strengthening and aiding sexual powers. The king reserves this for himself and does not allow anyone else to partake of it. He owns a enormous number of woman, and when he wants to make the round of them he warns them one day before, takes the medicine, and then takes them all in turn and scarcely flags. One of the neighbouring Muslim kings gave him precious gifts, requesting some of this plant in exchange. In return he gave presents of equal value and wrote a letter saying: "Muslims may lawfully wed only a few women, and I fear that if I sent you this medicine you would not be able to restrain yourself and you would commit excesses which your religion makes unlawful. I am however, sending you a herb which will enable an impotent man, if he eats it, to beget children." In the country of the Farwiyyūn salt is exchanged for gold.

Ghāna and the Customs of Its Inhabitants

Ghāna is a title given to their kings; the name of the region is Awkār, and their king today, namely in the year 460/1067–8, is Tunkā Manīn. He ascended the throne in 455/1063. The name of his predecessor was Basī and he became their ruler at the age of 85. He led a praiseworthy life on account of his love of justice and friendship for the Muslims. At the end of his life he became blind, but he concealed this from his subjects and pretended that he could see. When something was put before him he said: "This is good" or "This is bad". His ministers deceived the people by indicating to the king in cryptic words what he should say, so that the commoners could not understand. Basī was a maternal uncle of Tunkā Manīn. This is their custom and their habit, that the kingship is inherited only by the son of the king's sister. He has no doubt that his successor is a son of his sister, while he is not certain that his son is in fact his own, and he is not convinced of the genuineness of his relationship to him. This Tunkā Manīn is powerful, rules an enormous kingdom, and possesses great authority.

The city of Ghāna consists of two towns situated on a plain. One of these towns, which is inhabited by Muslims, is large and possesses twelve mosques, in one of which they assemble for the Friday prayer. There are salaried imams and muezzins, as well as jurists and scholars. In the environs are wells with sweet water, from which they drink and with which they grow vegetables. The king's town is six miles distant from this one and bears the name of Al-Ghāba. Between these two towns there are continuous habitations. The houses of the inhabitants are of stone and acacia (*sunt*) wood.

The king has a palace and a number of domed dwellings all surrounded with an enclosure like a city wall (*sūr*). In the king's town, and not far from his court of justice, is a mosque where the Muslims who arrive at his court (*yafid 'alayh*) pray. Around the king's town are domed buildings and groves and thickets where the sorcerers of these people, men in charge of the religious cult, live. In them too are their idols and the tombs of their kings. These woods are guarded and none may enter them and know what is there. In them also are the king's prisons. If somebody is imprisoned there no news of him is ever heard. The king's interpreters, the official in charge of his treasury and the majority of his ministers are Muslims. Among the people who follow the king's religion only he and his heir apparent (who is the son of his sister) may wear sewn clothes. All other people wear robes of cotton, silk, or brocade, according to their means. All of them shave their beards, and women shave their heads. The king adorns himself like a woman [wearing necklaces] round his neck and [bracelets] on his forearms, and he puts on a high cap (*ṭarṭūr*) decorated with gold and wrapped in a turban of fine cotton. He sits in audience or to hear grievances against officals (*maẓālim*) in a domed pavilion around which stand ten horses covered with gold-embroidered materials. Behind the king stand ten pages holding shields and swords decorated with gold, and on his right are the sons of the [vassal] kings of his country wearing splendid garments and their hair plaited with gold. The governor of the city sits on the ground before the king and around him are ministers seated likewise. At the door of the pavilion are dogs of excellent pedigree who hardly ever leave the place where the king is, guarding him. Round their necks they wear collars of gold and silver studded with a number of balls of the same metals. The audience is announced by the beating of a drum which they call *dubā*, made from a long hollow log. When the people who profess the same religion as the king approach him they fall on their knees and sprinkle dust on their heads, for this is their way of greeting him. As for the Muslims, they greet him only by clapping their hands.

Their religion is paganism and the worship of idols (*dakākir*). When their king dies they construct over the place where his tomb will be an enormous dome of *sāj* wood. Then they bring him on a bed covered with a few carpets and cushions and place him beside the dome. At his side they place his ornaments, his weapons, and the vessels from which he used to eat and drink, filled with various kinds of food and beverages. They place there too the men who used to serve his meals. They close the door of the dome and cover it with mats and furnishings. Then the people assemble, who heap earth upon it until it becomes like a big hillock and dig a ditch around it until the mound can be reached at only one place.

They make sacrifices to their dead and make offerings of intoxicating drinks.

On every donkey-load of salt when it is brought into the country their king levies one gold dinar, and two dinars when it is sent out. From a load of copper the king's due is five mithqals, and from a load of other goods ten mithqals. The best gold found in his land comes from the town of Ghiyārū, which is eighteen days' travelling distant from the king's town over a country inhabited by tribes of the Sūdān whose dwellings are continuous.

The nuggets (*nadra*) found in all the mines of his country are reserved for the king, only this gold dust (*al-tibr al-daqīq*) being left for the people. But for this the people would accumulate gold until it lost its value. The nuggets may weight from an ounce (*ūqiyya*) to a pound (*raṭl*). It is related that the king owns a nugget as large as a big stone. . . .

The king of Ghāna, when he calls up his army, can put 200,000 men into the field, more then 40,000 of them archers. The horses in Ghāna are very small. . . . The inhabitants sow their crops twice yearly, the first time in the moist earth (*tharā*) during the season of the Nīl flood, and later in the earth [that has preserved its humidity].

West of Ghiyārū, on the Nīl, is the town of Yarisnā, inhabited by Muslims surrounded by polytheists. In Yarisnā is a species of small goat. When a goat gives birth to a male it is slaughtered, only females being allowed to live. In this country is a certain tree against which the goats rub themselves and become fecundated by the wood without the medium of the male. This fact is well known to them; none of them deny it and it has been related by many trustworthy Muslims. From Yarisnā the Sūdān who speak an unintelligible language (*a'jam*, pl. *'ujm*) called the Banū Naghmārata, who are merchants, export gold to other countries. . . .

Beyond this country lies another called Malal, the king of which is known as *al-musulmānī*. He is thus called because his country became afflicted with drought one year following another; the inhabitants prayed for rain, sacrificing cattle till they had exterminated almost all of them, but the drought and the misery only increased. The king had as his guest a Muslim who used to read the Koran and was acquainted with the Sunna. To this man the king complained of the calamities that assailed him and his people. The man said; "O King, if you believed in God (who is exalted) and testified that He is One, and testified as to the prophetic mission of Muhammad (God bless him and give him peace) and if you accepted all the religious laws of Islam, I would pray for your deliverance from your plight and that God's mercy would envelop all the people of your country and that your enemies and adversaries might envy you on that account." Thus he continued to press the king until the latter accepted Islam and became a sincere Muslim. The man made him recite from the Koran some easy passages and taught him religious obligations and practices which no one may be excused from knowing. Then the Muslim made him wait till the eve of the following Friday, when he ordered him to purify himself by a complete ablution, and clothed him in a cotton garment which he had. The two of them came out towards a mound of earth, and there the Muslim stood praying while the king, standing at his right side, imitated him. Thus they prayed for part of the night, the Muslim reciting invocations and the king saying "Amen". The dawn had just started to break when God caused abundant rain to descend upon them. So the king ordered the idols to be broken and expelled the sorcerers from his country. He and his descendants after him as well as his nobles were sincerely attached to Islam, while the common people of the kingdom remained polytheists. Since then their rulers have been given the title of *al-musulmānī*.

Among the provinces (*a'māl*) of Ghāna is a region called Sāma, the inhabitants of which are known as al-Bukm. From that region to Ghāna is four days' travelling. The people there go naked; only the woman cover their sexual parts with strips of leather which they plait. They leave the hair on the pubis and only shave their heads. Abū ʿAbd Allāh al-Makkī related that he saw one of these women stop in front of an Arab, who had a long beard, and say something that he could not understand. He asked the interpreter about the meaning of her words. He replied that she wished that she had hair like that of his beard on her pubis. The Arab, filled with anger, called down curses upon her. . . .

From Būghrāt you go to Tīraqqā and from there across the desert plain to Tādmakka, which of all the towns of the world is the one that resembles Mecca the most. Its name means "the Mecca-like". It is a large town amidst mountains and ravines and is better built than Ghāna or Kawkaw. The inhabitants of Tādmakka are Muslim Berbers who veil themselves as the Berbers of the desert do. They live on meat and milk as well as on grain which the earth produces without being tilled. Sorghum and other grains are imported for them from the land of the Sūdān. They wear clothes of cotton, *nūlī*, and other robes dyed red. Their kings wears a red turban, yellow shirt, and blue trousers. Their dinars are called "bald" because they are of pure gold without any stamp. Their women are of perfect beauty, unequalled among people of any other country, but adultery is allowed among them. They fall upon any merchant [disputing as to] which of them shall take him to her house. . . .

When a traveller goes from the country of Kawkaw along the bank of the river in a westerly direction he reaches the kingdom called Damdam, the people of which eat anyone who falls into their hands. They have a great king to whom minor rulers are subject. In their country there is a huge fortress surmounted by an idol (*ṣanam*) in the form of a woman which they worship as their God and to which they go on pilgrimage.

Between Tādamakka and the town of Kawkaw is a distance of nine stages. The Arabs call the inhabitants of the latter the BZRKĀNYYN. This town consists of two towns, one being the residence of the king and the other inhabited by the Muslims. The king is called Qandā. The clothes of the people there are like those of the other Sūdān, consisting of a robe (*milḥafa*) and a garment of skins or some other material, according to each man's individual means. They worship idols (*dakākīr*) as do the other Sūdān. When their king sits down [to partake of a meal] a drum is beaten, the Sūdānese women dance with their thick hair flowing, and nobody in the town goes about his business until he has finished his repast, the remnants of which are thrown into the Nile. At this [the courtiers] shout out boisterously so that the people know that the king has finished his meal. When the king ascends the throne he is handed a signet ring, a sword, and a copy of the Koran which, as they assert, were sent to them by the Commander of the Faithful. Their king is a Muslim, for they entrust the kingship only to Muslims. . . .

STUDY QUESTIONS

1. What were the major features of the West African state? How did African kings use Muslims and Islam?
2. What were the major features of the West African economy?
3. What was the role of Islam in West Africa, and how did Muslims relate to other religions?

4. Where does al-Bakrí seem gullible in his accounts of West Africa? How would you explain these kinds of mistakes from a scholar who was overall trying to be accurate?

5. What, according to al-Bakrí, are the most significant features of the behavior of African women? How could you explain his emphasis?

6. For a reader, from al-Bakrí's account, what might be the major impressions about West Africa? What reasons does al-Bakrí provide for further contact with West Africa?

42 AFRICAN KINGDOMS AND ISLAM

The postclassical period formed a crucial stage in African history. Early civilization in Africa had focused in the northeast, in Egypt and the areas south of it (Kush, Axum, and ultimately Ethiopia) where major kingdoms formed. Agriculture and ironworking were widespread throughout much of the continent by the classical period. By the 5th century C.E., a second center of active trade and state building was developing in West Africa, in kingdoms such as Ghana and later Mali that stretched along the southern rim of the Sahara Desert. These "Sudanic kingdoms" (from the Arab world for black) built large regional holdings, with kings who claimed divine powers but who also maintained careful relations with more local rulers and military leaders. Extensive trade ran from the Sudanic kingdoms to North Africa and the Middle East, involving exchanges of gold, salt, some slaves, and other products in return for more manufactured goods and horses. Growing sophistication was applied to mining technology and other activities relating to commerce, and kings profited greatly from their ability to tax international trade from the region.

Contacts with North Africa included growing awareness of Islam. Mass conversions to Islam did not occur in sub-Saharan Africa at this point, but there was important interaction. Many Sudanic kings used Muslims as bureaucrats, benefiting among other things from their education and literacy. Many kings of Mali and other domains converted to Islam, establishing major educational centers and in one case making an elaborate pilgrimage to Mecca. At the same time, sub-Saharan Africa did not become a full part of Islamic civilization as North Africa did. Political institutions, popular religion, art, and gender roles were among the features of African society that remained partly distinct.

The society that was created during this period in many parts of Africa proved highly durable. Regional kingdoms, a mixture of Islam and popular religion, active internal trade, and strong family institutions continued to characterize this civilization for many centuries, surviving easily into the 19th century even amid additional new influences.

The following document is from an Arab traveler, who visited many African kingdoms during the 14th century. His observations indicate the range of contacts sub-Saharan Africa enjoyed with the Muslim world but also some of the differences that defined a separate civilization. Ibn Battuta (1304–1369), one of the great voyagers in world history, had been born in Morocco. He journeyed for almost 30 years in Asia, Europe, and Africa. His African accounts are extremely valuable, for no other comparable written sources exist for the period. He visited several parts of Africa, mainly through contacts with existing

From Ibn Battuta in Black Africa, translated and edited by Said Hamdum and Noël King, with an introduction by Ross Dunn (Noël King, 1975). Reprinted by permission of Markus Weiner Publishers, Inc.

Arab communities—the whites, in his account—in what was an established part of the Muslim trading orbit. This was a brave traveler, with some biases and a definite love of comfort, but also with an eager curiosity about the places he visited.

WRITINGS OF IBN BATTUTA

I went to the house of ibn Baddā', an excellent man of the people of Salā. I had written to him to rent a house for me and he had done that. Then the Overseer of Īwālātan, whose name was ManshāJū, invited those who had come in the caravan to his hospitality. I refused to attend that affair, but my friends insisted very much; so I went with the rest. Then the meal was brought out: a concoction of *anlī* mixed with a drop of honey and milk, which they placed in a half calabash like a deep wooden bowl. Those present drank and went away. I said to them, 'Was it for this the black invited us?' They said, 'Yes, this is great entertainment in their country.' I became sure then that there was no good to be expected from them. I wanted to travel back with the pilgrims of Īwālātan. Then it seemed good to me to go to see the capital [or residence, presence] of their King. My residence in Īwālātan was about fifty days. Its people were generous to me and entertained me. Among my hosts was its *qādī*, Muhammad ibn 'Abd Allāhibn Yanū-mar and his brother, the *faqīh* [qādī and faqīh were Muslim legal authorities] and teacher Yahyä. The town of Iwālātan is very hot and there are in it a few small date palms in whose shade they plant melons. They obtain water from the ground which exudes it. Mutton is obtainable in quantity there. The clothes of its people are of fine Egyptian material. Most of the inhabitants belong to the Massufa, and as for their women—they are extremely beautiful and are more important than the men.

Anecdote Concerning the Massūfa Who Inhabit Īwālātan

The condition of these people is strange and their manners outlandish. As for their men, there is no sexual jealousy in them. And none of them derives his genealogy from his father but, on the contrary, from his maternal uncle. A man does not pass on inheritance except to the sons of his sister to the exclusion of his own sons. Now that is a thing I never saw in any part of the world except in the country of the unbelievers of the land of Mulaībār [Malabar] among the Indians. As to the former [the Massūfa], they are Muslims keeping to the prayers, studying *fiqh* [Islamic jurisprudence], and learning the Koran by heart. With regard to their women, they are not modest in the presence of men, they do not veil themselves in spite of their perseverance in the prayers. He who wishes to marry among them can marry, but the women do not travel with the husband, and if one of them wanted to do that, she would be prevented by her family. The women there have friends and companions amongst men outside the prohibited degrees of marriage [other than brothers, fathers, etc.]. Likewise for the men, there are companions from amongst women outside the prohibited degrees. One of them would enter his house to find his wife with her companion and would not disapprove of that conduct. . . .

The sultan [emperor of Mali] has a raised cupola which is entered from inside his house. He sits in it a great part of the time. It has on the audience side a chamber with three wooden arches, the woodwork is covered with sheets of beaten silver and beneath these, three more covered with beaten gold, or, rather, it is silver covered with gilt. The windows have woolen curtains which are raised on a day when the sultan will be in session in his cupola: thus it is known that he is holding a session. When he sits, a silken cord is put out from the grill of one of the arches with a scarf of Egyptian embroidery tied to it. When the people see the scarf, drums are beaten and bugles sounded. Then from the door of the palace come out about three hundred slaves. Some have bows in their hands and some small spears and shields. Some of the spearmen stand on the right and some on the left, the bowmen sit likewise. Then they bring two mares saddled and bridled, and with them two rams. They say that these are effective against the evil eye. When the sultan has sat down three of his slaves go out quickly to call his deputy, Qanjā Musā. The *farāriyya* [commanders] arrive, and they are the *amīrs* [officers], and among them are the preacher and the men of *fiqh*, who sit in front of the armed men on the right and left of the place of audience. The interpreter Dūghā stands at the door of the audience chamber wearing splendid robes of *zardkhuāna* [official] and others. On his head is a turban which has fringes, they have a superb way of tying a turban. He is girt with a sword whose sheath is of gold, on his feet are light boots and spurs. And nobody wears boots that day except he. In his hands there are two small spears, one of gold and one of silver with points of iron. The soldiers, the district governors, the pages and the Massūfa and others are seated outside the place of audience in a broad street which has trees in it. Each *farārī* [commander] has his followers before him with their spears, bows, drums and bugles made of elephant tusks. Their instruments of music are made of reeds and calabashes, and they beat them with sticks and produce a wonderful sound. Each *farārī* has a quiver which he places between his shoulders. He holds his bow in his hand and is mounted on a mare. Some of his men are on foot and some on mounts.

Inside the audience chamber under the arches a man is standing; he who wants to speak to the sultan speaks to Dūghā, Dūghā speaks to the man who is standing, and he speaks to the sultan.

An Account of the Sessions in the Place of Audience

The sultan sits on certain days in the palace yard to give audience. There is a platform under a tree with three steps which they call *banbī*. It is covered with silk and has pillows placed on it. The *shatr* [umbrella] is raised, this is a shelter made of silk with a golden bird like a sparrowhawk above it. The sultan comes out from a gate in the corner of the palace, bow in hand, his quiver between his shoulders, and on his head a cap of gold tied with a golden band which has fringes like thin-bladed knives more than a span long. He often wears a robe which is soft and red, made from Roman cloth . . . *mutanfas*. The singers go out before him carrying gold and silver *qanābir* [guitars] and behind him come three hundred armed slaves. The sultan walks slowly and pauses often and sometimes he stops completely. When he comes to the *banbī* he stops and looks at the people. Then he mounts the steps with dignity in the manner of a preacher getting into the pulpit. When he sits down they beat the drums, blow the bugles and the horns, and three of the slaves go out in haste and call the deputy and the *farāriyya* [commanders]. They enter and sit down. The two mares are brought in with the two rams. Damūghā stands at the door while the rest of the people are in the street under the tree. The blacks are the most humble of men before their king and the most extreme in their self-abasement before him. They swear by his name, saying 'Mansā Sulaimānkī' [the law of Mansā Sulaimānkī]. When he calls one of them while he is in session in his cupola which we described above, the man invited takes off his clothes and wears patched clothes, takes off his turban, puts on a dirty cap, and goes in raising his clothes and trousers up his legs half-way to his knees. He advances with humility looking like a beggar. He hits the ground with his elbows, he hits it hard. He stands bowed, like one in the *ruku'* position in prayer, listening to what the king says. When one of them speaks to the sultan and he gives him an answer, he removes his clothes from his back and throws dust on his head and back, as a person does when bathing with water. I used to wonder how they do not blind their eyes. When the sultan speaks in his council, at his word those present take their turbans off their heads and listen to the speech. . . .

Amongst their good qualities is the small amount of injustice amongst them, for of all people they are the furthest from it. Their sultan does not forgive anyone in any matter to do with justice. Among these qualities there is also the prevalence of peace in their country, the traveller is not afraid in it nor is he who lives there in fear of the thief or of the robber by violence. They do not interfere with the property of the white man who dies in their country even though it may consist of great wealth, but rather they entrust it to the hand of someone dependable among the white men until it is taken by the rightful claimant.

Another of the good habits amongst them is the way they meticulously observe the times of the prayers and attendance at them, so also it is with regard to their congregational services and their beating of their children to instill these things in them.

When it is Friday, if a man does not come early to the mosque he will not find a place to pray because of the numbers of the crowd. It is their custom for every man to send his boy with his prayer mat. He spreads it for him in a place commensurate with his position and keeps the place until he comes to the mosque. Their prayer mats are made of the leaves of a tree like a date palm but it bears no fruit.

Among their good qualities is their putting on of good white clothes on Friday. If a man among them has nothing except a tattered shirt, he washes and cleans it and attends the Friday prayer in it. Another of their good qualities is their concern for learning the sublime Koran by heart. They make fetters for their children when they appear on their part to be falling short in their learning of it by heart, and they are not taken off from them till they do learn by heart. I went in to visit the *qādī* on an 'Id day and his children were tied up. I said to him, 'Why do you not release them?' He said, 'I shall not do so until they learn the Koran by heart.' One day I passed by a handsome youth from them dressed in fine clothes and on his feet was a heavy chain. I said to the man who was with me, 'What has this youth done—has he killed someone?' The youth heard my remark and laughed. It was told me, 'He has been chained so that he will learn the Koran by heart.'

Among the bad things which they do—their serving women, slave women and little daughters appear before people naked, exposing their private parts. I used to see many of them in this state in Ramaḍān, for it was the custom of the *farāriyya* [commanders] to break the fast in the sultan's house. Everyone of them has his food carried in to him by twenty or more of his slave girls and they are naked, every one. Also among their bad customs is the way women will go into the presence of the sultan naked, without any covering; and the nakedness of the sultan's daughters—on the night of the twenty-seventh of Ramadān, I saw about a hundred slave girls coming out of his palace with food, with them were two of his daughters, they had full breasts and no clothes on. Another of their bad customs is their putting of dust and ashes on their heads as a sign of respect. And another is the laughing matter I mentioned of their poetic recitals. And another is that many of them eat animals not ritually slaughtered, and dogs and donkeys.

STUDY QUESTIONS

1. How is it clear that Ibn Battuta assumes the presence of standard institutions of civilization in sub-Saharan Africa?
2. What kinds of government does Ibn Battuta describe?
3. What did he find strange? Are his observations likely to have been accurate, and if not, what might explain his exaggerations?
4. How do Ibn Battuta's impressions of Africa compare with those of al-Bakrí, in the previous chapter?
5. What are the advantages and disadvantages of using travelers' accounts for information about a past society?
6. Compare the evaluations of Africa by Ibn Battuta and in the earlier Sailer's story (Chapter 40). What features in Africa help explain differences and similarities in the two accounts?
7. What kind of ties did sub-Saharan Africa maintain with the Islamic world? What were the major differences between the two societies? Why did African leaders maintain distinctions along with their genuine appreciation of Islam?

A Major Artistic Tradition: The Sculptures of Benin

West African Art. A bronze head of a Benin king, dating from the 1500s. Leaders in Benin still wear caps and chokers similar to those worn by this figure. Benin bronzes began to emerge as an art form in the 15th century, as this important forest kingdom took shape. The art was influenced by earlier styles elsewhere in West Africa. It was designed to provide decoration, but also to project the power of the king (oba) and the state. The art also depended on the far-flung West African trade; copper to make bronze was imported on caravans from North Africa. (The Metropolitan Museum of Art, The Michael C. Rockerfeller Memorial Collection, Bequest of Nelson A. Rockerfeller, 1979. (1979. 206. 86.))

Benin became one of the earliest areas to gain contact with European traders and explorers, but its rulers decided not to become extensively involved with the slave trade. The state survived into the 19th century, by which time, however, royal power was in decline until takeover by the British in 1897.

STUDY QUESTIONS

1. How does this figure suggest a high level of artistic talent?
2. Which of the following terms best characterizes the style involved and why?
   a. caricature b. naturalistic c. abstract
3. What does this representation suggest about royal power? How does it convey the religious authority and divinity claimed by Benin kings?
4. How does this artistic representation of the king compare with the description of the emperor of Mali in the traveler's account by Ibn Battuta?
5. European "discovery" of West African art in the 19th century had a major impact on modern styles around 1900 and after. Does this figure suggest connections to modern art?

43

AFRICA THROUGH THE EYES OF AN EUROPEAN MERCHANT

Though the Romans had known quite a bit about Africa, even south of the northern rim which they controlled, postclassical Europe had far more limited contacts. In the 15th century, however, expanding trade brought more Europeans to Africa beyond the Mediterranean coast. Their comments, like those of other travelers, help us to learn more about postclassical Africa and of course about the attitudes of Europeans themselves in this period.

Antonius Malfante wrote from Tuat (Tawat) in the central Sahara in 1447, to a colleague in Genoa. Tawat was an important oasis on a trade route from the city-states of northern Nigeria. Malfante obviously traveled fairly widely in the region, and offered interesting comments on the diverse peoples of the area and on the kinds of trading activities they conducted. His observations also cover religious and political issues. We know nothing about Malfante himself. Genoa was increasingly active in Mediterranean trade, so we can surmise that he was involved in these endeavors, as he himself implies.

His account raises the usual questions about traveler's observations, as to which seem particularly accurate, and which are shaded by bias, exaggeration, or unacknowledged ignorance. He was certainly sympathetic in many ways, and in the process may tell us quite a bit about the nature of African civilization in and around the Sahara.

ANTONIUS MALFANTE

After we had come from the sea, we journeyed on horseback, always southwards, for about twelve days. For seven days we encountered no dwelling—nothing but sandy plains; we proceeded as though at sea, guided by the sun during the day, at night by the stars. At the end of the seventh day, we arrived at an oasis, where dwelt very poor people who supported themselves on water and a little sandy ground. They sow little, living upon the numerous date palms. At this [oasis] we had come into Tueto [Tawat, a group of oases]. In this place there are eighteen quarters, enclosed within one wall, and ruled by an oligarchy. Each ruler of a quarter protects his followers, whether they be in the right or no. The quarters closely adjoin each other and are jealous of their privileges. Everyone arriving here places himself under the protection of one of these

From *The Voyages of Cadamosto and Other Documents on Western Africa in the Second Half of the 15th Century*, trans. and edited by G. R. Crone (New York: Cambridge University Press, 1937), pp. 85–90.

rulers, who will protect him to the death: thus merchants enjoy very great security, much greater, in my opinion, than in other North African kingdoms such as Tunis.

Though I am a Christian, no one ever addressed an insulting word to me. They said they had never seen a Christian before. It is true that on my first arrival they were scornful of me, because they all wished to see me, saying with wonder "This Christian has a countenance like ours"—for they believed that Christians had disguised faces. Their curiosity was soon satisfied, and now I can go alone anywhere, with no one to say an evil word to me.

There are many Jews, who lead a good life here, for they are under the protection of the several rulers, each of whom defends his own clients. Thus they enjoy very secure social standing. Trade is in their hands, and many of them are to be trusted with the greatest confidence.

This locality is a mart of the country of the African Muslims, to which merchants come to sell their goods: gold is carried hither, and bought by those who come up from the coast. There are many rich men here. The generality, however, are very poor, for they do not sow, nor do they harvest anything, save the dates upon which they subsist. They eat no meat but that of castrated camels, which are scarce and very dear.

It is true that the Arabs with whom I came from the coast brought with them corn and barley which they sell throughout the year.

It never rains here: if it did, the houses, being built of salt in the place of reeds, would be destroyed. It is scarcely ever cold here: in summer the heat is extreme, wherefore they are almost all blacks. The children of both sexes go naked up to the age of fifteen. These people observe the religion and law of Muhammad. In the vicinity there are 150 to 200 oases.

In the lands of the blacks, as well as here, dwell the Tuareg, who live, like the Arabs, in tents. They are without number, and hold sway over the land from the borders of Egypt to the shores of the Ocean [present day Libya], and over all the neighbouring towns of the blacks. They are fair, strong in body and very handsome in appearance. They ride without stirrups, with simple spurs. They are governed by kings, whose heirs are the sons of their sisters—for such is their law. They keep their mouths and noses covered. I have seen many of them here, and have asked them through an interpreter why they cover their mouths and noses thus. They replied: "We have inherited this custom from our ancestors." Their faith is that of the Blacks. Their sustenance is milk and flesh, no corn or barley, but much rice. Their sheep, cattle, and camels are without number. One breed of camel, white as snow, can cover in one day a distance which would take a horseman four days to travel. Great warriors, these people are continually at war amongst themselves.

The states which are under their rule border upon the land of the Blacks. I shall speak of those known to men here, and which have inhabitants of the faith of Muhammad. In all, the great majority are Blacks, but there are a small number of whites [i.e. tawny Moors]. . . .

These adhere to the law of Muhammad.

To the south of these are innumerable great cities and territories, the inhabitants of which are all blacks and idolators, continually at war with each other in defence of their law and faith of their idols. Some worship the sun, others the moon, the seven planets, fire, or water; others a mirror which reflects their faces, which they take to be the images of gods; others groves of trees, the seats of a spirit to whom they make sacrifice; others again, statues of wood and stone, with which, they say, they commune by incantations. They relate here extraordinary things of this people.

The lord in whose protection I am, here, who is the greatest in this land, having a fortune of more than 100,000 *doubles* [a coin], a man worthy of credence, relates that he lived for thirty years in that town, and, as he says, for fourteen years in the land of the Blacks. Every day he tells me wonderful things of these peoples. He says that these lands and peoples extend endlessly to the south: they all go naked, save for a small loincloth to cover their privates. They have an abundance of flesh, milk, and rice, but no corn or barley.

The slaves which the blacks take in their internecine wars are sold at a very low price. These peoples, who cover the land in multitudes, are in carnal acts like the beasts. They breed greatly, for a woman bears up to five at a birth. Nor can it be doubted that they are eaters of human flesh, for many people have gone hence into their country. Neither there nor here are there ever epidemics.

When the blacks catch sight of a white man from a distance, they take to flight as though from a monster, believing him to be a phantom. They are unlettered, and without books. They are great magicians, evoking by incense diabolical spirits, with whom, they say, they perform marvels.

The wares for which there is a demand here are many: but the principal articles are copper, and salt in slabs, bars, and cakes. The copper of Romania [the Byzantine Empire], which is obtained through Alexandria, is always in great demand throughout the land of the Blacks. I frequently enquired what they did with it, but no one could give me a definite answer. I believe it is that there are so many peoples that there is almost nothing but is of use to them.

The Egyptian merchants come to trade in the land of the Blacks with half a million head of cattle and camels—a figure which is not fantastic in this region.

The place where I am is good for trade, as the Egyptians and other merchants come hither from the land of the Blacks bringing gold, which they exchange for copper and other goods. Thus everything sells well; until there is nothing left for sale. The people here will neither sell nor buy unless at a profit of one hundred per cent. For this reason, I have lost on the goods I brought here, two thousand *doubles*.

From what I can understand, these people neighbour on India. Indian merchants come hither, and converse through interpreters. These Indians are Christians, adorers of the cross. It is said that in the land of the Blacks there are forty dialects, so that they are unable to understand each other.

I often enquired where the gold was found and collected; my patron always replied "I was fourteen years in the land of the Blacks, and I have never heard nor seen anyone who could reply from definite knowledge. That is my experience, as to how it is found and collected. What appears plain is that it comes from a distant land, and, as I believe, from a definite zone." He also said that he had been in places where silver was as valuable as gold.

STUDY QUESTIONS

1. What was Malfante doing in Africa? How was he treated, and how would you explain the way Africans seem to have reacted to him?

2. What aspects of Malfante's observations about Africa seem most surprising? Where does he seem to lapse into stereotype or exaggeration? Overall, do you find him a sympathetic observer?

3. What were the main religious features of Saharan Africa and points south? What were the main political features?

4. According to Malfante's account, what kinds of contacts did this African region have with other parts of the world? What were the range and position of African merchants?

5. How does Malfante's account compare with the observations of other commentators on Africa, such as al-Bakrí or Ibn Battuta? Do his emphases differ? Is he more or less biased?

6. Is this a valuable source for understanding post-classical Africa? What other kinds of sources would help flesh out our grasp of this civilization in this period?

44 MAYAN AND AZTEC CREATION STORIES

Popol Vuh relates the Mayan story of creation. Literally translated as the "Council Book," it also served as a source of advice for the Lords of Quiché, a Mayan center of civilization located northwest of Guatemala City during the post-classical era about 1000 C.E. The lords used the Council Book at meetings to interpret signs, particularly omens related to death, famine, and conflict. Descendants of these ancient lineages wrote the only extant version of *Popol Vuh* between 1554 and 1558. They wrote in the Mayan language, using the Roman alphabet. Francisco Ximénez, a member of the Dominican Order, discovered and translated the manuscript into Spanish about 1701.

As related in the story, the gods of sky and water created the earth in one attempt. By contrast, the creation of humans took four attempts. The first three were defective and spawned other types of creatures. Even on the successful fourth try, the gods later changed the outcome because the humans were too perfect. Between the three failures and the fourth try, *Popol Vuh* relates numerous adventures of the gods and how they influenced cosmic and earthly conditions. They created the planets, sun, animals, trees, corn planting, artisan activities, and ball games. The first selection recounts the Mayan story of human creation.

The Aztecs appeared in the historical record much later than the Mayans. Originally barbarian migrants from northern Mexico, the Aztecs entered Central Mexico about 1300. There they inherited the cosmologies that had been passed down from previous civilizations, Teotihuacan (1–600), Toltec (900–1168) and the City-State Civilization that surrounded Lake Texcoco at their arrival. By the time the Aztecs created their own city-state (1322) and conquered the other city-states (1420–1480), they rewrote Central Mexican cosmology to suit their purposes of conquest and rule. In the Aztec version, Uitzilopochtli, an obscure God seldom mentioned, became the most important deity, although he was not the original creator. From the inherited stories, the Aztecs considered the God Ometeotl, who was both male and female, the creator of all the lesser Gods.

The Mayan story is from *Popol Vuh: The Mayan Book of the Dawn of Life*, by Dennis Tedlock. Copyright © 1985, 1996 by Dennis Tedlock. Reprinted by permission of Simon & Schuster. The Aztec account is taken from "Aztec Creation Story of the God Utzilopochtli" from *Bernardino de Sahagun General History of the Things of New Spain* (Florentine Codex) translated by Arthur J. O. Anderson and Charles Dibble, 2nd ed., Part IV (Santa Fe, New Mexico: The School of American Research and the University of Utah, 1978) pp. 1–4.

Ometeotl bore four sons, Red Tezcatlipoca, Black Tezcatlipoca, Quetzalcoatl and Uitzilopochtli. Similar to the Mayan story of multiple creations, Ometeotl's sons, plus the other Gods, created the heavens, earth, sea, fire and underworld, not once but four times. Black Tezcatlipoca ruled over the first, Quetzalcoatl the second, the rain God Tlaloc the third and Tlaloc's wife the fourth. Each new creation was preceded by a destructive struggle among the Gods. Thus, Aztec creation stories involved a series of conflicts among the Gods followed by new births. Uitzilopochtli created the world of the fifth sun. The second selection recounts his birth.

THE MAYAN STORY OF HUMAN CREATION FROM *POPOL VUH*

And here is the beginning of the conception of humans, and of the search for the ingredients of the human body. So they spoke, the Bearer, Begetter, the Makers, Modelers named Sovereign Plumed Serpent:

"The dawn has approached, preparations have been made, and morning has come for the provider, nurturer, born in the light, begotten in the light. Morning has come for humankind, for the people of the face of the earth," they said. It all came together as they went on thinking in the darkness, in the night, as they searched and they sifted, they thought and they wondered.

And here their thoughts came out in clear light. They sought and discovered what was needed for human flesh. It was only a short while before the sun, moon, and stars were to appear above the Makers and Modelers. Broken Place, Bitter Water Place is the name: the yellow corn, white corn came from there.

And these are the names of the animals who brought the food: fox, coyote, parrot, crow. There were four animals who brought the news of the ears of yellow corn and white corn. They were coming from over there at Broken Place, they showed the way to the break.

And this was when they found the staple foods.

And these were the ingredients for the flesh of the human work, the human design, and the water was for the blood. It became human blood, and corn was also used by the Bearer, Begetter.

And so they were happy over the provisions of the good mountain, filled with sweet things, thick with yellow corn, white corn, and thick with pataxte and cacao, countless zapotes, anonas, jocotes, nances, matasanos, sweets—the rich foods filling up the citadel named Broken Place, Bitter Water Place. All the edible fruits were there: small staples, great staples, small plants, great plants. The way was shown by the animals.

And then the yellow corn and white corn were ground, and Xmucane did the grinding nine times. Corn was used, along with the water she rinsed her hands with, for the creation of grease; it became human fat when it was worked by the Bearer, Begetter, Sovereign Plumed Serpent, as they are called.

After that, they put it into words:

the making, the modeling of our first mother-father,
with yellow corn, white corn alone for the flesh,

food alone for the human legs and arms,
for our first fathers, the four human works.
It was staples alone that made up their flesh.

• • •

These are the names of the first people who were made and modeled.
This is the first person: Jaguar Quitze.
And now the second: Jaguar Night.
And now the third: Mahucutah.
And the fourth: True Jaguar.

And these are the names of our first mother-fathers. They were simply made and modeled, it is said; they had no mother and no father. We have named the men by themselves. No woman gave birth to them, nor were they begotten by the builder, sculptor, Bearer, Begetter. By sacrifice alone, by genius alone they were made, they were modeled by the Maker, Modeler, Bearer, Begetter, Sovereign Plumed Serpent. And when they came to fruition, they came out human:

They talked and they made words.
They looked and they listened.
They walked, they worked.

They were good people, handsome, with looks of the male kind. Thoughts came into existence and they gazed; their vision came all at once. Perfectly they saw, perfectly they knew everything under the sky, whenever they looked. The moment they turned around and looked around in the sky, on the earth, everything was seen without any obstruction. They didn't have to walk around before they could see what was under the sky; they just stayed where they were.

As they looked, their knowledge became intense. Their sight passed through trees, through rocks, through lakes, through seas, through mountains, through plains. Jaguar Quitze, Jaguar Night, Mahucutah, and True Jaguar were truly gifted people.

And then they were asked by the builder and mason:

"What do you know about your being? Don't you look, don't you listen? Isn't your speech good, and your walk? So you must look, to see out under the sky. Don't you see the mountain-plain clearly? So try it," they were told.

And then they saw everything under the sky perfectly. After that, they thanked the Maker, Modeler:

"Truly now,
double thanks, triple thanks
that we've been formed, we've been given
our mouths, our faces,
we speak, we listen,
we wonder, we move,
our knowledge is good, we've understood
what is far and near,
and we've seen what is great and small
under the sky, on the earth.
Thanks to you we've been formed,

we've come to be made and modeled,
our grandmother, our grandfather,"

they said when they gave thanks for having been made and modeled. They under-stood everything perfectly, they sighted the four sides, the four corners in the sky, on the earth, and this didn't sound good to the builder and sculptor:

"What our works and designs have said is no good:

'We have understood everything, great and small,' they say." And so the Bearer, Begetter took back their knowledge:

"What should we do with them now? Their vision should at least reach nearby, they should see at least a small part of the face of the earth, but what they're saying isn't good. Aren't they merely 'works' and 'designs' in their very names? Yet they'll become as great as gods, unless they procreate, proliferate at the sowing, the dawn-ing, unless they increase."

"Let it be this way: now we'll take them apart just a little, that's what we need. What we've found out isn't good. Their deeds would become equal to ours, just because their knowledge reaches so far. They see everything," so said

the Heart of Sky, Hurricane,
Newborn Thunderbolt, Raw Thunderbolt,
Sovereign Plumed Serpent,
Bearer, Begetter,
Xpiyacoc, Xmucane,
Maker, Modeler,

as they are called. And when they changed the nature of their works, their designs, it was enough that the eyes be marred by the Heart of Sky. They were blinded as the face of a mirror is breathed upon. Their eyes were weakened. Now it was only when they looked nearby that things were clear.

And such was the loss of the means of understanding, along with the means of knowing everything, by the four humans. The root was implanted.

And such was the making, modeling of our first grandfather, our father, by the Heart of Sky, Heart of Earth.

AZTEC CREATION STORY OF THE GOD UTZILOPOCHTLI

TO UITZILOPOCHTLI the Mexicans paid great honor.

Thus did they believe of his beginning, his origin. At Coatepec, near Tula, there dwelt one day, there lived a woman named Coatl icue, mother of the Centzo-nuitznaua. And their elder sister was named Coyolxauhqui.

And this Coatl icue used to perform penances there; she used to sweep; she used to take care of sweeping. Thus she used to perform penances at Coatepec. And once, when Coatl icue was sweeping, feathers descended upon her—what was like a ball of feathers. Then Coatl icue snatched them up; she placed then at her waist. And when she had swept, then she would have taken the feathers which she had put at her waist. She found nothing. There-upon by means of them Coatl icue conceived.

And when the Centzonuitznaua saw that their mother was already with child, they were very wrathful. They said: 'Who brought this about? Who got her with child? She hath dishonored us' she hath shamed us. And their elder sister, Coyolxauhqui, said to them: 'My elder brothers, she hath dishonored us. We [can] only kill our mother, the wicked one who is already with child. Who is the cause of what is in her womb?'

And when Coatl icue learned of this, she was sorely afraid, she was deeply saddened. But her child, who was in her womb, comforted her. He called to her; he said to her: "Have no fear. Already I know [what I shall do]."

When Coatl icue heard the words of her child, she was much comforted by them she was satisfied [concerning] what had thus terrified her.

And upon this the Centzonuitznaua, when they had brought together all their considerations, when they had expressed their determination that they would kill their mother, because she had brought about an affront, much exerted themselves. They were very wrathful. As if her heart came forth, Coyolzauhqui greatly incited, aroused the anger of her elder brothers, that they would kill their mother. And the Centzonuitznaua thereupon arrayed themselves; they armed themselves for war.

And these Centzonuitznaua were like seasoned warriors. They twisted their hair; they wound their hair about their heads; they wound about their heads their hair, their forehead hair.

But one who was named Quauitl icac delivered information to both sides. That which the Centzonuitznaua said he then told, he informed Uitzilopochtli.

And Uitzilopochtli said to Quauitl icac: "Pay careful heed, my dear uncle; listen carefully. I already know [what I shall do]."

And upon this, when finally [the Centzonuitznaua] expressed their determination, when they were of one mind in their deliberations, that they would kill, that they would slay their mother, thereupon they went. Coyolxauhqui led them. Much did each one exert himself; each one persevered; each armed himself for war. Each one was provided. On them [selves] they placed their paper array, the paper crowns, their nettles hanging from the painted papers; and they bound little bells to the calves of their legs. These little bells were called *oyoualli.* And their arrows had notched heads.

Thereupon they went. They went each on in order. They went each one in his row. Each one wielded his weapons. They went crouching. Coyolxauhqui led them. . . .

Then Quauitl icac said to him: "At last they scale the heights here; at last they arrive here. Coyolxauhqui cometh leading them."

And Uitzilopochtli just then was born.

Then he had his array with him—his shield, *teueuelli;* and his darts and his blue dart thrower, called *xiuatlatl;* and in diagonal stripes was his face painted with his child's offal, called his child's face painting. He was pasted with feathers at his forehead and at his ears. And on his one thin foot, his left, he had the sole pasted with feathers. And he had stripes in blue mineral earth on both his thighs and both his upper arms.'

And one named Tochancalqui set fire to the [serpent] *xiuhcoatl.* Uitzilopochtli commanded it.

Then he pierced Coyolzauhqui, and then quickly struck off her head. It stopped there at the edge of Coatepetl. And her body came falling below; it fell breaking to pieces; in various places her arms, her legs, her body each fell.

And Uitzilopochtli then arose; he pursued, gave full attention to the Centzonuitznaua; he plunged, he scattered them from the top of Coatepetl.

And when he had come driving them to the ground below, thereupon he took after them; he pursued all of them around Coatepetl. Four times he chased them all around, pursued them all around. Yet in vain they went crying out at him, yet in vain they cried out against him, yet in vain they went striking their shields. No more could they do, no more could they achieve; no longer could they ward him off. Uitzilopochtli just set on all of them; he indeed made them turn tail; he indeed destroyed them; he indeed annihilated them; he indeed exterminated them.

And when even now he indeed did not leave them alone, when indeed he hung on to all of them, much did they importune him. They said to him: "Let this be enough!"

But Uitzilopochtli did not content himself with this. He was very bold against them as he took after them. And only very few fled his presence. Those who escaped his hands went there to the south. For indeed toward there these Centzonuitznaua went, the few who escaped the hands of Uitzilopochtli.'

And upon this when he had slain them, when he had taken his pleasure, he took from them their goods, their adornment, the paper crowns. He took them as his own goods, he took them as his own property; he assumed them as his due, as if taking the insignia to himself.

And Uitzilopochtli was also called an omen of evil, because only from a feather which fell, his mother Coatl icue conceived. For no one appeared as his father.'

This one the Mexicans respected. Hence they made offerings to him; hence they honored him, they exerted themselves for him. And they placed their trust in Uitzilopochtli. And this veneration was taken from there, Coatepec, as was done in days of yore.

Enough of this.

STUDY QUESTIONS

1. Mayan gods created humans from corn. What does this belief suggest about the Mayan world-view?
2. Why and how did Mayan gods alter their human creatures? What does this imply about the relationship between humans and gods?
3. What does the Uitzilopochtli story suggest about the Aztec view of life on earth?
4. What are the main similarities and differences between the accounts in terms of religious and scientific implications?
5. Compare the Ancient American accounts of the origins of humans, relations of humans to Gods and relations among the Gods to Mesopotamian (Chapter 1), Egyptian (Chapter 3), Hebrew (Chapter 4), and Hindu (Chapter 12) accounts. What do the comparisons suggest about the relationship of religion to politics and society?

45   TRIBUTE UNDER THE AZTECS

Aztec warriors, extending their rule outward from Tenochtitlan (Mexico City), conquered the other city-states of Central Mexico between C.E. 1420 and 1480. When the
Spaniards arrived in 1519, the Aztecs governed an area inhabited by about 18 million
people. Despite their recent military success, the Aztecs, when they first appeared on
the historical scene about 1250, were uncouth barbarian invaders from the north.
They were not responsible for creating civilization in Central Mexico but were its
inheritors.

Before the Aztec appearance, the rulers of Teotihuacan (C.E. 1–900) and the subsequent Toltec Empire (C.E. 1000–1200) established the essential features of civilization.
Cultivation of maize was highly developed, particularly through the use of irrigation
channels. Surplus production was obtained from local villages through a tribute system
that funneled grain, and other products, to central government warehouses. This surplus
supported a hierarchy of officials, who not only ran the government, but also devised
calendars, built monumental shrines, created a religious literature, and led ritual obser-
vances that bound society together. Although these societies succumbed to barbarian
invasions, civilization itself did not disappear.

After the demise of the Toltec Empire, civilization in Central Mexico consisted of
competing city-states scattered around Lake Texcoco in the Central Valley. When the
Aztecs conquered these city-states, they repeated the experience of pervious intruders.
Specifically the Aztecs took control of a centuries-old tribute system. Spanish observer
Gonzalo Fernández de Oviedo y Valdés (1478–1557) described that system and the
poverty it caused. Secondly, because they were unwelcome conquerors, the Aztecs
devised a politico-religious system that was based on terror. They demonstrated their
power by obtaining human sacrificial victims for their war god Huitzilipochtli. The statue
of Huitzilipochtli's mother, Coatlicue, expressed this style of rule.

OBSERVATIONS OF GONZALO FERNÁNDEZ
DE OVIEDO Y VALDÉS

The Indians of New Spain, I have been told by reliable persons who gained their
information from Spaniards who fought with Hernando Cortés in the conquest
of that land, are the poorest of the many nations that live in the Indies at the

From Benjamin Keen, ed. and trans., *Latin American Civilization*, Vol. 1, 3rd ed. (Boston:
Houghton Mifflin, 1974) pp. 19–22. Originally found in Gonzalo Fernandez de Oviedo y Valdes,
Historia General y Natural de las Indias, Vol. X (Asuncion, Paraguay: 1944–1945) pp. 110–114.

present time. In their homes they have no furnishings or clothing other than the poor garments which they wear on their persons, one or two stones for grinding maize, some pots in which to cook the maize, and a sleeping mat. Their meals consist chiefly of vegetables cooked with chili, and bread. They eat little—not that they would not eat more if they could get it, for the soil is very fertile and yields bountiful harvests, but the common people and plebeians suffer under the tyranny of their Indian lords, who tax away the greater part of their produce in a manner that I shall describe. Only the lords and their relatives, and some principal men and merchants, have estates and lands of their own; they sell and gamble with their lands as they please, and they sow and harvest them but pay no tribute. Nor is any tribute paid by artisans, such as masons, carpenters, feather-workers, or silversmiths, or by singers and kettle-drummers (for every Indian lord has musicians in his household, each according to his station). But such persons render personal service when it is required, and none of them is paid for his labor.

Each Indian lord assigns to the common folk who come from other parts of the country to settle on his land (and to those who are already settled there) specific fields, that each may know the land that he is to sow. And the majority of them have their homes on their land; and between twenty and thirty, or forty and fifty houses have over them an Indian head who is called *tiquitlato,* which in the Castilian tongue means "the finder (or seeker) of tribute." At harvest time this *tiquitlato,* inspects the cornfield and observes what each one reaps, and when the reaping is done they show him the harvest, and he counts the ears of corn that each has reaped, and the number of wives and children that each of the vassals in his charge possesses. And with the harvest before him he calculates how many ears of corn each person in that household will require till the next harvest, and these he gives to the Indian head of that house; and he does the same with the other produce, namely kidney beans, which are a kind of small beans, and chili, which is their pepper; and *chia,* which is as fine as mustard seed, and which in warm weather they drink, ground and made into a solution in water and used for medicine, roasted and ground; and cocoa, which is a kind of almond that they use as money, and which they grind, make into a solution, and drink; and cotton, in those places where it is raised, which is in the hot lands and not the cold; and pulque, which is their wine; and all the various products obtained from the maguey plant, from which they obtain food and drink and footwear and clothing. This plant grows in the cold regions, and the leaves resemble those of the cinnamon tree, but are much larger. Of all these and other products they leave the vassal only enough to sustain him for a year. And in addition the vassal must earn enough to pay the tribute of mantles, gold, silver, honey, wax, lime, wood, or whatever products it is customary to pay as tribute in that country. They pay this tribute every forty, sixty, seventy, or ninety days, according to the terms of the agreement. This tribute also the *tiquitlato* receives and carries to his Indian lord.

Ten days before the close of the sixty or hundred days, or whatever is the period appointed for the payment of tribute, they take to the house of the Indian lord the produce brought by the *tiquitlatos;* and if some poor Indian should prove unable to pay his share of tribute, whether for reasons of health or poverty, or lack of work, the *tiquitlato* tells the lord that such-and-such will not pay the proportion of the tribute that had been assigned to him; then the lord tells the *tiquitlato* to take the recalcitrant vassal to a *tianguez* or market, which they hold every five days in all the towns of the land, and there sell him into slavery, applying the proceeds of the sale to the payment of his tribute. . . .

All the towns have their own lands, long ago assigned for the provision of the *orchilobos* or *ques* or temples where they kept their idols; and these lands were and are the best of all. And they have this custom: At seeding time all would go forth at the summons of the town council to sow these fields, and to weed them at the proper time, and to cultivate the grain and harvest it and carry it to a house in which lived the pope and the *teupisques, pioches, exputhles* and *piltoutles* (or, as we would say, the bishops, archbishops, and the canons and prebendaries, and even choristers, for each major temple had these five classes of officials). And they supported them-selves from this harvest, and the Indians also raised chickens for them to eat.

In all the towns Montezuma had his designated lands, which they sowed for him in the same way as the temple lands; and if no garrison was stationed in their towns, they would carry the crops on their backs to the great city of Temistitan [Tenochtitlán]; but in the garrison towns the grain was eaten by Montezuma's sol-diers, and if the town did not sow the land, it had to supply the garrison with food, and also give them chickens and all other needful provisions.

STUDY QUESTIONS

1. What evidence can you find in this selection that shows social stratification prior to the arrival of the Aztecs?
2. How did the Aztec tribute system work? What does such a tribute system indi-cate about social organization in ancient Mexico?
3. After the Spanish conquest, how might the Spaniards view the operation of the tribute system? How might that view contribute to the structure of a new society?
4. How did Aztec social structure compare with social structures in other tradi-tional societies such as India or China?

AZTEC GODDESS

Aztec Sculpture: Coatlicue was the Aztec earth goddess and mother of the Aztec war god and chief deity, Huitzilipochtli. Through an outward display of terror, the eight-foot statue was designed to show the power of gods over mortals. Two snakes arise out of her neck to form her face. Blood serpents emerge from her wrists. She wears a skirt of snakes and a necklace of human hands, hearts and a human skull pendant. Of all the components of the statue, the necklace communicated clearly that human sacrifice sustained the gods and maintained cosmic order. Photo found in Michael C. Meyer, William L. Sherman, and Susan M. Deeds. *The Course of Mexican History.* 6th ed. (Museu National de Anthropologia, Mexico City, D. F., Mexico/Photo by Warner Forman/ Art Resource, NY)

STUDY QUESTIONS

1. What is your expectation of a portrayal of an earth mother goddess? How does this statue compare?
2. What does this statue convey about Aztec civilization?

46

THE ANDEAN KINGDOM
OF CHUQUITO IN 1567

The Inca Empire was formed at approximately the same time as the Aztec Empire. Incan military conquests began in 1438 when Incan armies subdued their home area of Cuzco in the highlands of southwestern Peru and ended with the conquest of Quito [Ecuador] in the 1520s. By the early 16th century, the Incan Empire stretched from Quito in the north to Chile in the south. The majority of the empire's 6 million inhabitants lived in the areas of present-day Peru and Bolivia. Three hundred years earlier the Incas were a small village community competing with other villages in the highlands of Cuzco. During the expansionary period, the Incas employed their traditional highland social practices as the model for imperial organization. The *ayllu,* the smallest Andean social unit, functioned on the basis of communal ownership of land, communal work practices and strong traditions of mutual aid for those unable to work. But *ayllus,* for many generations before the Incas began their imperial expansion, were also part of larger units, or chiefdoms. The organization of the chiefdom reflected a strong awareness of the economic potential of diverse ecological zones in the Andean area and revealed how the patterns of obligations to the chief enabled maximum exploitation of these areas. In the highlands (*altiplano*) staple products consisted of potatoes, quinua [a type of grain that only thrives in highland areas and is also known as altiplano rice], and llama and alpaca products. In lower areas on the Pacific coast and in semitropical valleys off the eastern escarpment of the Andean range, staple products consist of maize, cotton, fruits, and coca (used for chewing and in rituals). The economic goal of a highland chiefdom was to control as many ecological zones as possible. This same goal lay behind the Incan system of governance. The noteworthy characteristics of the Inca Empire, including forced migrations of people, road and bridge building, served not only to unite the empire but also to produce and distribute goods from all ecological zones.

The Kingdom of Chuquito was a pre-Inca chiefdom located on the western shore of Lake Titicaca that was subsequently incorporated into the Inca Empire. A Spanish governmental inquiry of 1567 clearly showed how the traditional patterns of obligations owed to the chief contributed to exploitation of various ecological zones. In order to verify accounts, Spanish officials took testimony not only from the chief but also from his subjects.

Selections taken from *Visita hecha a la procincia de Chuquito por Garci Diez de San Miguel en el año 1567*, paleography by Waldemar Espinoza Soriano, (Lima: Casa de la Cultura, 1964), pp. 20–22, 86. Translation from the Spanish by Erwin Grieshaber.

TESTIMONY OF MARTIN CARI, CHIEF (*CACIQUE PRINCIPAL*) OF THE LOWER DIVISION (*ANANSAYA*) OF CHUQUITO

Asked what tribute is given to him each year by his subjects, he replied that from the town of Chuquito his subjects cultivate in some years 100 *topos* [a *topo* is of indeterminate size but understood to be the minimum land needed for an Inca couple] of land and in other years 70 topos of potatoes, quinua, and canagua [similar to quinua] . . . in other towns [located on the western shore of Lake Titicaca and subject to Chuquito] of Acora, Ilave and Yunguyo his subjects cultivate 20 *topos* each and in the towns of Juli, Pomata and Zepita another 20 topos each . . . in each topo of land one can plant 3 *fanegas* [*fanega* as a grain measure is about 1.5 bushels] of seed . . . to plant one topo of land 16 Indian males and 8 Indian females are employed in plowing in one day . . . to seed 5 Indian males and 8 Indian females are employed in one day . . . to clean and weed the cultivated plots . . . 10 Indian females are employed for each *topo* of land in one day . . . to these Indian males and females who work the land it is customary to give meat, potatoes, *chuño* [freeze-dried potatoes], maize, quinua, coca, and *chicha* [maize beer] . . . from the town of Chuquito and the other towns subject to it each year 5 pieces of cloth are woven from wool supplied to each town . . . in addition the town of Chuquito provides 40 to 50 Indians each year to go with [pack] animals provided by the *cacique* to bring maize from Moquegua and Sama [Peruvian coastal locations] and Capinota and Larecaja [Bolivian valleys] and coca from Cuzco to his home [in Chuquito] . . . when the 40 Indians finish the trip they work no more on that road and others go . . . the round-trip takes two to three months and the Indians who are sent to these locations are given for their maintenance chuño, dried meat, quinua and coca and they are also given wool to exchange for food from those parts . . . from the town of Chuquito and its subject towns 60 Indians of service are provided each year and 10 are employed in guarding animals and 25 are employed in Moquegua working on maize lands and 15 are employed in guarding lands in Chuquito and 10 are employed in service in his home making cloth and taking care of household duties and beyond the 60 already mentioned are 2 more employed in gathering fodder and firewood . . . as well as another 20 who guard sheep . . . from the town of Juli 10 Indians of service were given to ancestors of the current cacique who guarded animals on the high plain and this group has now multiplied to 50 or 60 Indians including men, women and children and they now not only guard animals but also some have been sent to the Yunguas [steep valley off the eastern Andes] for maize and other necessities . . . another 2 Indians from Juli which were given to the ancestors have now multiplied to 9 who also guard animals . . . the town of Pomata does not provide one Indian because they do not wish to and the town of Yunguyo provides 1 Indian to guard land and the town of Zepita provides 1 to guard land and the towns of Acora and Ilave 3 each and all these Indians who serve are given coca, food and sheep that they raise for themselves.

Asked how many animals these servants guard, he replied 300.

Testimony of the Indians of Chuquito about Service to Their Cacique Principal

Asked what service and tribute they give to the cacique principal of Chuquito, his subjects answered that they provide 30 Indians for guarding land and another 20 for guarding animals and in some years 2 pieces of *cumbi* cloth [finest cloth made from vicuña wool] and in other years 3 pieces and sometimes even more . . . in addition 10 pieces of *auasca* [lesser quality cloth for commoners] are provided . . . in some years 4 pieces and in other years nothing . . . [since] auasca cloth is given voluntarily . . . and from the sheep of the community we give the cacique around 30 every year or a little more or less because in some years the cacique has guests and we give him more meat . . . we cultivate 150 *fanegas* [fanega as land measure is about 1.6 acres] of potatoes and in other years we cultivate the same amount in quinua and the harvesting and preparing are done by all the members of the community, except the Indians who have been given in service.

Asked what don Martin Cari gives to his subjects who serve and guard animals and land, they replied that those who guard animals are given coca, meat and other food plus wool so that they can make clothes for themselves and to those who serve in his house he gives food and wool to make clothes and to those who serve him very well he gives a live animal and to those who go and cultivate his lands he gives meat, *chicha,* potatoes, quinua and other food and to those who are cultivating his land he gives a good quantity because if he does not give it to them they will become angry.

STUDY QUESTIONS

1. What types of work and goods constituted tribute in Chuquito?
2. What practices indicated that the relationship between the subjects and the chief was reciprocal?
3. Compare Aztec methods of acquiring tribute to the methods used by the chiefs of Chuquito (see Chapter 46). What are the differences? What might account for the differences?
4. A tribute system reveals the basic forms of social stratification. What are they in Chuquito? How do they compare to social stratification in Babylonia (Chapter 2), India (Chapter 15), Mediterranean area (Chapter 19) and China (Chapter 31)?

FORCES OF CHANGE

47   CHINA "DISCOVERS" AFRICA

One of the intriguing aspects of the postclassical period involved the new contacts different societies began to acquire with each other, across Afro-Eurasia. Trade and travel provided many ties, as did missionary activity. But accounts of distant places could even precede direct contact, a sign of new horizons but also a preparation for more explicit interaction. This short set of documents, on China's first awareness of Africa, fits this description.

China had many contacts with other regions before the postclassical period, but interactions were more widely encouraged during the time of the Tang dynasty (618–907 C.E.) This is the first time in which information on regions beyond India began to appear in Chinese materials, and some views of Africa were part of this intellectual expansion. No Chinese directly visited Africa at this point; rather, information was gathered by writings by Persians, Arabs and other peoples with wide trading and missionary contacts. A few African slaves began to be sold in China as well.

The first source below was a general book of knowledge written by the scholar Duan Chengshi, who died in 863, writing about a region he called Bobali and which modern scholars have identified as Somalia. China's interest and information obviously centered on the eastern, Indian ocean parts of Africa.

The second source, The Xin Tangshu, written by Ouyang Xiu, appeared in 1060. It describes a region, Melinda or Malindi, in present-day Kenya and also, more briefly, the island of Madagascar.

Sources of this sort do not, by definition, provide direct information about Africa, but they are relevant to African history in terms of the impressions being conveyed by travelers and others, as filtered through the hands of foreign scholars. The sources reveal more about postclassical China itself: what aspects of a foreign region, in this case Africa, seem particularly interesting or noteworthy?

Accounts of Africa did not immediately stimulate a direct Chinese interest in the continent. But in the 15th century, huge expeditions were mounted, into the Indian Ocean, that did take Chinese officials and merchants to the Indian Ocean coast of Africa (as part of larger trips through southeast Asia, to India, and the Persian Gulf). Is

From *China's Discovery of Africa* by J. J. L. Duyvendak. Reprinted by permission of Arthur Probstain Publishers and Booksellers.

there anything in the general scholarly knowledge about Africa that would help explain why, for a brief period, a new kind of contact seemed desirable?

DUAN CHENGSHI AND XIN TANGSHU

1. DUAN CHENGSHI

The country of Bobali is in the southwestern sea. (The people) do not eat any of the five grains but eat only meat. They often stick a needle into the veins of cattle and draw blood which they drink raw, mixed with milk. They wear no clothes except that they cover (the parts) below their loins with sheep-skins. Their women are clean and of proper behaviour. The inhabitants themselves kidnap them, and if they sell them to foreign merchants, they fetch several times their price. The country produces only ivory and ambergris, a substance used for perfume. If Persian merchants wish to go into the country, they collect around them several thousand men and present them with strips of cloth. All, whether old or young draw blood and swear an oath, and then only do they trade their products. From olden times on they were not subject to any foreign country. In fighting they use elephants' tusks and ribs and the horns of wild buffaloes as lances and they wear armor and bows and arrows. They have twenty myriads of foot soldiers. The Arabs make frequent raids upon them.

2. XIN TANGSHU

South-west from Fulin [Egypt], after one traverses the desert for two thousand miles is a country called Malin. Its people are black and their nature is fierce. The land is pestilentious and has no herbs, no trees, and no cereals. They feed the horses on dried fish; the people eat *Humang;* the Humang is the Persian date. They are not ashamed of debauching the wives of their fathers or chiefs, they are (in this respect) the worst of the barbarians. They call this: to seek out the proper master and subject. In the seventh moon they rest completely [i.e. Ramadan]. They (then) do not send out nor receive (any merchandise) in trade and they sit drinking all night long. . . .

Madagascar is a large island in the sea. There are regularly great birds. When they fly they obscure the sun for a short time. There are wild camels, and if the birds meet them, they swallow them up. If one finds a feather of the great bird, by cutting the quill, one can make a water-jar of it.

The products of the country are big elephants' tusks and rhinoceros' horns.

There are many savages. Their bodies are black as lacquer and they have frizzled hair. They are enticed by (offers of) food and then captured and sold as slaves to the Arabic countries, where they fetch a very high price. They are employed as gate-keepers, and it is said that they have no longing for their kinsfolk.

STUDY QUESTIONS

1. Are these sources largely accurate concerning eastern Africa in the postclassical period? How do they compare with the accounts of people who traveled directly in Africa? Do the sources contribute to an understanding of some key characteristics of postclassical Africa?

2. Judging by these accounts, what kinds of contacts did eastern Africa have with other parts of the world during this period?

3. How do the accounts contradict each other? How might these contradictions be explained?

4. How would an educated Chinese reader, in the postclassical period, react to these accounts? Would these versions of Africa have seemed mostly interesting, or mostly strange?

5. Many historians argue that European accounts and stories about other regions like Africa and Asia, during the postclassical period, helped stimulate the European desire for contact. Would these accounts have had a similar impact on China? Why, or why not?

48

MERCHANTS AND TRADE: SOURCES AND COMPARISONS

Documents in this chapter focus on the relationship between commerce and cultural values in two major societies. The postclassical period witnessed an important expansion of trade within many civilizations and across their fluid boundaries. Merchants gained a growing role in West Africa, throughout the Islamic world, in Europe (both East and West), and in East Asia. Chapter 39 dealt with new merchant organizations in Europe, but the expansion of commerce had still wider reach.

Many merchants traded locally, although international merchants made the biggest impression. Chinese commercial centers grew rapidly, supporting a more urban environment. The search for wealth had never been so extensive, the willingness to take risks had never been so great, and the desire to promote commercial interests in government circles had never been so strong. At the same time, many societies had reservations about merchants. Aristocrats worried about their social claims; rulers might envy their wealth; priests and philosophers questioned their motives. Between religion and materialism, the clash of cultures was particularly intense because of the complex new forces at work in these centuries. A genuine ambivalence about merchants was common throughout the postclassical world—and it could affect merchants themselves and how they were treated, and it could also shift.

Comparison and assessment of change over time are both essential analytical approaches to the issue of the merchant's role. Christian tradition was uneasy with merchants' motives, fearing that they diverted people from religion. As trade increased, Christian concern relaxed somewhat. But efforts to find ways to accommodate the very different goals of capitalist trade and the holy life continued. Islam was initially more favorable to merchants, whose activities seemed compatible with religious obligations so long as they obeyed basic rules of fairness and gave to charity. It was no accident that Islam had up to that time sponsored the most intense merchant activity known in world history. The Middle East had long been a center of trade, even in the classical period. Muhammad, originally a merchant, praised the life of commerce, so long as it did not violate the primacy of religious goals, and so long as it was accompanied by active chants. But experience introduced greater caution, and toward the end of the postclassical period, as Muslim trade continued, though with slightly less dynamism, ambivalence

Selection I from *An Arab Philosophy of History: Selections from the Prolegomena of Ibn Khaldun*, edited and translated by Charles Issawi (London: John Murray, 1950), pp. 68–70, 78, 80–81. Reprinted by permission of the publisher. Selection II from Reginald of Durham, "Life of St. Godric," in *Social Life in Britain from the Conquest to the Reformation*, edited by G. G. Coulton (Cambridge: Cambridge University Press, 1918), pp. 415–420.

became more obvious. What value did Muslim thinkers see in trade? What were the danger signals? How do Christian and Muslim views compare at this point?

Given the attitudes and policies suggested for the two societies—Western Europe and the Middle East—which society in your judgment was becoming most favorable for merchant activity and why? Do cultural values really shape trade activities, or is a universal desire for profit more significant?

The values tensions surrounding merchant activity were very real in the postclassical period in both civilizations. They translated into individual ambiguities. Many European merchants—even some less holy than Godric—repented of their goals later in life and gave money away or entered a monastery.

The tensions also reflected a fascinating interaction between economic opportunities and cultural norms. None of the civilizations yielded entirely to one extreme or the other—which is why comparison must be subtle; a search for stark contrasts would be overly simple. The fact that some civilizations changed their balance over time adds another complexity. Nevertheless, certain differences were real, and they mattered in world history. China, to take the most obvious example, could have played a far larger trade role than it did, but it deliberately held back because of its own internal success—it did not need the outside world—and because of its cultural hostility to trade. Europe's growing commercial role required an adjustment of religious concerns, which did prove possible but caused wide anxiety about moral directions.

The description of the 12th-century British merchant Godric was written by a biographer attracted to his saintly life (most merchants did not, it should be emphasized, become saints). It suggests both actual activities and cultural values. The Muslim description of merchants' vices and merits comes from the great historian and philosopher Ibn Khaldun, a North African who wrote in the 14th century.

IBN KHALDUN, REGINALD OF DURHAM ON SAINT GODRIC

I. A MUSLIM VIEW: IBN KHALDUN

Characteristics of Traders

Commerce, as we have said before, is the increasing of capital by buying goods and attempting to sell them at a price higher than their cost. This is done either by waiting for a rise in the market price; or by transporting the goods to another place where they are more keenly demanded and therefore fetch a higher price; or, lastly, by selling them on a long-term credit basis. Commercial profit is small, relatively to the capital invested, but if the capital is large, even a low rate of profit will produce a large total gain.

In order to achieve this increase in capital, it is necessary to have enough initial capital to pay in cash the sellers from whom one buys goods; it is also necessary to sell for cash, as honesty is not widespread among people. This dishonesty leads on the one hand to fraud and the adulteration of goods, and on the other to delays in payment which diminish profits because capital remains idle during the interval.

It also induces buyers to repudiate their debts, a practice which is very injurious to the merchant's capital unless he can produce documentary evidence or the testimony of eyewitness. Nor are magistrates of much help in such cases, because they necessarily judge on evident proofs.

As a result of all this, the trader can only secure his meagre profits by dint of much effort and toil, or indeed he may well lose not only profits but capital as well. Hence, if he is known to be bold in entering law suits, careful in keeping accounts, stubborn in defending his point of view, firm in his attitude towards magistrates, he stands a good chance of getting his due. Should he not have these qualities, his only chance is to secure the support of a highly placed protector who will awe his debtors into paying him and the magistrates into meting justice out to him. Thus he gets justice spontaneously in the first case, and by compulsion in the second. Should a person, however, be lacking in boldness and the spirit of enterprise and at the same time have no protector to back him up, he had better avoid trade altogether, as he risks losing his capital and becoming the prey of other merchants. The fact of the matter is that most people, especially the mob and the trading classes, covet the goods of others; and but for the restraint imposed by the magistrates all goods would have been taken away from their owners. . . . The manners of trademen are inferior to those of rulers and far removed from manliness and uprightness. We have already stated that traders must buy and sell and seek profits. This necessitates flattery, and evasiveness, litigation and disputation, all of which are characteristic of this profession. And these qualities lead to a decrease and weakening in virtue and manliness. For acts inevitably affect the soul; thus good acts produce good and virtuous effects in the soul while evil or mean acts produce the opposite. Hence the effects of evil acts will strike root and strengthen themselves, if they should come early in life and repeat themselves; while if they come later they will efface the virtues by imprinting their evil effects on the soul; as is the case with all habits resulting from actions.

These effects will differ according to the conditions of the traders. For those of them who are of mean condition and in direct contact with the cheating and extortion of sellers will be more affected by these evils and further removed from manliness. . . . The other kind of traders are those who are protected by prestige and do not have to undertake directly such operations. Such persons are very rare indeed and consist of those who have acquired wealth suddenly, by inheritance or by other, unusual means. This wealth enables them to get in touch with the rulers and thus to gain prestige and protection so that they are released from practising these things [buying and selling] themselves; instead, they entrust such business to their agents. Moreover the rulers, who are not indifferent to the wealth and liberality of such traders, protect them in their right and thus free them from certain unpleasant actions and their resulting evil effects. Hence they will be more manly and honourable than the other kind of trader; yet certain effects will still make themselves felt behind the veil, inasmuch as they still have to supervise their agents and employees in their doings—but this only takes place to a limited extent and its effects are hardly visible. . . .

Consider, as an example, the lands of the East, such as Egypt, Syria, Persia, India, or China; or the lands lying North of the Mediterranean. Because social life is flourishing there, notice how wealth has increased, the state has grown stronger, towns have multiplied, trade has prospered, conditions have improved. . . .

As for Trade, although it be a natural means of livelihood, yet most of the methods it employs are tricks aimed at making a profit by securing the difference between the buying and selling prices, and by appropriating the surplus. This is why Canon Law allows the use of such methods, which, although they come under the heading of gambling, yet do not constitute the taking without return of other people's goods. . . .

Should their standard of living, however, rise, so that they begin to enjoy more than the bare necessities, the effect will be to breed in them a desire for repose and tranquillity. They will therefore co-operate to secure superfluities; their food and clothing will increase in quantity and refinement; they will enlarge their houses and plan their towns for defence. A further improvement in their conditions will lead to habits of luxury, resulting in extreme refinement in cooking and the preparation of food; in choosing rich clothing of the finest silk; in raising lofty mansions and castles and furnishing them luxuriously, and so on. At this stage the crafts develop and reach their height. Lofty castles and mansions are built and decorated sumptuously, water is drawn to them and a great diversity takes place in the way of dress, furniture, vessels, and household equipment.

Such are the townsmen, who earn their living in industry or trade. Their gains are greater than those working in agriculture or animal husbandry and their standard of living higher, being in line with their wealth. We have shown, then, that both the nomadic and the urban stages are natural and necessary.

II. A CHRISTIAN VIEW: REGINALD OF DURHAM ON SAINT GODRIC

This holy man's father was named Ailward, and his mother Edwenna; both of slender rank and wealth, but abundant in righteousness and virtue. They were born in Norfolk, and had long lived in the township called Walpole. . . . When the boy had passed his childish years quietly at home; then, as he began to grow to manhood, he began to follow more prudent ways of life, and to learn carefully and persistently the teachings of worldly forethought. Wherefore he chose not to follow the life of a husbandman, but rather to study, learn and exercise the rudiment of more subtle conceptions. For this reason, aspiring to the merchant's trade, he began to follow the chapman's [peddler's] way of life, first learning how to gain in small bargains and things of insignificant price; and thence, while yet a youth, his mind advanced little by little to buy and sell and gain from things of greater expense. For, in his beginnings, he was wont to wander with small wares around the villages and farmsteads of his own neighborhood; but, in process of time, he gradually associated himself by compact with city merchants. Hence, within a brief space of time, the youth who had trudged for many weary hours from village to village, from farm to farm, did so profit by his increase of age and wisdom as to travel with associates of his own age through towns and boroughs, fortresses and cities, to fairs and to all the various booths of the market-place, in pursuit of his public chaffer. He went along the high-way, neither puffed up by the good testimony of his conscience nor downcasting the nobler part of his soul by the reproach of poverty. . . .

Yet in all things he walked with simplicity; and, in so far as he yet knew how, it was ever his pleasure to follow in the footsteps of the truth. For, having learned the Lord's Prayer and the Creed from his very cradle, he oftentimes turned them over in his mind, even as he went alone on his longer journeys; and, in so far as the truth was revealed to his mind, he clung thereunto most devoutly in all his thoughts concerning God. At first, he lived as a chapman for four years in Lincolnshire, going on foot and carrying the smallest wares; then he travelled abroad, first to St. Andrews in Scotland and then for the first time to Rome. On his return, having formed a familiar friendship with certain other young men were eager for merchandise, he began to launch upon bolder courses, and to coast frequently by sea to the foreign lands that lay around him. Thus, sailing often to and fro between Scotland and Britain, he traded in many divers wares and, amid these occupations, learned much worldly wisdom. . . . He fell into many perils of the sea, yet by God's mercy he was never wrecked; for He who had upheld St. Peter as he walked upon the waves, by that same strong right arm kept this His chosen vessel from all misfortune amid these perils. Thus, having learned by frequent experience his wretchedness amid such dangers, he began to worship certain of the Saints with more ardent zeal, venerating and calling upon their shrines, and giving himself up by wholehearted service to those holy names. In such invocations his prayers were oftentimes answered by prompt consolation; some of which prayers he learned from his fellows with whom he shared these frequent perils; others he collected from faithful hearsay; others again from the custom of the place, for he saw and visited such holy places with frequent assiduity. Thus aspiring ever higher and higher, and yearning upward with his whole heart, at length his great labours and cares bore much fruit of worldly gain. For he laboured not only as a merchant but also as a shipman . . . to Denmark and Flanders and Scotland; in all which lands he found certain rare, and therefore more precious, wares, which he carried to other parts wherein he knew them to be least familiar, and coveted by the inhabitants beyond the price of gold itself; wherefore he exchanged these wares for others coveted by men of other lands; and thus he chaffered most freely and assiduously. Hence he made great profit in all his bargains, and gathered much wealth in the sweat of his brow; for he sold dear in one place the wares which he had bought elsewhere at a small price.

Then he purchased the half of a merchant-ship with certain of his partners in the trade; and again by his prudence he bought the fourth part of another ship. At length, by his skill in navigation, wherein he excelled all his fellows, he earned promotion to the post of steersman. . . .

For he was vigorous and strenuous in mind, whole of limb and strong in body. He was of middle stature, broad-shouldered and deep-chested, with a long face, grey eyes most clear and piercing, bushy brows, a broad forehead, long and open nostrils, a nose of comely curve, and a pointed chin. His beard was thick, and longer than the ordinary, his mouth well-shaped, with lips of moderate thickness; in youth his hair was black, in age as white as snow; his neck was short and thick, knotted with veins and sinews; his legs were somewhat slender, his instep high, his knees hardened and horny with frequent kneeling; his whole skin rough beyond the ordinary, until all this roughness was softened by old age. . . . In labour he was strenuous, assiduous above all men: and, when by chance his bodily strength proved insufficient, he compassed his ends with great ease by the skill which his daily labours had given, and by a prudence born of long experience. . . . He knew, from the aspect of sea and stars, how to foretell fair or foul weather. In his various voyages he visited many saints' shrines, to whose protection he was wont most devoutly to commend himself; more especially the church of St. Andrew in Scotland, where he most frequently made and paid his vows. On the way thither, he oftentimes touched at the island of Lindisfarne, wherein St. Cuthbert had been bishop, and at the isle of Farne, where that Saint had lived as an anchoret, and where St. Godric (as he himself would tell afterwards) would meditate on the Saint's life with abundant tears. Thence he began to yearn for solitude, and to hold his merchandise in less esteem than heretofore. . . .

And now he had lived sixteen years as a merchant, and began to think of spending on charity, to God's honour and service, the goods which he had so laboriously acquired. He therefore took the cross as a pilgrim to Jerusalem, and, having visited the Holy Sepulchre, came back to England by way of St. James [of Compostella]. Not long afterwards he became steward to a certain rich man of his own country, with the care of his whole house and household. But certain of the younger household were men of iniquity, who stole their neighbours' cattle and thus held luxurious feasts, whereat Godric, in his ignorance, was sometimes present. Afterwards, discovering the truth, he rebuked and admonished them to cease; but they made no account of his warnings; wherefore he concealed not their iniquity, but disclosed it to the lord of the household, who, however, slighted his advice. Wherefore he begged to be dismissed and went on a pilgrimage, first to St. Gilles and thence to Rome the abode of the Apostles, that thus he might knowingly pay the penalty for those misdeeds wherein he had ignorantly partaken. I have often seen him, even in his old age, weeping for this unknowing transgression. . . .

On his return from Rome, he abode awhile in his father's house; until, inflamed again with holy zeal, he purposed to revisit the abode of the Apostles and made his desire known unto his parents. Not only did they approve his purpose, but his mother besought his leave to bear him company on this pilgrimage; which he gladly granted, and willingly paid her every filial service that was her due. They came therefore to London; and they had scarcely departed from thence when his mother took off her shoes, going thus barefooted to Rome and back to London. Godric, humbly serving his parent, was wont to bear her on his shoulders. . . .

Godric, when he had restored his mother safe to his father's arms, abode but a brief while at home; for he was now already firmly purposed to give himself entirely to God's service. Wherefore, that he might follow Christ the more freely, he sold all his possessions and distributed them among the poor. Then, telling his parents of this purpose and receiving their blessing, he went forth to no certain abode, but whithersoever the Lord should deign to lead him; for above all things he coveted the life of a hermit.

STUDY QUESTIONS

1. What kinds of uneasiness did Muslim observers have about trade?
2. How did Islam offer a distinctive combination of trade and cultural goals—a combination relatively favorable to trade without slighting religion? In what ways

did Islam and Christianity, such similar religions in many respects, differ over the validity of trade? Would a story like Godric's have been probable in Islam?

3. What exceptions do the sources suggest, even as they emphasize high ideals? What kinds of activities in Europe clearly represented crasser motives than those of a holy merchant like Godric? Why, in fact, did Godric not enter a holy calling initially—what kinds of motives drew him to trade?

4. How did Christian attitudes on trade compare with actual merchant goals and values as indicated by merchant guilds (see Chapter 39)?

5. Do the sources demonstrate that Europe was becoming wealthier than the Islamic world by the late postclassical period?

6. In light of the postclassical sources and comparisons, how would you rate the argument that no matter what their professed values, most people and societies are motivated by a desire for profit and will expand commercially whenever they can? Is a desire for economic gain an inherent part of human nature?

7. Which came first in world history: concern about trade or economic limitations? Did Christianity cause Western Europe's initial commercial lag in the postclassical period, or did economic decline encourage Christian concerns? How did Islam affect actual Middle Eastern economic patterns in the postclassical period?

49 GLOBAL CONTACTS: TRAVELERS TO HOLY PLACES

BUDDHIST, CHRISTIAN, AND MUSLIM PILGRIMS

Buddhism, Christianity, and Islam spread widely in Afro-Eurasia during the postclassical period. As the number of converts increased, the tradition of pilgrimage—travel to holy places—became increasingly important. For Buddhists, the most sacred places were in northern India, the region where the Buddha was born, where he achieved enlightenment, and where he subsequently taught. Christian pilgrims sought to travel to Jerusalem, where Jesus was crucified and buried. Muslims were under the special injunction of the fifth pillar of Islam to make a pilgrimage (*hajj*) to Mecca, the Arabian city where Muhammad received his earliest revelations from God and where the Ka'bah is located.

Pilgrim narratives, the records of journeys to holy places left by religious travelers or their contemporaries, help historians to appreciate the power of religious ideals in the past. By examining pilgrim writing from different religions historians can also begin to obtain an understanding of religious beliefs and practices in comparative perspective. But pilgrim narratives are valuable for other reasons too. Despite having been written for essentially proselytizing purposes, they often contain valuable information for the student of world history about travel conditions, trade routes, and contacts between people from different cultures.

The selections that follow come from the experiences of four pilgrims, a Buddhist, two Muslims, and one Christian. Two Muslim pilgrims are included because of the special importance of pilgrimage in Islam. How do these documents help us to understand the experience of religious travelers in the postclassical world?

PILGRIMS' EXPERIENCES

I. XUANZANG IN THE TAKLAMAKAN DESERT, CA. 630

[Xuanzang is the best known of the several hundred Buddhist monks from China who traveled to India from the third through the 8th centuries. Journey to the West, *one of*

Selection I from Sramana Huili and Shi Yancong, *A Biography of the Tripitaka Master of the Great Ci'en Monastery of the Great Tang Dynasty.* Translated by Li Rongxi (Berkeley, Calif.: Numata Center for Buddhist Translation and Research, 1995), pp. 23–28. Selection II from Ibn Jubayr, *The Travels of Ibn Jubayr.* Translated by R. J. C. Broadhurst (London: Jonathan Cape, 1952), pp. 77–78, 85, 116–117. Selection III from *Corpus of Early African Sources for West African History,* edited by N. Levtzion and J. F. P. Hopkins and Translated by J. F. P. Hopkins (Cambridge: Cambridge University Press, 1981), pp. 269–271. Selection IV from *The Wanderings of Felix Fabri,* Vol. I (Part I), *The Library of the Palestine Pilgrims' Text Society,* Vol. VII (London: Committee of the Palestine Exploration Fund, 1897), pp. 37–41.

the great classics of Chinese fiction, is loosely based on his experiences in Central Asia and India. The following account of Xuanzang's difficulties in the Taklamakan Desert, located in today's western China, was written by one of his colleagues, a monk named Huili.]

After having packed his outfit, the Master [Xuanzang] started on the journey with the young Hu man [non-Chinese]. At about the third watch, they reached the river and saw the Yumen Pass at a distance. They went up the stream for about ten *li* from the pass and came to a place where the banks of the river were over ten feet apart, beside which there was a wood of tamarisks. The Hu man cut some branches and built a bridge, on which he spread grass and paved it with sand. Then they drove their horses across.

The Master was glad to have crossed the river, and he unsaddled his horse to take rest at a place more than fifty paces from the Hu man. They spread their quilts on the ground to sleep. After a little while the Hu man got up, unsheathed his knife, and slowly advanced toward the Master, but he retreated at a distance of about ten paces. Not knowing what he had in his mind and suspecting that he might have an evil intent, the Master got up and recited scriptures and repeated the name of Avalokiteśvara Bodhisattva [the Bodhisattva of mercy], whereupon the Hu man lay down and slept.

When it was nearly daybreak, the Master wakened the man to fetch some water for a wash. At the moment when they were about to continue the journey after having taken breakfast, the Hu man said, "Your disciple considers that the journey ahead is long and dangerous with neither water nor grass on the way. As water can be obtained only at the five towers [Chinese watch towers], we have to reach them at night to steal water and pass along. But once discovered we shall be dead men. So it is safer to turn back."

But the Master was determined not to go back, and so the Hu man proceeded with reluctance. He took out his sword and drew his bow, ordering the Master to go before him, but the Master refused to precede him. When they had gone a few *li*, the man stopped and said, "Your disciple cannot go any more. I have a big family to support, and moreover I dare not trespass against the law." The Master knew his mind and let him go back. The Hu man said, "You will certainly not be able to reach your destination. What shall I do if you are arrested and I am involved in the matter?" The Master replied, "Even if I am cut to pieces, I will never implicate you in my affair." He then took a solemn oath and the man was satisfied. The Master presented him with a horse out of gratitude for his service, and they parted.

After that the Master travelled alone in the desert, proceeding slowly along the trail marked by skeletons and horse dung. Shortly afterward he suddenly saw an army of several hundred men scattered all over the desert, moving forward or halting for a while. They were dressed in furs or coarse cloth, and their camels and horses, as well as banners, flags, and spears, kept on changing their shapes ever moment. They were quite clear at a distance but gradually disappeared as they approached. At first sight, the Master thought them to be bandits, but as they faded away then they came nearer, he realized that they were bogies and demons. He heard a voice in the air, saying, "Have no fear! Have no fear!" And then he felt a little better in his mind.

After travelling a distance of more than eighty *li* he came in sight of the first watchtower. Fearing that he might be seen by the watchmen, he hid himself in a sandy ditch and remained there until nightfall. Then he came to the west of the tower, where he saw water. He went down to have a drink and washed his hands, and when he was about to refill his water bag, an arrow whizzed through the air and nearly hit his knee. A moment later, another arrow was shot. Realizing that he had been seen, he said aloud, "I am a monk from the capital. Don't shoot at me!"

He led his horse to the tower, where the watchmen opened the door and came out to see him. Seeing that he was really a monk, they brought him in to see the captain, Wang Xiang, who ordered a lamp to be lit so he could see the Master. He said, "He is not a monk from our region of Hexi. It seems that he really comes from the capital." Then he inquired of the Master what the purpose of his travel was. The Master said in reply, "Did not the captain hear the people of Liangzhou say that a monk named Xuanzang intended to go to the Brahmanic countries to seek the Dharma?" The captain answered, "I head that the teacher Xuanzang has returned to the East. How is it that you have come here?" The Master took from his horse the petition he had written to the Emperor, in which his name was written, and showed it to the captain. The captain believed him but still said, "The road to the West is long and perilous, and you could never reach your destination. I shall not arrest you. But as I am a native of Dunhuang, I wish to send you back to that place. There is a reverend teacher named Zhangjiao, who esteems wise and virtuous people. I am sure he will be delighted to meet you. Please go to his place."

The Master said in reply, "My native place is Luoyang and I have admired the Dharma since my youth. I have studied under all the learned teachers of the two capitals and the talented monks in the regions of Wu and Shu, and have mastered all their knowledge. In explaining and discussing Buddhist teachings, I had the honor to be ranked among contemporary teachers. If I were interested in gaining personal benefit and reputation, those places would not be inferior to your Dunhuang. But it was because I regretted that the Buddhist scriptures were incomplete and that the doctrines were ambiguous that I made a vow to go to the West to seek the bequeathed Dharma at the risk of my life, without fearing the hardships and dangers of the journey. Now you do not encourage me but advise me to go back. Can that be a cause for us to free ourselves from worldly sufferings and realize nirvana? If you have to detain me, I am prepared to bear whatever punishment you may mete out to me. But I shall never go back a single step toward the East against my original intention."

On hearing this, the captain Wang Xiang said with sympathy, "I am lucky to have this chance to meet you. How can I do otherwise than comply with your wishes? You must be tired now and should take rest until tomorrow. I shall send you off and show you the way personally." A bamboo mat was then spread to accommodate the Master for the night. At dawn when the Master had taken his meal, Wang Xiang ordered his men to fill his water bag, provided him with wheat cakes, and escorted him for a distance of more than ten *li*. He said to the Master, "By this route you may go straight to the fourth watchtower. The man in charge there, by the name of Wang Bolong, is a man with a kind heart and a relative of mine. When you reach there you may say that I sent you." He took leave of the Master after paying homage to him with tears in his eyes.

After making his departure, the Master came to the fourth watchtower by nightfall. Fearing that he might be detained there, he intended to get some water and pass along silently. But before he could get down to fetch water, an arrow flew near him. So he made an announcement as before and went hurriedly to the tower, from which some men came down and took him in. In reply to the inquiries of the officer in charge of the tower, the Master said, "I am on my way to India, and Captain Wang Xiang of the first watchtower has sent me to come by this way." Being pleased to hear this, the officer lodged the Master for the night. He presented to the Master a large water bag with some wheat as fodder for his horse, saying, "You need not go to the fifth watchtower. The man there is an imprudent fellow and he might give you trouble. About a hundred *li* from here, there is Wild Horse Spring, where you can replenish your water bag."

Beyond this place was the Moheyan [Gobi] Desert, which stretched more than eight hundred *li*. This was what the ancients called the desert river, where there was no bird flying above, nor any beast roaming below; neither was there any water or grass. Now the Master had only his lonely shadow travelling with him, and all he could do was repeat the name of Avalokiteśvara Bodhisattva and recite the *Prajñāpāramitāhṛdaya Sūtra*. Formerly, when the Master was in the region of Shu, he once saw a sick man suffering from a foul skin ulcer and dressed in rags. With a feeling of pity, he took the man to his monastery and gave him money to purchase clothes and food. Being ashamed of himself, the sick man taught the Master this sutra, which he often recited. In the desert he met various evil spirits with strange appearances that surrounded him and refused to be dispelled completely, although he repeated the name of Avalokiteśvara Bodhisattva. But as soon as he uttered this sutra, all of them disappeared immediately. It was by depending upon this sutra that he was saved from many a peril.

After having travelled for more than a hundred *li*, he lost his way and could not find Wild Horse Spring. When he took down his water bag to have a drink, it was so heavy that it slipped from his hands and the water that was to sustain him during his journey of a thousand *li* was spilled all at once. He lost his way in the winding path and did not know which direction to proceed. So he wished to return eastward to the fourth watchtower. When he had gone about ten *li*, he said to himself, "I vowed not to turn back even one step to the East before I reached India. Why am I going back now? I would rather die on my way to the West than return to the East and live." Then he reined back his horse and proceeded toward the northwest, whilst repeating the name of Avalokiteśvara Bodhisattva.

He looked around and saw nothing but the vast desert, where there was not a man or even a bird to be seen. In the night the evil spirits and demons sparkled as brightly as stars in the sky. During the daytime surprising gales blew the sand up high, and it fell down like a shower. Although he encountered such circumstances, he had no fear in his mind. The trouble was the lack of water; he was so thirsty that he could proceed no more. For four nights and five days he had not a drop of water to moisten his throat, and his mouth and stomach became dried up. Being at the brink of death, he could no longer move forward. He lay down on the sand and repeated the name of Avalokiteśvara Bodhisattva, and did not give up the repetition even in such a desperate situation. He prayed to the Bodhisattva, saying, "I am undertaking this journey not for the purpose of gaining wealth nor for winning reputation. It was simply to acquire the supreme Right Dharma that I have come here. I sincerely pray that the Bodhisattva will have mercy upon all living beings and save those who are in distress. I am now in distress indeed! Cannot you hear my prayers?"

When he prayed in this manner, his mind was concentrated without distraction. At midnight on the fifth day a cool breeze suddenly came and made him feel as chilly as if he were taking a bath in cold water. He was able to open his eyes, and his horse also found its feet. Being refreshed by the cool air, he fell asleep for a while and dreamed that he saw a giant deity several tens of feet tall, holding a spear and a flag in his hands. The deity said to him, "Why are you sleeping here instead of forging ahead?"

The Master was startled and awakened from his sleep, and then he proceeded on his journey. Having gone for about ten *li*, his horse suddenly changed its course and could not turn back, though he pulled hard at the reins. A few *li* further on, he caught sight of a stretch of pasture several *mou* wide, and dismounted to graze his horse. When he had gone ten paces beyond the pasture and was about to turn back, he came to a pond of clean and sweet water. He went down to drink, and thus his life was preserved and both he and his horse were invigorated. One conjectures that this pasture and the water pond had not been there before but were produced out of compassion by the Bodhisattva. His sincerity of mind communicated with the divinities. This was one of many such instances. He rested for one day at the pasture and the pond, and after refilling his water bag and gathering some grass he continued his journey on the following day. Travelling for two more days, he came out of the desert and reached the country of Yiwu [Hami]. The hardships he experienced were numerous and cannot be related in full detail. . . .

II. IBN JUBAYR IN MECCA, 1183–1184

[Ibn Jubayr [b.1145] was serving as the secretary of the Muslim governor of Granada when he decided to go on pilgrimage to Mecca. His trip took him through much of the Mediterranean region and lasted more than two years.]

We entered Meccā—God protect it—at the first hour of Rabi', being the 4th of August, by the 'Umrah Gate. As we marched that night, the full moon had thrown its rays upon the earth, the night had lifted its veil, voices struck the ears with the *Talbiyat*[1] ['Here am I, O God, here am I'], from all sides, and tongues were loud in invocation, humbly beseeching God to grant them their requests, sometimes redoubling their *Talbiyat*, and sometimes imploring with prayers. Oh night most happy, the bride of all the nights of life, the virgin of the maidens of time.

And so, at the time and on the day we have mentioned, we came to God's venerable Haram, the place of sojourn of Abraham the Friend (of God), and found the Ka'bah, the Sacred House, the unveiled bride conducted (like a bride to her groom) to the supreme felicity of heaven, encompassed by the deputations (pilgrims) of the All-Merciful. We performed the *tawaf*[2] of the new arrival, and then prayed at the revered Maqam.[3] We clung to the covering of the Ka'bah near the Multazam, which is between the Black Stone and the door, and is a place where prayers are answered. We entered the dome of Zamzam[4] and drank of its waters which is 'to the purpose for which it is drunk,' as said the Prophet—may God bless

---

[1] *Talbiyat*. The cry which pilgrims utter as they approach Mecca.
[2] *Tawaf*. The rite of walking around the Ka'bah seven times.
[3] *Maqam*. A sacred building associated with Abraham, the Hebrew patriarch who Muslims believe built the Ka'bah.
[4] *Zamzam*. The sacred well, which Muslims believe was dug by the Angel Gabriel; its water is used to wash the Ka'bah.

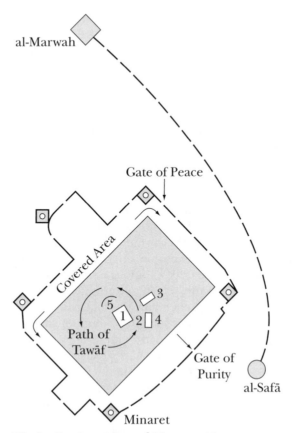

al-Marwah

Gate of Peace

Covered Area

Path of
Tawāf

5

1

2 4

3

Gate of
Purity

al-Safā

Minaret

Pilgrim Routes at Sacred Mosque, Mecca.
(1) Ka'bah. (2) Corner of the Black Stone.
(3) Maqām. (4) Well of Zamzam. (5) Al-Hijr.
From Mircea Eliade, ed. *The Encyclopedia of
Religion* (New York: Macmillan, 1987), 11:342.

and preserve him—and then performed the *sa'i*[5] between al-Safa and al-Marwah. After this we shaved and entered a state of *halal*.[6] Praise be to God for generously including us in the pilgrimage to Him and for making us to be of those on whose behalf the prayers of Abraham reach. Sufficient He is for us and the best Manager. We took lodging in Mecca at a house called al-Halal near to the Haram and the Bab al-Suddah, one of its gates, in a room having many domestic conveniences and overlooking the Haram and the sacred Ka'bah. . . .

The blessed Black Stone is enchased in the corner facing east. The depth to which it penetrates it is not known, but it is said to extend two cubits into the wall. Its breadth is two-thirds of a span, its length one span and a finger joint. It has four pieces, joined together, and it is said that it was the Qarmata [Carmathians]—may

---

[5] *Sa'i.* The ceremony of running seven times between the hills of al-Safa and al-Marwah in commemoration of Hagar, who in doing so attracted the attention of the Angel Gabriel and saved her son Ishmael from dying of thirst.
[6] *Halal.* That which is lawful.

God curse them—who broke it. Its edges have been braced with a sheet of silver whose white shines brightly against the black sheen and polished brilliance of the Stone, presenting the observer a striking spectacle which will hold his looks. The Stone, when kissed, has a softness and moistness which so enchants the mouth that he who puts his lips to it would wish them never to be removed. This is one of the special favors of Divine Providence, and it is enough that the Prophet—may God bless and preserve him—declare to be a covenant of God on earth. May God profit us by the kissing and touching of it. By His favor may all who yearn fervently for it be brought to it. In the sound piece of the stone, to the right of him who presents himself to kiss it, is a small white spot that shines and appears like a mole on the blessed surface. Concerning this white mole, there is a tradition that he who looks upon it clears his vision, and when kissing it one should direct one's lips as closely as one can to the place of the mole. . . .

The *Kiswah* [lit. 'robe,' covering] of the sacred Ka'bah is of green silk as we have said. There are thirty-four pieces: nine on the side between the Yemen and Syrian corners, nine also on the opposite side between the Black corner and the 'Iraq corner, and eight on both the side between the 'Iraq and Syrian corners and on that between the Yemen and the Black. Together they come to appear as one single cover comprehending the four sides. The lower part of the Ka'bah is surrounded by the projecting border built of stucco, more than a span in depth and two spans or a little more in width, inside which is wood, not discernible. Into this are driven iron pegs which have at their ends iron rings that are visible. Through these is inserted a rope of hemp, thick and strongly made, which encircles the four sides, and which is sewn with strong, twisted, cotton, thread to a girdle, like that of the *sirwal* [loose cotton trousers], fixed to the hems of the covers. At the juncture of the covers at the four corners, they are sewn together for more than a man's stature, and above that they are brought together by iron hooks engaged in each other. At the top, round the sides of the terrace, runs another projecting border to which the upper parts of the covers are attached with iron rings, after the fashion described. Thus the blessed *Kiswah* is sewn top and bottom, and firmly buttoned, being never removed save at its renewal year by year. Glory to God who perpetuates its honour until the Day of Resurrection. There is no God but He. . . .

This blessed town and its peoples have from ancient times profited from the prayers of the friend of God, Abraham. . . .

The proof of this in Mecca is manifest, and will continue to the Day of Resurrection, for the hearts of men yearn towards it from far countries and distant regions. The road to it is a place of encounter for those, coming and going, to whom the blessed claims (of Islam) have reached. From all parts produce is brought to it, and it is the most prosperous of countries in its fruits, useful requisites, commodities, and commerce. And although there is no commerce save in the pilgrim period, nevertheless, since people gather in it from east and west, there will be sold in one day, apart from those that follow, precious objects such as pearls, sapphires, and other stones, various kinds of perfume such as musk, camphor, amber and aloes, Indian drugs and other articles brought from India and Ethiopia, the products of the industries of 'Iraq and the Yemen, as well as the merchandise of Khurasan, the goods of Maghrib, and other wares such as it is impossible to enumerate or correctly assess. Even if they were spread over all lands, brisk markets could be set up with them and all would be filled with the useful effects of commerce. All this is within the eight days that follow the pilgrimage, and exclusive of what might suddenly arrive throughout the year from the Yemen and other countries. Not on the face of the world are there any goods or products but that some of them are in Mecca at this meeting of the pilgrims. This blessing is clear to all, and one of the miracles that God has worked in particular for this city. . . .

III. MANSA MŪSĀ: A WEST AFRICAN MONARCH ON PILGRIMAGE, 1324

[Mansa Mūsā (reigned 1312–1337) ruled the West African kingdom (or empire) of Mali at its peak of prosperity and influence. The following account of Mansa Mūsā's famous pilgrimage to Mecca comes from the writings of al-Umari, a 14th-century Arab scholar who lived in Cairo. Much of al-Umari's information came from interviews of Egyptian officials who had met Mansa Mūsā.]

From the beginning of my coming to stay in Egypt I heard talk of the arrival of this sultan Mūsā on his Pilgrimage and found the Cairenes eager to recount what they had seen of the Africans' prodigal spending. I asked the emir Abū 'l-'Abbās Ahmad b. al-Hāk the *mihmandar* [official guide] and he told me of the opulence, manly virtues, and piety of this sultan. "When I went out to meet him (he said), that is, on behalf of the mighty sultan al-Malik al-Nāsir, he did me extreme honour and treated me with the greatest courtesy. He addressed me, however, only through an interpreter despite his perfect ability to speak in the Arabic tongue. Then he forwarded to the royal treasury many loads of unworked native gold and other valuables. I tried to persuade him to go up to the Citadel to meet the sultan, but he refused persistently, saying: 'I came for the Pilgrimage and nothing else. I do not wish to mix anything else with my Pilgrimage.' He had begun to use this argument but I realized that the audience was repugnant to him because he would be obliged to kiss the ground and the sultan's hand. I continued to cajole him and he continued to make excuses but the sultan's protocol demanded that I should bring him into the royal presence, so I kept on at him till he agreed.

"When we came in the sultan's presence, we said to him: 'Kiss the ground!' but he refused outright saying: 'How may this be?' Then an intelligent man who was with him whispered to him something we could not understand and he said: 'I make obeisance to God who created me!' then he prostrated himself and went forward to the sultan. The sultan half rose to greet him and sat him by his side. They conversed together for a long time, then sultan Mūsā went out. The sultan sent to him several complete suits of honour for himself, his courtiers, and all those who had come with him, and saddled and bridled horses for himself and his chief courtiers. His robe of honor consisted of an Alexandrian open-fronted cloak embellished with *tard wahsh* cloth containing much gold thread and miniver fur, bordered with beaver fur and embroidered with metallic thread, along with golden fastenings, a silken skull-cap with caliphal emblems, a gold-inlaid belt, a damascened sword, a kerchief [embroidered] with pure gold, standards, and two horses saddled and bridled and equipped with mule [-type] saddles. He also furnished him with accommodation and abundant supplies during his stay.

"When the time to leave for the Pilgrimage came round the sultan sent to him a large sum of money with ordinary and thoroughbred camels complete with saddles and equipment to serve as mounts for him, and purchased abundant supplies for his entourage and others who had come with him. He arranged for deposits of fodder to be placed along the road and ordered caravan commanders to treat him with honour and respect.

"On his return I received him and supervised his accommodation. The sultan continued to supply him with provisions and lodgings and he sent gifts from the Noble Hijaz [the western coast and highlands of Arabia] to the sultan as a blessing. The sultan accepted them and sent in exchange complete suits of honour for him and his courtiers together with other gifts, various kinds of Alexandrian cloth, and other precious objects. Then he returned to his country.

"This man flooded Cairo with his benefactions. He left no court emir nor holder of royal office without the gift of a load of gold. The Cairenes made incalculable profits out of him and his suite in buying and selling and giving and taking. They exchanged gold until they depressed its value in Egypt and caused its price to fall."

The *mihmandār* spoke the truth, for more than one has told this story. When the *mihmandār* died the tax office found among his property which he left thousands of dinars' [gold coins] worth of native gold which he had given to him, still just as it had been in the earth, never having been worked.

Merchants of Cairo have told me of the profits which they made from the Africans, saying that one of them might buy a shirt or cloak or robe or other garment for five dinars when it was not worth one. Such was their simplicity and trustfulness that it was possible to practice any deception on them. They greeted anything that was said to them with credulous acceptance. But later they formed the very poorest opinion of the Egyptians because of the obvious falseness of everything they said to them and their outrageous behaviour in fixing the prices of the provisions and other good which were sold to them, so much so that were they to encounter today the most learned doctor of religious science and he were to say that he was Egyptian they would be rude to him and view him with disfavour because of the ill treatment which they had experienced at their hands.

[A]l-Ujrumi the guide informed me that he accompanied sultan Mūsā when he made the Pilgrimage and that the sultan was very open-handed towards the pilgrims and the inhabitants of Holy Places. He and his companions maintained great pomp and dressed magnificently during the journey. He gave away much wealth in alms. "About 200 mithqals [gold coins] of gold fell to me" said Muhanna' "and he gave other sums to my companions." Muhanna' waxed eloquent in describing the sultan's generosity, magnanimity, and opulence.

Gold was at a high price in Egypt until they came in that year. The mithqal did not go below 25 *dirhams* [silver coins] and was generally above, but from that time its value fell and cheapened in price and has remained cheap till now. The mithqal does not exceed 22 *dirhams* or less. This has been the state of affairs for about twelve years until this day [in the year 1337 or 1338] by reason of the large amount of gold which they brought into Egypt and spent there.

A letter came from this sultan to the court of the sultan in Cairo. It was written in the Maghribī style of handwriting on paper with wide lines. In it he follows his own rules of composition although observing the demands of propriety. It was written by the hand of one of his courtiers who had come on the Pilgrimage. Its contents comprised greetings and a recommendation for the bearer. With it he sent 5,000 mithqals of gold by way of a gift.

IV. FELIX FABRI ENCOUNTERS A STORM, 1480s

[Felix Fabri, a Swiss-German monk, made two pilgrimages to Jerusalem in the 1480s. From the time of the first crusade, Christian pilgrims had favored the sea route to the Holy Land. Like most of his co-religionists, Fabri arranged for his passage in Venice and sailed to the port of Accra (today's Akko on the coast of Israel). Although this route was well traveled, the dangers were real. In the following excerpt from his richly informative book, Fabri remembers the storm in the Adriatic Sea that he encountered while returning to Venice from his first pilgrimage.]

But while it was yet dark, and no stars could be seen, as we tacked to windward there arose a most frightful storm, and a terrible disturbance of the sea and air. Most furious winds tossed us aloft, lightning flashed, thunder roared dreadfully; moreover, on either side of us fearful thunderbolts fell, so that in many places the sea seemed to be on fire. The rain, too, fell in such torrents as though entire rain-clouds had burst and fallen upon us. Violent squalls kept striking the galley, covering it with water, and beating upon the sides of it as hard as though great stones from some high mountains were sent flying along the planks. I have often wondered when at sea in storms how it can be that water, being as it is a thin, soft and weak body, can strike such hard blows against whatever it meets, for it makes a noise when it runs against the ship as though millstones were being flung against her; and one cannot wonder at its breaking up a ship even though she were built of iron. Waves of sea-water are more vehement, more noisy, and more wonderful than those of other water. I have had great pleasure in sitting or standing on the upper deck during a storm, and watching the marvellous succession of gusts of wind and the frightful rush of the waters. Storms are endurable by day, but at night they are too cruel, especially when they are violent ones like that of which I am now speaking: for this was a very fierce storm, and the darkness was intense, nor was there any light save the continual flashes of lightning. So fierce a wind kept tossing the galley up and down, rolling it from side to side and shaking it about, that no man could lie in his berth, much less sit, and least of all stand. We were obliged to hang on to the pillars which stood in the middle of the cabin supporting the upper works, or else to crouch on our bended knees beside our chests, embracing them with our hands and arms, and so holding ourselves still; and while doing so, sometimes big heavy chests would be upset, together with the men who were clinging to them. For the galley moves so violently, and in such different directions, that it upsets everything that stands, and, which sounds miraculous but is perfectly true, even things which were hanging up against the bulk-heads came off their hooks and fell down. Although the ship was everywhere dressed with pitch and the other things which are used to prevent leakage and to keep out the water, yet during this storm the water came in through unsuspected leaks everywhere, so that there was nothing in the whole ship which was not wet; our beds and all our things were sopping, our bread and biscuit all spoiled by the sea water. On the lower deck was terror and misery; on the upper deck toil and trouble. The wind blew our mainsail all to pieces, so the sailors lowered the yard, and bent to it another sail, for use in storms, which they call 'papafigo'; but after they had hoisted up the yard with the sail furled along it, while the sailors were sitting along the yard letting the ties go, and the sail was falling down, and the sailors on deck were holding in their hands the 'polistrelum,' that is, the rope by which the lower corners of the sail are held, lo! the wind rushed into the sail and filled it with such force that it tore the sheet out of the hands of the sailors, and blew it and the sail itself above the mast-head and above the 'keba,' or 'top,' high into the air: and it blew out so strongly in the wind that the yard bent like a bow, and the very mast itself, although it was big and strong, formed of many beams fastened together, creaked loudly as though it was already split and broken. At this time we were in the greatest danger, for had the mast broken during such a storm, we should soon have been overwhelmed by the sea, galley and all. As a bird cannot fly without its feathers and wings, even so a ship of the greatest burthen cannot move without sails, which are its wings and feathers. So when the poets speak of winged horses, they merely mean ships, as, for instance, Perseus came from Greece on a winged horse, and saved Andromeda from the rock at Joppa, etc. So our mast made many dreadful noises, and the yard likewise; and every joint in the whole galley seemed to be coming to pieces. Nothing ever frightened me in storms so much as the loud groans of the ship, which are so intense that one thinks that the ship must be broken somewhere. Nor can a man refrain from crying out, because of the sudden and dreadful noise of these groans. So there we stood, beholding a sad sight and in imminent danger. As the sail flapped thus in the air, the galley-slaves and other sailors ran to and fro with as much noise and shouting as though they were just about to be run through with swords; some climbed up the shrouds on to the yard, and tried to draw the sail down to them; some on deck below ran about trying to catch hold of the sheet again; some rove ropes through blocks and put brails round the sail. Meanwhile the pilgrims and those who were useless at this work prayed to God and called upon the saints. Some made their confessions as though already at the very point of death; some made great vows that they would travel from hence to Rome, to St. James (at Compostella), or to the house of the Blessed Virgin (at Loretto), if only they might escape from this death; for it is only when death is present before our eyes that we fear it. I thought of the aphorisms of Anacharsis the philosopher, who said that those who are at sea cannot be counted among either the living or the dead. Moreover, he said that they were only removed from death by the space of four fingers, four fingers being the thickness of the sides of a ship. Also, when asked which ships were the safest, he replied: 'Those which lie on dry ground, and not in the sea,' declaring that there was no safety at sea, because of its numerous and sudden perils. In the course of this terrible storm, lo! of a sudden there came an unhoped-for help from heaven. Amid the flashing of the lightning there appeared a light which stood fixed in the air above the prow for some time. Thence it slowly moved throughout the whole length of the galley as far as the stern, where it vanished. This light was a ray of fire about a cubit in width. As soon as the officers, the galley-slaves, and the other sailors, and such of the pilgrims as were on deck, saw this light, they all left off working, ceased their noise and shouting, and kneeling down with their hands raised to heaven, cried out in a low voice nothing except 'Holy, holy, holy.' We who were below, not knowing what was happening, were scared at the sudden quiet and silence, and the unwonted prayer. We imagined that they had given up working in despair, and were crying 'Holy' because they were on the point of death, and we stood astonished, waiting to see what should be the end of this. So someone opened a door which covered the main hatchway of the galley, through which men come down from the deck into the cabin, and called to us in Italian, saying: *O, Signori pellegrini, ñon habeate paura que questo note non avereto fortuna,* which is, being interpreted: 'Pilgrims, my masters, fear not, for this night and in this storm we shall suffer no evil, for we have received help from heaven.' After this, as the storm continued, the galley-slaves returned to their accustomed labours, and now they no longer howled as before, but worked with joyous shouts; for they never work without shouting. Let no man suppose that what I have told about the light is false, for it is as true as possible, and I could prove it by the oaths of more than two hundred witnesses who are alive at this day; for the arm of the Lord is not shortened that He should be unable to save those who are in distress. . . .

STUDY QUESTIONS

1. What dangers did Xuanzang face in the desert? Do you see evidence that he was following a route that was at least partially secured by Chinese soldiers? Who would have been likely to use such a route? Did Xuanzang have a passport?

2. Does Xuanzang seem to have been inspired by the Four Noble Truths or by later expressions of Buddhism (see Chapters 13 and 26)? Was he probably closer to the Mahayana or the Hinayana school of Buddhism? Were there aspects of non-Buddhist traditions in his beliefs? How do you explain this? Why did he not turn back?

3. What does Ibn Jubayr emphasize in his account of his time in Mecca? Why does he take such care in describing the Ka'bah and its surroundings? Was he writing a guidebook for future pilgrims?

4. What evidence does Ibn Jubayr provide regarding commerce in Mecca following the end of the formal pilgrimage period? From what countries did the merchants come? Might some of the pilgrims have financed their journeys by engaging in trade?

5. What does the account of Mansa Musa's pilgrimage suggest about the prosperity of the Malian court in the 14th century? How does the report of his trip reinforce suggestions in Ibn Jubayr of an extensive Islamic trade network? What does Mansa Musa's journey suggest about the use of currency in the Islamic world?

6. In what ways does Felix Fabri's book provide information about the realities of maritime travel in the 15th century? How was his ship powered? How many pilgrims did it carry? How did Fabri and his shipmates respond to the storm?

7. What similarities or differences do you see in the way Xuanzang and Fabri reacted to difficulties they encountered while traveling? Which of them responded more realistically? How do you explain this? How do you account for their fortitude?

MUSLIM PILGRIMS IN MECCA

"Exhort all men to make the pilgrimage." This famous verse from the Koran (Koran 22:27) urges Muslims to travel to Mecca to visit the holy places of Islam. In making the pilgrimage (*hajj*) to Mecca, Muslims follow the example set by Muhammad and also reenact events in the lives of the Muslim patriarch Abraham, his wife Hagar, and their son Ishmael. Muslims believe that Abraham originally built the Ka'bah, the huge black cube

Pilgrims Performing the *Tawaf* in Mecca, ca. 1980 (1358 A.H.). (Camerapix Ltd., Nairobi, Kenya)

depicted in this photograph, and that the black stone inside the Ka'bah was given to him by the Angel Gabriel.

Present-day pilgrims to Mecca, as in the time of Ibn Jubayr, travel to the holy places in carefully organized "tour" groups and are subject to strict rules. Pilgrimage takes place between the eighth and the thirteenth days of *Dhu al-Hijah,* the last month of the Muslim lunar year. As they approach Mecca, men don garments of simple white cotton cloth and women put on plain dresses, clothing that is intended to symbolize purity and unity. Once at the sacred sites, pilgrims follow much the same practices engaged in by Ibn Jubayr 800 years ago. A highlight of the *hajj* is the *tawaf,* the rite of walking counter-clockwise around the Ka'bah seven times and pointing to it or kissing it to mark the continuity of Islam.

For a thousand years or more the *hajj* has probably been the largest routine gathering of people in the world. Currently, about 2 million Muslims participate in this rite annually. The Sacred Mosque in Mecca, which houses the Ka'bah, has room for 1 million worshippers.

STUDY QUESTIONS

1. What features of the *hajj* are illustrated in the photograph?
2. How has the *hajj* strengthened Muslim unity?
3. How has the *hajj* contributed to cross-cultural contacts?

50 GLOBAL CONTACTS: SAILING TO CALICUT
CHINESE AND PORTUGUESE VOYAGES

Contacts between widely separated regions in the world greatly intensified during the 15th century C.E. Columbus's first voyage across the Atlantic at the end of the century brought the earth's two great islands—Afro-Eurasia and the Americas—into direct and permanent contact with one another. The changes that resulted from the new trans-Atlantic connections were massive in both the "New World" of the Americas and the "Old World" of Afro-Eurasia.

There was also a great leap forward in contacts between the major regions within Afro-Eurasia, a continuation of the trend that had begun with the establishment of the overland Silk Roads and the Indian Ocean voyages of the classical period. Between 1405 and 1433 the Ming emperors in China dispatched seven huge naval expeditions into the Indian Ocean under the admiralship of Zheng He. The Chinese ships were the largest and most technologically advanced vessels in the early 15th-century world. They made many successful landings at ports in Southeast Asia, India, Arabia, and the East African coast. Then, for reasons that are somewhat unclear, the Ming government called a halt to the maritime expeditions and cut off funds for shipbuilding, sending the greatest navy in the world into sharp decline.

While the Ming voyages were in full swing, the Portuguese government (which knew nothing about the maritime activities of the Chinese) began to sponsor its own, much smaller, overseas expeditions. During the course of the 15th century Portuguese mariners were sent, very tentatively, down the west coast of Africa with the aim of discovering a sea route to Asia. (Muslim states now blocked the traditional routes from Christian Europe to Asia via the Red Sea and the Persian Gulf.) Finally, in 1497 and 1498, Vasco da Gama led a fleet of three Portuguese ships and a crew of about 170 sailors around the Cape of Good Hope and up the East African coast. Assisted by an experienced Indian Ocean pilot, the Portuguese ships then sailed across the Arabian Sea to Calicut, a major port on the southwest coast of India (which the Chinese fleet had visited several times earlier in the century). Europeans were now able to sail directly to Asian ports. A new era of world history had begun.

Selection I from Ma Huan, *Ying-Yai Sheng-Lan: "The Overall Survey of the Ocean's Shores,"* translated by J. V. G. Mills (Cambridge: Cambridge University Press, 1970), pp. 138, 140–141, 143, 146. Reprinted by permission of David Higham Associates. Selection II excerpt from *A Journal of the First Voyage of Vasco da Gama, 1497–1499*, translated by E. G. Ravenstein (New York: Burt Franklin, n.d.), pp. 49–50, 56–63. Reprinted by permission of the Hakluyt Society.

The two selections that follow focus on the visits of the Chinese and Portuguese fleets to Calicut at different times in the 15th century. In the first reading Ma Huan, who traveled with Zheng He on several of the great maritime expeditions, records his impressions of the Indian port in the early 15th century. The second selection is taken from the record of the Portuguese voyage made by an anonymous member of Vasco da Gama's crew in 1497 and 1498. How do these selections illustrate the growth of maritime commerce in the Indian Ocean in the 15th century? In what ways were the Chinese and Portuguese voyages similar? How did they differ?

JOURNAL OF THE FIRST VOYAGE OF VASCO DA GAMA

I. A CHINESE REPORT ON CALICUT

In the fifth year of the Yonglo [period; 1408] the court ordered: the principal envoy the grand eunuch Zheng He and others to deliver an imperial mandate to the king of this country [Calicut] and to bestow on him a patent conferring a title of honour, and the grant of a silver seal, [also] to promote all the chiefs and award them hats and girdles of various grades.

[So Zheng He] went there in command of a large fleet of treasure-ships, and he erected a tablet with a pavilion over it and set up a stone which said 'Though the journey from this country to the Central Country [China] is more than a hundred thousand *li*, yet the people are very similar, happy and prosperous, with identical customs. We have here engraved a stone, a perpetual declaration for ten thousand ages.'

The king of the country is a NanKun [upper caste] man; he is a firm believer in the Buddhist religion [In fact, the king was a Hindu.]; [and] he venerates the elephant and the ox.

The population of the country includes five classes, the Muslim people, the Nan-k'un people, the Zhedi people, the Geling people, and the Mugua people.

The king of the country and the people of the country all refrain from eating the flesh of the ox. The great chiefs are Muslim people; [and] they all refrain from eating the flesh of the pig. Formerly there was a king who made a sworn compact with the Muslim people, [saying] 'You do not eat the ox; I do not eat the pig; we will reciprocally respect the taboo'; [and this compact] has been honoured right down to the present day. . . .

The king has two great chiefs who administer the affairs of the country; both are Muslims.

The majority of the people in the country all profess the Muslim religion [In fact, most of the people were Hindus.]. There are twenty or thirty temples of worship, and once in seven days they go to worship. When the day arrives, the whole family fast and bathe, and attend to nothing else. In the *si* and *wu* periods [times of the day], the menfolk, old and young, go to the temple to worship. When the *wei* period arrives, they disperse and return home; thereupon they carry on with their trading, and transact their household affairs.

The people are very honest and trustworthy. Their appearance is smart, fine, and distinguished.

Their two great chiefs received promotion and awards from the court of the Central Country.

If a treasure-ship goes there, it is left entirely to the two men to superintend the buying and selling; the king sends a chief and a Zhedi Weinuoji [a trader or broker] to examine the account books in the official bureau; a broker comes and joins them; [and] a high officer who commands the ships discusses the choice of a certain date for fixing prices. When the day arrives, they first of all take the silk embroideries and the open-work silks, and other such goods which have been brought there, and discuss the price of them one by one; [and] when [the price] has been fixed, they write out an agreement stating the amount of the price; [this agreement] is retained by these persons.

The chief and the Zhedi, with his excellency the eunuch, all join hands together, and the broker then says 'In such and such a moon on such and such a day, we have all joined hands and sealed our agreement with a hand-clasp; whether [the price] be dear or cheap, we will never repudiate it or change it.'

After that, the Zhedi and the men of wealth then come bringing precious stones, pearls, corals, and other such things, so that they may be examined and the price discussed; [this] cannot be settled in a day; [if done] quickly, [it takes] one moon; [if done] slowly, [it takes] two or three moons.

Once the money-price has been fixed after examination and discussion, if a pearl or other such article is purchased, the price which must be paid for it is calculated by the chief and the Weinuoji who carried out the original transaction; [and] as to the quantity of the hemp-silk or other such article which must be given in exchange for it, goods are given in exchange according to [the price fixed by] the original hand-clasp—there is not the slightest deviation. . . .

The people of the country also take the silk of the silk-worm, soften it by boiling, dye it in all colours, and weave it into kerchiefs with decorative stripes at intervals; the breadth is four or five *chi*, and the length one *zhang* two or three *chi;* [and] each length is sold for one hundred gold coins.

As to the pepper: the inhabitants of the mountainous countryside have established gardens, and it is extensively cultivated. When the period of the tenth moon arrives, the pepper ripens; [and] it is collected, dried in the sun, and sold. Of course, big pepper-collectors come and collect it, and take it up to the official storehouse to be stored; if there is a buyer, an official gives permission for the sale; the duty is calculated according to the amount [of the purchase price] and is paid in to the authorities. Each one *bone* of pepper is sold for two hundred gold coins.

The Zhedi mostly purchase all kinds of precious stones and pearls, and they manufacture coral beads and other such things.

Foreign ships from every place come there; and the king of the country also sends a chief and a writer and others to watch the sales; thereupon they collect the duty and pay it in to the authorities.

The wealthy people mostly cultivate coconut trees—sometimes a thousand trees, sometimes two thousand or three thousand—; this constitutes their property.

The coconut has ten different uses. The young tree has a syrup, very sweet, and good to drink; [and] it can be made into wine by fermentation. The old coconut has flesh, from which they express oil, and make sugar, and make a foodstuff for eating. From the fibre which envelops the outside [of the nut] they make ropes for ship-building. The shell of the coconut makes bowls and makes cups; it is also good for burning to ash for the delicate operation of inlaying gold or silver. The trees are good for building houses, and the leaves are good for roofing houses. . . .

On the day when the envoy returned, the king of the country wished to send tribute; [so] he took fifty *liang* of fine red gold and ordered the foreign craftsmen to draw it out into gold threads as fine as a hair; these were strung together to form a ribbon, which was made into a jewelled girdle with incrustations of all kinds of precious stones and large pearls; [and the king] sent a chief, Naibang, to present it as tribute to the Central Country.

II. A PORTUGUESE REPORT ON CALICUT

[*A description of Calecut.*] The city of Calecut is inhabited by Christians [*sic*]. They are of a tawny complexion. Some of them have big beards and long hair, whilst others clip their hair short or shave the head, merely allowing a tuft to remain on the crown as a sign that they are Christians. They also wear moustaches. They pierce the ears and wear much gold in them. They go naked down to the waist, covering their lower extremities with very fine cotton stuffs. But it is only the most respectable who do this, for the others manage as best they are able.

The women of this country, as a rule, are ugly and of small stature. They wear many jewels of gold round the neck, numerous bracelets on their arms, and rings set with precious stones on their toes. All these people are well-disposed and apparently of mild temper. At first sight they seem covetous and ignorant.

[*A messenger sent to the King.*] When we arrived at Calecut [in May 1498] the king was fifteen leagues away. The captain-major [Vasco da Gama] sent two men to him with a message, informing him that an ambassador had arrived from the King of Portugal with letters, and that if he desired it he would take them to where the king then was.

The king presented the bearers of this message with much fine cloth. He sent word to the captain bidding him welcome, saying that he was about to proceed to Qualecut [Calecut]. As a matter of fact, he started at once with a large retinue. . . .

[*A Royal Audience, May 28.*] The king was in a small court, reclining upon a couch covered with a cloth of green velvet, above which was a good mattress, and upon this again a sheet of cotton stuff, very white and fine, more so than any linen. The cushions were after the same fashion. In his left hand the king held a very large golden cup [spittoon], having a capacity of half an almude [8 pints]. At its mouth this cup was two palmas [16 inches] wide, and apparently it was massive. Into this cup the king threw the husks of a certain herb which is chewed by the people of this country because of its soothing effects, and which they call *atambor* [betel nut]. On the right side of the king stood a basin of gold, so large that a man might just encircle it with his arms: this contained the herbs. There were likewise many silver jugs. The canopy above the couch was all gilt.

The captain, on entering, saluted in the manner of the country: by putting the hands together, then raising them towards Heaven, as is done by Christians when addressing God, and immediately afterwards opening them and shutting the fists quickly. The king beckoned to the captain with his right hand to come nearer, but the captain did not approach him, for it is the custom of the country for no man to approach the king except only the servant who hands him the herbs, and when anyone addresses the king he holds his hand before the mouth, and remains at a distance. When the king beckoned to the captain he looked at us others, and ordered us to be seated on a stone bench near him, where he could see us. He ordered that water for our hands should be given us, as also some fruit, one kind of which resembled a melon, except that its outside was rough and the inside sweet, whilst another kind of fruit resembled a fig, and tasted very nice. There were men who prepared these fruits for us; and the king looked at us eating, and smiled; and talked to the servant who stood near him supplying him with the herbs referred to. . . .

And the captain told him he was the ambassador of a King of Portugal, who was Lord of many countries and the possessor of great wealth of every description, exceeding that of any king of these parts; that for a period of sixty years his ancestors had annually sent out vessels to make discoveries in the direction of India, as they knew that there were Christian kings there like themselves. This, he said, was the reason which induced them to order this country to be discovered, not because they sought for gold or silver, for of this they had such abundance that they needed not what was to be found in this country. He further stated that the captains sent out travelled for a year or two, until their provisions were exhausted, and then returned to Portugal, without having succeeded in making the desired discovery. There reigned a king now whose name was Dom Manuel, who had ordered him to build three vessels, of which he had been appointed captain-major, and who had ordered him not to return to Portugal until he should have discovered this King of the Christians, on pain of having his head cut off. That two letters had been intrusted to him to be presented in case he succeeded in discovering him, and that he would do so on the ensuing day; and, finally, he had been instructed to say by word of mouth that he [the King of Portugal] desired to be his friend and brother.

In reply to this the king said that he was welcome; that, on his part, he held him as a friend and brother, and would send ambassadors with him to Portugal. This latter had been asked as a favour, the captain pretending that he would not dare to present himself before his king and master unless he was able to present, at the same time, some men of this country. . . .

[*Presents for the King.*] On Tuesday [May 29] the captain got ready the following things to be sent to the king, viz., twelve pieces of *lambel* [striped cloth], four scarlet hoods, six hats, four strings of coral, a case containing six wash-hand basins, a case of sugar, two casks of oil, and two of honey. And as it is the custom not to send anything to the king without the knowledge of the Moor, his factor, and of the *bale,* the captain informed them of his intention. They came, and when they saw the present they laughed at it, saying that it was not a thing to offer to a king, that the poorest merchant from Mecca, or any other part of India, gave more, and that if he wanted to make a present it should be in gold, as the king would not accept such things. When the captain heard this he grew sad, and said that he had brought no gold, that, moreover, he was no merchant, but an ambassador; that he gave of that which he had, which was his own [private gift] and not the king's; that if the King of Portugal ordered him to return he would intrust him with far richer presents; and that if King Camolim would not accept these things he would send them back to the ships. Upon this they declared that they would not forward his presents, nor consent to his forwarding them himself. When they had gone there came certain Moorish merchants, and they all depreciated the present which the captain desired to be sent to the king. . . .

[*A Second Audience, May 30.*] When he had entered, the king said that he had expected him on Tuesday. The captain said that the long road had tired him, and that for this reason he had not come to see him. The king then said that he had told him that he came from a very rich kingdom, and yet had brought him nothing; that he had also told him that he was the bearer of a letter, which had not yet been delivered. To this the captain rejoined that he had brought nothing, because the object of his voyage was merely to make discoveries, but that when other ships came he would then see what they brought him; as to the letter, it was true that he had brought one, and would deliver it immediately.

The king then asked what it was he had come to discover: stones or men? If he came to discover men, as he said, why had he brought nothing? Moreover, he had been told that he carried with him the golden image of a Santa Maria. The captain said that the Santa Maria was not of gold, and that even if she were he would not part with her, as she had guided him across the ocean, and would guide him back to his own country. The king then asked for the letter. The captain said that he begged as a favour, that as the Moors wished him ill and might misinterpret him, a Christian able to speak Arabic should be sent for. The king said this was well, and at once sent for a young man, of small stature, whose name was Quaram. The captain then said that he had two letters, one written in his own language and the other in that of the Moors; that he was able to read the former, and knew that it contained nothing but what would prove acceptable; but that as to the other he was unable to read it, and it might be good, or contain something that was erroneous. As the Christian was unable to *read* Moorish, four Moors took the letter and read it between them, after which they translated it to the king, who was well satisfied with its contents.

The king then asked what kind of merchandise was to be found in his country. The captain said there was much corn [wheat], cloth, iron, bronze, and many other things. The king asked whether he had any merchandise with him. The captain replied that he had a little of each sort, as samples, and that if permitted to return to the ships he would order it to be landed, and that meantime four or five men would remain at the lodgings assigned them. The king said no! He might take all his people with him, securely moor his ships, land his merchandise, and sell it to the best advantage. Having taken leave of the king the captain returned to his lodgings, and we with him. As it was already late no attempt was made to depart that night. . . .

STUDY QUESTIONS

1. What does Ma Huan report about the people of Calicut? What aspects of life in Calicut interested him the most? What do we learn about the local economy from his report? How do you explain his confusion about religion in Calicut? What seems to have been the purpose of the Chinese visit to Calicut?

2. How does the Portuguese report compare with that of Ma Huan? What similarities and differences do you see? What explains the discord between the Portuguese and their hosts?

3. How important were Muslim merchants in Calicut? Where did they come from? What evidence do you see of an Islamic trade network in these documents? How did the level of Indian Ocean commerce in the 15th century compare with that during the classical period?

4. Was the long experience the Chinese had in dealing with pastoral nomads such as the Xiongnu an asset or a liability for Ma Huan and his shipmates when they docked in Calicut? How does Ma Huan's account of Calicut compare with Sima Qian's report on the Xiongnu (see Chapter 24)?

5. What do the Chinese decisions to sponsor and then terminate the Zheng He voyages suggest about the political leadership of China during the Ming dynasty? Why was the decision to end the voyages significant?

6. Suppose the Portuguese naval program had been ended after Vasco da Gama returned home. Would such a decision have altered the course of world history in important ways?

7. Does the Portuguese document suggest a shift in the European attitude toward trade and merchants?

51

THE CRUSADES:
CHRISTIAN AND MUSLIM VIEWS

In 1096, spurred by a call from Pope Urban II, a variety of Christians, including many knights from several parts of Western Europe, launched the first Crusade to recover Jerusalem and the Christian Holy Land from Muslim control. Their opponents were primarily Saracen Turks, who had been moving into the Abbasid caliphate. For a time, the Christians managed to carve out a Christian kingdom in Jerusalem. But by the late 12th century, a Turkish leader, Saladin, had largely dispersed the European forces.

The Crusades demonstrate the importance of religious goals to Europeans during the Middle Ages, though there were other motives as well. Growing European strength in a reviving economy also supported the effort. However, despite some political disarray, the balance of power still favored the Muslims, and in the long run the Crusades had little impact on the Middle East except perhaps in increasing mutual hostilities between the two religious sides.

The Crusades did, however, provide an intriguing set of contacts between two different cultures. Europeans came away from the experience with a knowledge of more sophisticated urban and commercial systems, including a specific taste for many products available in the Middle East such as sugar and spices.

Key questions about the Crusades involve causation and motivation, on the Christian side, and the nature of contacts and mutual impressions. The following documents take up both these topics.

Documents I–III involve Christian accounts, and they suggest a range of motivations plus some change over time as the Crusades began to bog down. In the first document, a German historian Ekkehard, who had visited Jerusalem in 1101, reports on the First Crusade. His account has a clear emphasis, but it already suggests some complexity in the factors involved and some real disputes about the whole enterprise. A letter from crusader Stephen of Blois, in the First Crusade, adds some detail about motives on the spot. The third document is from a later account, as Turkish resistance stiffened: an anonymous German annalist, in the city of Wuerzburg, wrote the passage around 1147.

Documents IV and V turn to the Muslim side. The first selection comes from a Muslim official in Jerusalem, writing about the Third Crusade in the later 12th century, when the European kings were negotiating with the Turkish Sultan, Saladin. The second

Selections I and II from James Harvey Robinson, *Readings in European History,* Vol. I (New York: Ginn and Company, 1904), pp. 316–318, 321; Selection III from *The Crusades: A Documentary History* (Milwaukee: Marquette University Press, 1962) pp. 1, 222; Selection IV from T. A. Archer, ed. *The Crusade of Richard I* (New York: G.P. Putnams, 1885), pp. 128–129; Selection V from ibn-Munqidh, Usamah, *Memoirs: An Arab-Syrian Gentleman and Warrior in the Period of the Crusades,* ed. Philip Hitti, pp. 162–165 (Princeton, NJ: Princeton University Press, 1987).

account deals with the Christian occupation of Jerusalem during the 12th century. It comes from the memoirs of Usamah ibn-Munqidh, an Arab soldier.

THE CRUSADES

I. EKKEHARD, C. 1102

Here I am very anxious to add certain details concerning these military undertakings, which are due to divine rather than human inspiration. This I do for the especial purpose of refuting those imprudent—or, better, impudent—critics, who, bound by prejudice, take it upon themselves with insolent lips to blame this novel enterprise, so necessary to a world that is growing old and nearing its end. They, like the Epicureans, prefer the broad way of pleasure to the narrow way of God's service. To them love of the world is wisdom and those who despise it are fools. . . . I, however, since I trust in the Lord and strive not for present but for future things, would, although only as an idle spectator yet a kindly well-wisher, exalt the glorious men of our time who have overcome the kingdoms of this world and who, for the sake of the blessed Shepherd who sought the hundredth sheep that was lost, have left wife and child, principalities and riches, and have taken their lives in their hands . . .

[After [Pope] Urban had aroused the spirits of all by the promise of forgiveness to those who undertook the expedition with single-hearted devotion,] toward one hundred thousand men were appointed to the immediate service of God from Aquitaine and Normandy, England, Scotland, Ireland, Brittany, Galicia, Gascony, France, Flanders, Lorraine, and from other Christian peoples, whose names I no longer retain. It was truly an army of "crusaders," for they bore the sign of the cross on their garments as a reminder that they should mortify the flesh, and in the hope that they would in this way triumph over the enemies of the cross of Christ . . . Thus, through the marvelous and unexampled working of divine dispensation, all these members of Christ, so different in speech, origin, and nationality, were suddenly brought together as one body through their love of Christ.

While they were all under one king, Christ, the several peoples nevertheless were led by their several leaders, namely Godfrey of Lorraine and his brothers Baldwin and Eustace, Robert of Flanders, Robert of Normandy, Count Regimund of St. Gilles, Hugh, brother of King Philip of France, and other warriors of similar energy, rank, and bravery. Over all of these the above-mentioned pope placed Bishop Hademar, a man of venerable holiness and wisdom. To him the pope granted the right to exercise in his stead the power transmitted by St. Peter to the Roman see [to make religious rulings]. . . .

The West Franks were easily induced to leave their fields, since France had, during several years, been terribly visited now by civil war, now by famine, and again by sickness. . . . Among the other nations, the common people, as well as those of higher rank, related that, aside from the apostolic summons, they had in some instances been called to the land of promise by certain prophets who had appeared among them, or through heavenly signs and revelations. Others confessed that they had been induced to pledge themselves by some misfortune. A great part of them started forth with wife and child and laden with their entire household equipment.

[But] almost the whole German people were, at the beginning of the expedition, quite unacquainted with the reasons for it. Consequently the many legions of horsemen who passed through their land, the hosts of people on foot, the crowds of country people, women and children, were viewed by them with contempt as persons who had altogether lost their wits.

Those bound for the Holy Land seemed to them to be leaving the land of their birth and sacrificing what they already had for a vain hope. The promised land offered no certainty but danger, yet they deserted their own possessions in a greedy struggle for those of others. Nevertheless, . . . after [the Germans] had thoroughly discussed the matter with the multitude of pilgrims, they too inclined their hearts.

Moreover the signs in the sun and the wonders which appeared, both in the air and on the earth, aroused many who had previously been indifferent. It seems to us useful to interweave an account of a few of these signs, although it would carry us too far to enumerate them all. For example, we beheld a comet on the 7th of October to the south, and its brilliancy slanting down seemed like a sword. . . . Some who were watching horses in the fields reported that they had seen the image of a city in the air and had observed how various troops from different directions, both on horseback and on foot, were hastening thither.

Many, moreover, displayed, either on their clothing, or upon their forehead, or elsewhere on their body, the sign of the cross, which had been divinely imprinted, and they believed themselves on this account to have been destined to the service of God. Others likewise were induced, through some sudden change of spirit or some nocturnal vision, to sell all their property and possessions and to sew the sign of mortification on their mantles. Among all these people who pressed into the churches in incredible numbers, swords were distributed with the priestly benediction, according to the new usage, along with the pilgrim's staff and wallet.

I may also report that at this time a woman after two years gestation finally gave birth to a boy who was able to talk; and that a child with a double set of limbs, another with two heads, and some lambs with two heads were also born; and that colts came into the world with great teeth, which we ordinarily call horses' teeth and which nature only grants to three-year old horses.

II. LETTER FROM A CRUSADER, 1098

You may be very sure, dearest, that the messenger whom I sent to you left me before Antioch safe and unharmed and, through God's grace, in the greatest prosperity. And already at that time, together with all the chosen army of Christ, endowed with great valor by him, we had been continuously advancing for twenty-three weeks toward the home of our Lord Jesus. You may know for certain, my beloved, that of gold, silver, and many other kinds of riches, I now have twice as much as you, my love, supposed me to have when I left you. . . .

III. A GERMAN ANNALIST, C. 1147

God allowed the Western church, on account of its sins, to be cast down. There arose, indeed, certain pseudo prophets, sons of Belial [the Devil], and witnesses of anti-Christ, who seduced the Christians with empty words. They constrained all sorts of men, by vain preaching, to set out against the Saracens [Turks] in order to liberate Jerusalem. The preaching of these men was so enormously influential that the inhabitants of nearly every region, by common vows, offered themselves freely for common destruction. Not only the ordinary people, but kings, dukes, marquises, and other powerful men of this world as well, believed that they thus showed their allegiance to God. The bishops, archbishops, abbots, and other ministers and prelates of the church joined in this error, throwing themselves headlong into it to the great peril of bodies and souls. . . . The intentions of the various men were different. Some, indeed, lusted after novelties and went in order to learn about new lands. Others there were who were driven by poverty, who were in hard straits at home; these men went to fight, not only against the enemies of Christ's cross, but even against the friends of the Christian name, wherever opportunity appeared, in order to relieve their poverty. There were others who were oppressed by debts to other men or who sought to escape the service due to their lords, or who were even awaiting the punishment merited by their shameful deeds. Such men simulated a zeal for God and hastened chiefly in order to escape from such troubles and anxieties. A few could, with difficulty, be found who had not bowed their knees to [the Devil], who were directed by a holy and wholesome purpose, and who were kindled by love of the divine majesty to fight earnestly and even to shed their blood for the holy of holies.

IV. BEH-EL-DIN, OFFICIAL IN JERUSALEM

Then the king of England, seeing all the delays interposed by the Sultan to the execution of the treaty, acted perfidiously as regards his Muslim prisoners. On their yielding the town he had engaged to grant them life, adding that if the Sultan carried out the bargain he would give them freedom and suffer them to carry off their children and wives; if the Sultan did not fulfill his engagements they were to be made slaves. Now the king broke his promises to them and made open display of what he had till now kept hidden in his heart, by carrying out what he had intended to do after he had received the money and the Frank prisoners. It is thus that people of his nation ultimately admitted.

In the afternoon of Tuesday . . . about four o'clock, he came out on horseback with all the Frankish army; knights, footmen, Turcoples, and advanced to the pits at the foot of the hill of Al 'Ayâdîyeh, to which place he had already sent on his tents. The Franks, on reaching the middle of the plain that stretches between this hill and that of Keisân, close to which place the sultan's advanced guard had drawn back, ordered all the Muslim prisoners, whose martyrdom God had decreed for this day, to be brought before him. They numbered more than three thousand and were all bound with ropes. The Franks then flung themselves upon them all at once and massacred them with sword and lance in cold blood. Our advanced guard had already told the Sultan of the enemy's movements and he sent it some reinforcements, but only after the massacre. The Muslims seeing what was being done to the prisoners, rushed against the Franks and in the combat, which lasted till nightfall, several were slain and wounded on either side. On the morrow morning our people gathered at the spot and found the Muslims stretched out upon the ground as martyrs for the faith. They even recognized some of the dead, and the sight was a great affliction to them. The enemy had only spared the prisoners of note and such as were strong enough to work.

The motives of this massacre are differently told; according to some, the captives were slain by way of reprisal for the death of those Christians whom the Muslims had slain. Others again say that the king of England, on deciding to attempt the conquest of Ascalon, thought it unwise to have so many prisoners in the town after his departure. God alone knows what the real reason was.

V. USAMAH IBN-MUNQIDH

A few days after the departure of my uncle, the public announcer called us to arms, and I started at the head of a small band, hardly amounting to twenty horsemen, with full conviction that Afāiyah had no cavalry in it. Accompanying me was a great body of pillagers and Bedouins [shepherds]. As soon as we arrived in the Valley of Bohemond, and while the pillagers and the Arabs were scattered all over the planted fields, a large army of the Franks set out against us. They had been reinforced that very night by sixty horsemen and sixty footmen. They repulsed us from the valley, and we retreated before them until we joined those of our number who were already in the fields, pillaging them. Seeing us, the Franks raised a violent uproar. Death seemed an easy thing to me in comparison with the loss of that crowd [24] in my charge. So I turned against a horseman in their vanguard, who had taken off his coat of mail in order to be light enough to pass before us, and thrust my lance into his chest. He instantly flew off his saddle, dead. I then faced their horsemen as they followed, and they all took to flight. Though a tyro in warfare, and having never before that day taken part in a battle, I, with a mare under me as swift as a bird, went on, now pursuing them and plying them with my lance, now taking cover from them.

In the rear guard of the Franks was a cavalier on a black horse, large as a camel, wearing a coat of mail and the full armor of war. I was afraid of this horseman, lest he should be drawing me further ahead in order to get an opportunity to turn back and attack me. All of a sudden I saw him spur his horse, and as the horse began to wave its tail, I knew that it was already exhausted. So I rushed on the horseman and smote him with my lance, which pierced him through and projected about a cubit in front of him. The lightness of my body, the force of the thrust and the swiftness of my horse made me lose my seat on the saddle. Moving backward a little, I pulled out my lance, fully assuming that I had killed him . . .

I once witnessed in an encounter between us and the Franks one of our cavaliers, named Badi ibn-Talīl al-Qushayri, who was one of our brave men, receive in his chest, while clothed with only two pieces of garment, a lance thrust from a Frankish knight. The lance cut the vein in his chest and issued from his side. He turned back right away, but we never thought he would make his home alive. But as Allah (worthy of admiration is he!) had predestined, he survived and his wound was healed. But for one year after that, he could not sit up in case he was lying on his back unless somebody held him by the shoulders and helped him. At last what he suffered from entirely disappeared and he reverted to his old ways of living and riding. My only comment is: How mysterious are the works of him whose will is always executed among his creatures! He giveth life and he causeth death, but he is living and dieth not. In his hand is all good, and he is over all things potent. . . .

A case illustrating their [the Europeans] curious medicine is the following:

The lord of al-Munaytirah wrote to my uncle asking him to dispatch a physician to treat certain sick persons among his people. My uncle sent him a Christian physician named Thābit. Thābit was absent but ten days when he returned. So we said to him, "How quickly hast thou healed thy patients!" He said:

> They brought before me a knight in whose leg an abscess had grown; and a woman afflicted with imbecility. To the knight I applied a small poultice until the abscess opened and became well; and the woman I put on diet and made her humor wet. Then a Frankish physician came to them and said, "This man knows nothing about treating them." He then said to the knight, "Which wouldst thou prefer, living with one leg or dying with two?" The latter replied, "Living with one leg." The physician said, "Bring me a strong knight and a sharp ax." A knight came with the ax. And I was standing by. Then the physician laid the leg of the patient on a block of wood and bade the knight strike his leg with the ax and chop it off at one blow. Accordingly he struck it—while I was looking on—one blow, but the leg was not severed. He dealt another blow, upon which the marrow of the leg flowed out and the patient died on the spot. He then examined the woman and said, "This is a woman in whose head there is a devil which has possessed her. Shave off her hair." Accordingly they shaved it off and the woman began once more to eat their ordinary diet—garlic and mustard. Her imbecility took a turn for the worse. The physician then said, "The devil has penetrated through her head." He therefore took a razor, made a deep cruciform incision on it, peeled off the skin at the middle of the incision until the bone of the skull was exposed and rubbed it with salt. The woman also expired instantly. Thereupon I asked them whether my services were needed any longer, and when they replied in the negative I returned home, having learned of their medicine what I knew not before.

I have, however, witnessed a case of their medicine which was quite different from that.

The king of the Franks had for treasurer a knight named Bernard [*barnād*], who (may Allah's curse be upon him!) was one of the most accursed and wicked among the Franks. A horse kicked him in the leg, which was subsequently infected and which opened in fourteen different places. Every time one of these cuts would close in one place, another would open in another place. All this happened while I was praying for his perdition. Then came to him a Frankish physician and removed from the leg all the ointments which were on it and began to wash it with very strong vinegar. By this treatment all the cuts were healed and the man became well again. He was up again like a devil. . . .

Newly arrived Franks are especially rough: One insists that Usāmah should pray eastward.—Everyone who is a fresh emigrant from the Frankish lands is ruder in character than those who have become acclimatized and have held long association with the Moslems. Here is an illustration of their rude character.

Whenever I visited Jerusalem I always entered the Aqṣa Mosque, beside which stood a small mosque which the Franks had converted into a church. When I used to enter the Aqṣa Mosque, which was occupied by the Templars [*al-dāwiyyah*], who were my friends, the Templars would evacuate the little adjoining mosque so that I might pray in it. One day I entered this mosque, repeated the first formula, "Allah is great," and stood up in the act of praying, upon which one of the Franks rushed on me, got hold of me and turned my face eastward saying, "This is the way thou shouldst pray!" A group of Templars hastened to him seized him, and repelled him from me. I resumed my prayer. The same man, while the others were otherwise busy, rushed once more on me and turned my face eastward, saying, "This is the way thou shouldst pray!" The Templars again came in to him and expelled him. They apologized to me, saying, "This is a stranger who has only recently arrived from the land of the Franks and he has never before seen anyone praying except eastward." Thereupon I said to myself, "I have had enough prayer." So I went out and have ever been surprised at the conduct of this devil of a man, at the change in the color of his face, his trembling and his sentiment at the sight of one praying towards the *qiblah* [direction of Mecca].

Another wants to show God as a child to a Moslem.—I saw one of the Franks come to al-Amīr Mu'īn-al-Dī (may Allah's mercy rest upon his soul!) when he was in the Dome of the Rock and say to him, "Dost thou want to see God as a child?" Mu'īn-al-Dīn said, "Yes." The Frank walked ahead of us until he showed us the picture of Mary with Christ (may peace be upon him!) as an infant in her lap. He then said, "This is God as a child." But Allah is exalted far above what the infidels say about him!

The Franks are void of all zeal and jealousy. One of them may be walking along with his wife. He meets another man who takes the wife by the hand and steps aside to converse with her while the husband is standing on one side waiting for his wife to conclude the conversation. If she lingers too long for him, he leaves her alone with the conversant and goes away.

Here is an illustration which I myself witnessed:

When I used to visit Nāblus, I always took lodging with a man named Mu'izz, whose home was a lodging house for the Moslems. The house had windows which opened to the road, and there stood opposite to it on the other side of the road a house belonging to a Frank who sold wine for the merchants. He would take some wine in a bottle and go around announcing it by shouting, "So and so, the merchant, has just opened a cask full of this wine. He who wants to buy some of it will find it in such and such a place." The Frank's pay for the announcement made would be the wine in that bottle. One day this Frank went home and found a man with his wife in the same bed. He asked him, "What could have made thee enter into my wife's room?" The man replied, "I was tired, so I went in to rest." "But how," asked he, "didst thou get into my bed?" The other replied, "I found a bed that was spread, so I slept in it." "But," said he, "my wife was sleeping together with thee!" The other replied, "Well, the bed is hers. How could I therefore have prevented her from using her own bed?" "By the truth of my religion," said the husband, "if thou shouldst do it again, thou and I would have a quarrel." Such was for the Frank the entire expression of his disapproval and the limit of his jealousy.

STUDY QUESTIONS

1. What were the various motives that spurred Europeans to join the crusades? Were different kinds of people involved, or could a given individual operate from conflicting motives?
2. Did European motivations change over time, and if so, why?
3. How did Muslims perceive the Christian crusaders? Were their perceptions accurate?
4. How did the experience of the Crusades change some Christian views?
5. Judging by these documents, what long-term impact do you think the Crusades had on Christian-Muslim relations?

THE MONGOLS

52 CHINGIS KHAN AND THE RISE OF THE MONGOLS

The sudden rise of the Mongols under the leadership of Chingis Khan, the greatest of the nomad conquerors to come galloping out of the grasslands of Central Asia, has long excited the imagination of historians. When Chingis Khan was born around 1165 (and given the name Temujin), the Mongol region was politically fragmented. The Mongols were one of a half-dozen major tribes of migratory herders who claimed sovereignty over parts of the grasslands north of China. Conflict between the various tribes, none of whom had any particular advantage over the others, was endemic.

Temujin's early life, so far as we know, was little different from that of many of his contemporaries. His father, known as Yesugei the Brave, was a minor Mongol leader. When Temujin was about 10 years old, Yesugei was murdered by members of a rival tribe. The death of Yesugei was a disaster for Temujin, his brothers, and their mother, Hogelun Ujin. The family was abandoned by the other members of their clan, the Tayichiguds, and experienced much hardship for the next several years.

Somehow Temujin overcame these obstacles. He had a talent for establishing close ties with other nomads, some of whom were tribal elders. His ability as a military leader was extraordinary. Around 1185, when he was about 20, some of the Mongol elders elected him as their khan (tribal chief). Two decades later, following his leadership in the conquest of much of Central Asia, a Great Assembly (*Khuriltai*) of the Mongols designated Temujin as Chingis Khan (Universal Ruler). He spent the rest of his life expanding the boundaries of his conquests—westward toward Persia and southward into China.

Much of Chingis Khan's life will always be a mystery. Our best source for his life is a book called *The Secret History of the Mongols* that was written shortly after the death of the Great Khan. The author of the *Secret History* is unknown, but the book is clearly the work of someone who was a contemporary of Chingis, perhaps even a member of his household. Written to glorify Chingis and having some of the characteristics of an epic

From Paul Kahn, *The Secret History of the Mongols: The Origin of Chingis Khan: An Adaptation of the Yuan Ch'ao Pi Shih, Based Primarily on the English Translation by Francis Woodman Cleaves.* Expanded edition (Boston: Cheng and Tsui, 1998), pp. 3, 18, 40–41, 44–45, 96–97, 128–134, 146, 160.

poem, the *Secret History* must be used carefully. Despite its limitations, however, the *Secret History* remains the best entry point into the world of Chingis Khan.

How does the *Secret History* help us to understand the reasons for the rise of Chingis Khan?

THE SECRET HISTORY OF THE MONGOLS

I. LEGENDARY ORIGINS: THE MONGOL CREATION STORY

There came into the world a blue-gray wolf
whose destiny was Heaven's will.
His wife was a fallow deer.
They travelled together across the inland sea
and when they were camped near the source of the Onan River
in sight of Mount Burkhan Khaldun
their first son was born, named Batachikhan. . . .

II. CHILDHOOD EXPERIENCES

After the Tayichigud brothers had abandoned the old camp,
leaving only Hogelun Ujin,
her sons and her little ones,
after the Tayichigud had taken all of the people away,
leaving only the mothers and sons,
Hogelun Ujin, a woman born with great power,
took care of her sons.
Proudly she put on her headdress and gathered the folds of her skirt.
She went up and down the banks of the Onan
and gathered pears and wild fruit.
Day and night she found food for their mouths.
Mother Hogelun, a woman born with great courage,
took care of her sons.
Taking a juniper stick in her hands
she fed them by digging up roots.
These boys who were nourished on the wild onion and pear,
who were fed by Ujin, the Mother,
became the great Lords of all men.
These boys who lived on the roots that she dug for them,
who were cared for with pride by Mother Ujin,
became the wise men who gave us our laws.
These boys who were nourished on the wild onion and pear,
who were fed by the beautiful Ujin,
grew up to be fine, daring men.
Once they'd grown into men,
they pledged to themselves: "Now we'll feed our mother."
They sat on the banks of the Mother Onan

and bent needles they'd found into fishhooks.
With these hooks they caught a few misshapen fish.
They made nets to sweep through the river
and they caught tiny fish.
With these in their turn they helped feed their mother. . . .

III. ANDA

[The bond established between Temujin and Jamugha described here eventually broke down, a frequent occurrence among the fractious nomads of the Mongolian steppe. Nonetheless, it is clear from many passages in the Secret History, *that the Mongols attached great importance to anda.]*

Temujin and Jamugha pitched their tents in the Khorkonagh Valley.
With their people united in one great camp,
the two leaders decided they should renew their friendship,
their pledge of anda.
They remembered when they'd first made that pledge,
and said, "We should love one another again."
That first time they'd met Temujin was eleven years old.
In those days
when he and his family had been abandoned by the Tayichigud,
he'd first met Jamugha,
a young noble of the Jadaran clan,
and they'd played at games of knucklebone dice on the banks of the Onan,
casting bones on the frozen waters of the Onan.
Jamugha had given Temujin the knucklebone of a roebuck
and in return Temujin gave Jamugha a knucklebone of brass.
With that exchange the two boys had pledged themselves anda forever.
Then later that spring
when the two were off in the forest together shooting arrows,
Jamugha took two pieces of calf-horn.
He bored holes in them,
glued them together to fashion a whistling arrowhead,
and he gave this arrow as a present to Temujin.
In return Temujin gave him a beautiful arrow with a cypress wood tip.
With that exchange of arrows
they declared themselves anda a second time.
So Temujin and Jamugha said to each other:
"We've heard the elders say,
'When two men become anda their lives become one.
One will never desert the other and will always defend him.'
This is the way we'll act from now on.
We'll renew our old pledge and love each other forever."
Temujin took the golden belt he'd received
in the spoils from Toghtoga's defeat
and placed it around Anda Jamugha's waist.
Then he led out the Merkid chief's warhorse,

a light yellow mare with black mane and tail,
and gave it to Anda Jamugha to ride.
Jamugha took the golden belt he'd received
in the spoils from Dayir Usun's defeat
and placed it around the waist of Anda Temujin.
Then he led out the whitish-tan warhorse of Dayir Usun
and had Anda Temujin ride on it.
Before the cliffs of Khuldaghar
in the Khorkhonagh Valley,
beneath the Great Branching Tree of the Mongol,
they pledged their friendship and promised to love one another.
They held a feast on the spot
and there was great celebration.
Temujin and Jamugha spent that night alone,
sharing one blanket to cover them both. . . .

IV. TEMUJIN BECOMES A MONGOL KHAN, 1185

Then they moved the whole camp
to the shores of Blue Lake in the Gurelgu Mountains.
Altan, Khuchar, and Sacha Beki conferred with each other there,
and then said to Temujin:
"We want you to be Khan.
Temujin, if you'll be our Khan
we'll search through the spoils
for the beautiful women and virgins,
for the great palace tents,
for the young virgins and loveliest women,
for the finest geldings and mares.
We'll gather all these and bring them to you.
When we go off to hunt for wild game
we'll go out first to drive them together for you to kill.
We'll drive the wild animals of the steppe together
so that their bellies are touching.
We'll drive the wild game of the mountains together
so that they stand leg to leg.
If we disobey your command during battle
take away our possessions, our children, and wives.
Leave us behind in the dust,
cutting off our heads where we stand and letting them fall to the ground.
If we disobey your counsel in peacetime
take away our tents and our goods, our wives and our children.
Leave us behind when you move,
abandoned in the desert without a protector."
Having given their word,
having taken this oath,
they proclaimed Temujin Khan of the Mongol. . . .

V. PREPARING FOR BATTLE, 1204

[Temujin's defeat of the Naimans in 1204 gave the Mongols control of much of the steppe and paved the way for his election as Chingis Khan at the Khuriltai in 1206.]

He divided the men into thousands to form troops of a thousand,
and appointed for each troop a captain of thousands,
captains of hundreds, and captains of tens.
He appointed six men to be stewards of the army,
giving them the title of Cherbi,
including Dodai and Ogele Cherbi among them.
Then having divided the army to form troops of a thousand,
having divided it further to form troops of a hundred,
having divided these further to form troops of ten,
he chose from among them his personal guard,
the eighty nightguards and seventy dayguards.
For this he inspected the sons and relations of all his captains,
and the sons and relations of all common soldiers,
and he selected those with the greatest ability,
those most fit and pleasant to look at.
He had Arkhai Khasar help him, saying:
"Let's pick the bravest men and form a troop of a thousand.
On the days of battle these will fight in front of me.
On the other days they will be my dayguard.
Ogele Cherbi will be their commander
and Khudus Khalkhan will advise him."
Then Chingis Khan established these regulations:
"Let the archers,
the solders of the dayguard,
the cooks,
the door keepers,
and the keepers of the geldings
each take his turn at their post during daylight.
Before sunset let the nightguards relieve them.
The men who've served me in daylight
will go spend the night with their horses.
Let the nightguard assign men to lie in the grass around my tent in the
    darkness,
and assign others to be the door sentries.
Then at daylight when I arise for my morning drink
let the archers and dayguards tell the nightguards they're here
and let the archers,
the soldiers who are dayguards,
the cooks, and door keepers
each go to their job.
Let them each be seated in his proper place.
They'll each finish their assigned tasks,
which will last three days and nights,

spending each of the nights the same way with their horses,
then they'll trade places with the men who've relieved them,
becoming the nightguards on the following night,
beginning as the men who lie in the grass around my tent."

So having divided his army to form troops of a thousand,
having appointed his stewards,
having chosen his eighty nightguards,
and seventy soldiers as dayguards,
having selected the bravest among them for Arkhai Khasar to lead,
having made his camp near Keltegi Cliffs on the Khalkha,
it being the sixteenth day of the summer's first moon,
the Red Circle day in the Year of the Rat,
having sprinkled libations of mare's milk on his standard of nine tails
as a signal to Heaven that he was going to war,
Chingis Khan set out with his army against the Naiman. . . .

VI. AFTER 1206: CREATING THE MONGOL STATE

He rewarded all those who had helped him establish the Nation
by appointing them Mingghan-u Noyan [rulers of a thousand households].
He divided the people into bands of one thousand households,
appointing captains of thousands,
captains of hundreds, and captains of tens to rule over them.
He divided the people into units of ten thousand
and appointed captains of ten thousand for each unit.
Then Chingis Khan made this decree:
"Before I had eighty nightguards and seventy dayguards.
Now thanks to Eternal Blue Heaven
my power has been increased by Heaven and Earth.
I've straightened out the lives of the entire Nation
and they're controlled by the reins in my hands.
From the thousands of people in the Nation
I'll select men to serve me as nightguards, archers, and dayguards
until I've filled a unit of ten thousand."
When Chingis Khan proclaimed that he would select his new guard
he issued this decree to the entire Nation:
"Let the ablest and best-looking men step forward,
the sons of captains of ten thousand,
of thousands, of hundreds, of tens,
and the sons of common soldiers,
any man who is worthy to serve in my presence.
The sons of captains of thousands
should bring ten companions and one younger brother.
The sons of captains of hundreds
should bring five companions and one younger brother.
The sons of captains of tens or common soldiers
should bring three companions and one younger brother,

along with their own horses.

When the son of a captain of thousands comes to serve me,

the ten companions he brings will be given to him to command,

along with any animals and property given to them by their fathers.

All this will be redistributed from the units they've come from.

The same will hold true for the sons of captains of hundreds,

of tens, and of common soldiers.

Their companions and their property will be redistributed.

Any person who does not obey this order will be punished.

Any person who's accepted to serve in my presence and doesn't serve properly,

I'll send such a man out of my sight and exile him to a distant land."

Because Chingis Khan had originally chosen eighty nightguards

from among the sons of the captains of thousands, of hundreds, and tens,

now he chose eight hundred nightguards.

Then he said:

"In addition to these eight hundred

fill out the guard to make it a unit of one thousand.

No one shall stop a man who wishes to volunteer for the nightguard.

Yeke Negurin will be their captain

and he will command a thousand men."

Previously he had chosen four hundred archers.

Now he said:

"Jelme's son, Yesun Tege, will be captain of the archers,

and Yesun Tege, Bugidai, Horkhudagh, and Lablakha

will each command one company taken from the various units."

In addition to the thousand dayguards he had chosen before,

commanded by Ogele Cherbi, he said:

"Select one thousand dayguards from Mukhali's people and let Bukha
 command them.

Select a thousand from Ilugei's people for Alchidai to command.

Both Dodai Cherbi and Dokholkhu Cherbi will command a thousand dayguards.

Chanai will command a thousand chosen from Jurchedei's people.

Akhutai will command a thousand chosen from Alchi's people.

Arkhai Khasar will command a band of a thousand chosen heroes,

and these heroes will be the dayguards on usual days.

During battles this band of heroes will surround me."

From the tens of thousands of people eight thousand dayguards were chosen,

along with two thousand nightguards and archers.

The guard was a band of ten thousand soldiers.

Then Chingis Khan made this decree:

"This band of ten thousand soldiers will serve in my presence

and become the great middle army.

Bukha, Alchidai, Dodai Cherbi, and Dokholkhu Cherbi

will be their senior commanders."

Then he established these rules for men who served in the guard:

"When a soldier enters service in the guard

he'll serve in his place for three nights
and then change places with his relief.
If a soldier breaks the rules once
he'll be corrected with three lashes.
If the same soldier breaks the rules again
he'll be corrected with seven lashes.
If that same soldier breaks the rules a third time
he'll receive thirty-seven lashes.
We'll assume that he's found his duties too difficult to perform
and he'll be exiled to some distant place.
The company commanders will see to it
that the guard hear these rules every third turn of service.
If these rules aren't repeated the commanders will be punished.
Having heard these rules
if a guard breaks them he'll be punished.
Let no commander hold himself above the members of my guard.
The soldiers who serve me are equal to any man.
If they cause offense to any man let him come to me.
If they've done something that should cost them their lives
then I will behead them.
If they've done something they should be beaten for
then I will order them to lie down and see that they're beaten.
If any man lays a hand on a member of my guard
his lashes will be paid back with lashes
and his fists will be paid back with fists.
The members of my guard are superior to the captains of thousands.
The companions of my guard are superior to the captains of hundreds and
   the captains of tens.
If the captains of thousands argue or fight with my guard
it's the captain of thousands who'll be punished."

Then Chingis Khan spoke to the captains of his guard
and made this decree:
"The archers, dayguards, and cooks
will each perform their appointed duties,
and then when the sun sets
they'll give their places to the nightguard,
leaving the tent to pass the night elsewhere.
When the archers leave they'll give their quivers to the nightguard,
and when the cooks leave they'll give up their utensils and bowls.
The next morning the archers, dayguards, and cooks will return
and wait at the place where the horses are kept
until I've had my morning broth.
Then they'll announce themselves to the nightguard
and return to their places,
the archers taking back their quivers,
the dayguards going back to their seats,
and the cooks taking back their utensils and bowls.

This is the procedure that will be followed.
Once the sun has set
any person found near the palace tent will be seized by the nightguard,
held through the night and questioned the next morning.
When one company changes place with another
the nightguard coming in will present their passes and take their place,
and the nightguard being relieved will present their passes and leave.
The nightguard who lie around the outside of the tent and guard the door
will cut in two any person who tries to enter the tent at night.
If someone comes with an urgent message
let them present it to the nightguard.
They can stand to the north of the tent
and announce that they have a message to present.
No one may sit above the nightguard's seat.
No one may enter the tent without the nightguard's permission.
No one may walk between the nightguard and the tent.
No one may walk between the nightguard's posts.
No one may ask how many soldiers are in the nightguard.
The nightguard will arrest any person who walks between their posts.
The nightguard will arrest any person who asks their numbers
and will confiscate the gelding the person rode that day,
along with the person's saddle and bridle,
along with the clothes the person was wearing."
And these orders were strictly followed,
so that one evening
when Eljigedei tried to walk between the nightguard and the tent
even though he was a trusted soldier
he was arrested by the nightguard. . . .
Once again Chingis Khan spoke, saying:
"The nightguard will supervise my servants,
the sons and daughters of my Palace Tent.
They'll watch after those who tend to my camels and oxen
and see that all the tent carts are in order.
The nightguard will collect all the weapons
and keep them beside the standard and drums.
They'll also collect all the utensils and bowls,
supervising all that's eaten and drunk.
Let them see to it that the sides of meat are cooked properly
and that all other food is prepared well.
If I need any food or drink I'll get it from the nightguard.
The archers are forbidden from distributing any food
without permission from the nightguard.
And when they do divide the food
the nightguard are first to be served.
The nightguard can command anyone who enters or leaves the Palace Tent.
They'll be posted at the door
and two of them will be in charge of the great wine table.
Other nightguard will be responsible for putting up the Palace Tent.

When I go out with my falcons to hunt
the nightguard will go along with me.
They'll separate into two divisions
and one division will remain with the carts in the Great Camp.
If I don't go off to fight in a war
then no member of the nightguard may go to war without me.
Any commander in my army who becomes jealous of this
and tries to break this law will be punished.
If you say to yourselves,
'How can the nightguard be excused from warfare?'
the answer is that the nightguard must always protect
the golden life of Chingis Khan.
When I hunt, they hunt with me.
When the Palace Tent moves or stops to make camp,
they must oversee all the work.
Don't imagine it's an easy job to guard me constantly.
Don't think it's easy to oversee all the carts
when my Great Camping Circle is on the move or at rest.
I say to myself,
'The nightguard must work twice as hard as the rest of the army.'
That's why I can say,
'Let them not go to war unless I go to war.'"
Then finally Chingis Khan made this decree:
'Some of the nightguard will serve as judges
and hear cases under Shigi Khutukhu.
Some will gather and distribute the weapons and armor.
These nightguard will also gather the nets used for hunting on the steppe.
Others, along with the stewards,
will divide and distribute the satins. . . .

VII. CONQUERING NORTHERN CHINA, 1211–1215

After this in the Year of the Sheep
Chingis Khan set out to fight the people of Cathay [northern China].
First he took the city of Fuzhou
then marching through the Wild Fox Pass
he took Xuandefu.
From here he sent out an army under Jebe's command
to take the fortress at the Zhuyongguan.
When Jebe arrived he saw the Zhuyongguan was well defended,
so he said:
"I'll trick them and make them come out in the open.
I'll pretend to retreat
and when they come out I'll attack them."
So Jebe retreated and the Cathayan army cried:
"Let's go after them!"
They poured out of their fortifications

until the valleys and mountainsides were full of their soldiers.
Jebe retreated to Sondi-i-wu Ridge
and there he turned his army around to attack
as the enemy rushed towards him in waves.
The Cathayan army was beaten
and close behind Jebe's forces
Chingis Khan commanding the great Middle Army attacked as well,
forcing the Cathayan army to retreat,
killing the finest and most courageous soldiers of Cathay,
the Jurchin and Khara Khitan fighters,
slaughtering them along the sides of Zhuyongguan
so that their bodies lay piled up like rotting trees. . . .

VIII. RECRUITING ADMINISTRATORS, 1220s

Once he had conquered the Moslem people
Chingis Khan appointed agents to govern in each of their cities.
From the city of Gurganj came two Khwarezm [present-day Uzbekistan]
    Moslems,
a father and son named Yalavech and Masgud,
who explained to Chingis Khan the customs and laws of these cities
and the customs by which they were governed.
Chingis Khan appointed the Khwarezm Masgud head of the agents
who governed the cities of the Turkestan:
Bukhara, Samarkand, Guranj, Khotan, Kashgar, Yarkand, and Kusen Tarim.
And his father Yalavech he made governor of the city of Zhongdu in Cathay.
Since among all the Moslems Yalavech and Masgud
were the most skilled at the customs and laws for governing cities,
he appointed them the governors of Cathay,
along with our own agents. . . .

STUDY QUESTIONS

1. What did the Mongols mean by "anda"? Why was anda important to the Mongols? What does the importance of anda suggest about the strength of kinship ties, tribal loyalties, and the stability of Mongol systems of governance?
2. How does the *Secret History* explain the rise of Chingis Khan? What were his strengths? Does the *Secret History* reveal any of his weaknesses?
3. How would you evaluate Chingis Khan as a manager/administrator? How did he select advisers and generals? What evidence do you find regarding the importance of familial, tribal, or religious loyalties to Chingis Khan?
4. Why were the Mongol armies so successful?
5. What does the *Secret History* reveal about Mongol beliefs and habits of mind?
6. Does the *Secret History* help us to understand why the era of Mongol power was so brief?
7. How does Chingis Khan compare to the Xiongnu leader Modun in Chapter 24?

PERSIAN PAINTING OF CHINGIS KHAN LEADING THE CHARGE

Chingis Khan and his soldiers relied on methods of fighting on horseback that, for the most part, had been pioneered during the first millennium B.C.E. by the Xiongnu and other Central Asian nomads. From the time of the Xiongnu onward the military success of the nomads was based on the use of small but powerful compound bows, mass-produced socketed arrowheads made of iron, and improved saddles that provided stability for the riders. Early in the Common Era the nomads added the stirrup to their horseriding paraphernalia.

An additional reason for the effectiveness of the nomad cavalries was their ability to fight as a cohesive force, a trait that was clearly evident among the Xiongnu and the Mongols. Perhaps the occasional emergence of an unusually talented leader such

Chingis Khan in Battle. Illustration from the *History of the Mongols,* by Rashid al-Din (ca. 1247–1317). (Bibliothèque Nationale de France/www.bridgeman.co.uk)

as Mo-tun among the Xiongnu or Chingis Khan was the decisive factor in bringing unity to the chronically feuding nomads. It may be that the anonymous Persian book illustrator who painted this picture of Chingis Khan leading the Mongols in battle meant to capture some of the cohesion that the Great Khan was able to establish among his soldiers.

STUDY QUESTIONS

1. What military equipment is illustrated in the painting?
2. Did the Mongols have the ability to produce all the equipment illustrated in this painting, or was it necessary for them to obtain some of it from sedentary peoples?
3. In what ways has the artist depicted skill in horseriding?
4. Does the artist seem to have been biased, either toward or against the Mongols? Is this painting an example of pro-Mongol propaganda?

53 THE MONGOL EMPIRE TAKES SHAPE

In the last chapter we looked at the rise of Chingis Khan through the eyes of the Mongols. Now, in this chapter, we turn to Persian, Korean, Russian, and Western European sources in order to see how "outsiders" viewed the conquering nomads.

The documents that follow focus on the decades from the 1220s though the 1250s, a decisive time for the Mongols. At the beginning of this period Chingis Khan had already conquered part of northern China and was in the process of leading an invasion of the Central Asian region centering on present-day Uzbekistan. The Uzbek steppe, which included the flourishing caravan cities of Samarkand, Bukhara, and Balkh, was the midpoint of the overland Silk Road and the heartland of a vibrant Islamic culture. In conquering northern China and the Uzbek territory, Chingis Khan created one of the most extensive empires in world history.

But there were many more Mongol conquests to come. A nearly continuous string of military victories under the leadership of Chingis's son and successor, Ogedei (Great Khan, 1229–1241), and grandson, Mongke (Great Khan, 1251–1259), created an empire of truly unprecedented size. At the time of Mongke's death the Mongol boundaries included all of Central Asia, Persia, and most of Russia. When another of Chingis Khan's grandsons, Khubilai, succeeded as Great Khan in 1260, the Mongols were prepared to realize their greatest dream, the completion of their conquest of China.

How do the documents in this chapter help us to understand why the Mongol empire grew so extensively in the 13th century? Did the Mongol conquests inadvertently strengthen a sense of religious, ethnic, or national identity among their victims?

ASIAN AND EUROPEAN SOURCES

I. THE DESTRUCTION OF BUKHARA, 1220

[The author of the following selection, Ala-ad-Din Ata-Malik Juvaini (1226–1283), was a Persian historian who served the Mongols as governor of Baghdad.]

Selection I from *Genghis Khan: The History of the World Conqueror* by Ala-ad-Din Ata-Malik Juvaini, translated by J. A. Boyle (Manchester University of Manchester Press, 1997), pp. 102–107. Reprinted by permission of Manchester University Press. Selection II from *Sources of Korean Tradition*, edited by Peter Lee and Theodore de Bary. Copyright © 1997 Columbia University Press. Reprinted with permission of the publisher. Selection III from *Medieval Russia: A Sourcebook 850–1700*, 3rd Edition, translated by Basil Dmtryshyn. (pp. 146–148.) Reprinted by permission of Academic International Press. Selection IV excerpt from "The Mongols in the West" by Denis Sinor from *Journal of Asian History* (33)1 (1999), pp. 7–18. Reprinted by permission of the Journal of Asian History. Selection V from *The Mission of Friar William of Rubruck: His Journey to the Court of the Great Khan Mongke 1253–1255*, translated by Peter Jackson (London: Hakluyt Society, 1990) pp. 74, 90–92, 209.

And from thence Chingiz-Khan proceeded to Bokhara [Bukhara, in Uzbekistan], and in the beginning of Muharram, 617 [March, 1220], he encamped before the gates of the citadel. . . .

And his troops were more numerous than ants or locusts, being in their multitude beyond estimation or computation. Detachment after detachment arrived, each like a billowing sea, and encamped round about the town. At sunrise twenty thousand men from the Sultan's [Muhammad II, Sultan of Khwarazm, 1200–1220] auxiliary army issued forth from the citadel together with most of the inhabitants; being commanded by Kök-Khan and other officers such as Khamid-Bur, Sevinch-Khan and Keshli-Khan. Kök-Khan was said to be a Mongol and to have fled from Chingiz-Khan and joined the Sultan (*the proof of which statements must rest with their author*); as a consequence of which his affairs had greatly prospered. When these forces reached the banks of the Oxus, the patrols and advance parties of the Mongol army fell upon them and left no trace of them. . . .

On the following day when from the reflection of the sun the plain seemed to be a tray filled with blood, the people of Bokhara opened their gates and closed the door of strife and battle. The *imams* and notables came on a deputation to Chingiz-Khan, who entered to inspect the town and the citadel. He rode into the Friday mosque and pulled up before the *maqsura* [the part of mosque reserved for the *imam*], whereupon his son Toli dismounted and ascended the pulpit. Chingiz-Khan asked those present whether this was the palace of the Sultan; they replied that it was the house of God. Then he too got down from his horse, and mounting two or three steps of the pulpit he exclaimed: 'The countryside is empty of fodder; fill our horses' bellies.' Whereupon they opened all the magazines in the town and began carrying off the grain. And they brought the cases in which the Korans were kept out into the courtyard of the mosque, where they cast the Korans right and left and turned the cases into mangers for their horses. After which they circulated cups of wine and sent for the singing-girls of the town to sing and dance for them; while the Mongols raised their voices to the tunes of their own songs. Meanwhile, the *imams, shaikhs, sayyids*, doctors and scholars of the age kept watch over their horses in the stable under the supervision of the equerries, and executed their commands. After an hour or two Chingiz-Khan arose to return to his camp, and as the multitude that had been gathered there moved away the leaves of the Koran were trampled in the dirt beneath their own feet and their horses' hoofs. . . .

When Chingiz-Khan left the town he went to the festival *musalla* [place of public prayer outside a city] and mounted the pulpit; and, the people having been assembled, he asked which were the wealthy amongst them. Two hundred and eighty persons were designated (a hundred and ninety of them being natives of the town and the rest strangers, viz. ninety merchants from various places) and were led before him. He then began a speech, in which, after describing the resistance and treachery of the Sultan (of which more than enough has been said already) he addressed them as follows: 'O people, know that you have committed great sins, and that the great ones among you have committed these sins. If you ask me what proof I have for these words, I say it is because I am the punishment of God. If you had not committed great sins, God would not have sent a punishment like me upon you.' When he had finished speaking in this strain, he continued his discourse with words of admonition, saying, 'There is no need to declare your property that is on the face of the earth; tell me of that which is in the belly of the earth.' Then he asked them who were their men of authority; and each man indicated his own people. To each of them he assigned a Mongol or Turk as *basqaq* [his representative] in order that the soldiers might not molest them, and, although not subjecting them to disgrace or humiliation, they began to exact money from these men; and when they delivered it up they did not torment them by excessive punishment or demanding what was beyond their power to pay. And every day, at the rising of the greater luminary, the guards would bring a party of notables to the audience-hall of the World-Emperor.

Chingiz-Khan had given orders for the Sultan's troops to be driven out of the interior of the town and the citadel. As it was impossible to accomplish this purpose by employing the townspeople and as these troops, being in fear of their lives, were fighting, and doing battle, and making night attacks as much as was possible, he now gave orders for all the quarters of the town to be set on fire; and since the houses were built entirely of wood, within several days the greater part of the town had been consumed, with the exception of the Friday mosque and some of the palaces, which were built with baked bricks. Then the people of Bokhara were driven against the citadel. And on either side the furnace of battle was heated. On the outside, mangonels were erected, bows bent and stones and arrows discharged; and on the inside, ballistas and pots of naphtha were set in motion. It was like a red-hot furnace fed from without by hard sticks thrust into the recesses, while from the belly of the furnace sparks shoot into the air. For days they fought in this manner; the garrison made sallies against the besiegers, and Kök-Khan in particular, who in bravery would have borne the palm from male lions, engaged in many battles: in each attack he overthrew several persons and alone repelled a great army. But finally they were reduced to the last extremity; resistance was no longer in their power; and they stood excused before God and man. The moat had been filled with animate and inanimate and raised up with levies and Bokharians; the outworks had been captured and fire hurled into the citadel; and their khans, leaders and notables, who were the chief men of the age and the favourites of the Sultan and who in their glory would set their feet on the head of Heaven, now became the captives of abasement and were drowned in the sea of annihilation. . . .

When the town and the citadel had been purged of rebels and the walls and outworks levelled with the dust, all the inhabitants of the town, men and women, ugly and beautiful, were driven out on to the field of the *musalla*. Chingiz-Khan spared their lives; but the youths and full-grown men that were fit for such service were pressed into a levy for the attack on Samarqand and Dabusiya. Chingiz-Khan then proceeded against Samarqand; and the people of Bokhara, because of the desolation, were scattered like the constellation of the Bear and departed into the villages, while the site of the town became like '*a level plain*'. . . .

II. THE BATTLE OF KUJU, 1231

[Although the Mongols eventually conquered Korea, they were stymied by the Koreans at Kuju in 1231. The account of the battle of Kuju is taken from a history of Korea written by leading Korean scholars in the 15th century.]

Pak Soˇ was from Chukchu, and in 1231 he became military commissioner of the Northwestern Frontier District. The Mongol commander Sartaq swept over Ch'oˇlchu and reached Kuju. Pak Soˇ, as well as the general of Sakchu subcircuit, Kim Chungon; the general of Choˇngju subcircuit, Kim Kyoˇngson; and the magistrates of Choˇngju, Sakchu, Wiju, and T'aeju, all leading troops, met at Kuju. Pak Soˇ had General Kim Chungon's troops defend the town on the east and west; Kyoˇngson's army defended the south; the special patrol troops of the regional military command and the special patrol troops of Wiju and T'aeju, numbering more than two hundred and fifty men, defended three sides.

The Mongols encircled the town in several layers and attacked the west, south, and north gates day and night. The troops in the city went out at once and attacked them. The Mongol troops captured Wiju Deputy Commissioner Pak Munch'ang and ordered him to enter the town to persuade the defenders to surrender. Pak Soˇ beheaded him. The Mongols selected three hundred crack cavalrymen and attacked the north gate. Pak Soˇ counterattacked and checked them.

The Mongols constructed wheeled observation towers as well as a great platform wrapped with cowhide in which they hid soldiers, using it to approach the base of the town walls to excavate a tunnel. Pak Soˇ bored through the city walls and poured molten iron to burn the wheeled observation towers. The ground also collapsed, crushing more than thirty Mongols to death. Pak Soˇ then burned rotten thatch to ignite the wooden platform, alarming the Mongols and causing them to scatter.

The Mongols suddenly attacked the south of the town with fifteen large catapults. Pak Soˇ constructed platforms on the town walls, and mounting catapults on them, he hurled stones and drove the attackers off. The Mongols also piled up faggots soaked with human fat and used them to attack the town with fire. When Pak Soˇ tried to put them out by pouring water on them, the fire burned even more fiercely. Pak Soˇ then had his men throw mud mixed with water to stop the fire. The Mongols also ignited a cart loaded with grass to attack the gate tower. As Pak Soˇ had prepared water reserves in the tower and poured these from the top of the tower onto the flames, the fire subsequently went out. The Mongols encircled the town for thirty days and attacked it in every conceivable way. Pak Soˇ, quickly responding to the changing situation, steadfastly defended the town. Unable to win, the Mongols retreated, and then, deploying troops regrouped from assaults on various northern frontier district towns, they attacked Kuju again. Lining up thirty catapults for the attack, they destroyed a fifty-*kan*-long corridor in the town wall. As quickly as the walls were smashed, Pak Soˇ chained iron links across the holes and repaired them. The Mongols did not dare attack again.

Then when Pak Soˇ went out fighting and won a great victory, the Mongols attacked Kuju again with a great catapult. But as Pak Soˇ, too, set catapults flinging rocks and killing the enemy in endless numbers, the Mongol troops retreated and camped in a wooded palisade in order to protect themselves.

The next year, the king sent the administrator of the Military Commission of the Rear Army and Junior Policy Critic Ch'oe Imsu, as well as Investigating Censor Min Huˇi. They led the Mongols to a point outside the Kuju wall to order the town's surrender, saying: "We have already sent Choˇng, the Lord of Hŭian, to discuss peace with the Mongol troops, and our three armies have already surrendered. You may cease fighting and come out to surrender." They tried to persuade them four times, but Pak Soˇ would not surrender. Min Huˇi was exasperated by the firm refusal and wanted to draw his sword and stab himself. Ch'oe Imsu again ordered Pak Sŏ to surrender, stressing that he was seriously violating the king's orders. Only then did he surrender.

When the Mongols encircled Kuju, there was a Mongol general whose age was about seventy, and he went below the city wall and looked around at the fortress's ramparts and military weapons and sighed, saying: "Since my youth I have followed the army, and I am accustomed to seeing the cities of the world fought over and defended, but I have never seen anyone being attacked like this and to the end not surrendering. Certainly those military leaders in the city will later become distinguished generals and ministers of the state." Later Pak Sŏ in fact became executive of the Chancellery.

III. THE CONQUEST OF RUSSIAN CITIES, 1237–1238

[The Mongol campaigns in Russia are recorded in contemporary Russian chronicles, from which the following passages are drawn.]

It happened in 1237. That winter, the godless Tatars [the Mongols], under the leadership of Batu, came to the Riazan principality from the East through the forests. Upon arriving they encamped at Onuza, which they took and burned. From here they despatched their emissaries—a woman witch and two men—to the princes of Riazan demanding a tithe from the princes and complete armor and horses from the people. The princes of Riazan, Iurii Igorevich and his brother Oleg, did not allow the emissaries to enter the city, and [together with] the Murom and Pronsk princes [they] moved against the Tatars in the direction of Voronezh. The princes replied: "When we are gone, everything will be yours." . . . The princes of Riazan sent a plea to Prince Iurii of Vladimir, begging him to send aid or to come in person. Prince Iurii, however, did not go; neither did he listen to the plea of the princes of Riazan, as he wanted to fight the Tatars alone. . . .

The princes of Riazan, Murom, and Pronsk moved against the godless and engaged them in a battle. The struggle was fierce, but the godless Mohammedans [Note: The Mongols were animists; later, some of them converted to Islam.] emerged victorious with each prince fleeing toward his own city. Thus angered, the Tatars now began the conquest of the Riazan land with great fury. They destroyed cities, killed people, burned, and took [people] into slavery. On December 6 [1237], the cursed strangers approached the capital city of Riazan, besieged it, and surrounded it with a stockade. The princes of Riazan shut themselves up with the people of the city, fought bravely, but succumbed. On December 21 [1237], the Tatars took the city of Riazan, burned it completely, killed Prince Iurii Igorevich, his wife, slaughtered other princes, and of the captured men, women, and children, some they killed with their swords, others they killed with arrows and [then] threw them into the fire; while some of the captured they bound, cut, and disemboweled their bodies. The Tatars burned many holy churches, monasteries, and villages, and took their property.

On Tuesday, February 3 [1238], . . . the Tatars approached Vladimir. The inhabitants of Vladimir, with their princes and military commander, Peter Osliadiukovich, shut themselves up in the city. The Tatars came to the Golden Gates, brought with them Prince Vladimir, the son of the Grand Prince Iurii Vsevolodovich, and inquired: "Is the Grand Prince Iurii in the city?" But the inhabitants of Vladimir began to shoot at them. They, however, shouted: "Do not shoot!" And, having approached very close to the gates, they showed the inhabitants of Vladimir their young Prince Vladimir, son of Iurii, and asked: "Do you recognize your young Prince?" As a result of privation and misfortune, his face was sad and he looked weak. Vsevolod and Mstislav stood atop the Golden Gates and recognized their brother Vladimir. Oh, how sad and tearful it is to see one's brother in such a condition! Vsevolod and Mstislav, with their *boyars* and all the inhabitants, wept as they looked at Vladimir. And the Tatars departed from the Golden Gates, circled the entire city, examined it, and encamped at Zremany in front of the Golden Gates and about the entire city; and there were many of them. . . .

After they made camp around Vladimir, the Tatars went and occupied the city of Suzdal. . . . They brought a multitude of prisoners into their camp, approached the city of Vladimir on Saturday, and from early morning till evening they built scaffolds and set up rams, and during the night they surrounded the entire city with a fence. In the morning, the princes, Bishop Mitrophan, military leader Peter Osliadiukovich, and all the *boyars* and the people realized that their city would be taken and they all began to weep. . . . On Sunday, February 8 [1238], . . . early in the morning the Tatars approached the city from all sides and began to hit the city [walls] with rams, and began to pour great stones into the center of the city from far away, as if by God's will, as if it rained inside the city; many people were killed inside the city and all were greatly frightened and trembled. The Tatars broke through the wall at the Golden Gates, also from the Lybed [side] at the Orininy and the Copper Gates, and from the Kliazma [direction] at the Volga Gates, and in other places; they destroyed the whole city, threw stones inside, and . . . entered it from all sides like demons. Before dinner they took the new city which they set on fire; and there they killed Prince Vsevolod with his brother, many *boyars* and people, while other princes and all the people fled into the middle city. Bishop Mitrophan and the Grand Duchess with her sons and daughters, daughters-in-law, grandchildren, *boyars,* and their wives, and many people fled into a church, locked the church gates, and climbed inside the church to the choir loft. The Tatars took this city too, and began to search after the princes and their mother, and found that they were inside the church. . . . The Tatars broke the gates of the church and slaughtered those who were inside and resisted. And they begin to ask the whereabouts of the princes and their mother and found they were in the choir loft. They began to entice them to come down. But they did not listen to them. The Tatars then brought many fire logs inside the church and set it on fire. Those present in the choir loft, praying, gave their souls to God; they were burned and joined the list of martyrs. And the Tatars pillaged the holy church, and they tore the miracle-making icon of the Mother of God.

IV. CROSSING THE DANUBE RIVER, FEBRUARY 1242

[After capturing and destroying Kiev in 1240, the huge Mongol army commanded by Batu moved west to Poland and Hungary. A 13th-century Roman Catholic monk provides the following description of Mongol guile.]

Lo! in the winter, the snow and ice came in such abundance that the Danube was frozen over, which had not occurred in times reaching very far back. But the Hungarians from the inside broke the ice every day and guarded the Danube thus, so that there was a continual fight by the foot-soldiers against the ice. However, when the hard frost came, the whole Danube was frozen over, yet the Mongols by no means tried to cross with their horses. Listen to what they did. They led many horses and beasts up to the banks of the Danube, but for three days they sent no one to look after them, so that the beasts seemed to be left without keepers; and none of those people made an appearance in those regions. Then the Hungarians, thinking that the Tartars had retreated, suddenly crossed over and led the animals over the ice. When the Tartars observed this, they thought they could cross freely over the ice on horseback. Which was done, and so many crossed in one charge that from that part of the Danube they filled the surface of the earth.

V. THE REPORT OF A EUROPEAN VISITOR, 1250s

V. A. Karakorum

[William of Rubruck, the author of the following two selections, was a Franciscan friar who visited the Great Khan Mongke at his capital in Karakorum during the 1250 on behalf of King Louis of France.]

1. Regarding the city of Caracorum, you should know that, discounting the Chan's [Khan's] palace, it is not as fine as the town of St. Denis [near Paris], and the monastery of St. Denis is worth ten of the palace. It contains two quarters [*vici*]: one for the Saracens [Muslims], where there are bazaars and where many traders gather due to the constant proximity of the camp and to the great number of envoys; the other is the quarter of the Cataians [Chinese], who are all craftsmen. Set apart from these quarters lie large palaces belonging to the court secretaries. There are twelve idol temples belonging to different peoples, two mosques where the religion of Mahomet is proclaimed, and one Christian church at the far end of the town. The town is enclosed by a mud wall and has four gates. At the east gate are sold millet and other kinds of grain, though they are seldom imported; at the western, sheep and goats are on sale; at the southern, cattle and wagons; and at the northern, horses. . . .

2. At Caracorum Mangu has a large encampment, near the city walls and enclosed by a brick wall just as are the priories of our own monks. Here there is a great palace where he holds his drinking sessions twice a year, once at Easter when he passes by there and once in the summer when he is on his way back. The latter occasion is the more important, inasmuch as then there gather at his court all the nobles from any place up to two months' journey away; and he then confers on them garments and presents, and parades his great grandeur. There are numerous other buildings there the length of barns, where his supplies and treasure are stored.

3. At the entrance to this great palace, since it was unfitting that skins of milk and other drink should be brought through there, Master William of Paris has constructed for him a large tree made of silver, with four silver lions at its roots, each one containing a conduit-pipe and spewing forth white mare's milk. There are four conduits leading into the tree, right to the top, with their ends curving downwards, and over each of them lies a glided serpent with its tail twined around the trunk of the tree. One of the pipes discharges wine, a second *caracomos* (refined mare's

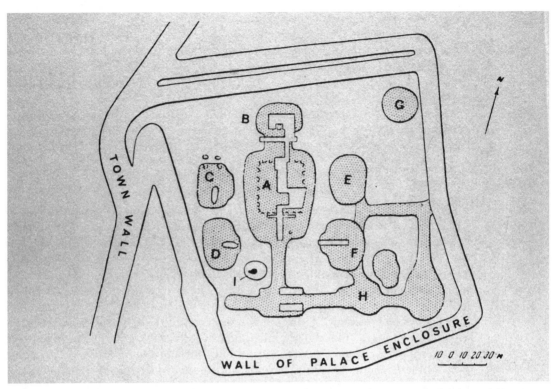

Plan of the Mongol Palace at Karakorum. From David Morgan, The Mongols (Malden, MA: Blackwell, (1986)), p. 116.

milk), a third *boal* (a drink made from honey), and a fourth rice ale, known as *terracina*. Each beverage has its own silver vessel at the foot of the tree, ready to receive it. Between the four pipes, at the top, he made an angel holding a trumpet, and beneath the tree a cavity capable of concealing a man; and there is a pipe leading up to the angel through the very core of the tree. (Originally he had constructed bellows, but they failed to blow with sufficient force.) Outside the palace there is a chamber where drink is stored and where stewards stand ready to pour when they hear the angel sound the trumpet. The branches, leaves and fruit of the tree are of silver.

4. So when drink is required, the head butler calls to the angel to sound the trumpet. On hearing this, the man concealed in the cavity then blows strongly on the pipe that leads to the angel, the angel puts the trumpet to its mouth, and the trumpet gives out a very loud blast. When the stewards in the chamber hear this, each pours his drink into the appropriate pipe, and the pipes spurt it out, down into the vessels designed for the purpose; whereupon the butlers draw it up and convey it through the palace to the men and women.

5. The palace resembles a church, with a middle nave and two sides beyond two rows of pillars and three doors on the south side. The tree stands inside, opposite the middle door, and the Chan sits at the northern end, in an elevated position so that he is visible to all. There are two stairways leading up to him, and the man

who brings him his cup goes up the one and comes down the other. The space in the middle, between the tree and the stairways that give access to him, is clear: there stands the cup-bearer, and also envoys bringing gifts, while he sits up above like some god. To the right, namely on the west side, are the men, and to the left the women; for the palace extends from north to south. Near the pillars on the right there are raised pews rather like a balcony, where his son and his brothers are seated; and there is a corresponding arrangement on the left, occupied by his wives and daughters. Only one wife is seated up there by his side, though not at such a high level as he is himself. . . .

B. GENDER RELATIONS

The married women make themselves very fine wagons, which I could describe to you only by drawing—and indeed I should have drawn everything for you had I known how to draw. One rich Mo'al [Mongol or Tartar] has easily a hundred or two hundred such wagons with chests. Baatu has twenty-six wives, each of whom has a large dwelling, not counting the other, smaller ones placed behind the large one, which are chambers, as it were, where the maids live: to each of these dwellings belong a good two hundred wagons. When they unload the dwellings, the chief wife pitches her residence [curia] at the westernmost end, and the others follow according to rank, so that the last wife will be at the eastern end: there is a space of a stone's throw between the residence of one lady and the next. Hence the court [curia] of one wealthy Mo'al will have the appearance of a large town, though there will be very few males in it.

One woman will drive twenty or thirty wagons, since the terrain is level. The ox- or camel-wagons are lashed together in sequence, and the woman will sit at the front driving the ox, while all the rest follow at the same pace. If at some point the going happens to become difficult, they untie them and take them through one at a time. For they move slowly, at the pace at which a sheep or an ox can walk. . . .

It is the women's task to drive the wagons, to load the dwellings on them and to unload again, to milk the cows, to make butter and *grut* [curds or cheese], and to dress the skins and stitch them together, which they do with a thread made from sinew. They divide the sinew into tiny strands, and then twist them into a single long thread. In addition they stitch shoes, socks and other garments. They never wash clothes, for they claim that this makes God angry and that if they were hung out to dry it would thunder; in fact, they thrash anyone doing laundry and confiscate it. (They are extraordinarily afraid of thunder. In that event they turn out of their dwellings all strangers, and wrap themselves up in black felt, in which they hide until it has passed.) They never wash dishes either, but instead, when the meat is cooked, rinse the bowl in which they are to put it with boiling broth from the cauldron and then pour it back into the cauldron. In addition [the women] make the felt and cover the dwellings.

The men make bows and arrows, manufacture stirrups and bits, fashion saddles, construct the dwellings and the wagons, tend the horses and milk the mares, churn the *comos* (that is, the mare's milk), produce the skins in which it is stored, and tend and load the camels. Both sexes tend the sheep and goats, and they are milked on some occasions by the men, on others by the women. The skins are dressed with curdled ewe's milk, thickened and salted.

When they want to wash their hands or head, they fill their mouths with water and let it trickle slowly from their mouths onto their hands, using it to wet their hair and wash their heads.

Regarding their marriages, you should know that the only way to have a wife there is to purchase her, and for this reason the girls are sometimes very mature before they are married, for the parents always keep them until they sell them. They observe the first and second degrees of consanguinity, but none of affinity, for they can have two sisters at the same time or in succession. Widows among them do not marry, on the grounds of their belief that all who serve them in this life will do so in the one to come; and so in the case of a widow they think that after death she will always revert to her first husband. Consequently, there is to be found among them the shameful practice whereby a son sometimes marries all his father's wives except his own mother. The residence [*curia*] of the father and mother always devolves upon the youngest son, and so he himself is obliged to provide for all his father's wives who pass to him along with his father's household; then, if he wishes, he treats them as his own wives, since he reckons he has made no loss if they revert to his father after death.

So, then, when someone makes a contract with someone else to take his daughter, the girl's father holds a banquet, and she flees to her relatives in order to lie in hiding. Then the father says, 'Behold, my daughter is yours; take her, wherever you may find her.' At this the man searches for her with his friends until he discovers her, and he is required to take her by force and carry her off with a semblance of violence to his own home.

STUDY QUESTIONS

1. What evidence does Juvaini provide regarding the importance of trade and Islam in 13th-century Bukhara? According to Juvaini, what was the Mongols' attitude toward Islam? Does Juvaini appear to have been a Muslim?

2. How might Juvaini's religious beliefs have shaped his account of the Mongols in Bukhara? Could the fire that destroyed the city's wooden buildings have been an inadvertent result of the fighting? What became of the people of Bukhara?

3. Were religious considerations a factor in the Korean resistance to the Mongols? How does the Korean document shed light on the methods of warfare used in the 13th century? How did the Mongols, as pastoral nomads, learn the siege techniques they employed against cities in Central Asia and Korea?

4. What feature of Russian political life worked to the advantage of the Mongols? How do you explain the chronicler's description of the Mongols as both "godless" and "Mohammedan"? What was the likely religion of the chronicler?

5. How might the Persian, Korean, and Russian accounts of the Mongols have reinforced a sense of national or religious identity in these countries? Which seems stronger in these reports, a sense of national or religious identity?

6. How does the description of the Mongols in Hungary reveal their cleverness? Why did the Mongols evacuate Hungary shortly after their arrival?

7. What features of Karakorum impressed Rubruck? What did not impress him? How do think the Mongols obtained the resources to build Karakorum? Why did they not move their center of operations to one of the cities they conquered?

8. What did Rubruck observe about gender relations among the Mongols? Does his report imply anything about gender in Western Europe?

9. How do the views of the "outsiders" in this chapter compare with the "insider" point of view expressed in the *Secret History* in Chapter 52? What differences do you see? Are there any similarities? In general, which is a more valuable aid to understanding the past, an "insider" or an "outsider" account?

10. How do the Mongols compare to the Xiongnu (see Chapters 24 and 25)? In what ways had the lifeways of the nomads changed from the time of the Xiongnu? What were the continuities?

54

MONGOL RULE IN RUSSIA

Mongol armies conquered most of Russia, including Kievan Rus', early in the 13th century. Their rule lasted until the middle of the 15th century. It had considerable impact in limiting Russian contacts with other societies, reducing trade and educational levels, and shifting political emphasis more toward central Russia. Many Russians copied Mongol habits in matters such as dress, and Russian leaders may have learned more about an authoritarian political model. Russia's Asian elements, certainly, gained ground in this period. But Russia was not completely changed, and among other things orthodox religious emphasis remained intact.

The following documents describe Mongol conquest and rule (Russians called the Mongols Tatars). They are a bit fragmentary, coming from snippets in Russian chronicles and travelers' accounts. They are also not entirely harmonious, in talking both about atrocities and about considerable political and religious latitude. How do the documents, in combination, help explain why Mongol rule lasted so long? How do they also help explain why ultimately Russian leaders sought to drive the Mongols out?

Document I comes from the First Novgorian Chronicle, dealing with the year 1238. The passage provides another account of the attacks on Riazan and the city Vladimir, already discussed in document III in the previous chapter. Chronicles were written by orthodox priests, and this authorship explains some of the terms used in the chronicle and might raise questions about factual accuracy.

Document II is from another religious source, a Catholic (Franciscan) monk, Giovanni de Plano, describing a visit to Kiev in 1244.

Document III is from a message sent to his people by the Prince of Novgorod, between 1266 and 1272.

Document IV deals with a Mongol decree, issued by Khan Mengu-Emir around 1308, sent to the Metropolitan (archbishop) of the Russian Church.

Document V comes from fragments of chronicles in the 13th century, on dealings between Russian princes and their Tatar overlords.

Document VI, finally, comes from another chronicle, the Voskresnesk, in 1262, discussing Muslim agents that Mongols used to collect taxes in Russia.

Collectively, the documents deal with a major episode in the occupation of one society by conquerors from another. They encourage assessment of changes and continuities between initial conquest and consolidation of rule in Russia, and they allow analysis of methods of rule and of the impact of the conquest period.

From A *Source Book for Russian History From Early Times to 1917*, 2 vols., edited by George Vernadsky, (New Haven, Conn.: Yale University Press, 1972), Vol. I, pp. 45–46, 49–50. Copyright © Yale University Press, 1972. Reprinted by permission.

CHRONICLES AND OTHER ACCOUNTS

I. NOVGORODIAN CHRONICLE

Having taken Riazan', the pagan and godless Tatars—a host of shedders of Christian blood—then went to Vladimir. Prince Iurii left Vladimir and fled to Iaroslavl', while his son Vsevolod, with his mother and the bishop and the whole [population] of the province, shut themselves up in Vladimir. The lawless Ishmaelites approached the town, and surrounded the town in force, and fenced it all round with a stockade. And the next morning Prince Vsevolod and Bishop Mitrofan saw that the town would be taken, and they entered the Church of the Holy Virgin, and Bishop Mitrofan sheared them all into monasticism and into the *skhima* [the strictest monastic vows]—the prince and the princess their daughter and daughter-in-law, and good men and women. And when the lawless ones had already come near and set up battering rams, they took the town and set it on fire on Friday before Sexagesima Sunday. The prince and the bishop and the princess, seeing that the town was on fire and that the people were already perishing, some by fire and others by the sword, took refuge in the Church of the Holy Virgin and shut themselves in the sacristy. The pagans, breaking down the doors, piled up wood, and set fire to the sacred church, and slew them all. Thus they perished, giving up their souls to God. . . . And [the people of] Rostov and Suzdal' dispersed in various directions. Having come from there, the accursed ones took Moscow, Pereiaslavl', Iur'ev [northeast of Moscow], Dmitrov, Volok [Volokolamsk], and Tver'. . . . Then the accursed, godless ones pushed on from Torzhok, cutting down everyone like grass, to within one hundred versty [about sixty-six miles] of Novgorod. God, however, and the great and sacred apostolic cathedral Church of Sancta Sophia . . . protected Novgorod.

II. GIOVANNI DI PLANO CARPINI, CATHOLIC MONK

They [the Mongols] attacked Russia, where they made great havoc, destroying cities and fortresses and slaughtering men; and they laid siege to Kiev, the capital of Russia; after they had besieged the city for a long time, they took it and put the inhabitants to death. When we were journeying through that land we came across countless skulls and bones of dead men lying about on the ground. Kiev had been a very large and thickly populated town, but now it has been reduced almost to nothing, for there are at the present time scarce two hundred houses there and the inhabitants are kept in complete slavery. Going on from there, fighting as they went, the Tartars destroyed the whole of Russia.

· · ·

When the inhabitants of Kiev became aware of our arrival, they all came to meet us rejoicing and they congratulated us as if we were risen from the dead. We met with the same reception throughout the whole of Poland, Bohemia and Russia. Daniel [Prince of Galicia] and his brother Vasilko [Prince of Volynia] made a great feast for us and kept us, against our will, for quite eight days. In the meantime they discussed between themselves and with the bishop and other worthy men the matter about which we had spoken to them when we were setting out for the Tartars. They answered us jointly declaring that they wished to have the Lord Pope as their special lord and father, and the Holy Roman Church as their lady and mistress, and they also confirmed everything which they had previously despatched by their abbot concerning this matter. In addition they sent with us a letter and envoys.

III. MESSAGE FROM THE PRINCE OF NOVGOROD

The word of Mengu-Temir to Prince Iaroslav: give foreign merchants passage into your domain. From prince Iaroslav to the small people of Riga, and to the great and the small [*bol'shie i molodye*], and to those who come to trade, and to everyone: you shall have free passage through my domain; and if anyone comes to me with arms, him I shall deal with myself; but the merchant has free passage through my domain.

IV. RECONSTRUCTED CHARTER FROM KHAN MENGU TEMIR

And this third iarlyk Tsar [Khan] Mengu-Temir gave to Metropolitan Peter, in the year 6816 [1308].

. . .

Tsar [Khan] Chingis [ordered] that in the future: [in exacting] tribute [*dan'*] or subsistence for officials [*korm*], do not touch [the clergy]; may they pray to God with righteous hearts for us and for our tribe, and give us their blessing. . . . And past tsars [khans] have granted [privileges] to priests and monks by the same custom. . . . And we who pray to God have not altered their charters and, in keeping with the former custom, say thus: let no one, whoever it may be, demand tribute, or tax on land [*popluzhnoe*], or transport [*podvoda*], or korm; or seize what belongs to the church: land, water, orchards, vineyards, windmills; . . . and if anything has been taken, it shall be returned; and let no one, whoever he may be, take under his protection what belongs to the church: craftsmen, falconers, huntsmen; or seize, take, tear, or destroy what belongs to their faith: books, or anything else; and if anyone insults their faith, that man shall be accused and put to death. Those who eat the same bread and live in the same house with a priest—be it a brother, be it a son—they shall likewise be granted [privileges] by the same custom, so long as they do not leave them; if they should leave them, they shall give tribute, and everything else. And you priests, to whom we granted our previous charter, keep on praying to God and giving us your blessings! And if you do not pray to God for us with a righteous heart, that sin shall be upon you. . . . Saying thus, we have given the charter to this metropolitan; having seen and heard this charter, the *baskaki* [tax inspectors], princes, scribes, land-tax collectors, and customs collectors shall not demand or take tribute, or anything else from the priests and from the monks; and if they should take anything, they shall be accused and put to death for this great crime.

V. FROM THE CHRONICLES

[From the Suzdalian Chronicle:]
    [A.D. 1234:] Grand Prince Iaroslav went to the Tatar land to Batu and sent his son Konstantin to the khan [in Mongolia]. Batu honored Iaroslav and his men with

great honor and in dismissing him said: "Iaroslav, be you the senior among all the princes of the Russian people." Iaroslav returned to his land with great honor.

[A.D. 1244:] The princes Vladimir Konstantinovich, Boris Vasilkovich, and Vasilii Vsevolodovich went with their men to the Tatar land to Batu, concerning their patrimony [*otchina*]. Batu honored them with due honor and dismissed them, adjudging to each his patrimony; and they returned to their lands with honor.

[A.D. 1245:] . . . Grand Prince Iaroslav went to the Tatar land to Batu, with his brothers and sons.

[A.D. 1246:] . . . Mikhailo, prince of Chernigov, went to the Tatar land with his grandson Boris, and while they were in the camp, Batu sent to Prince Mikhailo, ordering him to bow to the fire and to their idols. Prince Mikhailo did not obey his command but reproached his false gods, and thus was slain without mercy by the heathen and reached the end of his life.

• • •

[A.D. 1249:] Prince Gleb Vasilkovich went to the Tatar land to Sartak. Sartak honored him and dismissed him to his patrimony. That same winter, Aleksandr and Andrei returned from the khan, who ordered that Kiev and the entire Russian land be given to Aleksandr and that Andrei sit on the throne in Vladimir [Russian capital].

• • •

[A.D. 1252:] Aleksandr Iaroslavich [Aleksandr Nevskii], prince of Novgorod, went to the Tatar land, and they dismissed him with great honor, giving him seniority over all his brothers. . . . Grand Prince Aleksandr returned from the Tatar land to the city of Vladimir, and the metropolitan and all the abbots and the townspeople met him with crosses at the Golden Gate and seated him on the throne of his father Iaroslav . . . and there was great rejoicing in the city of Vladimir and in all the land of Suzdal'.

[From the Voskresensk Chronicle:]

[A.D. 1339:] Grand Prince Ivan Danilovich [called Kalita or "Purse"] went to the Horde, and with him his sons Semen [Simon] and Ivan. . . . That same autumn, on October 29, the accursed Tatars killed Prince Aleksandr Mikhailovich of Tver' and his son Feodor in the Horde, by command of the godless tsar Azbiak; and he had summoned him [the Russian prince] deceitfully, saying: "I want to bestow my favor upon you"; and he [the Russian] had obeyed the deceitful words of the pagan, and upon their arrival they were killed and their bodies dismembered. That same winter the sons of Grand Prince Ivan Danilovich, Semen, Ivan, and Andrei, were dismissed from the Horde in favor and in peace.

• • •

[A.D. 1341:] Grand Prince Ivan Danilovich departed this life. . . . And all the Russian princes went to the Horde: Prince Semen Ivanovich with his brothers, and Prince Vasilii Davydovich of Iaroslavl', Prince Konstantin of Tver', Prince Konstantin Vasilievich of Suzdal', and other Russian princes. . . . That same autumn Prince Semen Ivanovich left the Horde as grand prince, and with him his brothers Ivan and Andrei; and all the Russian princes were placed under his rule, and he took his place upon the throne in Vladimir.

VI. FROM THE VOSKRESENSK CHRONICLE

[A.D. 1262:] God delivered the people of the Rostov land from the savage torture of the Moslems through the prayers of the Holy Virgin and instilled fury in the hearts of Christians, unable to endure any longer the oppression of the pagans; and they convoked a veche and drove them from the towns: from Rostov, from Vladimir, from Suzdal', from Iaroslavl', from Pereiaslavl'; these accursed Moslems had farmed tribute from the Tatars and had brought much ruin upon men thereby, enslaving Christian men for [nonpayment of] interest [on loans], and many men were taken to various places; but God, who loves mankind, in his mercy delivered his people from great misfortune. . . . That same summer Grand Prince Aleksandr [Nevskii] decided to go to the tsar in the Horde, so that his entreaties might avert misfortune from his people.

STUDY QUESTIONS

1. What were the worst aspects of Mongol conquest and rule?
2. What were the best aspects? Why and how did Russian commentary ultimately go beyond the initial horror stories?
3. What did Mongols seek in conquering Russia? How do their goals compare with those of other major conquests in world history?
4. Are there biases in the sources available, and do they distort our picture of Mongol rule?
5. Why did Mongol rule last so long without a huge occupying force? Why did Russian leaders ultimately decide to contest the occupation and push the Mongols out?
6. What were the long-term implications of Mongol rule for the nature of Russian culture and politics, including foreign policy? What were the impacts on Russian identity?
7. How does the Mongol period in Russia compare with Mongol impact on other parts of Asia and Europe?